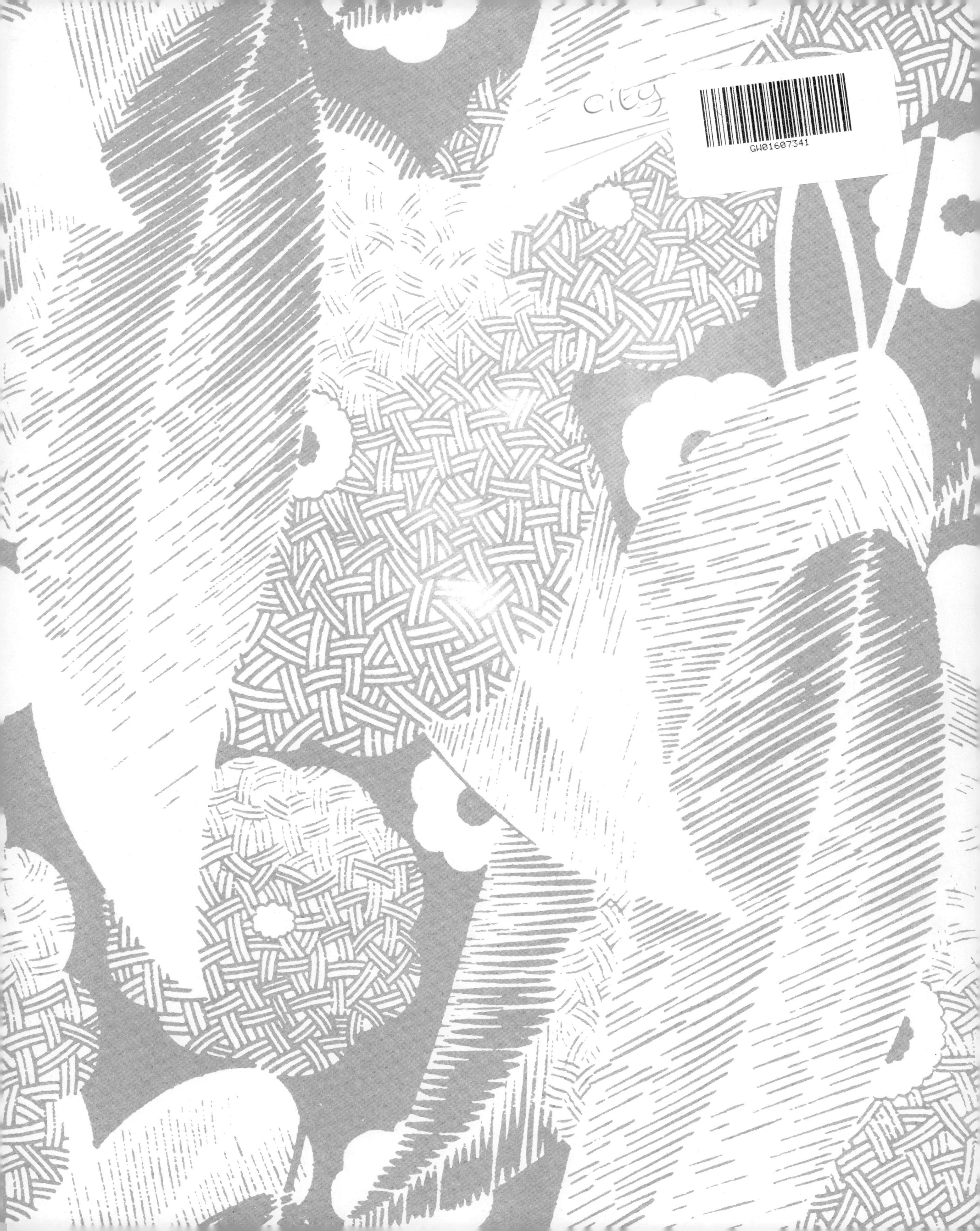

THE BRILLIANCE OF ART DECO

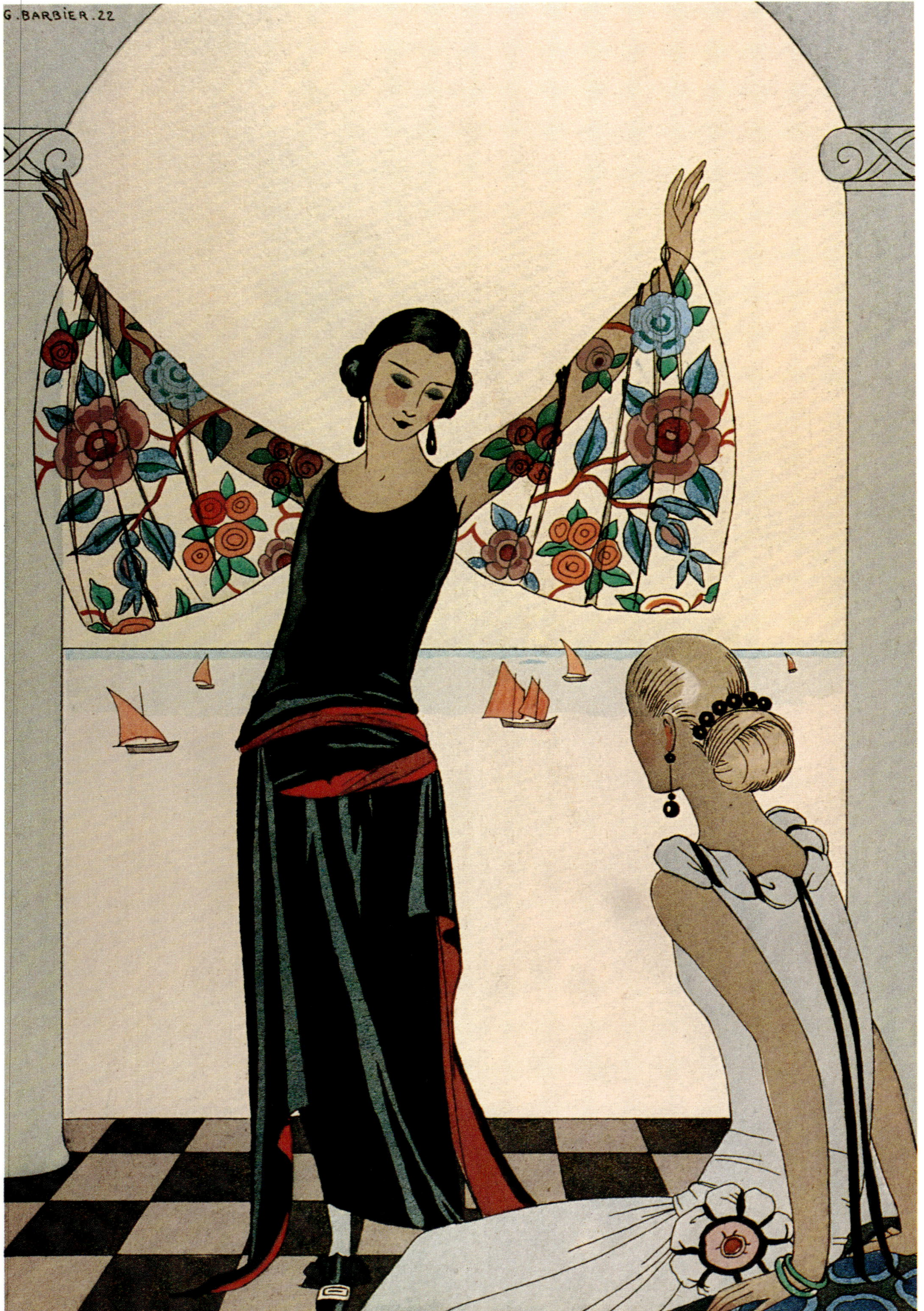

Pochoir illustration *Voici mes ailes!* by George Barbier, for *Falbalas et Fanfreluches*. Published by Editions Meynial, Paris.

THE BRILLIANCE OF ART DECO

JULIAN ROBINSON, DesRCA, FRSA

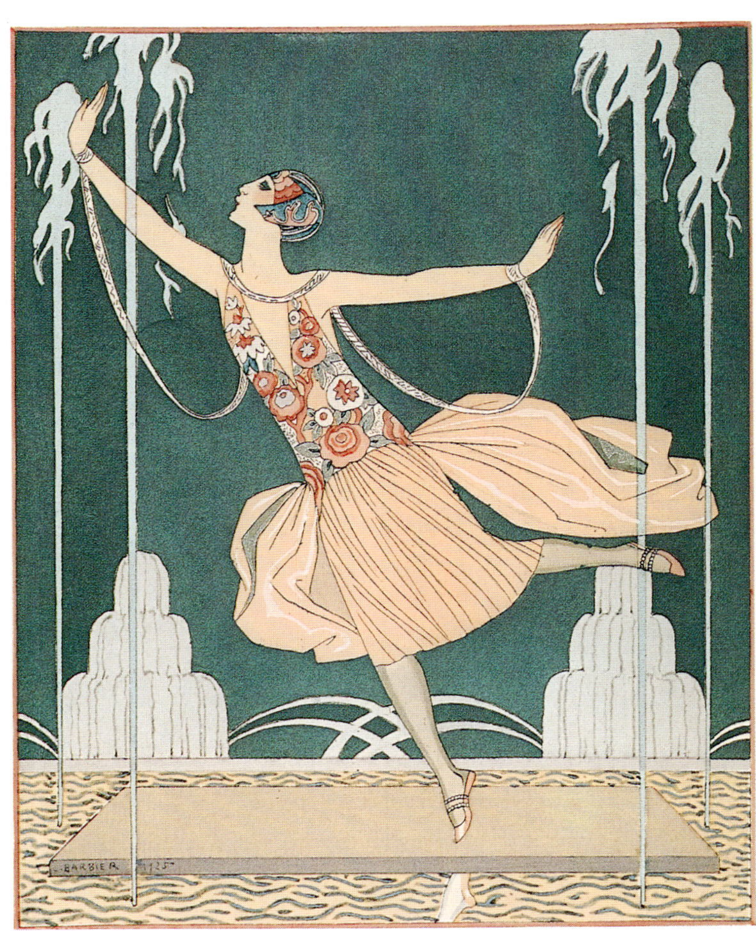

Pochoir illustration *La Danseuse aux jets d'eau* by George Barbier, for *La Gazette du bon ton*. Paris. 1925.

Border design by Kay Nielsen from *East of the Sun West of the Moon*, Hodder & Stoughton, London 1913.

The endpapers are from a textile design featured in the July 1932 edition of *Art-Goût-Beauté.*

Publisher: George Barber,

Published by Bay Books
61–69 Anzac Parade, Kensington
Sydney, NSW 2033, Australia

National Library of Australia
Card No and ISBN 1 86256 1117

Designed by Susan Kinealy
Typeset by Savage Type Pty Ltd, Brisbane
Printed in Singapore by Toppan Printing

BB87N

C·O·N·T·E·N·T·S

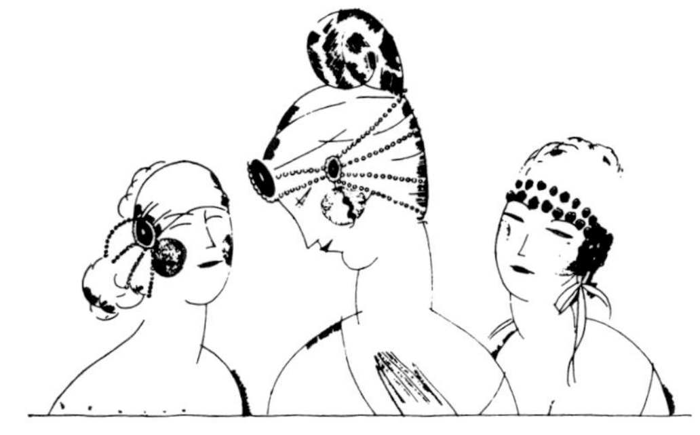

Unless otherwise credited all illustrations are from Julian Robinson's private collection.

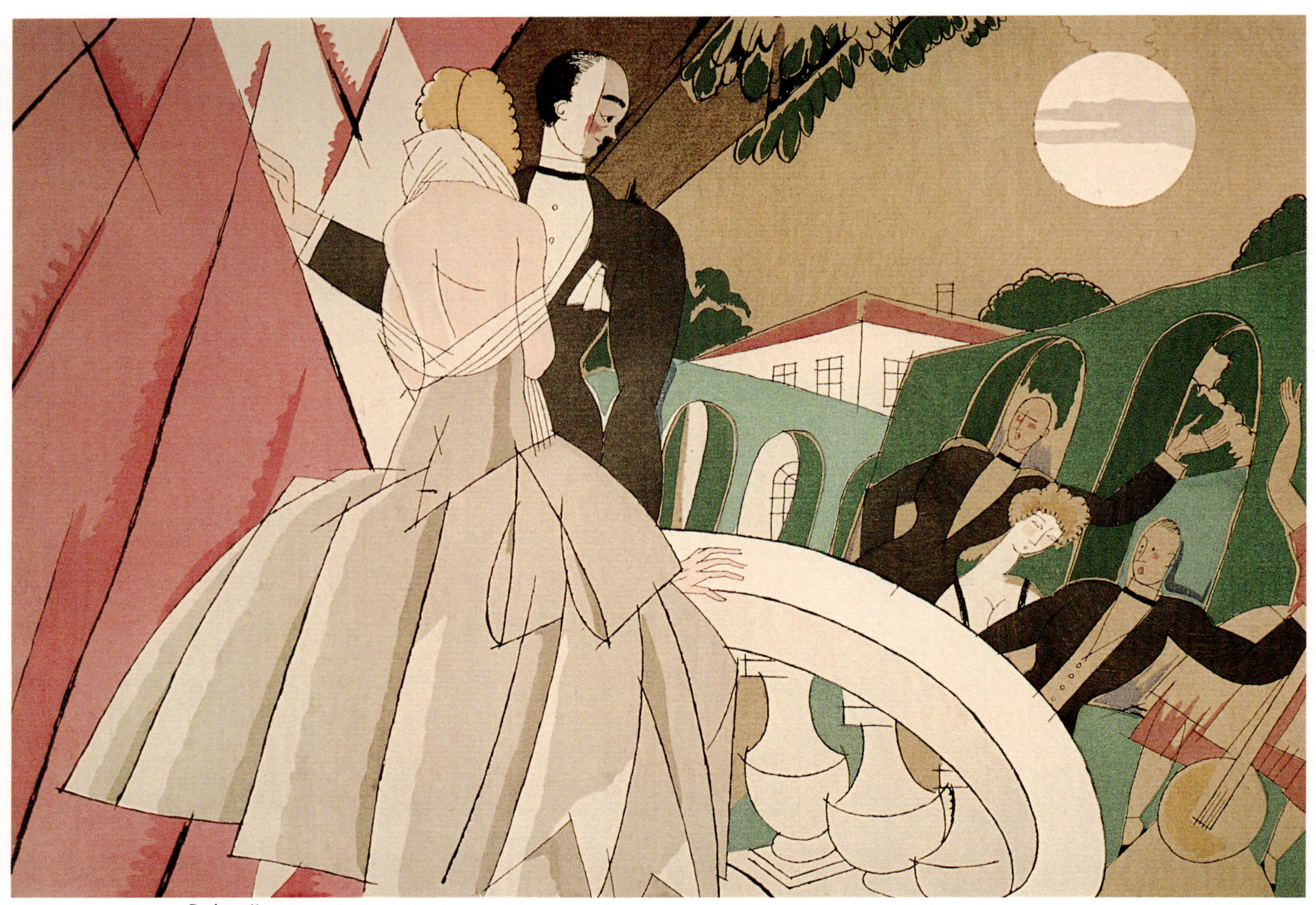

Pochoir illustration *La Mariée* by Charles Martin, for *Sports et divertissements,* with music by Erik Satie. Deluxe edition of 225 copies. Lucien Vogel, Paris. 1920.

P·R·E·F·A·C·E

Earlier this century, in the twenty-five turbulent years between 1910 and 1935, the revolutionary Art Deco style of design reached a pinnacle of aesthetic achievement which for a time rivalled that of the Italian Renaissance. This revolutionary style of design was created in France by leading artists, designers and master-craftsmen from all over the Western world, who worked in Paris with a single-minded passion, producing objects, artifacts and clothes worthy of their illustrious predecessors. During this period the Paris ateliers, costume houses and artists' studios were at the zenith of their international reputation, and nowhere else in the world could be found such an abundance of beautiful things.

The illustrative style used to promote this array of Art Deco merchandise also changed dramatically. It became an accepted art form in its own right, and attracted many of the leading pictorial artists of the day — Bakst, Barbier, Lepape, Picasso, Drian, Dufy, Martin, Benito, Erté, Delaunay and many others. Their Art Deco illustrations were not simply line-by-line representations of the new design styles. The artists captured the very spirit of each new design and portrayed it in their own idiosyncratic style, pointing out its individual features, nuances and subtleties and capturing the creative flavour for future generations to admire and enjoy. This book is about these magnificent illustrations; a celebration of the splendid achievements of the great Art Deco image-makers. Their work comes first, the literary substance explains the social background to this fascinating period, and endeavours to persuade the reader to look again, long and attentively, at the products of this illustrative oeuvre.

And if this looking and re-looking persuades a new generation of talented image-makers that there is far more to an illustrative commission than a simple line-by-line rendering, then we may once again have our lives brightened by the idiosyncratic styles of a new generation of illustrators. This would be a fitting epitaph to the work of all those talented artists, designers and master-craftsmen who helped to create the brilliance and splendour of this wonderful Art Deco period.

Julian Robinson.

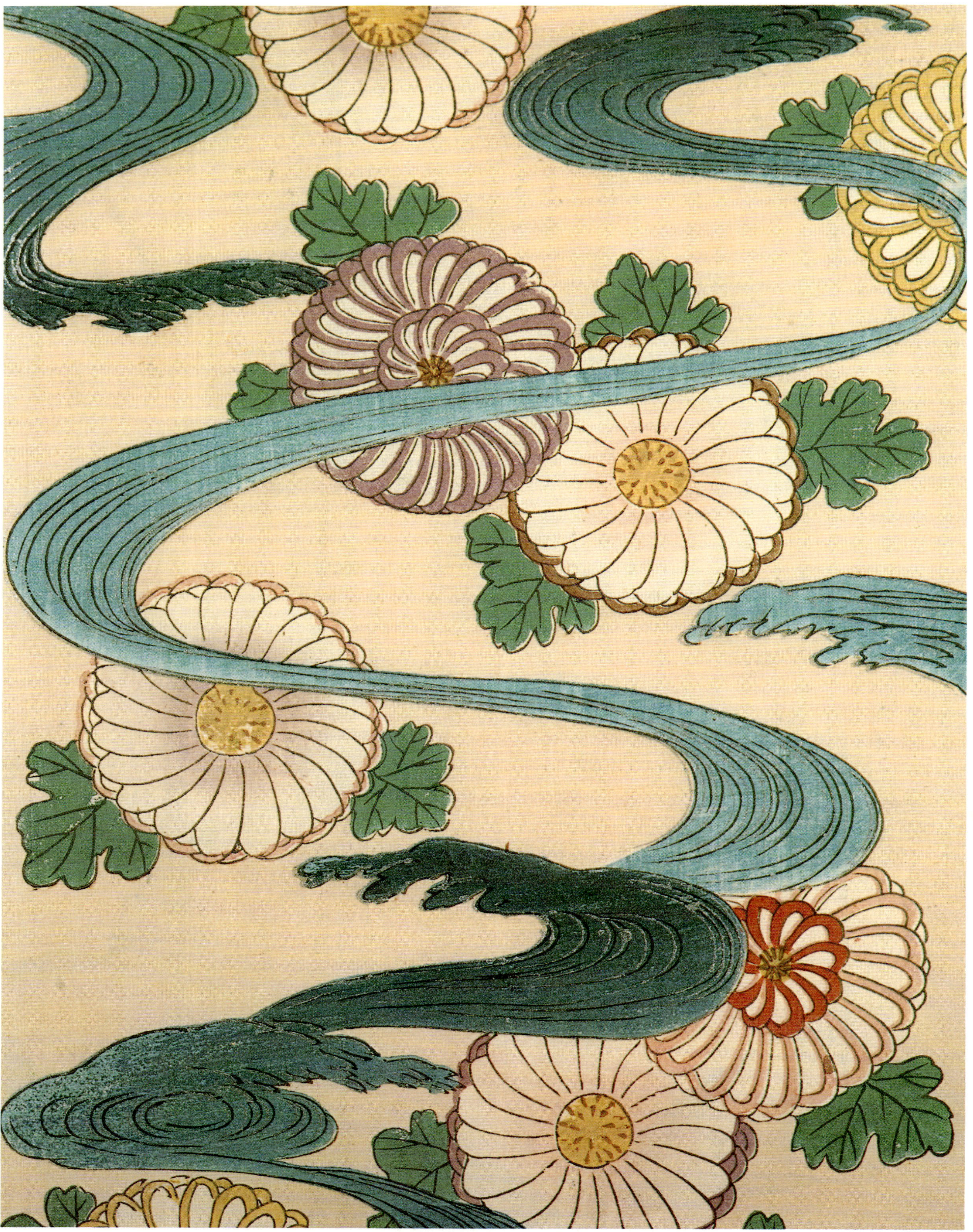

Japanese textile design, coloured woodcut. Early nineteenth century.

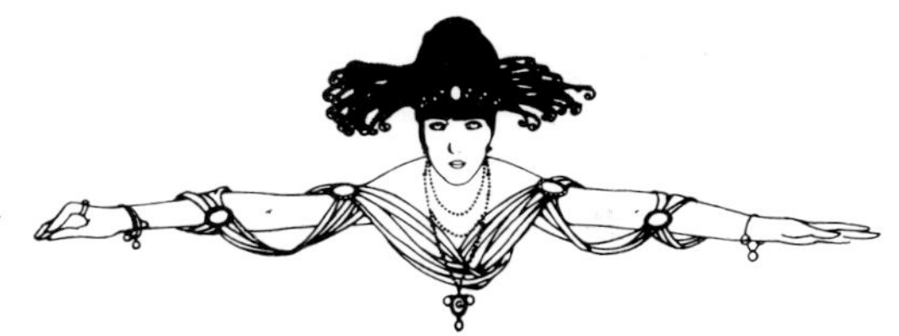

THE ORIGINS OF THE WORLD OF ART DECO

The civil strife, revolution, war and dramatic social change that afflicted the Western world during the years from 1905 to 1930 were accompanied by the emergence and flourishing of a revolutionary style of design and illustration — a burst of creative energy in response to changing times. Gone was the overpowering opulence and claustrophobic clutter of the Belle Epoque, which had dominated fashion since the early 1890s; in its place were the clear, clean lines of a new style that emphasised angular geometric shapes, bright acid colours, refined detailing, and superb draftsmanship. Today we refer to this new impulse as 'Art Deco', a term first used in the mid-1920s to describe the designs typical of the leading artists, designers and master-craftsmen whose works were displayed in the famous Exposition Internationale des Arts Décoratifs et Industriels Modernes, held in Paris in 1925.

Not since the golden age of the Italian Renaissance, when the great artists of the period — Cellini, Bramante, Bellini, da Vinci and Michelangelo — had been employed by the princes and merchants of Venice and Florence to beautify their clothing, adornments and surroundings, had so much creative talent been devoted to the designing, making and promoting of an abundance of artifacts and fashions. These objects were intended to adorn the bodies and beautify the houses of a dedicated clientele who, despite the changes that were taking place, still had time and funds to devote to an exclusive and expensive way of life.

The beginning of this period of stylistic change was in fact a time unique in Western history. Europe was at peace. New discoveries and liberalised forms of education were changing the traditional mores of much of Western society, and egalitarian ideals were beginning to triumph over many aristocratic habits. Inventions such as the telephone, electric lighting, moving

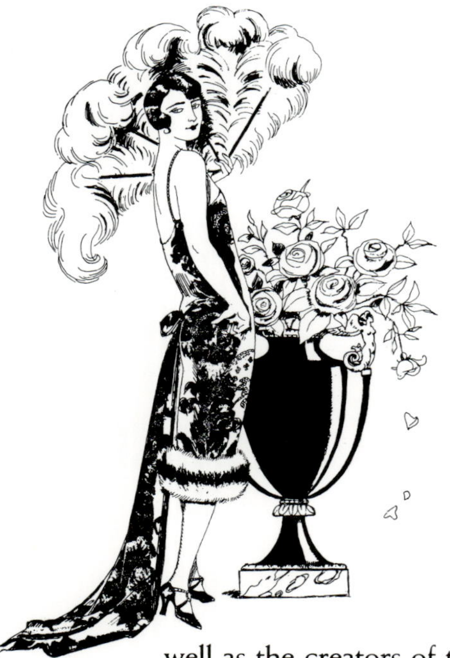

pictures, and the automobile were changing people's aspirations and ways of life. The working classes were uniting as never before, in search of political freedom and social justice.

And yet, in the first decade of the twentieth century, despite widespread poverty and continual civil unrest, the Belle Epoque was at the height of its popularity and extravagance. Paris was the unquestioned cultural centre of the Western world, and the arbiters of taste, as well as the creators of the current fashions, were the great Paris couturiers — Doeuillet, Doucet, Redfern, Worth, Paquin, Chéruit and Callot Soeurs. The couturiers promoted their most recent creations twice a year, in February and August. Their salons bulged with the haut monde of Europe, the Americas, Russia, South Africa, and Australia, who travelled to Paris to satisfy all their sartorial needs and to see the latest ideas in jewellery, furs, furnishings and novelties. Every comfort that these couturiers could devise was to be found in the salons: their wealthy international clientele could scarcely be expected to judge the effect of the new creations in an inappropriate or unfashionable setting.

Whilst in Paris these wealthy members of world society also visited the famous ateliers and designers — Lalique, Gallé, de Feure, Gaillard, Grasset,

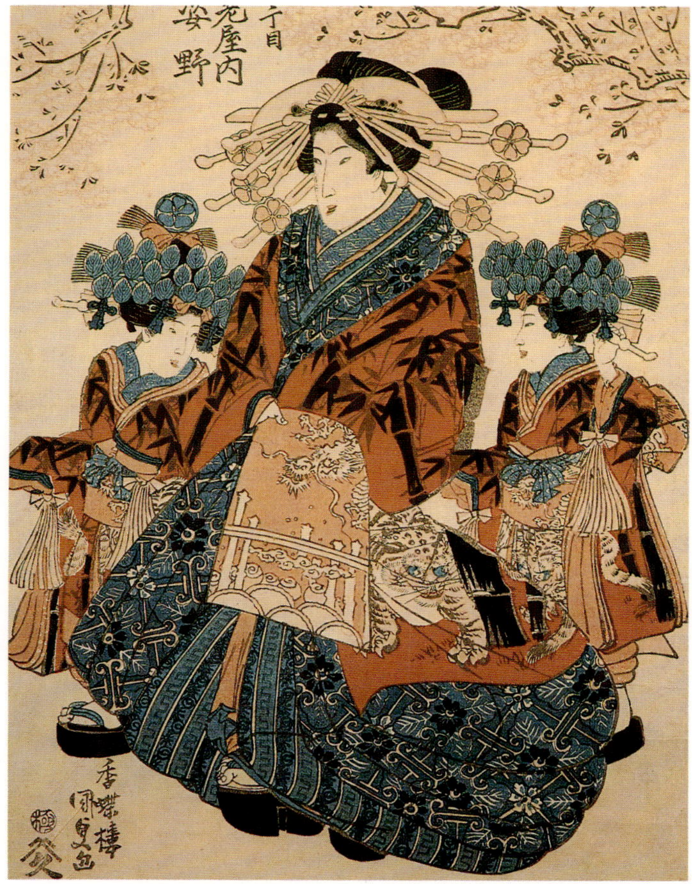

Japanese *ukiyo-e* coloured woodcut print by Kunisada, Tokyo. Early nineteenth century.

and Majorelle Frères — who specialised in unique forms of glassware, furniture, ceramics, tapestries, carpets, lacquer work, textiles, silverware, and deluxe edition books. The designers and master-craftsmen pursued their goal with passion: they wished to create expensive and exclusive products for the members of this rich international elite, a section of society unembarrassed by splendour and unopposed to luxury.

In 1900 the Exposition Universelle had been held in Paris to commemorate the arrival of the twentieth century and to celebrate French pre-eminence in the decorative and fashionable arts. Everybody who was anybody visited Paris that year to see the vast array of exhibits from the twenty-four contributing nations and their numerous colonies. The work of the 75 000 exhibitors was on view and by the time the exhibition closed, towards the end of September, nearly 50 million visitors had passed through the turnstiles. It was one of the most successful exhibitions ever held in the world.

The Exposition Universelle had been built in the very heart of Paris, bordered by the gardens of the Champs Elysées, the Trocadéro, the Boulevard des Invalides, and the Champs de Mars. The Champs de Mars was, and still is, dominated by Alexander Eiffel's great steel tower, constructed as the centrepiece of the earlier 1889 Exposition, which heralded the beginning of the Belle Epoque. The 1900 Exhibition's centrepiece, also built on the Champs de Mars facing the great Eiffel Tower, was the magnificent Palais de l'Eléctricité, decorated with over 10 000 multi-coloured electric lights.

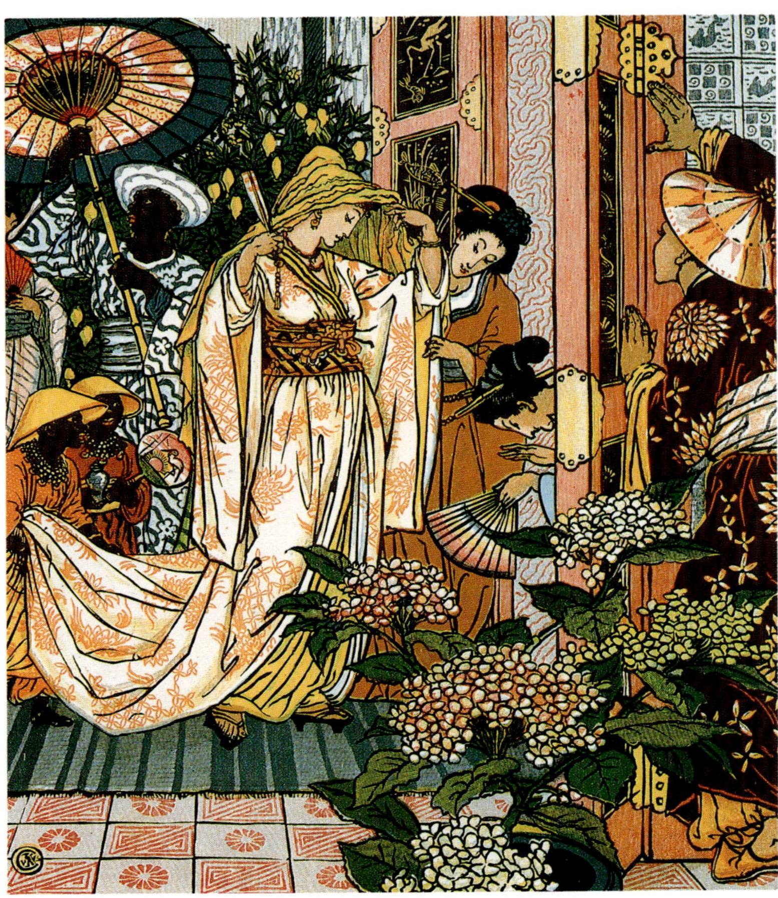

Chromo-litho illustration by Walter Crane, from *Aladdin and his Wonderful Lamp*. Published by George Routledge & Sons, London. 1876.

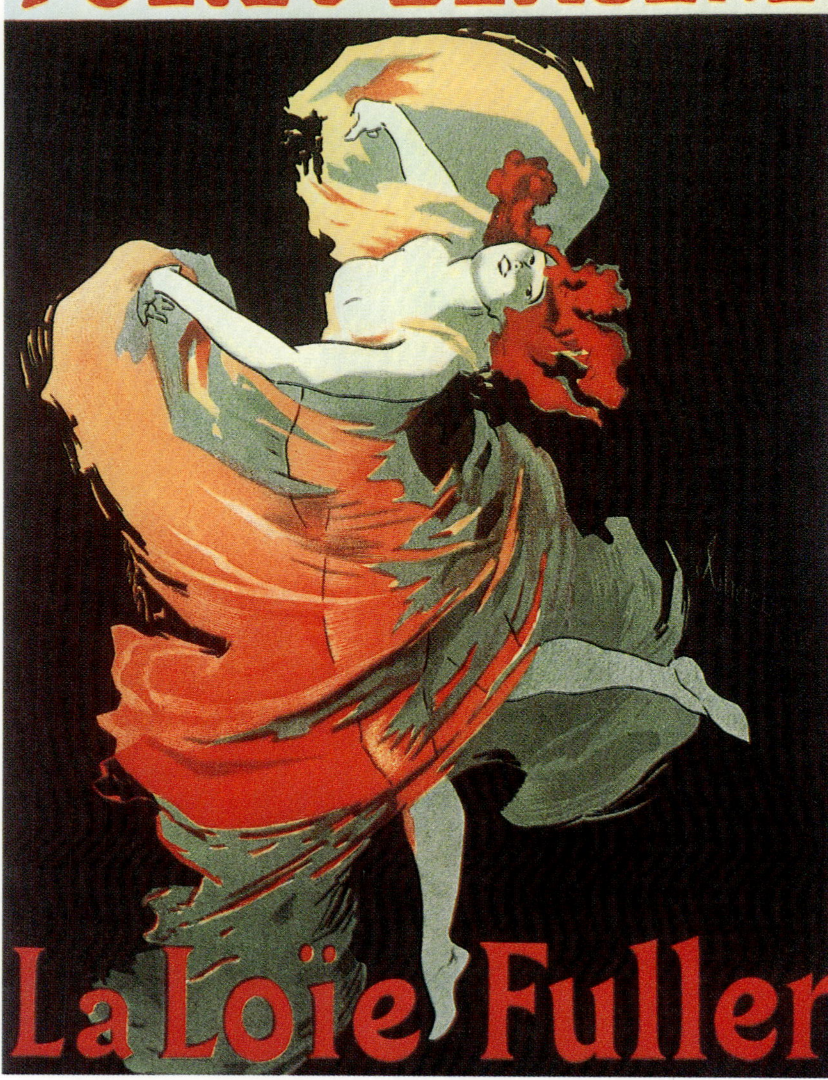

Loie Fuller at the Folies Bergère, Paris. Late nineteenth century.

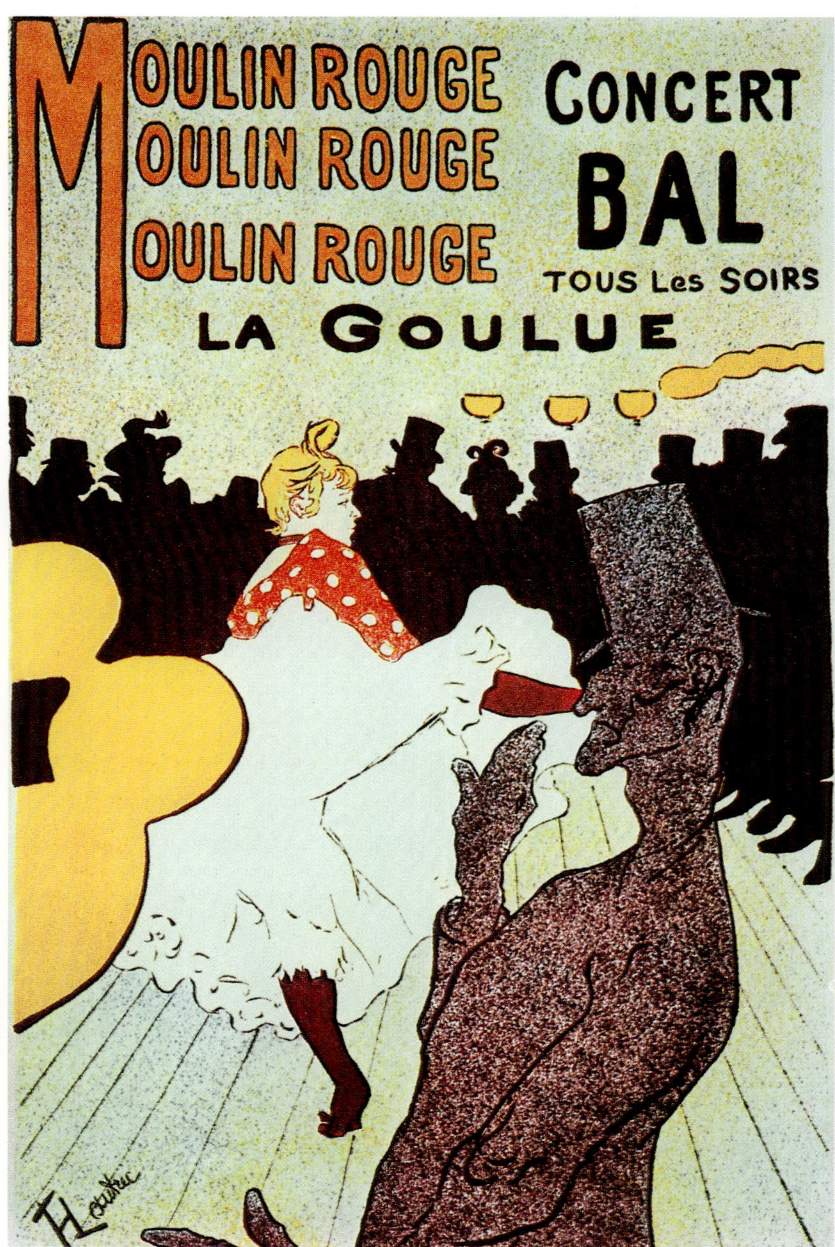

Chromo-litho poster for the Moulin Rouge, Paris, by Henri de Toulouse-Lautrec. Late nineteenth century.

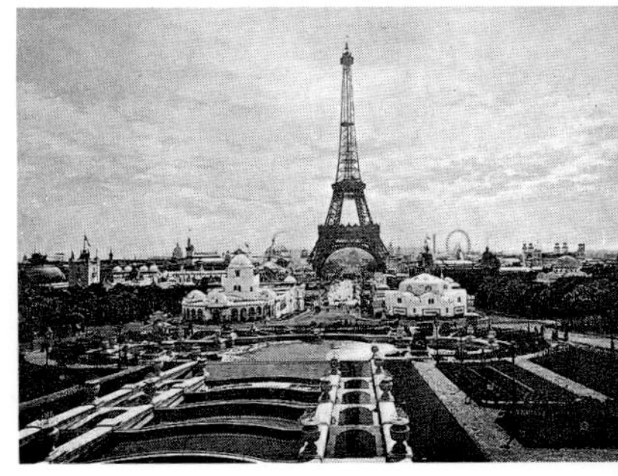

In reviewing the 1900 Exhibition in the prestigious *British Art Journal*, the editor declared it to be 'the greatest Exhibition the world has ever seen', and the art critic Herbert E. Butler wrote,

The art-loving people from throughout the world found in the Paris exhibition a collection of works such as has rarely, if ever, been brought together in the history of the human race. From north, south, east and west, treasures hitherto scattered over the whole world were gathered for education and delight.

The Exhibition covered a huge area, spanning the Seine from the Pont d'Iéna to the specially constructed Pont Aléxandre III. Exhibiting countries were housed in specially constructed pavilions and galleries with linking esplanades; their exhibits included fine leather bookbindings, large bronze statues, electrical gadgetry of all sorts, glassware, jewellery, gold and silver work, porcelain, ceramics and pottery, stained glass, wall decorations of all types, furniture, wood carvings, ivory pieces, works in marble, and paintings by such artists as Renoir, Gainsborough, Degas, Turner, Delacroix, Constable, Watteau, Corot and many others of European, American, African, Asian, oriental and Islamic descent.

Although some countries displayed retrospective examples of work by their more traditional manufacturers and craftsmen, the general tenor of the Exhibition was one of orientation towards the new century. The American section, for instance, was noteworthy for the contemporary work of Charles Lewis Tiffany of New York, whose jewellery, gold and silverware, and glass pieces (many by his son Louis Comfort Tiffany) were considered outstanding, and for the work of two of the more fashionable artists of the period, James Abbot McNeill Whistler and John Singer Sargent.

The Austrian exhibit contained some fine and very modern furniture by Niedermoser of Vienna. There were excellent examples of contemporary leather bookbindings by Jacob Baden of Copenhagen and some unusual art pottery by Rozenburg of The Hague. Fine porcelain with stylised decoration was exhibited by Gustafsberg of Stockholm and Meissen of Dresden. There were examples of the best work in wrought iron by Paul Kruger of Berlin, and unusual silk and gold tapestries by Mlle Karlickova of Prague. And there were marqueterie pieces by Spindler of Strasbourg.

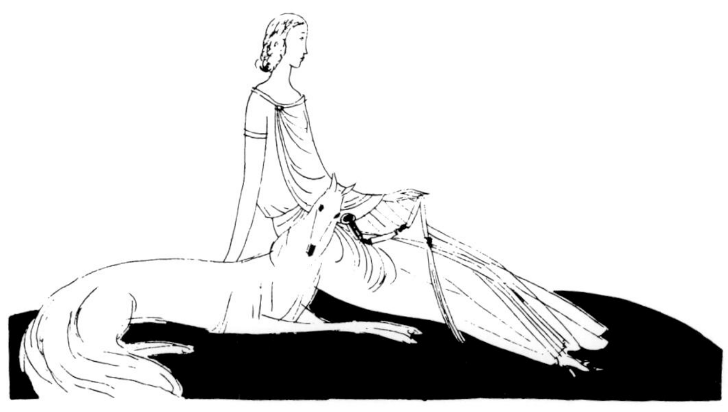

The British exhibits, however, were still markedly influenced by the revivalist 'medieval style', established in the late 1870s by the members of the Arts and Crafts Movement as a reaction against the overly ornate mid-Victorian designs that dominated the London exhibitions of 1851 and 1862.

In 1900 Queen Victoria was still head of a vast British Empire, with one quarter of the world's inhabitants being her subjects, and the British Government had decided to demonstrate this world dominance in its Colonial Pavilion, which featured selected artifacts from the Queen's realm. These exhibits, and those featured in the main British Pavilion, emphasised many of Britain's traditional nineteenth century moral and cultural values. The more talented experimental designers of the time — Christopher Dresser, Charles Rennie Mackintosh, Arthur Mackmurdo and Herbert McNair, for example — were not permitted to display their most creative verve.

The Exhibition also contained items from Japan, Turkey, China, Persia and other oriental countries whose varied visual styles had influenced many of the younger European artists and designers during the latter part of the nineteenth century. They also formed the aesthetic base of many of the new designs exhibited by the Dutch, Austrian, Hungarian, Danish, Italian and French designers, who variously termed their new aesthetic styles as *Jugendstil, Stile floreale, Sezessionsstile, Baudwurmstil, Le Style moderne* and *L'Art nouveau Bing.*

The Art Nouveau style of design had been inspired by the increasing array of oriental artifacts arriving in Europe after the introduction in the late 1870s of the large steel-hulled steamships that replaced the wooden-hulled sailing ships on many of the world's trading routes. The simplified oriental aesthetic style appealed to many designers who were reacting against the European drift towards industrialisation and the ornate artifacts that manufacturers tended to produce when they confused design with choice of ornamentation.

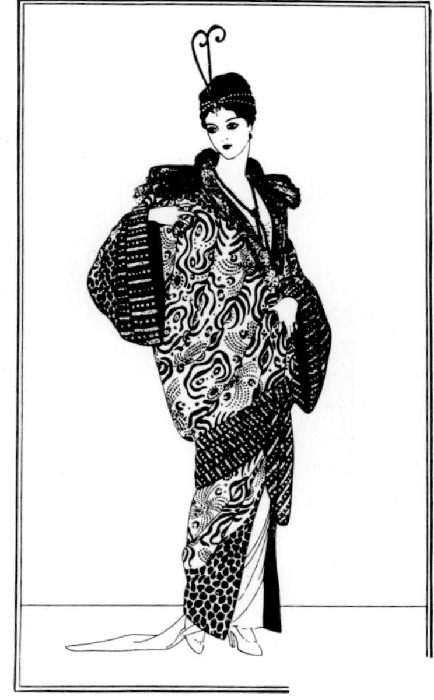

Among the best examples of this new orientally inspired Art Nouveau style, with its distinctive use of free-flowing curves, irregular and often asymmetrical shapes, naturalistic surface treatments and pastel colours, were those displayed by the French designers Gallé, Colonna, de Feure, and Gaillard, whose work had been co-ordinated by Samuel Bing. Bing was very influential in introducing into France oriental works of art, especially those from Japan: in the early 1890s he had opened his Maison de L'Art Nouveau Bing in the Rue Provence, and it is from this enterprise that the term 'Art Nouveau' derives.

In the two decades preceding the 1900 Exhibition, Bing had also introduced into France examples of the British Aesthetic Style, designed by William Morris, Edward Burne-Jones, Walter Crane, and the younger members of the Arts and Crafts Movement, and the American Louis Comfort Tiffany's experimental and stylish Favrile glass pieces, all of which were greatly admired at the 1900 Exhibition.

In addition, Bing had arranged a special exhibition of jewellery by René Lalique, who was described as 'displaying more variety, more originality, and

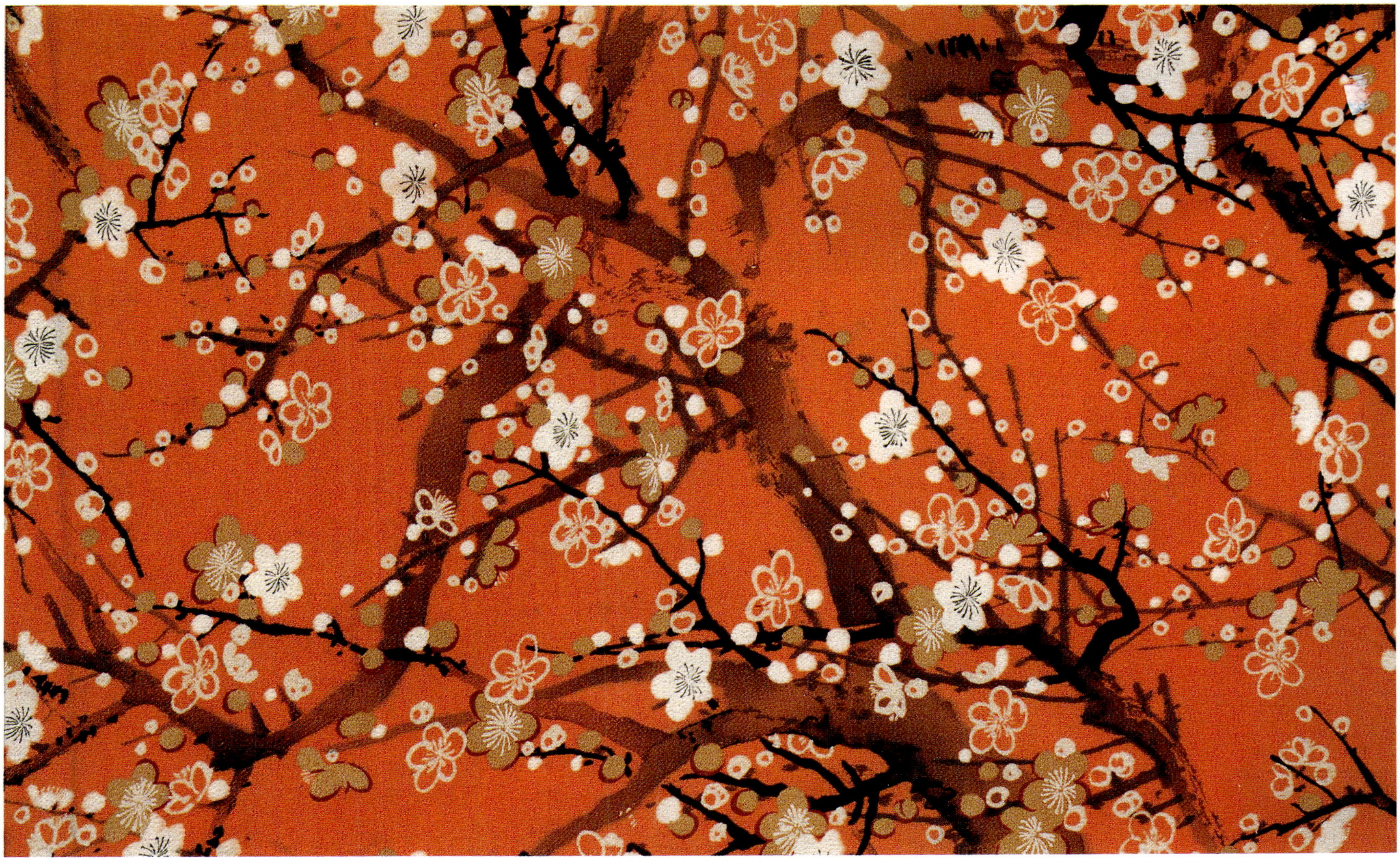

Japanese silk textile printed by stencil. Early nineteenth century.

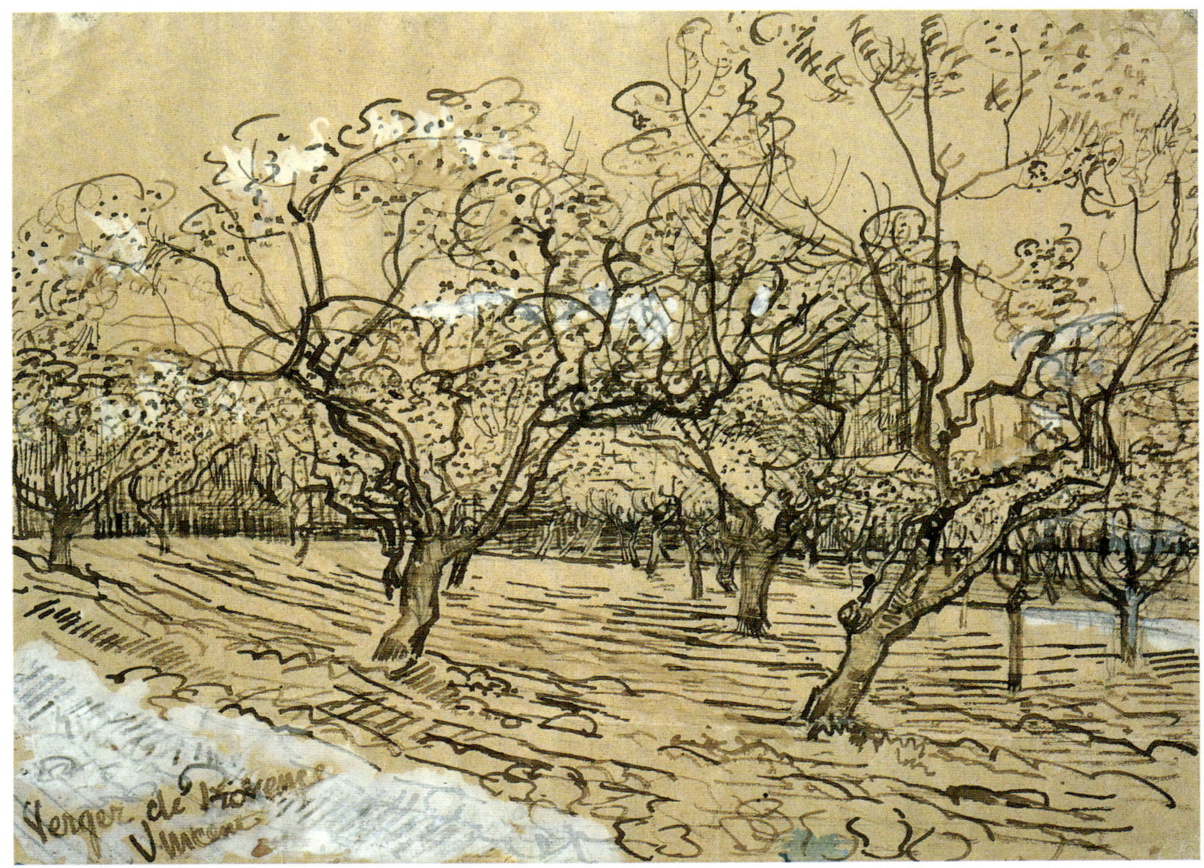

Vincent van Gogh's reed-pen drawing *Orchard in Provence.* (Vincent van Gogh Foundation, National Museum van Gogh, Amsterdam, Rijksmuseum.) 1888.

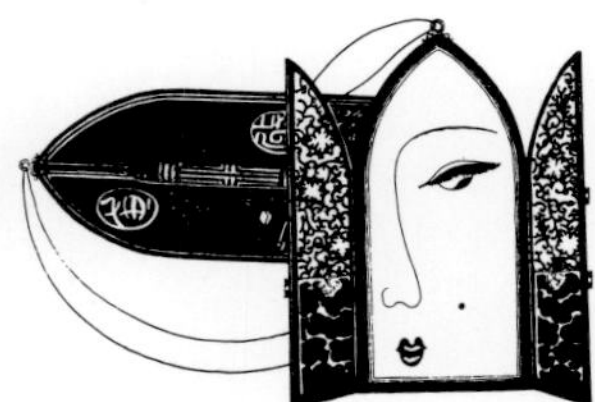

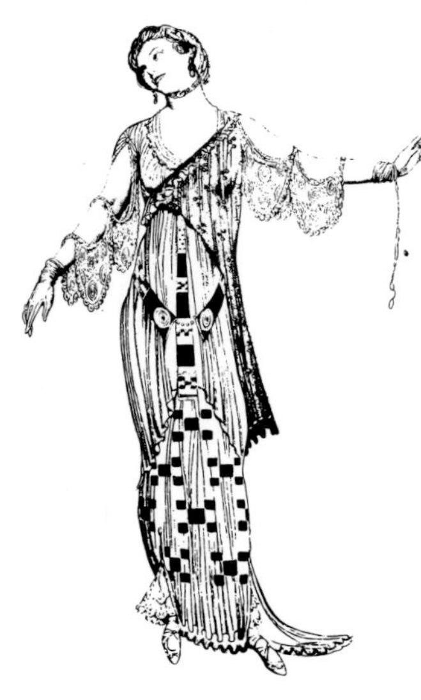

more style' than any other jeweller of his day; his new pieces inspired by Art Nouveau were said to demonstrate 'the imagination and the fancifulness which are the special property of the French race in all that relates to articles of luxury and modishness'. Similar superlatives were used for the Art Nouveau glass pieces displayed by Emile Gallé, the furniture of Eugène Gaillard and Eugène Colonna, and the designs of Georges de Feure, Louis Majorelle, and Eugène Grasset. In his review of the 1900 Exhibition Herbert E. Butler wrote, *Any publication dealing with the artistic side of the Paris exhibition which omitted to give some words of appreciation to the exhibits by the 'Art Nouveau' designers would be quite incomplete. For we may say without hesitation, that in this exhibition the French decorative artists have reached a new high-water mark of originality and excellence.*

Two years later, in 1902, the Italian Government staged its own international exhibition in Turin. This firmly established Art Nouveau as the most fashionable and sought after design style of the early twentieth century. Italy's designers, led by Carlo Bugatti, and designers from Vienna, New York, Glasgow, Nancy, London, Paris, Brussels, Cologne and numerous other centres, were developing interesting, sometimes nationalistic, variations, incorporating specific idiomatic and historical themes into their work. The French Art Nouveau variation had obviously been inspired by the visual opulence of the eighteenth century rococo period; the flat patterning of traditional Celtic manuscripts was without doubt the inspiration of Glasgow designers such as Mackintosh and McNair; the designer Henry van de Velde was proud to admit his conscious use of the medieval Gothic concepts of line and space. Other leading designers, such as Victor Horta, Adolf Loos and Richard Riemerschmid, refused to adopt any form of historic influence, using a local cultural or demotic variation instead.

The style of design developed by Liberty of London (one that lingers on in their Regent Street store) was a mixture of Tudor, Celtic and oriental influences as interpreted for Arthur Lasenby Liberty by his team of designers — Archibald Knox, Jessie M. King, Rex Silver and Walter Crane — who established 'Le Style Liberty' as one of the most admired design styles of the period. Other designers, such as Carlo Bugatti, the Czech artist Alphonse Mucha, the Austrian Josef Hoffmann, the German August Endell, and the Englishman Christopher Dresser, added their individual vision and skill to produce even greater diversity. But it was the universal use of the Japanese-inspired curvilinear shapes, the love of the irregular and the exotic, and the accepted iconography — lily, peacock, sunflower, flowing tendrils, the idealised ambivalent female form — that gave Art Nouveau its universal cohesion.

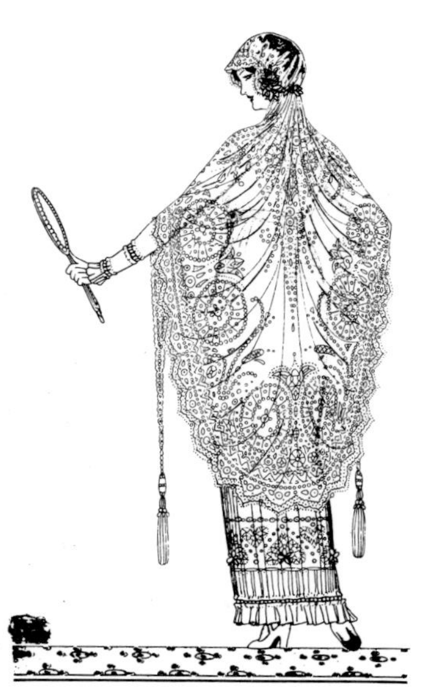

The Japanese influence on Western modes of design, art and graphic illustration, first noted by the French art critic Philippe Burty in the mid-1860s, had been growing in importance ever since the Japanese ports had been forcibly opened to international trade by Commodore Matthew C. Perry and a contingent of American naval gunboats on 31 March 1854, after two centuries of self-imposed isolation during what has become known as the Edo period.

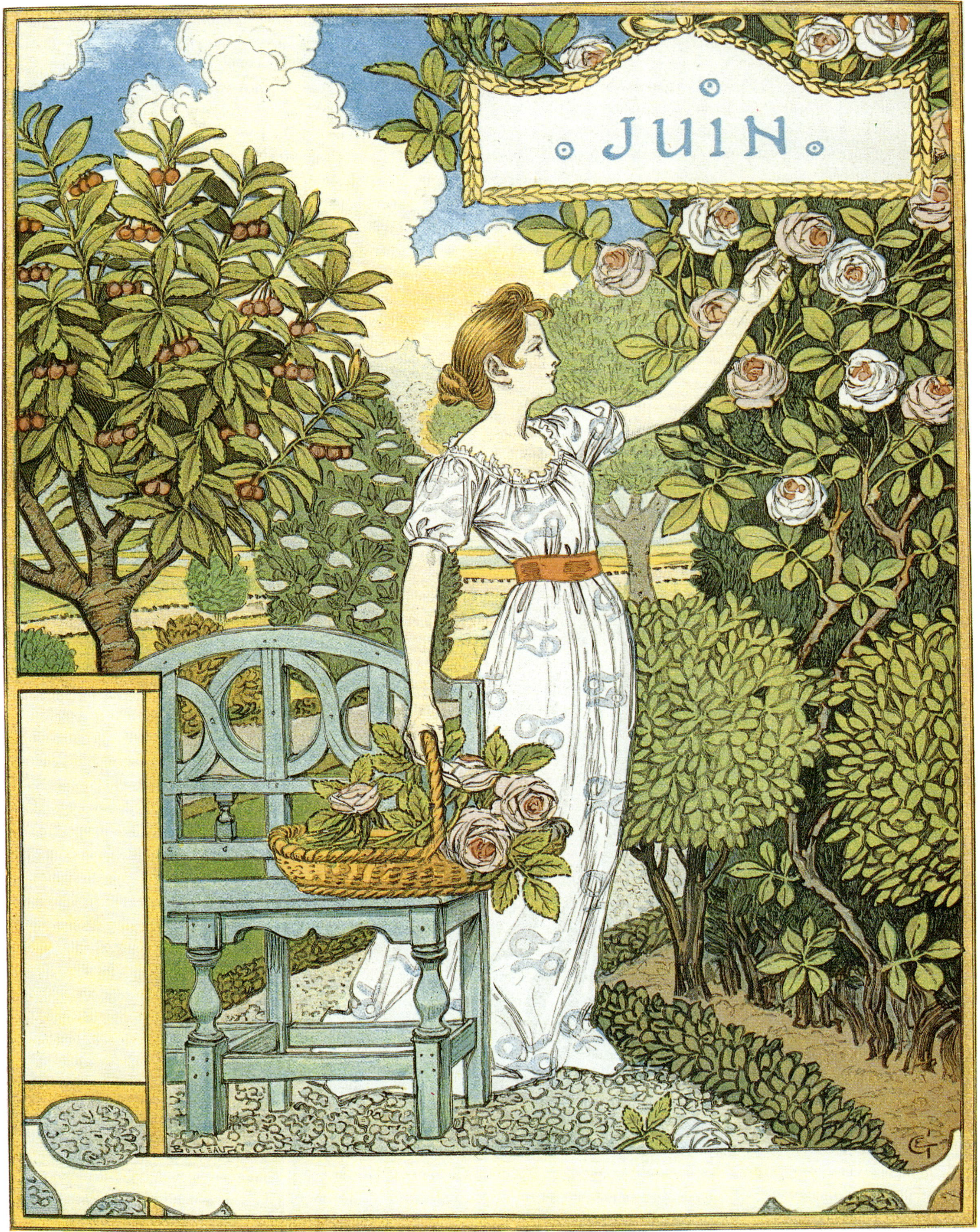

Chromo-litho illustration by Eugène Grasset, from *Les Mois*. Published by G. de Malherbe, Paris.
Late nineteenth century.

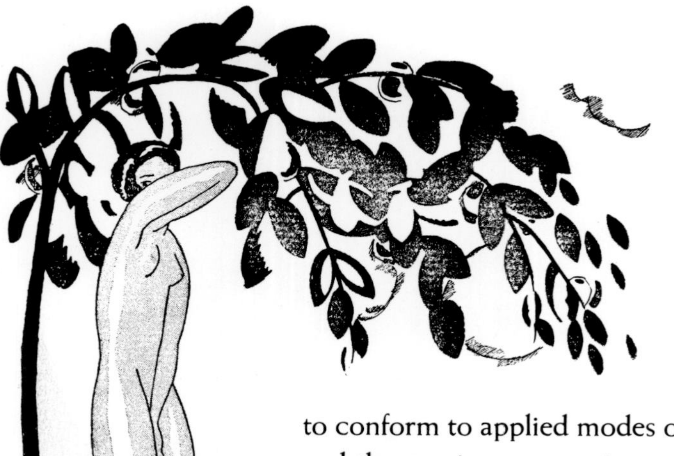

And just as the expanded eighteenth century trade with India and China had led to the introduction of the Chinoiserie style in Great Britain (which remains in the world of Chippendale-style antiques), so it was that the new Japanese trade led to the formulation of the Art Nouveau style: it rekindled in the younger artists and designers an interest in fine craftsmanship that had its own aesthetic integrity, in individuality of design without having to conform to applied modes of commercial ornamentation, and in the unusual and the exotic as a reaction against mass-produced merchandise of British and European origins.

In 1862 an exhibition of Japanese art objects had been displayed at the second International Exhibition held in London; it created much interest, especially among the younger artists, illustrators and designers who were beginning to embark on their professional careers. This exhibition was followed by numerous others of kimonos, lacquer work, examples of calligraphy, *ukiyo-e* prints, samurai armour, ceramics, and other artifacts and works of art, and it culminated in the spectacular displays of Japanese works at the famous Paris Exhibitions of 1878 and 1889.

In fact, by the end of the 1870s many Impressionist painters and designers had become avid collectors of Japanese *ukiyo-e* coloured woodcut prints, small carved *netsuke* figurines, ceramics, lacquer work, and all sorts of other artifacts that had transported to the West a wealth of information about the oriental traditions of fine craftsmanship, modes of design, visual composition, and details of line, colour and decoration. Many of these collectors used in their own work the inspiration gleaned from these Japanese artifacts and works of art: one has only to see an Impressionist painting by Monet, Degas, Manet or Gauguin, a piece of *marqueterie sur verre* or cameo glassware by Gallé, a lithographic print by Toulouse-Lautrec, an enamelled brooch by Lalique, or a book illustrated by Beardsley side by side with its Japanese source, to understand how influential Japan had become for many British, American and European artists, designers and master-craftsmen of the period.

At first, artists such as Edouard Manet simply used an assortment of Japanese objects to enliven their traditional European style of painting, as in his *Portrait of Emile Zola* painted in 1868; Claude Monet did the same thing in his painting of *Madame Monet in a Kimono* in 1876. But by the late 1870s many European artists had begun to depict Japanese-style poses, grouping of individuals and pictorial compositions. This can be clearly seen if one com-

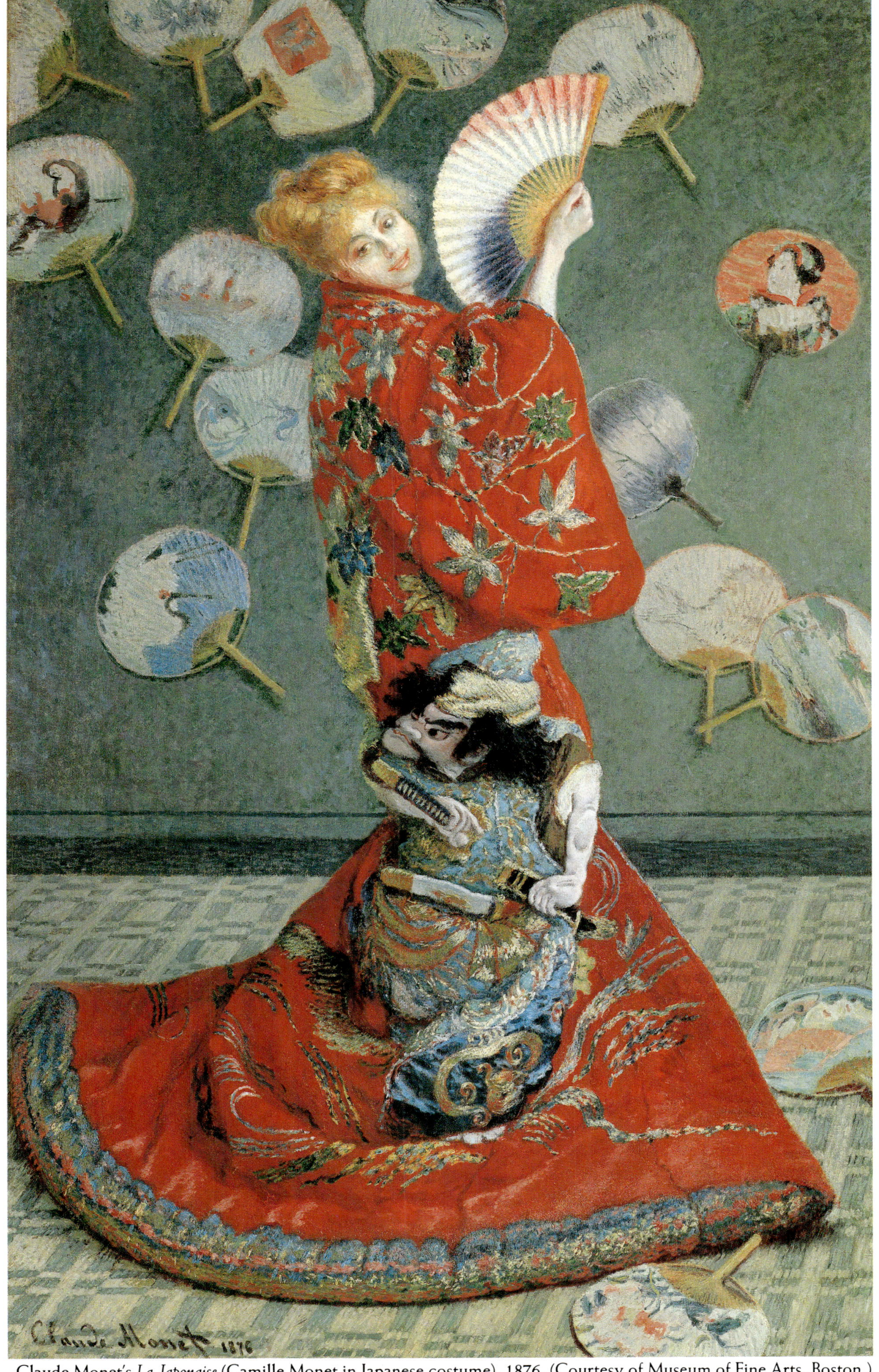

Claude Monet's *La Japonaise* (Camille Monet in Japanese costume). 1876. (Courtesy of Museum of Fine Arts, Boston.)

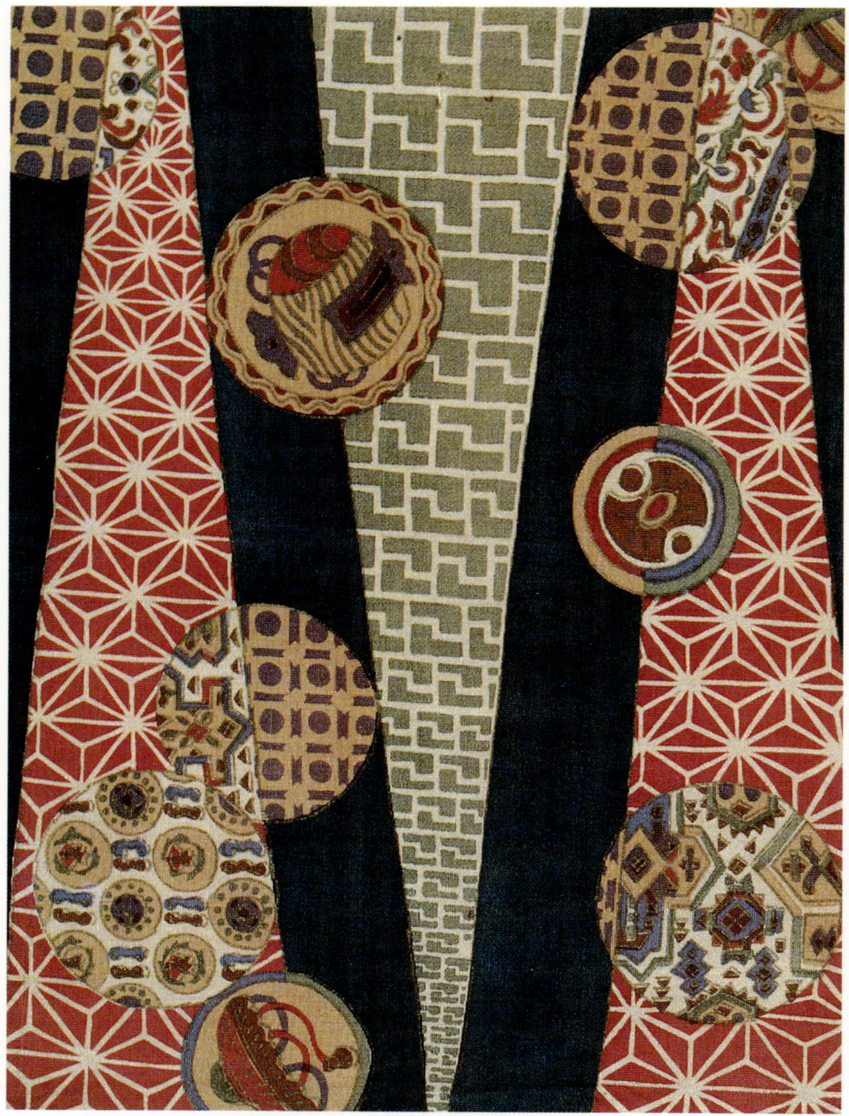

Japanese silk textile printed by stencil. Early nineteenth century.

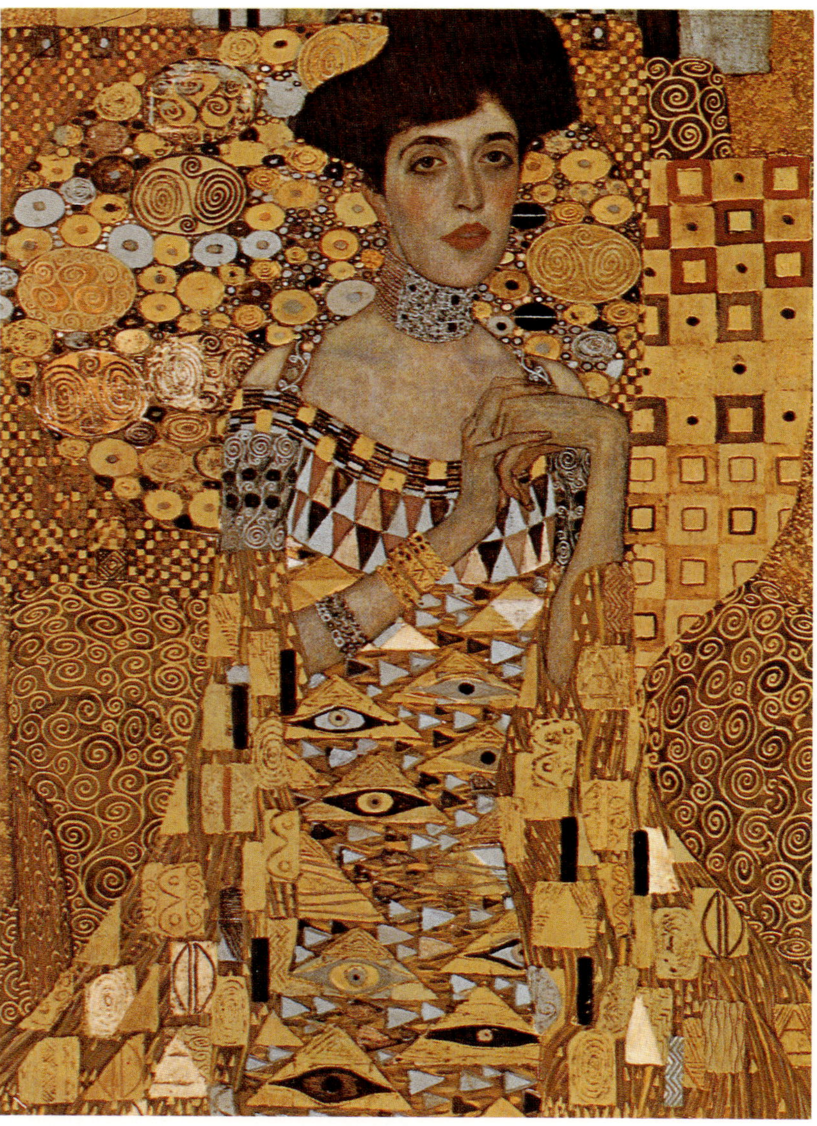

Gustav Klimt's painting of Adèle Block-Bauer I. Osterreichische Galerie, Vienna. 1907. (Reproduced with permission of Galerie Welz, Salzburg.)

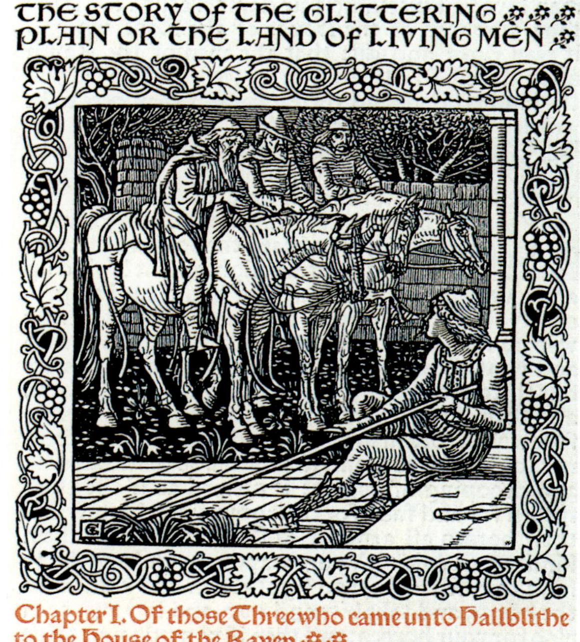

THE STORY OF THE GLITTERING PLAIN OR THE LAND OF LIVING MEN

Chapter I. Of those Three who came unto Hallblithe to the House of the Raven

THAS been told that there was once a young man of free kindred and whose name was Hallblithe: he was fair, strong, and not untried in battle; he was of the House of the Raven of old time. This

Title page of *The Story of the Glittering Plain* with decorations by William Morris and Walter Crane. Printed by the Kelmscott Press, London. 1894.

pares Degas' drawings and paintings of ballet dancers with Hokusai's *ukiyo-e* woodcut prints. The similarity is also evident in Degas' series of women bathing.

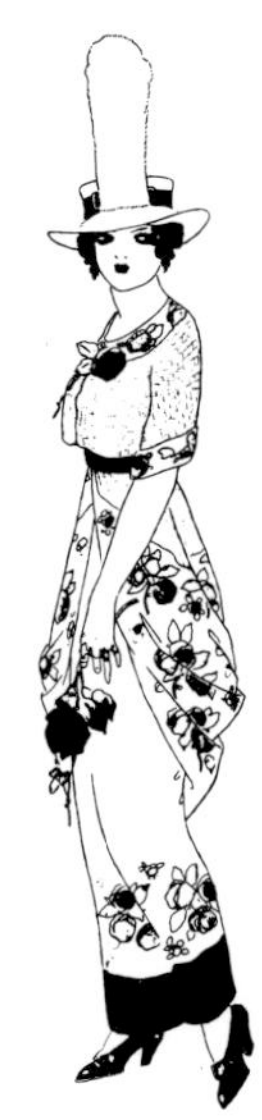

The American artist James Abbot McNeill Whistler is among those known to have been directly influenced by *ukiyo-e* prints; his famous *Nocturne in Blue and Gold*, a painting of old Battersea Bridge in 1875, is obviously inspired by Hiroshige's woodcut *Edo Bridge*, from the *Hundred Views of Famous Places in Edo* published in Tokyo earlier in that century. Vincent van Gogh was also greatly influenced by the works of Hiroshige and Hokusai and he was an enthusiastic collector of *ukiyo-e* prints, which he purchased from a small Paris gallery owned by Samuel Bing. At that stage Bing was importing the prints from Tokyo, for collectors such as van Gogh, Degas, Whistler and Monet.

But, although they derived much of their inspiration and many of their aesthetic principles from Japanese art, these artists and designers never imitated its style in a servile manner. The influence is beyond question, but nothing could be more unlike a piece of Japanese art than one of Degas' paintings, a Beardsley drawing, a brooch by Lalique, or a glass vase by Gallé. The artists and designers had developed their own aesthetic style, using their individual instincts and abilities, yet never losing sight of the Japanese mode within which they worked. They combined this mode with their inherited cultural and dialectic variations in an entirely personal way, stamping each piece of work with their own recognisable and idiosyncratic style.

By the early twentieth century, the Japanese aesthetic influence was being mellowed by a wide variety of other influences and traditions, from China, India, Turkey, Persia, Russia, and by the work of earlier artists of Celtic, Byzantine, Roman, Greek, Egyptian, African and pre-Columbian origin. The Viennese painter Gustav Klimt, for instance, combined his love for Japanese kimonos and stencilled textile designs with ideas taken from the great Byzantine mosaics of Ravenna, which he had visited in 1903. Henri Matisse and the Fauves — Braque, Vlaminck, Derain, Rouault and van Dongen — the 'wild beasts of colour', as this group of painters had been named after their exhibition at the Paris Salon d'Automne in 1905, carried on where van Gogh's colourful Japanese-inspired paintings had left off after his untimely death in 1890. This in turn inspired the German Expressionists and many other individuals such as Kandinsky and Picasso.

After the success of the 1902 Turin Exhibition, the Italian Goverment decided in 1906 to stage another international exhibition, this time in Milan, to celebrate the opening of the Simplon Tunnel, one of the greatest engineering feats attempted during that decade. But much had happened in the world of fashionable design since 1902. In their continual fight for commercial gain, many producers of large quantity low quality merchandise had begun to apply an exuberance of Art Nouveau-style ornamentation to their otherwise uninteresting wares. Unfortunately, many of the products displayed at the 1906 exhibition were of this calibre and were thus not Art Nouveau in the

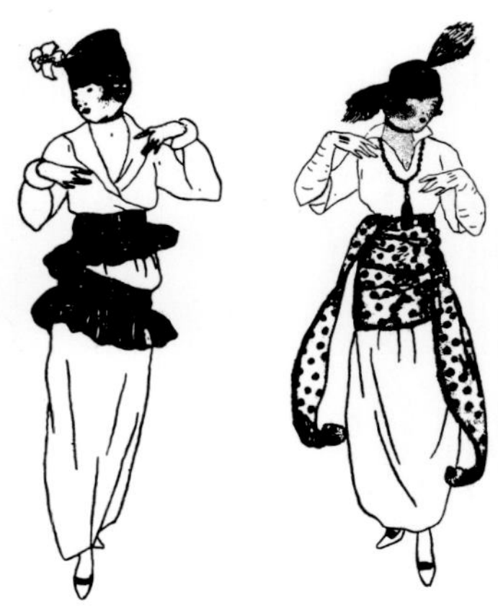

true sense: the decorative aspects were not an essential part of the construction, the applied stylisation making the products only superficially different from those of the late nineteenth century.

Originally, the creators of the Art Nouveau movement had begun their work with the hope of evoking meaning as well as feeling through shape and form, and to a certain degree many designers and craftsmen had succeeded in embodying this hope in their work. But when the Art Nouveau style was merely applied to a product, it became no better than the nineteenth century applied modes of design against which the designers had rebelled.

Nevertheless, during its brief flowering the unique style had fulfilled a valuable liberating function in allowing its creators to discard many of the outdated conventions and strictures of the nineteenth century. And, having once managed to shake off the ungentle compulsions of unthinking manufacturers, many of the younger avant-garde designers began experimenting with the simpler relationships to be found in geometric shapes, textural surfaces and angular forms of construction; they started to combine this with their continuing admiration for the oriental ideals of quality and superb craftsmanship.

During the next four years, between 1906 and 1910, a new twentieth century style of design began to develop which involved the intellectual as well as the visual sense of both designer and purchaser — a style that was to become what we now know as 'Art Deco'. In retrospect, however, it appears that the wealthy members of world society (the designers' most ardent patrons) were not yet ready for such a dramatic change, and the famous ateliers of Gallé, Lalique, Gaillard, Colonna, and de Feure continued to produce expensive merchandise in the Art Nouveau style — although Emile Gallé had died in 1904 and his atelier was now under the direction of the less talented Victor Prouvé.

The British designer Christopher Dresser had also died in 1904, and between 1900 and 1906 so had Gauguin, Cézanne, Toulouse-Lautrec, Chekhov, Zola and Ibsen. During this six-year period there had been many new developments throughout the Western world: the American Wright brothers had successfully flown the first engine-propelled aeroplane; the Nobel Prize for Physics had been awarded to Pierre and Marie Curie for their work on uranium radiation and for isolating radium from pitchblende; and the young

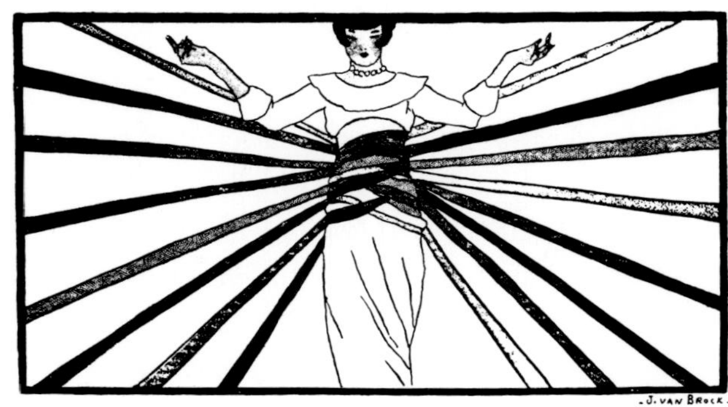

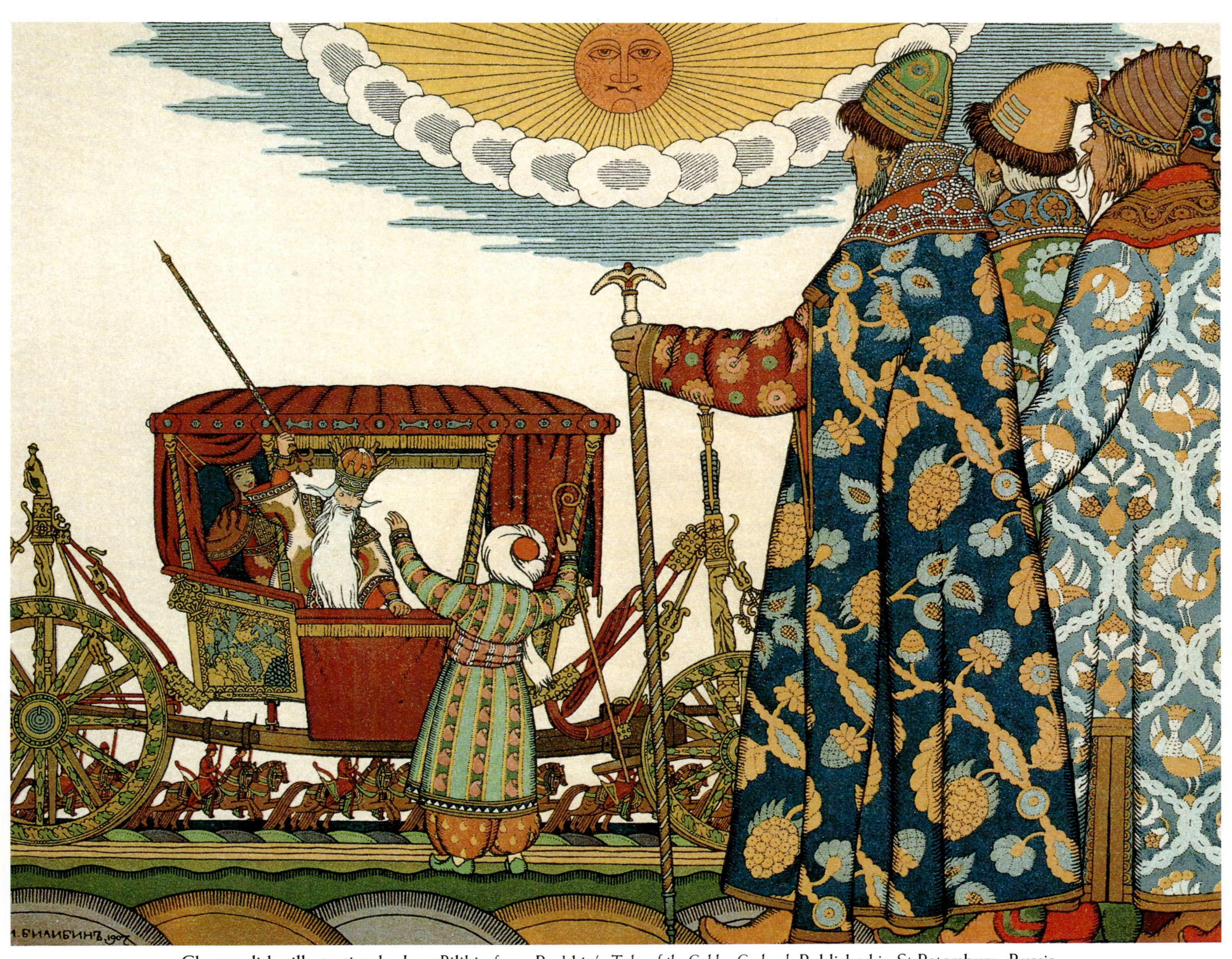

Chromo-litho illustration by Ivan Bilibin from Pushkin's *Tales of the Golden Cockerel*. Published in St Petersburg, Russia. 1907.

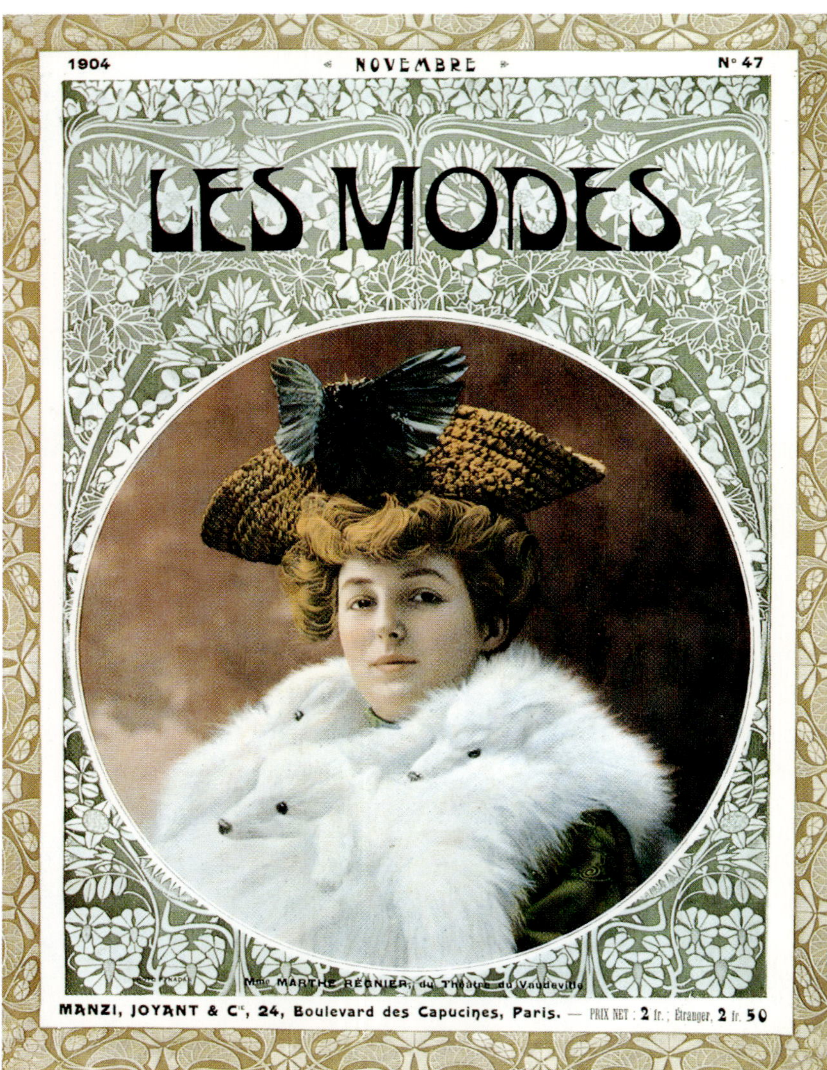

Les Modes, November 1904. Photo by P. Nadan of the actress Mme Marthe Régier, Théâtre du Vaudeville.

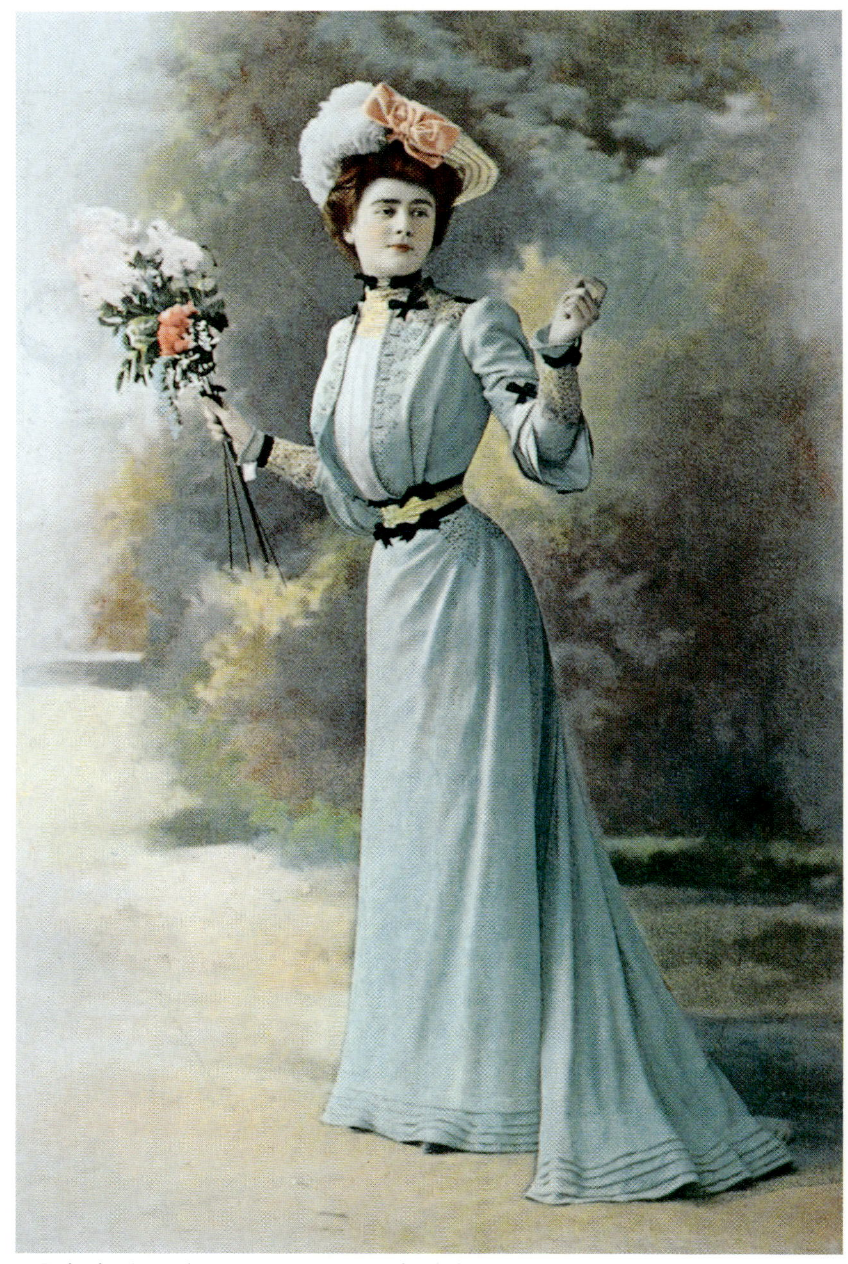

Robe d'après-midi featured in *Les Modes*, July 1901. Photograph by Reutlinger.

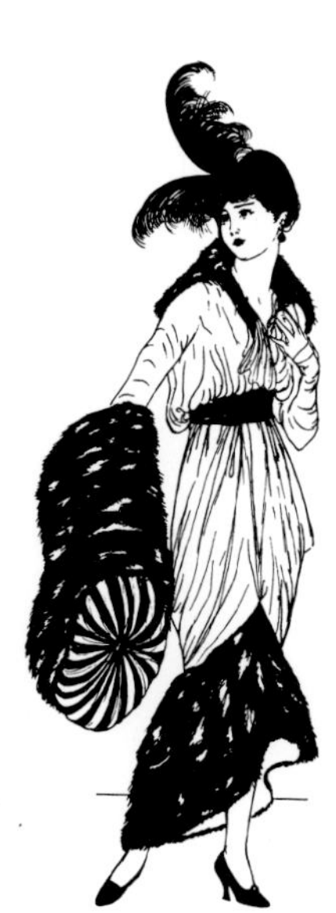

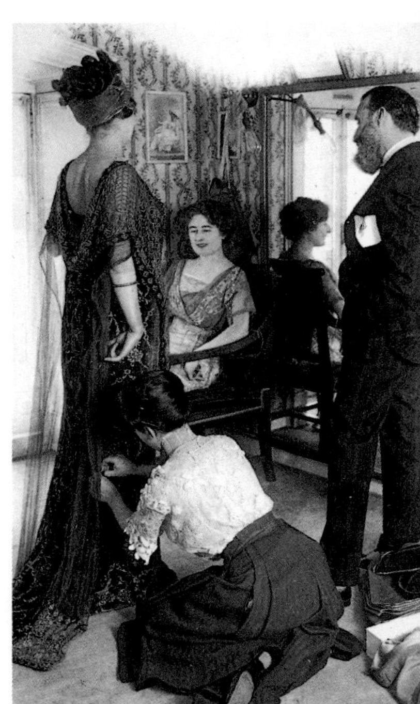

Albert Einstein had worked out the basis for his theory of relativity. In addition, many people had begun to read about the curious sexual emotions of the Victorian psyche in Sigmund Freud's *Interpretation of Dreams*, about previously unmentionable aspects of their own sexuality in Havelock Ellis's *Studies in the Psychology of Sex*, about the social problems of the underprivileged members of the Western world in Nikolai Lenin's book *What is to be Done?*, and about the conspicuous waste of the wealthy elite in Thorstein Veblen's *Theory of the Leisure Classes*.

Another dramatic change was beginning to take effect at this time. In the late 1890s the half-tone process of reproducing coloured and monochrome photographs had been developed. (It involves the use of a fine, dotted screen and is still the process by which most pictorial images are reproduced today.) The consequences of this change are exemplified in the development of fashion photography.

Until the introduction in 1901 of the glossy magazine *Les Modes*, the latest fashionable styles had been promoted by the use of hand-coloured engravings. These had first been used in magazine form in a 1771 edition of the British *Lady's Magazine*; the method relied solely on the depictive skills of the illustrator and the engraver, who endeavoured to convey their perception of the latest mode. During its first seventy or so years of use, the method worked admirably at the hands of artists and entrepreneurs such as Claude-Louis Desrais, Antoine Watteau, Horace Vernet, Nicklaus von Heideloff, Rudolph Ackermann, Philippe-Louis Debucourt and Pierre La Mésangère, but its quality degenerated in the mid-nineteenth century, under the influence of artists of mediocre talent. By the first decade of the present century, however, the haut monde could actually see coloured photographs of the newest styles, and they were able to make their selections in the comfort of their own homes. This, in turn, influenced the styles themselves.

In England, the recalcitrant Edward VII had ascended the throne on the death of his mother, Queen Victoria, in 1901. The new King was the antithesis of his mother, and by 1906 the English palaces, gloomy and lifeless during the latter part of Queen Victoria's reign, had become models of activity and style. They influenced the courts of Europe; also the 'courts' of the British and American millionaires whose company the new King enjoyed, inspiring a seemingly endless spree of opulence and self-indulgence among the wealthy of the Western world.

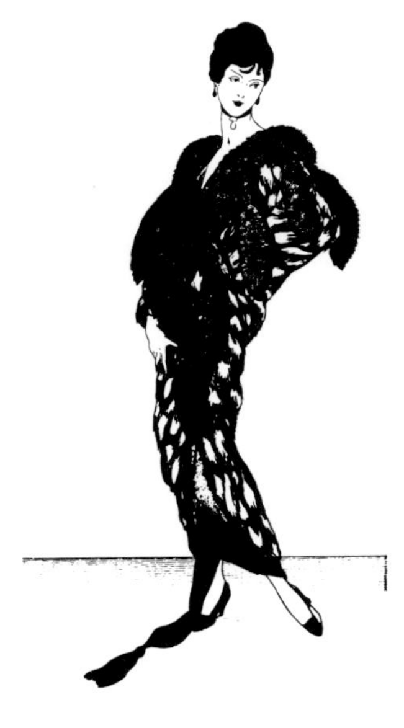

In the courts of Edward VII, Kaiser Wilhelm II and the Tsar, and of Norway, Belgium, Austria, Hungary, Italy, Rumania and Spain, whenever receptions were held it seemed that all the world's supply of diamonds, rubies, turquoises, emeralds and pearls was sprinkled over the wealthy and aristocratic guests as they mixed with ambassadors and field marshals in gold-encrusted uniforms and maharajahs adorned with brilliant silk turbans.

France had no royal courts, so the sumptuous Paris *châteaux* of the aristocrats took their place. Having no political power, the French aristocrats had

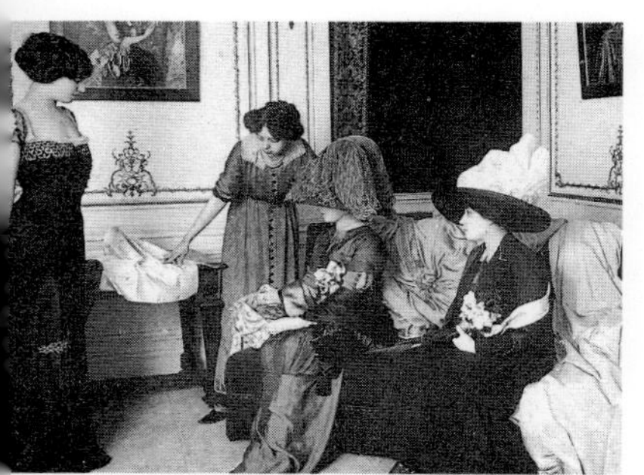

learnt to devote their time, money and energy to other pleasures, and they openly consorted with the fashionable demi-mondaines — the great courtesans and cocottes of the day. And when they held a reception it was far from the formal affair normally associated with matters of State.

Not that the English aristocracy and the American millionaires were above diversions of the flesh, as the 'actress' Lillie Langtry knew very well, having first been Prince Edward's favourite mistress before he became King and then becoming the mistress of American millionaire Freddie Gebhard. Whilst married to the Duke of Malborough Lady Randolph Churchill is also reputed to have had many passionate love affairs as did many other society women of that period.

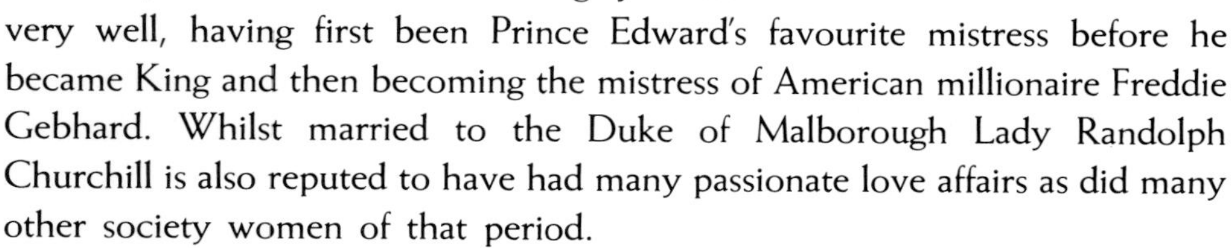

It had become the accepted role of the demi-mondaines not only to look attractive at all times but also to keep the wealthy and powerful members of French society happy and contented in all respects. In so doing, these professional beauties lived a life of extraordinary luxury, enjoying everything their wealthy patrons could possibly afford.

Naturally, rivalry between them was intense, and when it caused friction the public watched with great interest and amusement. During a period of rivalry between La Belle Otero and the equally beautiful Liane de Pougy the public was thrilled and gossip abounded. It is reported, for instance, that on one particular evening La Belle Otero wore her entire collection of rubies; Liane de Pougy is said to have worn even more costly ones the next day. When La Belle Otero's famous pearls were worn to her waist, her rival could be seen wearing hers as a belt. Finally, when it was rumoured that La Belle Otero had been given a diamond necklace which would have made that of Liane de Pougy look insignificant by comparison, the latter appeared in a stunning white silk dress without a single jewel. Her maid, who followed her, was covered in diamonds and other jewels worth far more than those worn on that occasion by La Belle Otero.

Most demi-mondaines also loved making spectacular entrances at the theatre, the opera, or the great restaurants of the period, especially at Maxim's at suppertime, where they regularly dined in one of the private suites with their latest devoted millionaire or aristocrat. They invariably arrived in a new dress, supplied that afternoon by one of the great couture houses, with jewels glistening and wearing a hat shimmering with plumes.

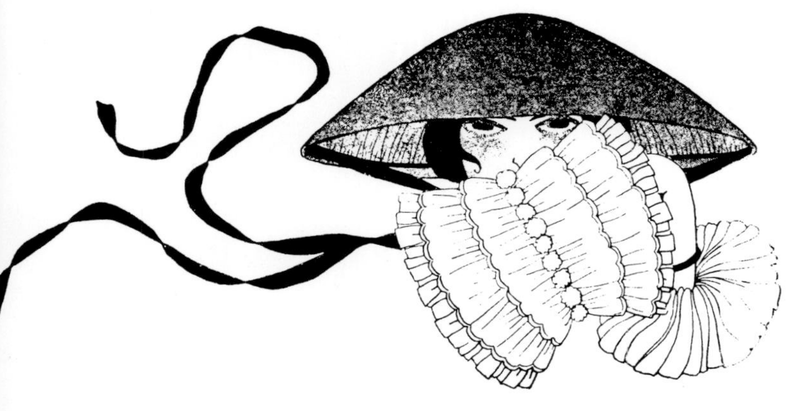

In the streets outside, more straightforward forms of prostitution had never been as

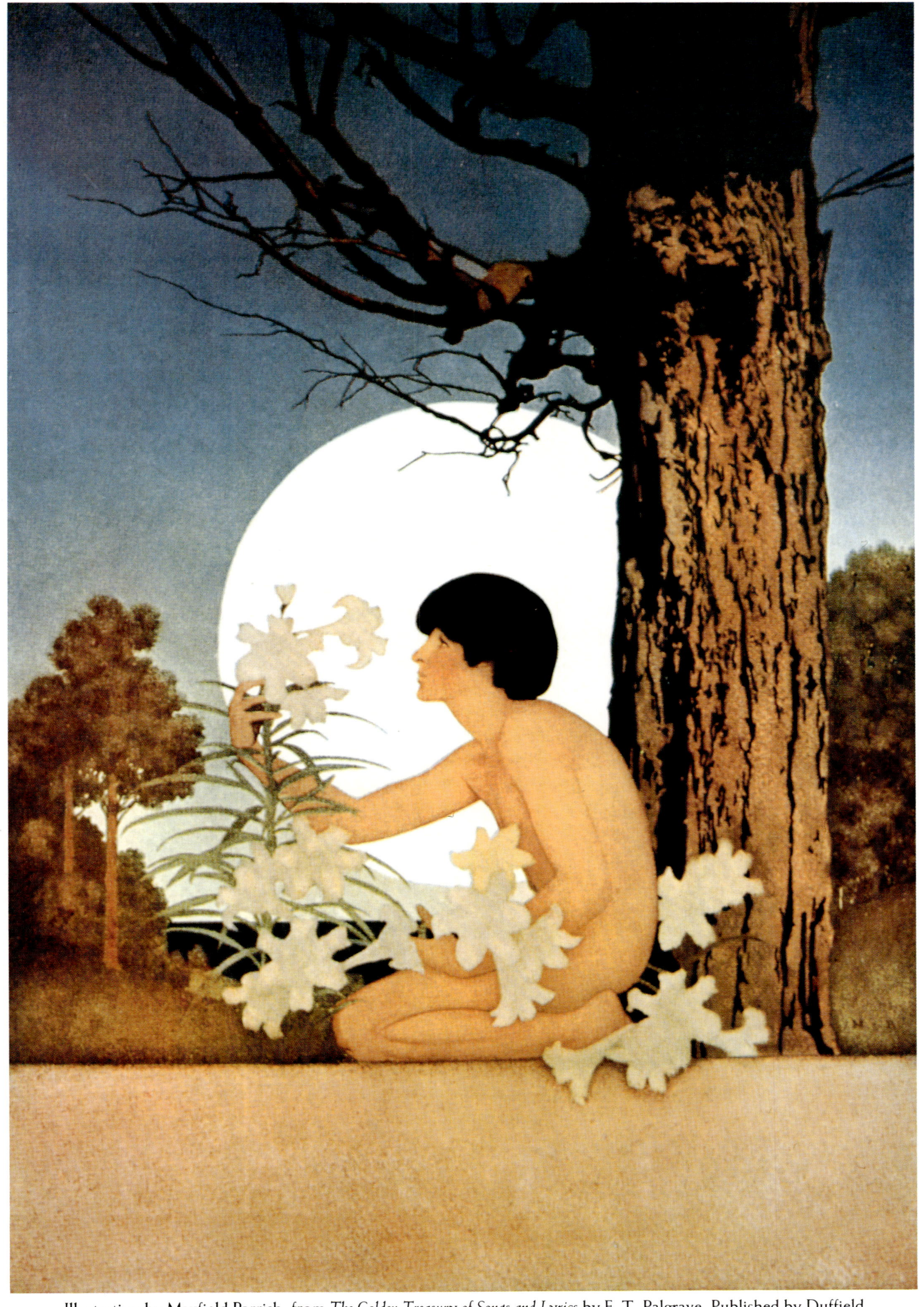

Illustration by Maxfield Parrish, from *The Golden Treasury of Songs and Lyrics* by F. T. Palgrave. Published by Duffield & Co., New York. 1911.

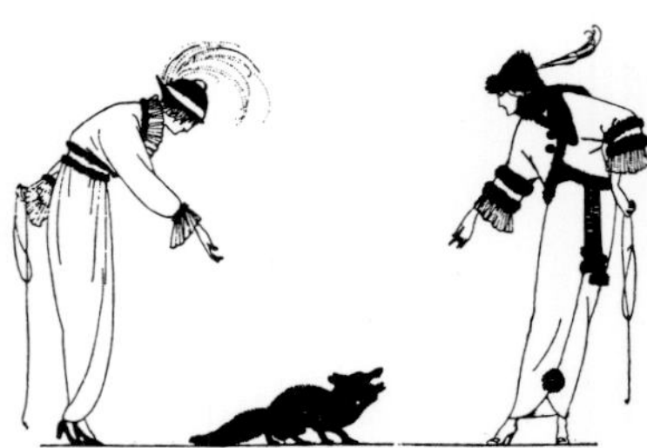

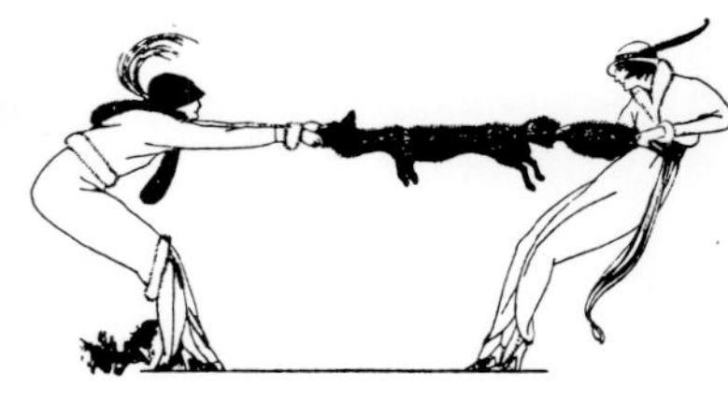

well organised, nor offered in such variety, since the decline of the Roman Empire. There were young, inexperienced girls who strolled the outer boulevards, a great many experienced women who frequented the minor boulevards, and there were the great madams of Montmartre, offering in their luxurious bordellos every variety of sexual delight that man or beast could devise.

The couture houses used the demi-mondaines as promoters of the latest fashionable ideas, often offering them their latest styles for little more than cost price, so that they would be able to sell similar styles to their established clientele, who would then be seen to be keeping up with the trends. When a particular couture house lost the patronage of one of the more avant-garde demi-mondaines its sales would plummet alarmingly, prompting it to pay handsomely for the return of that particular beauty, or her greatest rival. It would seem that even during the golden age of the Belle Epoque, when women's clothing had rarely, if ever, been so elaborate and so all-concealing, the respectable woman of society still wished to be associated with a risqué mode of dressing, by being seen wearing the fashionable styles that had just been set by the professional beauties of somewhat questionable virtue.

Throughout this period the theatre also played an important part in entertaining, surprising, enthralling, amusing and outraging Western society. This was the era of Loie Fuller, Eleonora Duse, Isadora Duncan, the Gibson Girls, and Sarah Bernhardt, whose private lives appear to have been as full of sex and scandal as their public lives had been full of adulation.

In the latter part of the decade, strikes, riots, attempted revolutions, assassinations and indiscriminate bombings had plagued many of the major cities of Italy, Hungary, Germany, Austria, Russia and France. In Serbia, King Alexander and Queen Drago had been killed in a bloody uprising. In Russia, hundreds of civilians had been killed in riots against the Tsar. The King and Crown Prince of Portugal had been assassinated. Suffragettes throughout the Western world were strident in their demand for the vote. In Turkey, a new constitution had been granted after months of civil strife. And in America the city of Baltimore had been burnt to the ground, 950 children had died in a shipping accident in New York harbour, San Francisco had been completely destroyed by an earthquake, and accusations of fraud and corruption implicated almost every major city.

Western society began to change under the pressure of the times, and so did its expressive needs. Artists and designers responded by developing a new visual language that aimed at expressing their perceptions of the new era. In America, Frank Lloyd Wright and the brothers Charles and Henry Greene had already begun to replace the opulence and clutter of the few remaining interiors of the Belle Epoque with clear, clean lines and unfussy furnishings. The European designers Henry van de Velde, Josef Hoffmann and Peter Behrens were doing likewise.

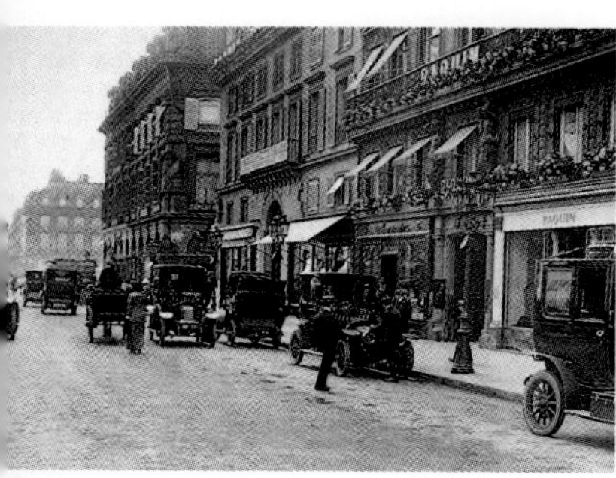

Many product designers were also experimenting with new variations of purely functional forms of design, following Adam Smith's eighteenth century

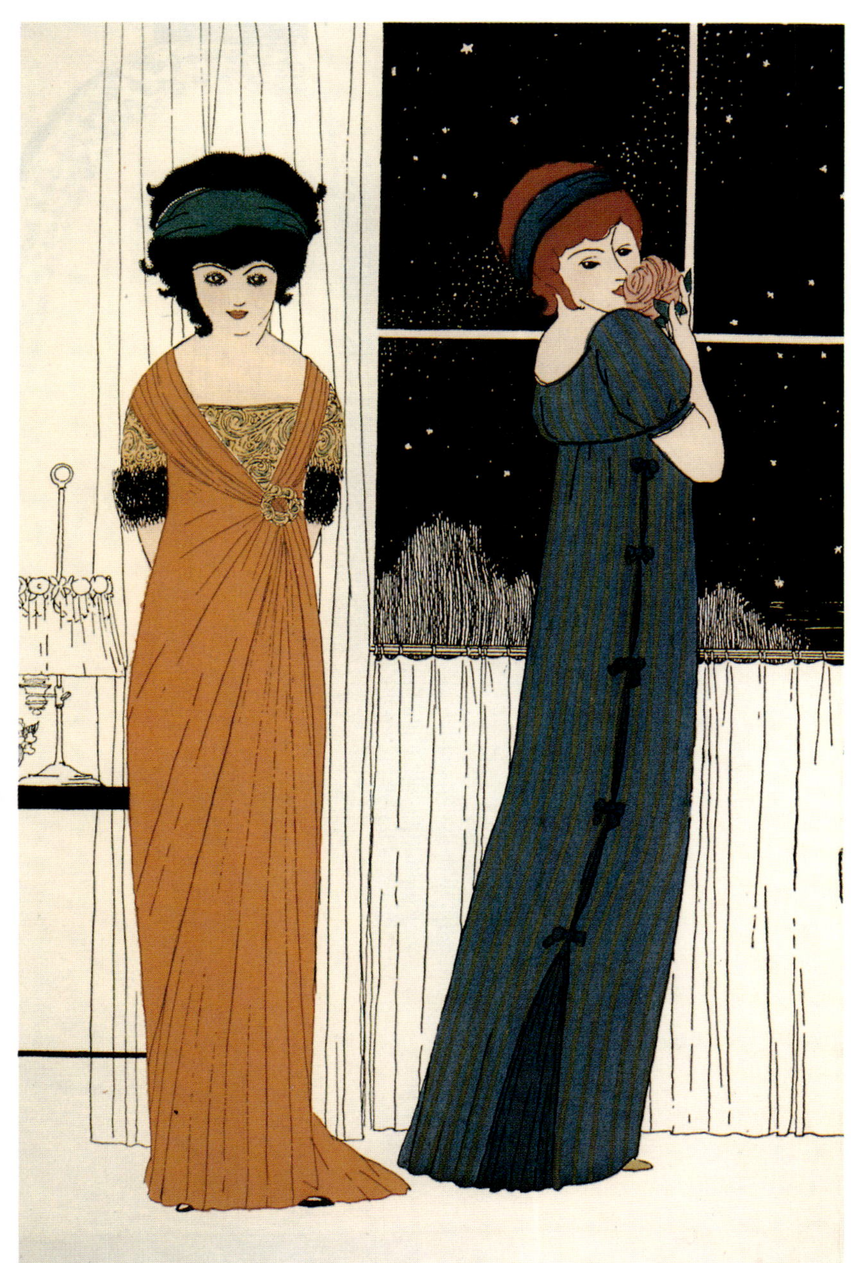

Pochoir illustration by Paul Iribe, from *Les Robes de Paul Poiret*. Published for Paul Poiret by La Société Générale d'Impression, Paris. 1908.

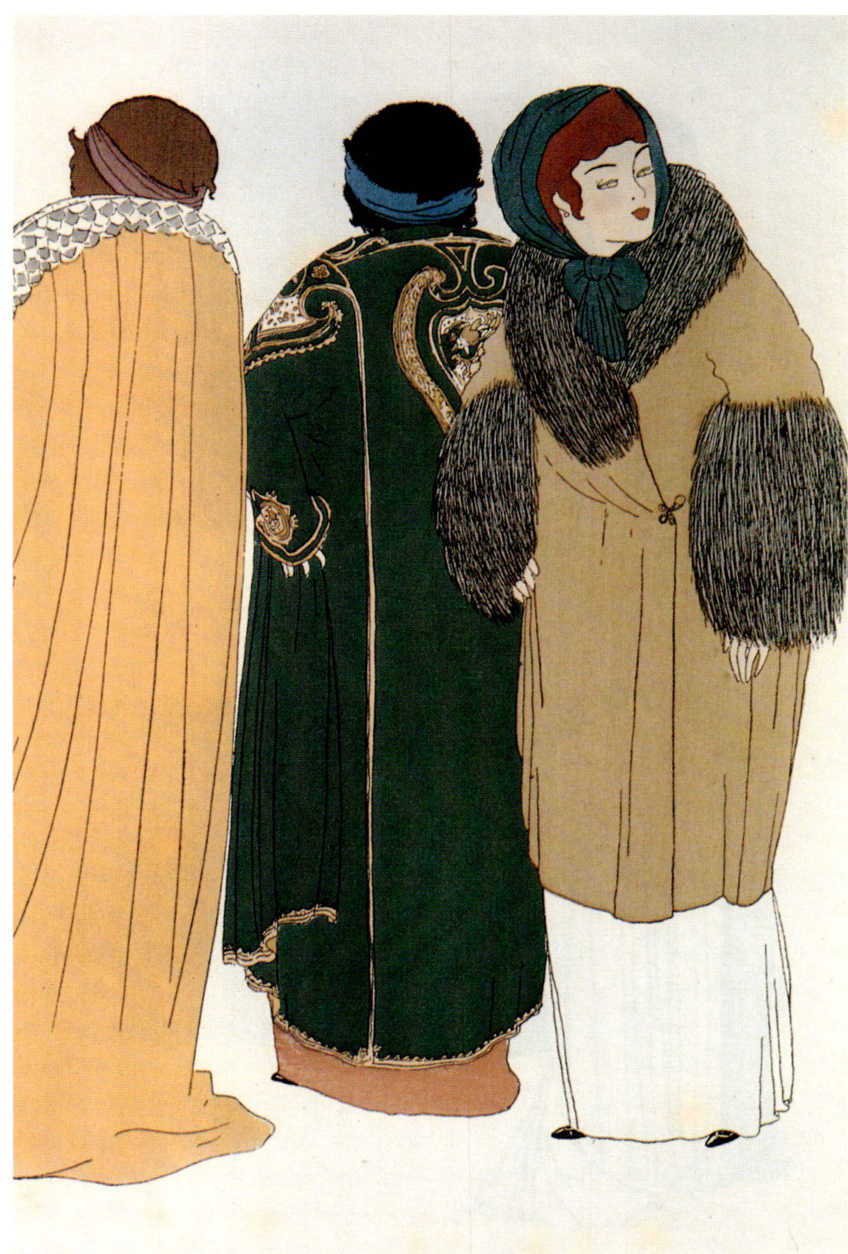

Pochoir illustration by Paul Iribe, from *Les Robes de Paul Poiret*. Published for Paul Poiret by La Société Générale d'Impression, Paris. 1908.

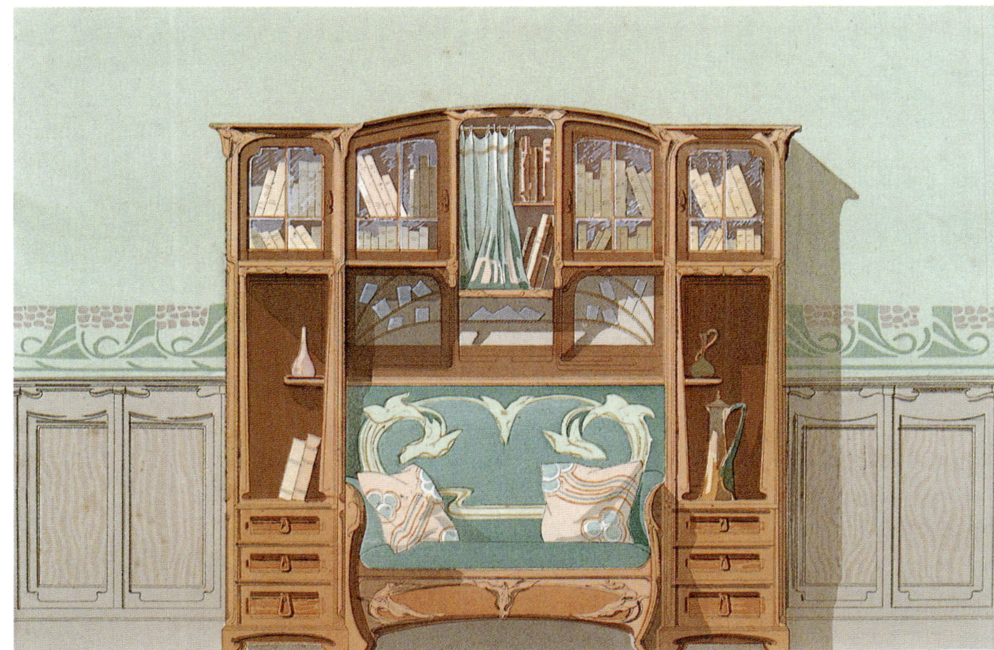

Pochoir illustration in the Art Nouveau style by Gustave Raynal, from *Le Meuble au XXme siècle*. Librairie Centrale d'Architecture, Paris. Very early twentieth century.

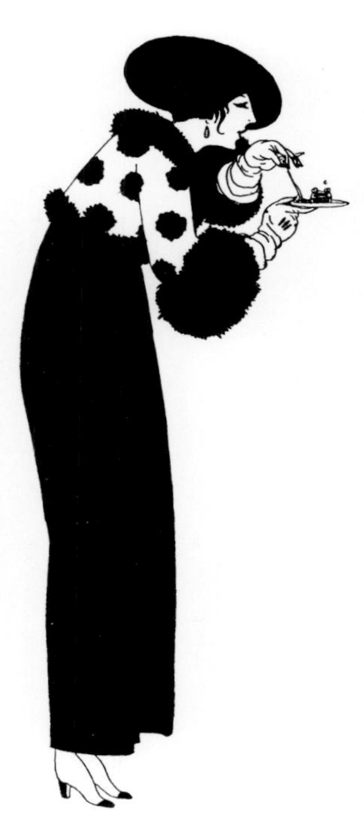

dictum that 'utility is one of the principal sources of beauty'. During the nineteeth century this had been forgotten by all but a few individuals whose work belongs to what is best described as the 'proto-modern movement'. Notable in this group were the English designer Christopher Dresser, whose designs were being rediscovered and admired for their clean, uncluttered shapes and functional detailing; the Austrian designer Michael Thonet, who had founded the Gebruder Thonet furniture company in 1849 and whose early experimental work in bentwood was being rediscovered by the new avant-garde designers; Sir George Cayley, who had been a pioneer in streamlining at the beginning of the nineteenth century; and the craftsmen–designers responsible for many of the vernacular forms, such as farm carts, everyday utensils and tools, farmhouse furnishings, and an array of unpretentious utilitarian objects such as ploughs, rakes, cane baskets, and storage casks.

Many of the avant-garde designers thought that they were on the threshold of a new, more permanent mode of design that would be incapable of becoming outmoded. They declared that 'beauty was not an essential ingredient in the design of a manufactured object, as the eventual aesthetic attractiveness of such an object is the result of the observer's perceived relationship between the object and its function', echoing the thoughts of many British industrial philosophers of the mid-eighteenth century.

In the belief that they were in fact creating an entirely new twentieth century mode of design, many young designers attempted to purge their work of the influence of all the 'pecuniary-style' beauty that they considered had plagued European design since the beginnings of the Industrial Revolution and had given reputability to objects only by virtue of their obvious uselessness and honorific waste. They began to produce objects in time-honoured vernacular tradition.

Proto-modern designs in silver plate by Christopher Dresser c.1875–90.

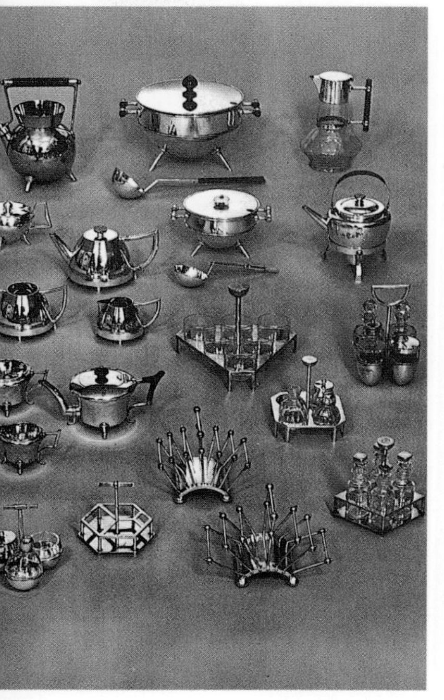

But it was not very long before many of these designers began to realise that pure functionalism was too austere and emotionally barren for all but the most devoted, and that most of their potential customers required a certain amount of fantasy, luxury and embellishment in order to fulfil their aesthetic dreams — these dreams being more real to them, and more emotionally fulfilling, than the designers' ideals of pure functionalism could ever be. Thus it became the task of these designers to proclaim function as the determining factor of their new design forms, yet to be guided by other values when actually designing.

But the dichotomy became less and less important: the new twentieth century style of design achieved wider acceptance and started to progress and change into Art Deco, which is today regarded as the most influential, the most original, the most visually coherent, and the most aesthetically complete style of design created in this or the previous century.

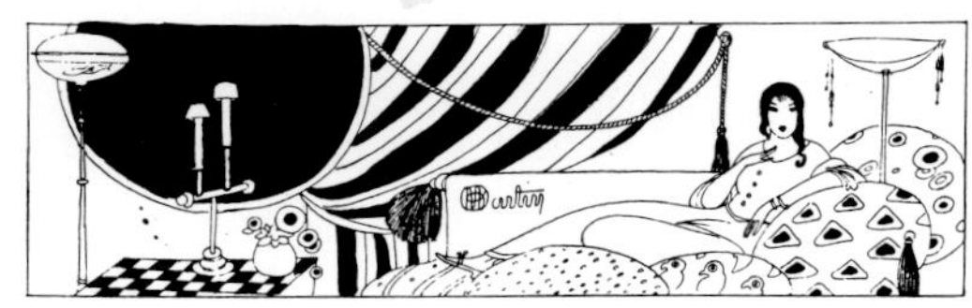

Pochoir illustration in the Art Nouveau style by M. P. Verneuil, from *La Plante et ses applications ornementales* by Eugène Grasset. Published by F. Lyon-Claesen, Brussels. 1895.

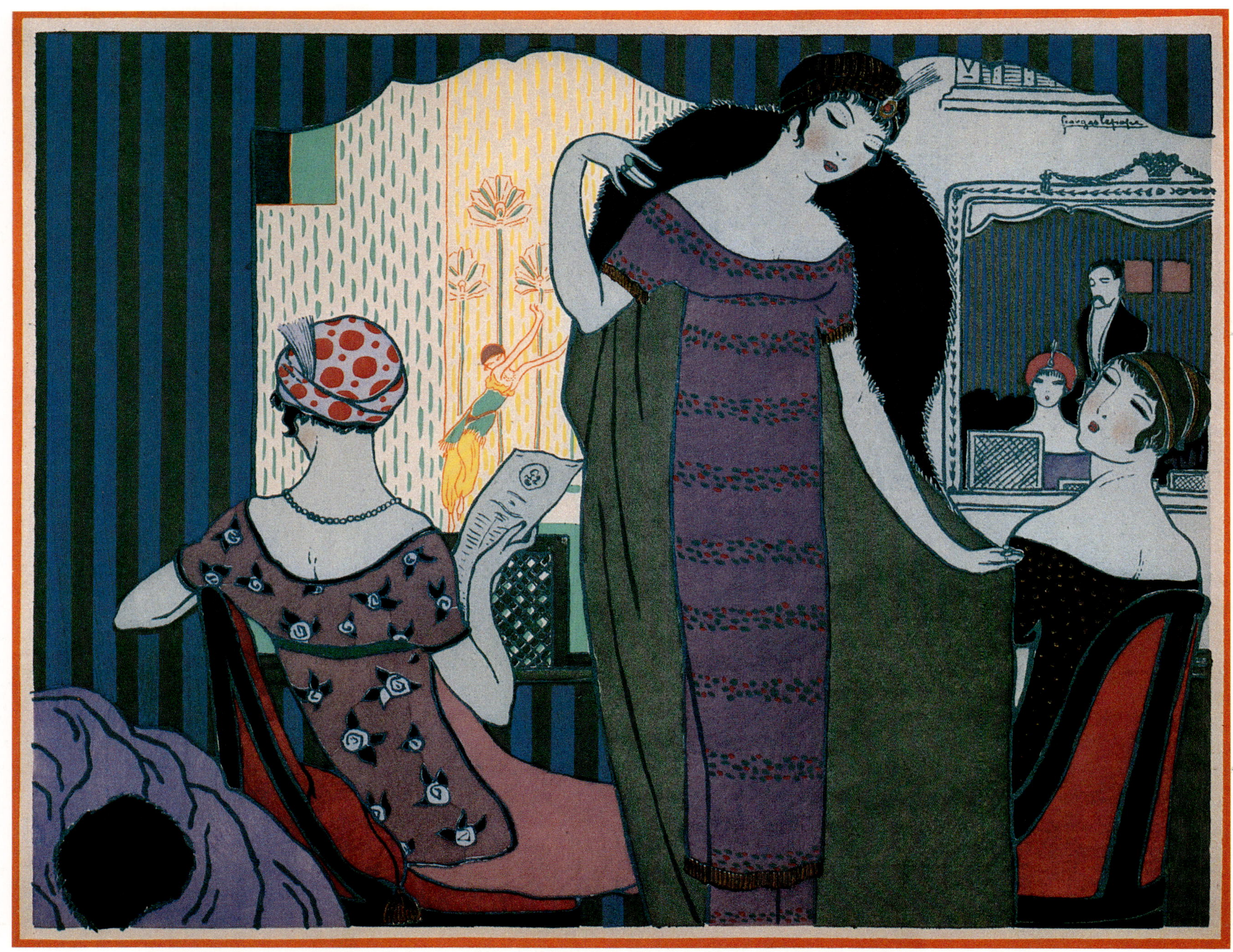

Pochoir illustration by Georges Lepape, from *Les Choses de Paul Poiret*. Published for Paul Poiret by Maquet et Cie, Paris. 1911.

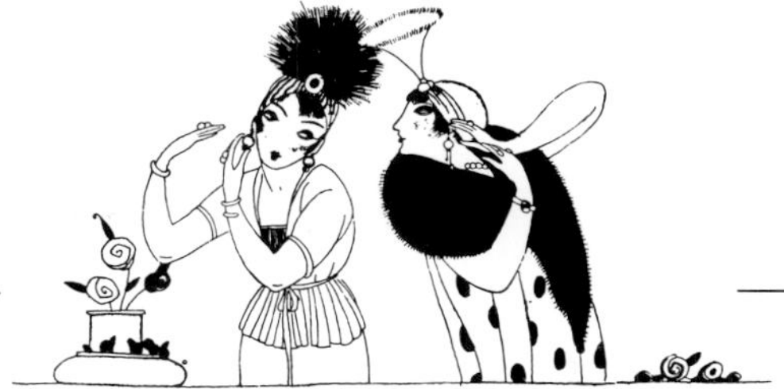

THE EARLY EXPERIMENTAL STYLE

Experimental forms of Art Deco developed fitfully during the latter part of the first decade of the twentieth century, nurtured by a small group of avant-garde designers who, in an attempt to achieve a new visual honesty in their work, had discarded all traditional European forms of decoration and the opulence and clutter associated with the Belle Epoque. In their determination to produce a design style that would transcend the fickleness of fashion, they began to produce a range of high quality products that would appeal to the intellect as well as the visual senses of their discerning customers, who had begun to tire of the curvilinear shapes and pastel colours of the Art Nouveau style.

Initially, the designers found that many of their established customers regarded the experimental Art Deco designs as too austere. Even though the Art Nouveau style had somewhat diminished their ardour for the opulence they had enjoyed during the latter part of the nineteenth century, they still felt that the new designs lacked the necessary aesthetic appeal to fit in with their collections of eighteenth century antiques and paintings and their nineteenth century bric-a-brac.

But by the end of the first decade of the twentieth century, as society began to change in response to the times, and a new generation of potential customers had come of age, the uncluttered shapes and angular forms of the experimental Art Deco style were beginning to find favour with these new members of the haut monde. Not that the Art Nouveau style came to an abrupt end — it lingered on for several more years — but it had slowly begun to degenerate into an applied decorative stylism that no longer reflected the lifestyles, design ideals, or aesthetic dreams of its most influential supporters.

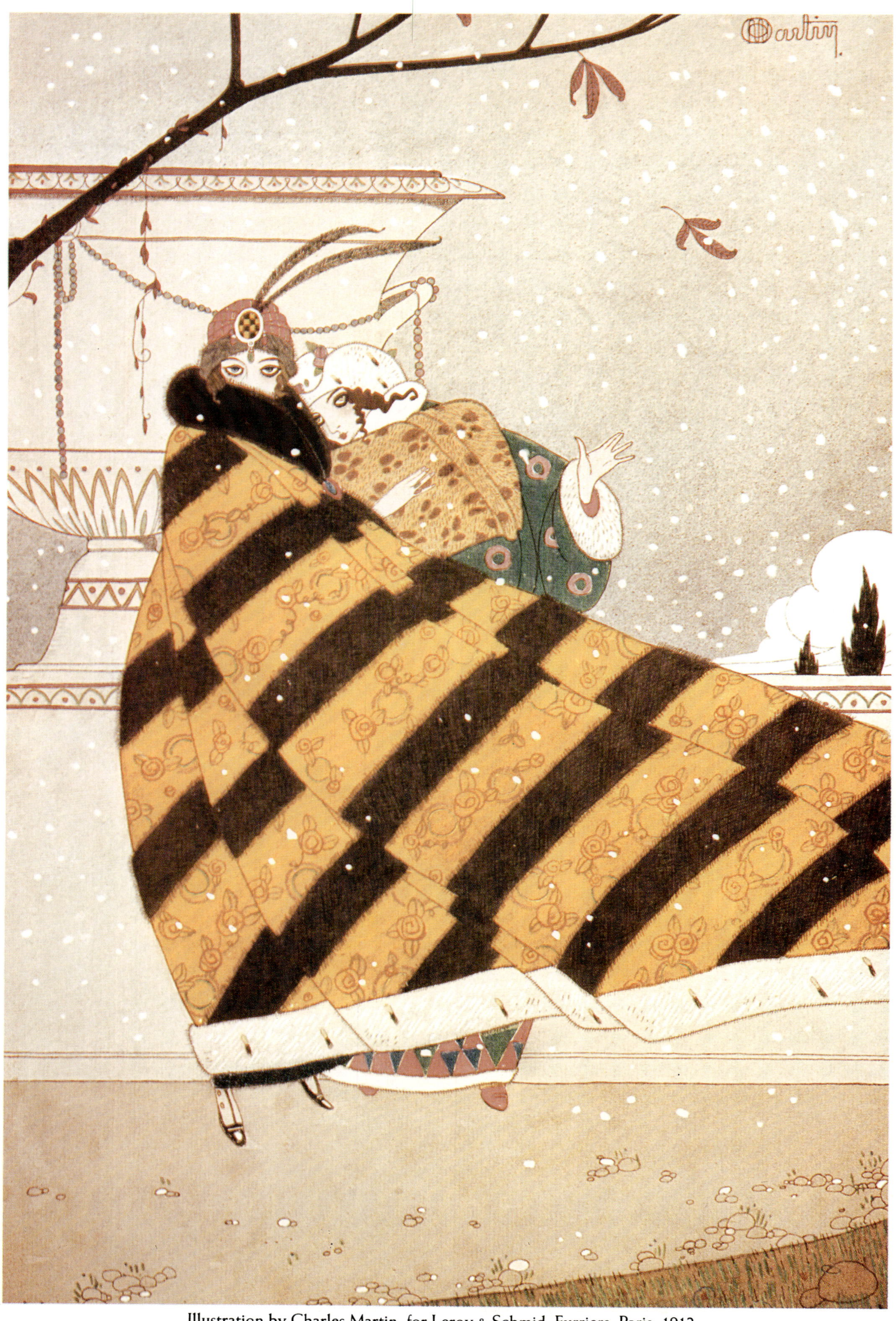

Illustration by Charles Martin, for Leroy & Schmid, Furriers, Paris. 1912.

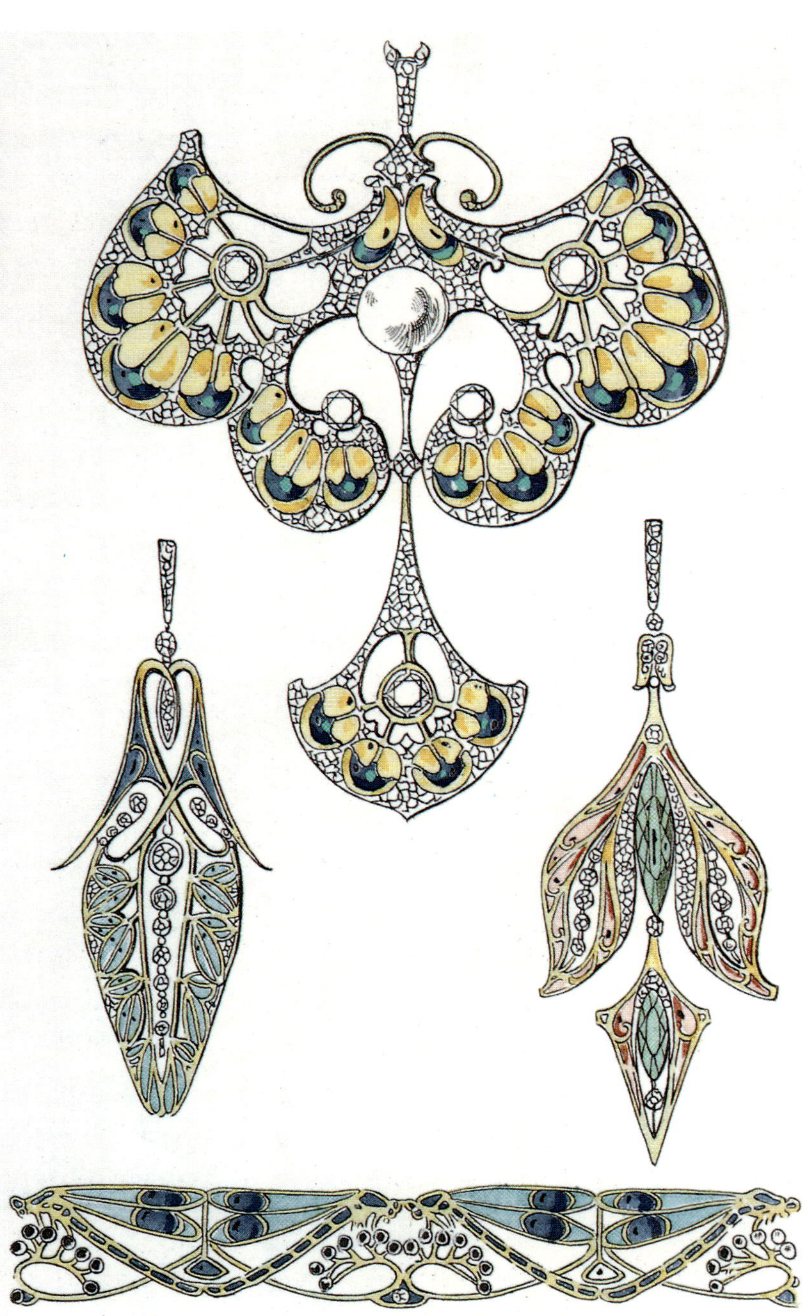

Pochoir illustration of jewellery by Véver, for *Le Journal des dames et des modes*. Paris. 1912.

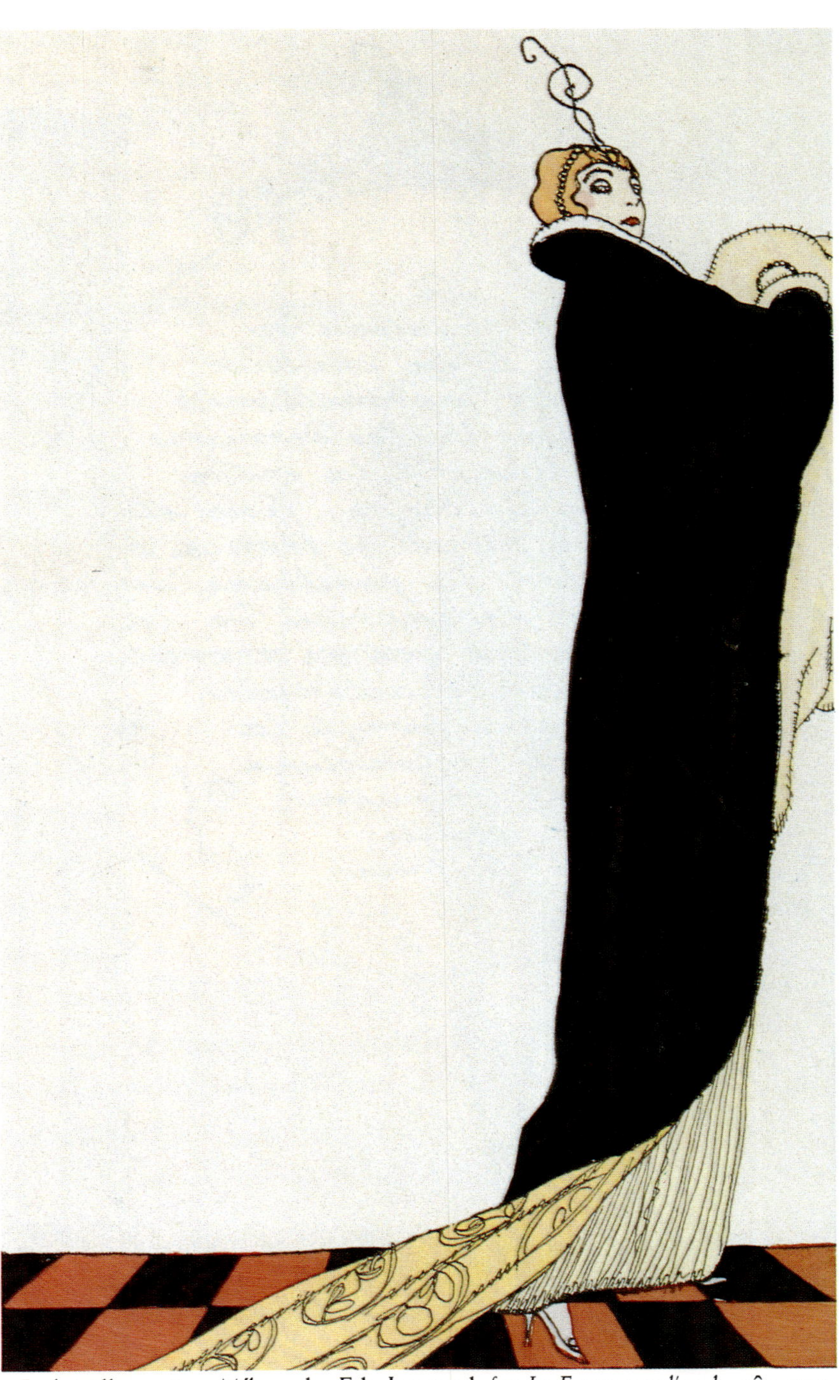

Pochoir illustration *Mélusine* by Edy Legrand, for *La Fourrure en l'an de grâce 1914* by François Seynoha. Paris. 1913.

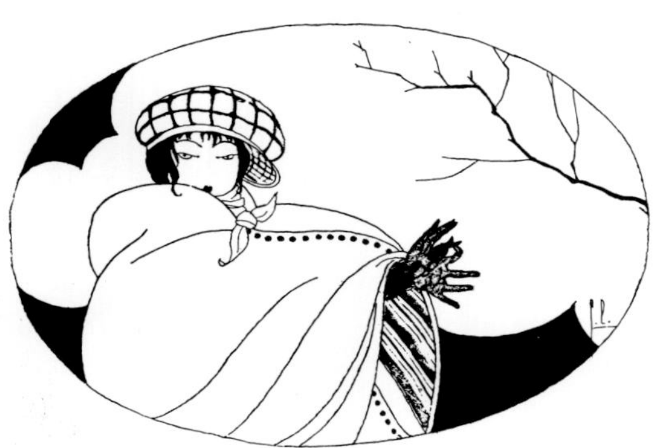

The principal patrons of the newly fashionable Art Deco style were not the leading intellectuals of the period, as one might expect, although many of them had openly admired the functionalist approach of the early Art Deco designers and the aesthetics of many of the individual pieces. But these intellectuals were usually too poor to afford such items; they certainly did not possess the vast mercantile fortunes of those who had supported the opulence and clutter of the Belle Epoque and had come to accept the less flamboyant Art Nouveau style. Purchasers of the new Art Deco style were often themselves involved in some aspect of the style — the couturiers Jacques Doucet, Madeleine Vionnet, Jeanne Lanvin and the young Paul Poiret, for example, were starting to design revolutionary Art Deco fashions as well as buying Art Deco objects.

Knowledgeable patrons expressed their admiration for the artistic integrity of the new group of designers, whom they perceived to be pursuing their aesthetic dreams with a single-mindedness worthy of the master-craftsmen of the past. Under their patronage the designers began to create a completely new range of products that demonstrated their love for angular geometric shapes, clear bright colours, unusual surface treatments, rare and often exotic materials, refined detailing, and superb craftsmanship. As a result of the active patronage of many of the leading couturiers of the period, who were still regarded as the arbiters of taste as well as the creators of the new fashions, an ever-growing group of influential clients and design converts was encouraged to purchase selected Art Deco items. Soon the new style was being widely worn and widely collected by the haut monde. The increasing success of the Art Deco style and the diminishing interest in Art Nouveau products led designers to produce a greater range of high quality Art Deco merchandise and fashions, encouraging the belief that Western design was on the threshold of a new era of artistic achievement: a 'twentieth century Renaissance' which would soon rival the great Italian Renaissance.

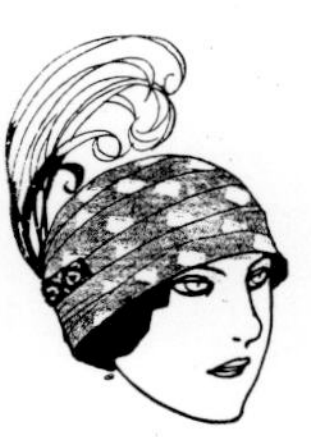

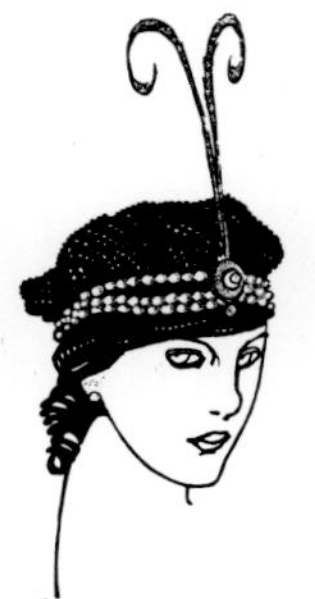

'Not since that "Golden Age" of 500 years earlier,' it was proclaimed, 'had so many artists, designers and master-craftsmen devoted so much creative energy to such an abundance of beautiful artifacts.' The Commissaire-Général de l'Exposition Internationale, who had been responsible for the Paris Exhibition of 1900, and a number of other influential art authorities were prompted to propose that an Exposition Internationale des Arts Décoratifs be held in Paris in 1914; this would be the culmination of the Art Deco movement.

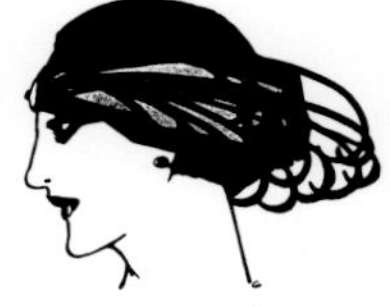

The French Government established a cultural committee to consider this proposal and it decided that such an exhibition should be held

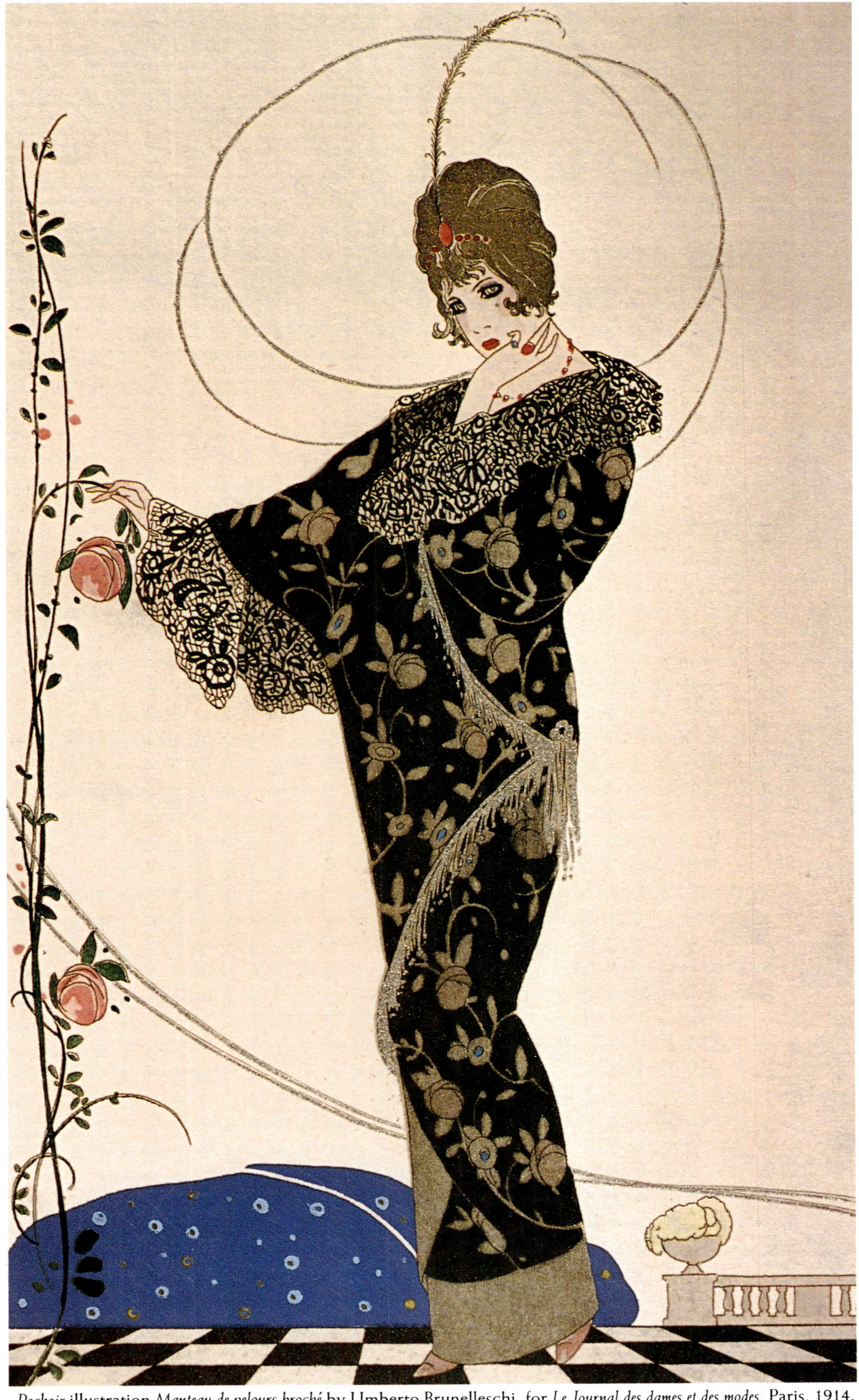

Pochoir illustration *Manteau de velours broché* by Umberto Brunelleschi, for *Le Journal des dames et des modes*. Paris. 1914.

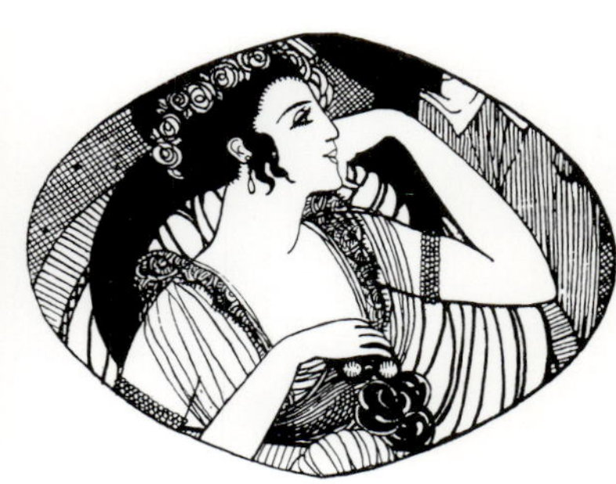

in 1915, rather than 1914. The committee also suggested that only original works of an artistic or decorative nature and with twentieth century origins be allowed, that such exhibits be made from the finest natural materials by master craftsmen, and that they be entirely modern in concept. No traditional styles were to be permitted.

Unfortunately, the outbreak of World War I in 1914 led to the postponement of the exhibition until 1925, when it was enlarged to include industrially made products. In the meantime, the Art Deco style underwent a dramatic change in response to changing ideals created by changing times, and in 1925 it was represented by an entirely new group of designers and craftsmen who had established a visual language, a stylistic logic, and an aesthetic dream that differed from the language, logic and dreaming of the earlier period.

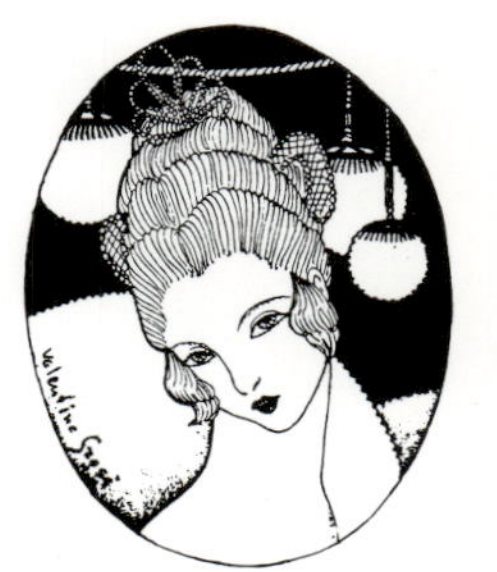

In this context, it is important to understand the use of the word 'dream': stylistic changes come about not only because designers' ideas change, but also because society itself changes, and along with this people's own hopes, aspirations and 'dreams'. Stylistic changes are in fact the most visually conspicuous of the mechanisms by which we hope to alter ourselves and our way of life. We think that by creating a new kind of environment and by wearing different clothes we will become different people, closer to the ideal we have formulated in our 'dreams'. Each attempted transformation seems to be at least partly successful; social commentators have noted with interest that our bodies actually seem to change in response to the times and the new designs and fashions that are created, provided that these have been created in response to the collective dreams of a particular group of influential people.

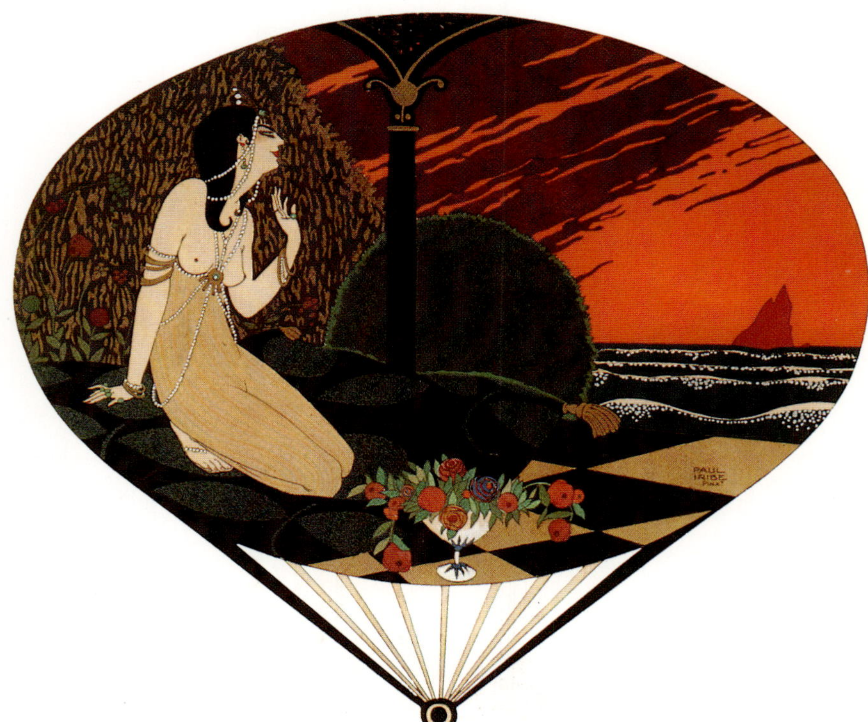

Pochoir illustration by Paul Iribe, for *L'Eventail et la fourrure par Paquin*. Published for Madame Paquin by Maquet et Cie, Paris. 1911.

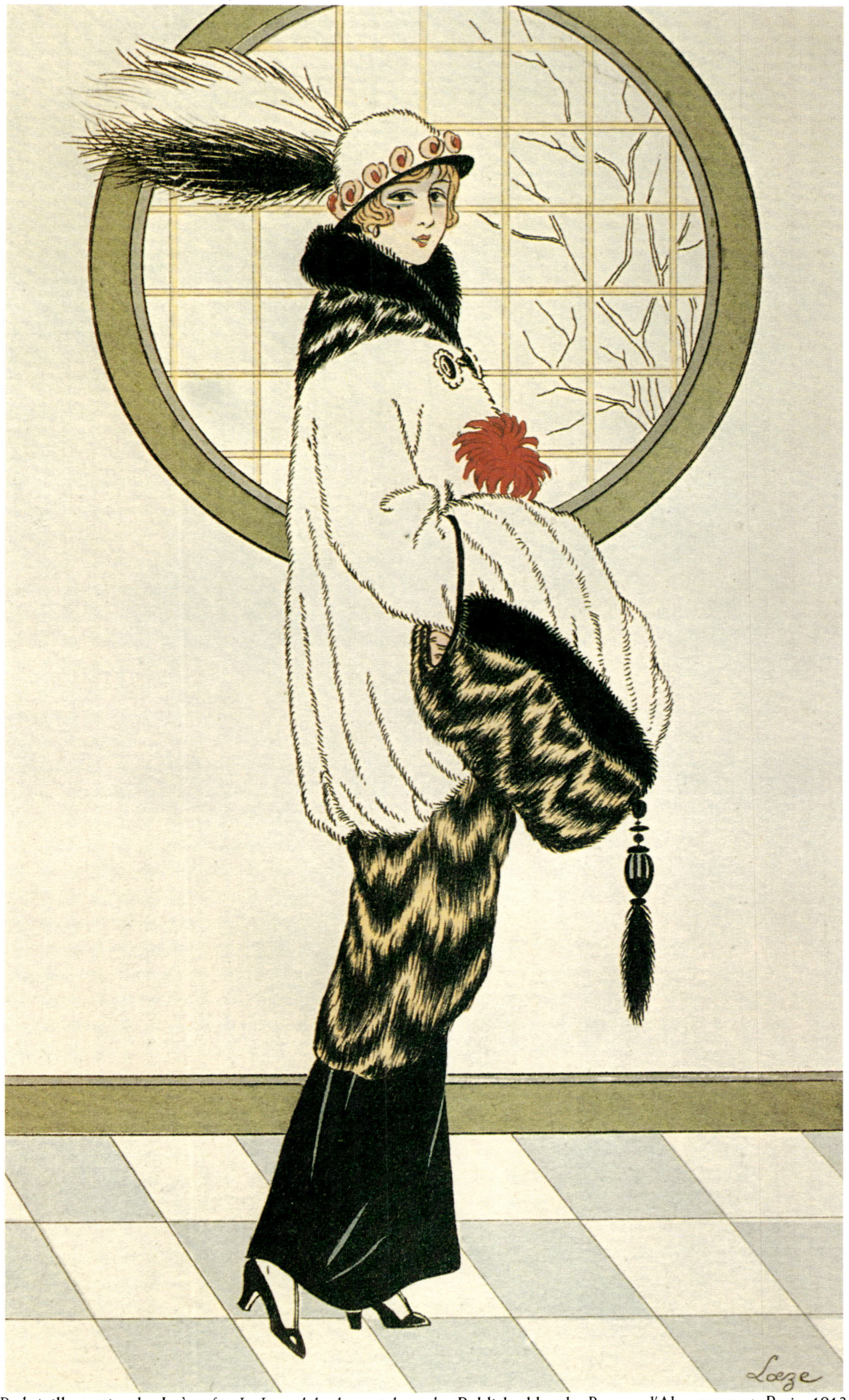

Pochoir illustration by Loèze for *Le Journal des dames et des modes*. Published by the Bureau d'Abonnement, Paris. 1913.

In 1910 one of the great arbiters of taste, a man who fully understood the needs and the dreams of his elite clientele, was Jacques Doucet. He had been one of the foremost Paris couturiers since the mid-1870s and was particularly noted for his unostentatiously luxurious clothes, a most unusual quality during the *fin de siècle* period but one that appealed to many of the leading actresses and demi-mondaines of the time: they did not wish to be confused with the rich and flashy dowagers who displayed their wealth in their clothes.

Doucet was also a famous collector of eighteenth century antiques and works of art, and by the turn of the century he had acquired a solid reputation as a connoisseur of all kinds of fine artifacts and objets d'art. In addition, he was a patron of the Impressionists and a collector of African sculpture and oriental artifacts. Being an ardent supporter of Picasso, he purchased a number of his early works, among them the controversial *Les Demoiselles d'Avignon,* today regarded as one of Picasso's most important works.

During the first decade of the twentieth century Doucet had also started collecting early Art Deco pieces, and at the end of the decade,

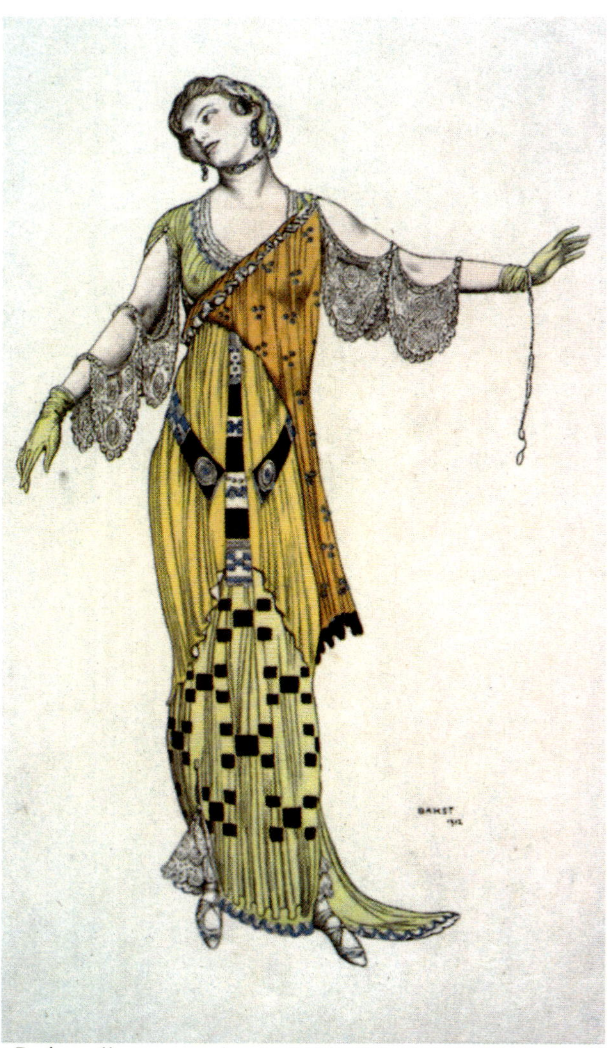

Pochoir illustration by Bakst for Madame Paquin, for *Le Journal des dames et des modes.* Paris. 1913.

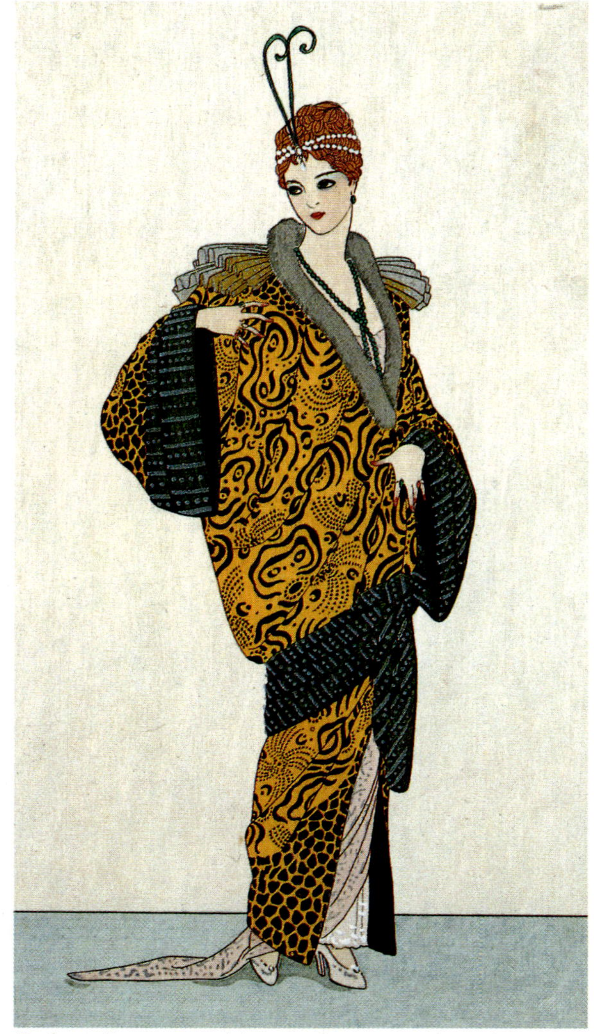

Pochoir illustration *Manteau de soir en velours frappé* by Francesco Gosé, *Le Journal des dames et des modes.* Paris. 1914.

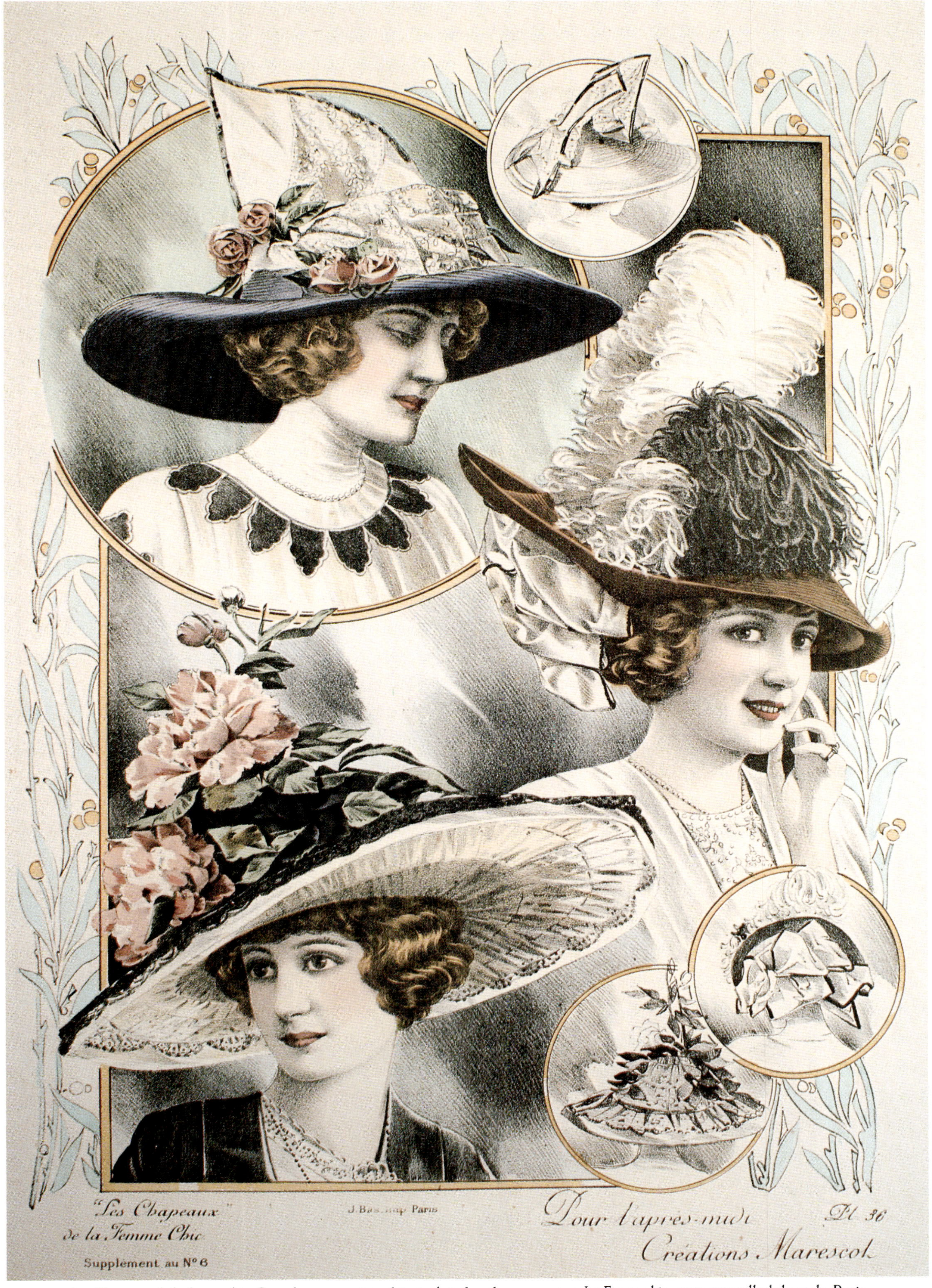

Les Chapeaux de la femme chic. Supplement printed in *pochoir* for the magazine *La Femme chic: revue mensuelle de la mode*, Paris. 1911.

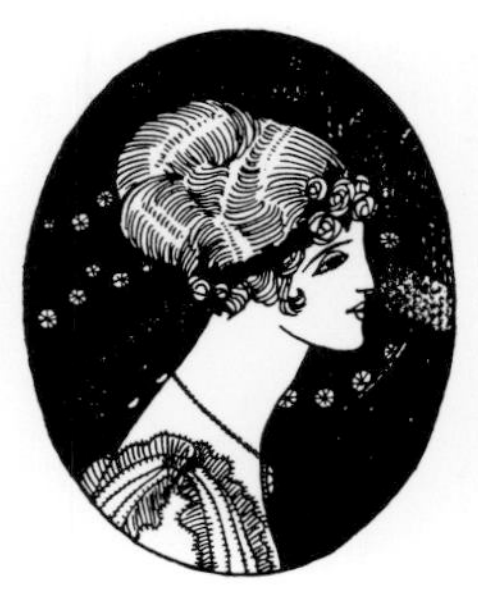

having wearied of his collection of eighteenth century antiques and paintings, he had them auctioned. With the revenue, he bought fine examples of the current Art Deco mode, more Impressionist and post-Impressionist works, Cubist paintings and experimental pieces by the Fauves, and he added to his collection of African, Islamic and oriental art. In typically grand style, he had the entire setting for this unique collection designed and made in the most luxurious Art Deco style, by the leading designers and craftsmen of the period under the direction of the young Paul Iribe.

One of Doucet's outstanding protégés was the couturier Madeleine Vionnet, who had worked from 1903 to 1908 as his design assistant in his *maison de couture* in the Rue de la Paix. Vionnet was born in 1876, in the Jura Mountains near Lake Geneva, and became an apprentice dressmaker at the age of twelve. She arrived in Paris in the year of the great 1889 Exhibition, to work as a seamstress in a small dressmaking atelier that specialised in casual day garments. During the next ten years, she worked for a number of minor couture houses before becoming an assistant designer, specialising in expensive lingerie, at the renowned Callot Soeurs, where she was responsible for making dresses *déshabillé* for many of the famous demi-mondaines. This is the area of design in which she continued to specialise after joining Doucet.

While she was working for Callot Soeurs and then Jacques Doucet, Vionnet developed the belief that it was the natural body shape, with its changing contours and subtle curves, that was of paramount importance to her clients, not the imposition of a stereotyped shape achieved by the use of a whalebone corset, a fashion created by the dowagers of the mid-nineteenth century. She is credited with persuading many of her younger clients, before 1910, to dispose of their corsets and wear one of her flowing dresses that showed to advantage their natural feminine attributes. Such a style of dressing was condemned as indecent, lewd, licentious, and even obscene by many moralists at the time, but has persisted throughout this century.

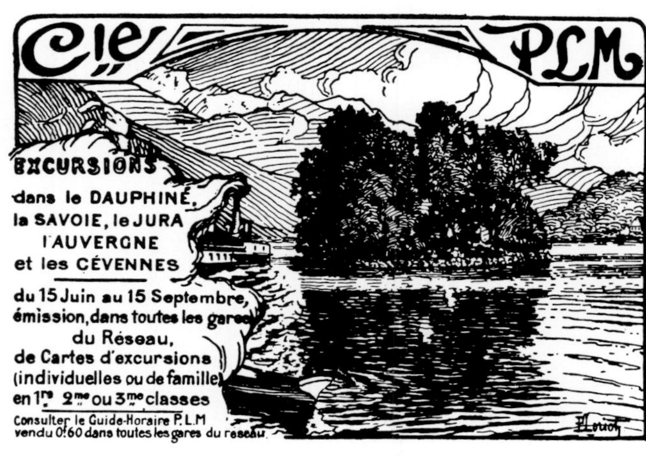

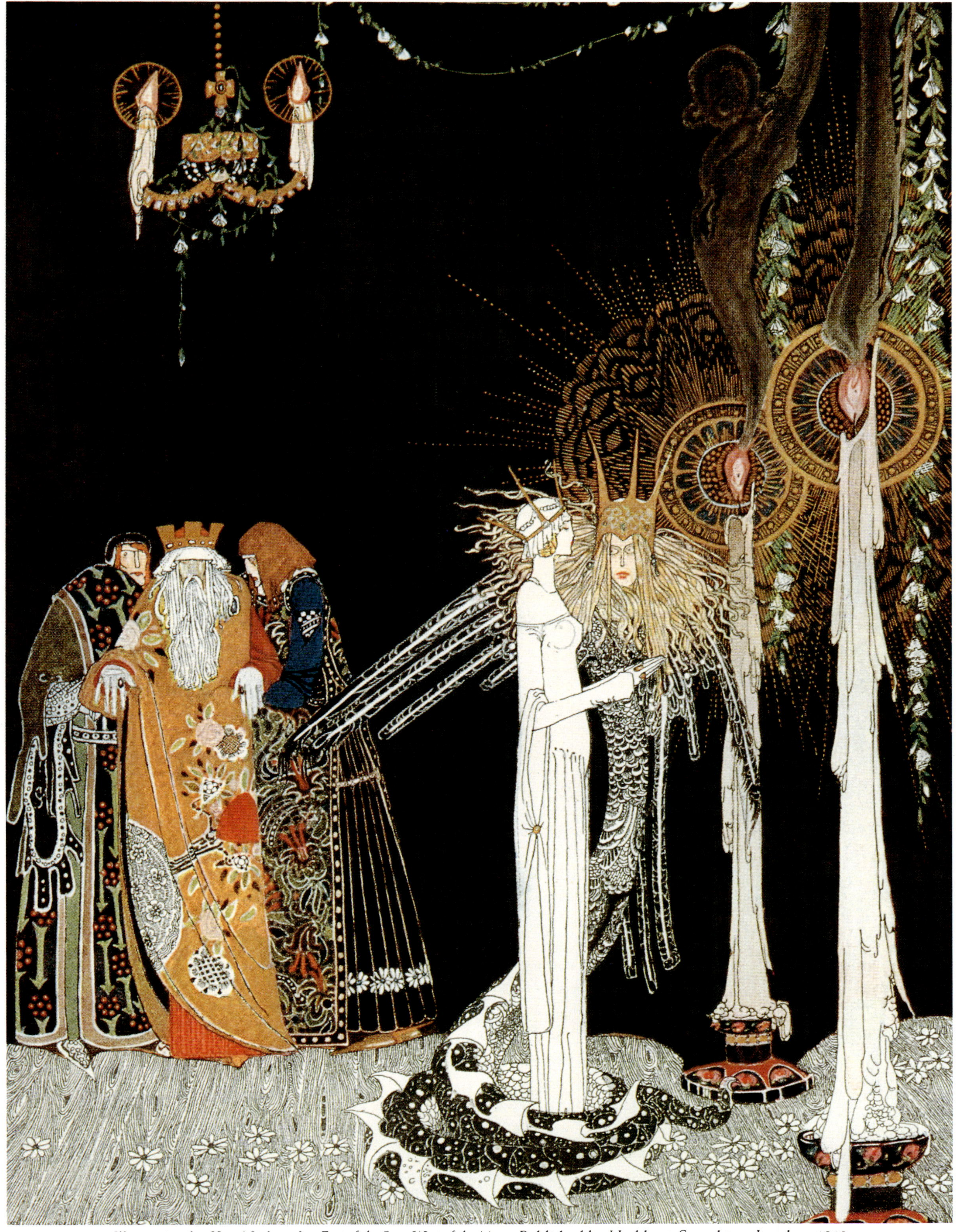

Illustration by Kay Nielsen for *East of the Sun, West of the Moon*. Published by Hodder & Stoughton, London. 1913.

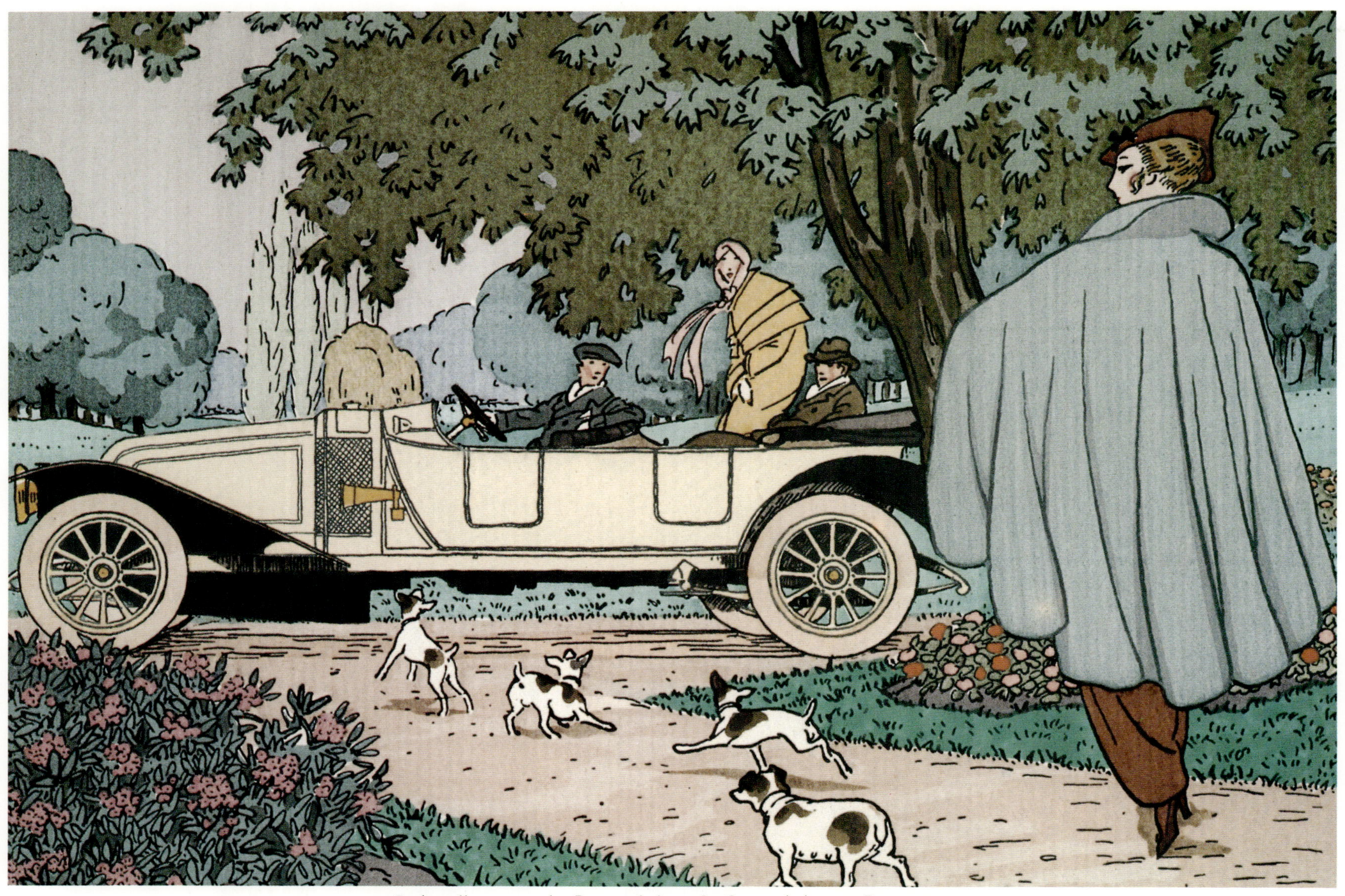

Pochoir illustration by Brissaud, from *La Gazette du bon ton*. Paris. 1914.

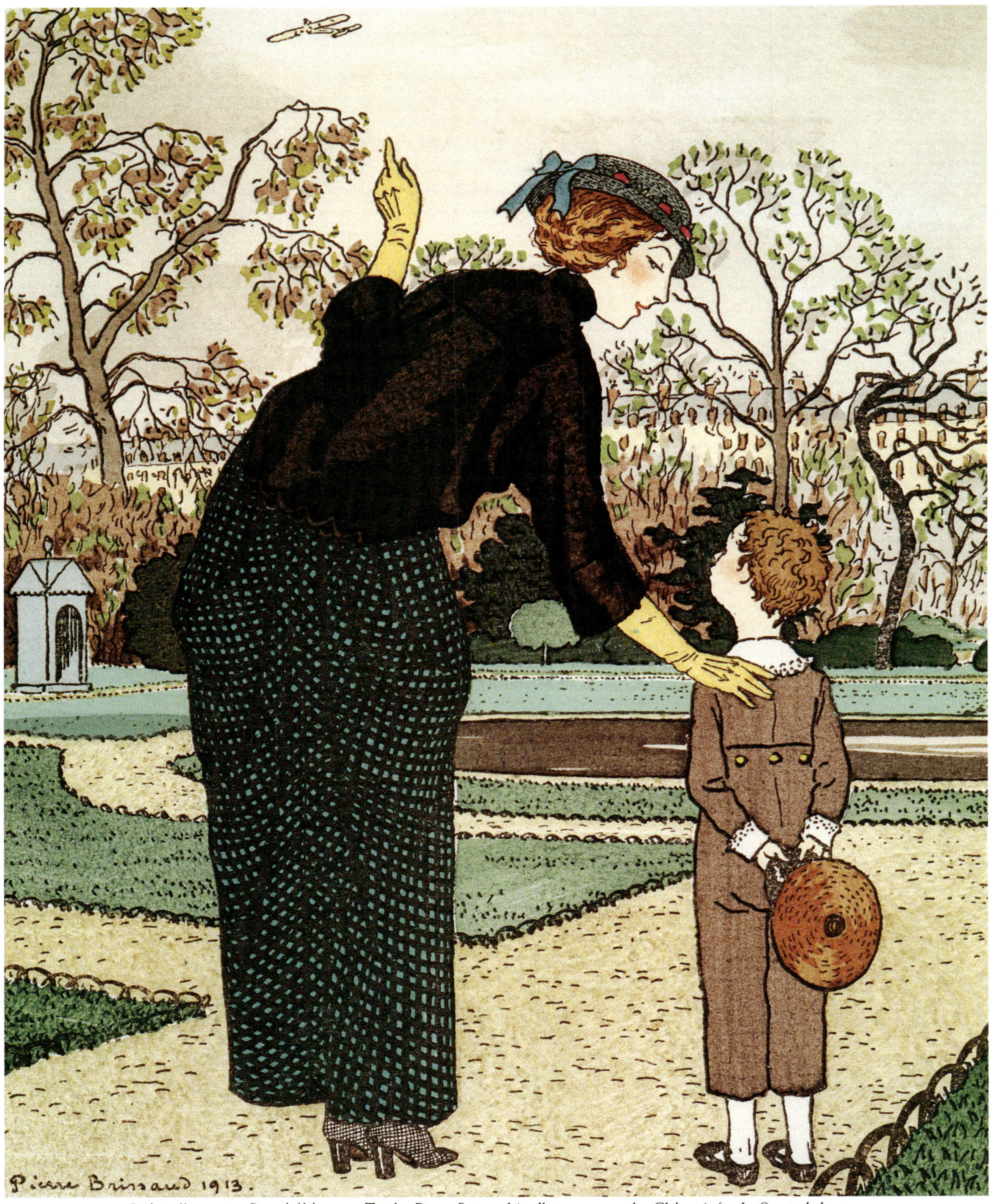

Pochoir illustration *Regarde là-haut . . . Toto* by Pierre Brissaud (walking costume by Chéruit), for *La Gazette du bon ton*. Paris. 1913.

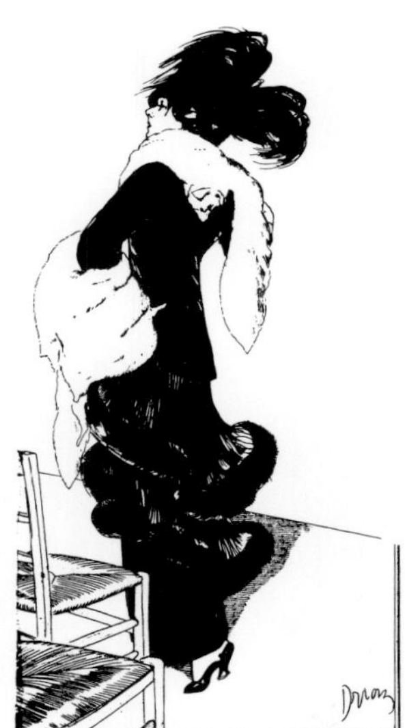

Madeleine Vionnet opened her own *maison de couture* in the Rue de Rivoli in 1912, using money she had saved whilst making dresses *déshabillé* and lingerie for the famous demi-mondaines and younger actresses after leaving Doucet in 1908. Soon she was attracting the attention of many of the avant-garde, who loved a hint of sinfulness in their dresses and for whom she developed her famous figure-clinging 'bias cut', which was to revolutionise dressmaking in the 1930s. As her couture house prospered she became a great collector of Art Deco objects and she had her show-rooms and private apartment totally refurbished in Art Deco style by the best designers and master-craftsmen, many of whom were her personal friends.

Vionnet personally designed all of her collections until the outbreak of World War II, when she closed her couture house. She continued to live in her private world of Art Deco splendour in the Place Antoine-Arnauld until she died in 1975, shortly before her ninety-ninth birthday. And although she always claimed that she never created any new fashions — she simply made what she felt was right for the time — examples of her Art Deco clothes are collector's items today, and selected pieces are now housed in major museum collections around the world.

Another Doucet protégé — and one whose Art Deco fashions were just as controversial as those of Vionnet — was the flamboyant Paul Poiret, who worked as Doucet's assistant between 1897 and 1900. Poiret was a true Parisian, born in Les Halles in 1879 and possessed of a love for visiting the great art galleries and seeing the continually changing exhibitions of paintings that were to be found in Paris throughout the 1880s and 1890s. He was also a frequent visitor to the theatre, where he would sketch the costumes worn by the actresses and the dresses worn by the fashionable women in the audience; these he would use as a guide for his own designs.

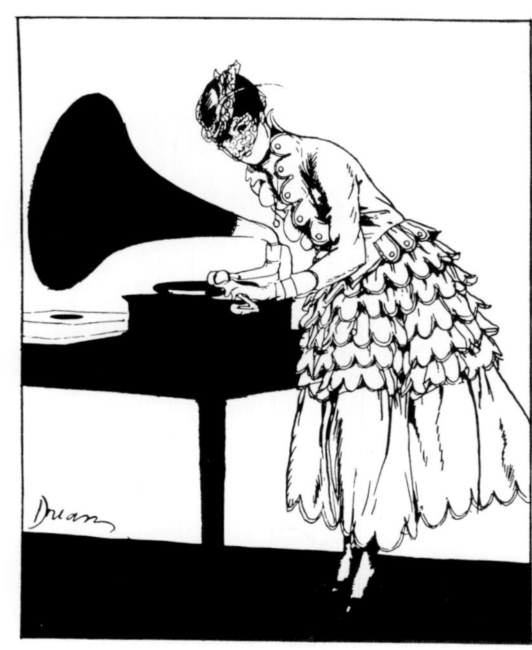

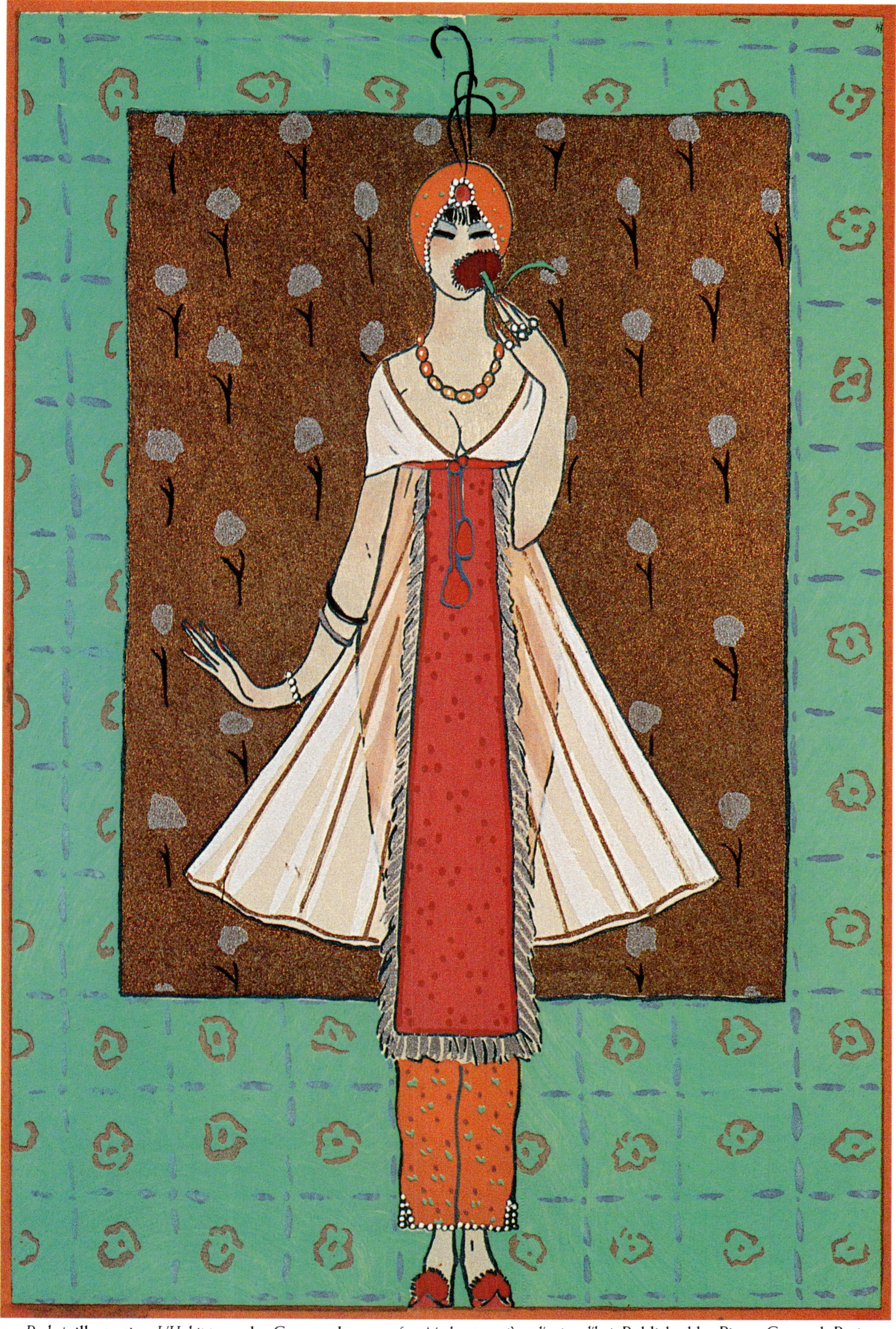

Pochoir illustration *L'Habit persan* by Georges Lepape, for *Modes et manières d'aujourd'hui*. Published by Pierre Corrard, Paris. 1912.

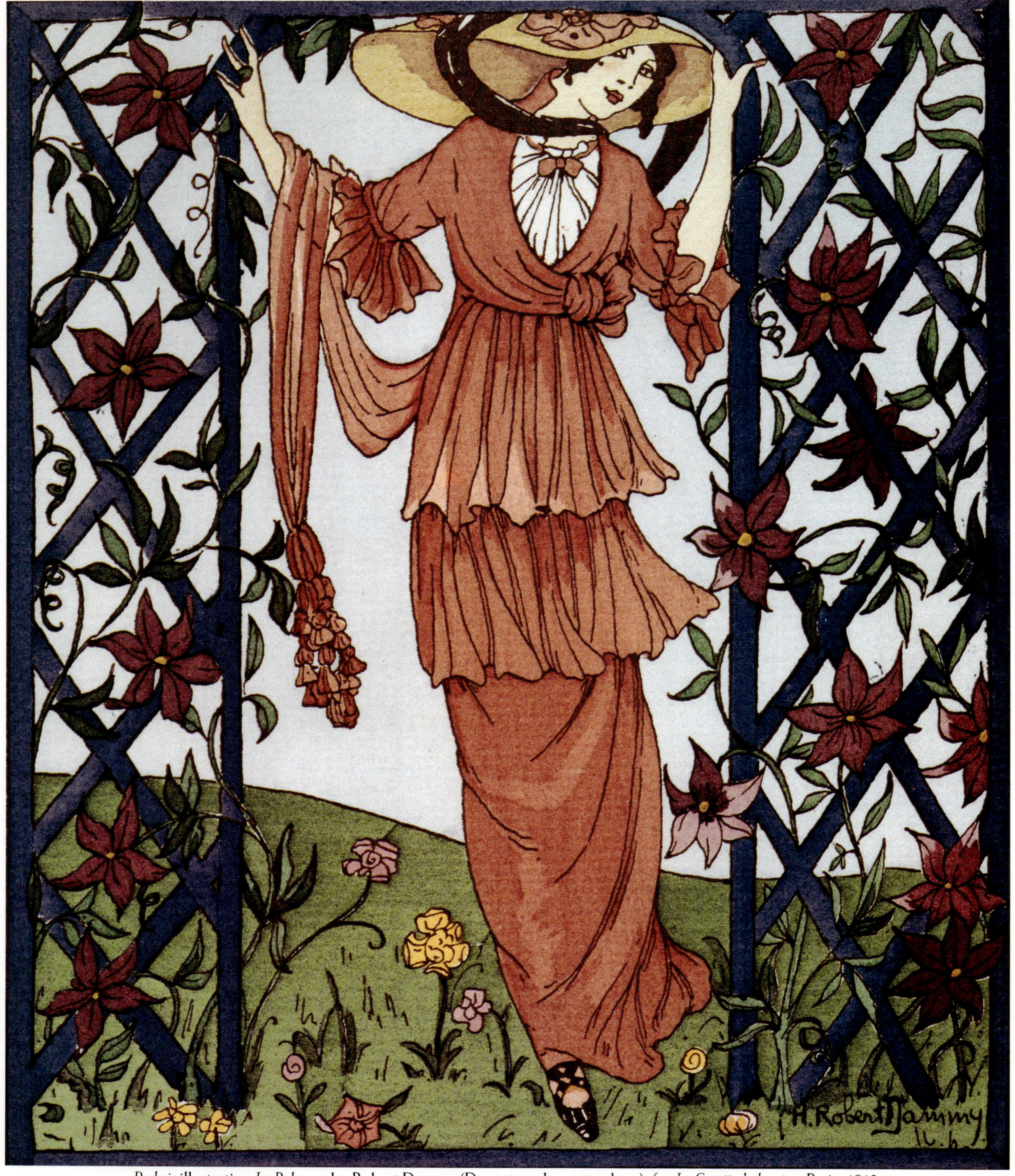

Pochoir illustration *La Robe rose* by Robert Dammy (Doucet garden party dress), for *La Gazette du bon ton*. Paris. 1913.

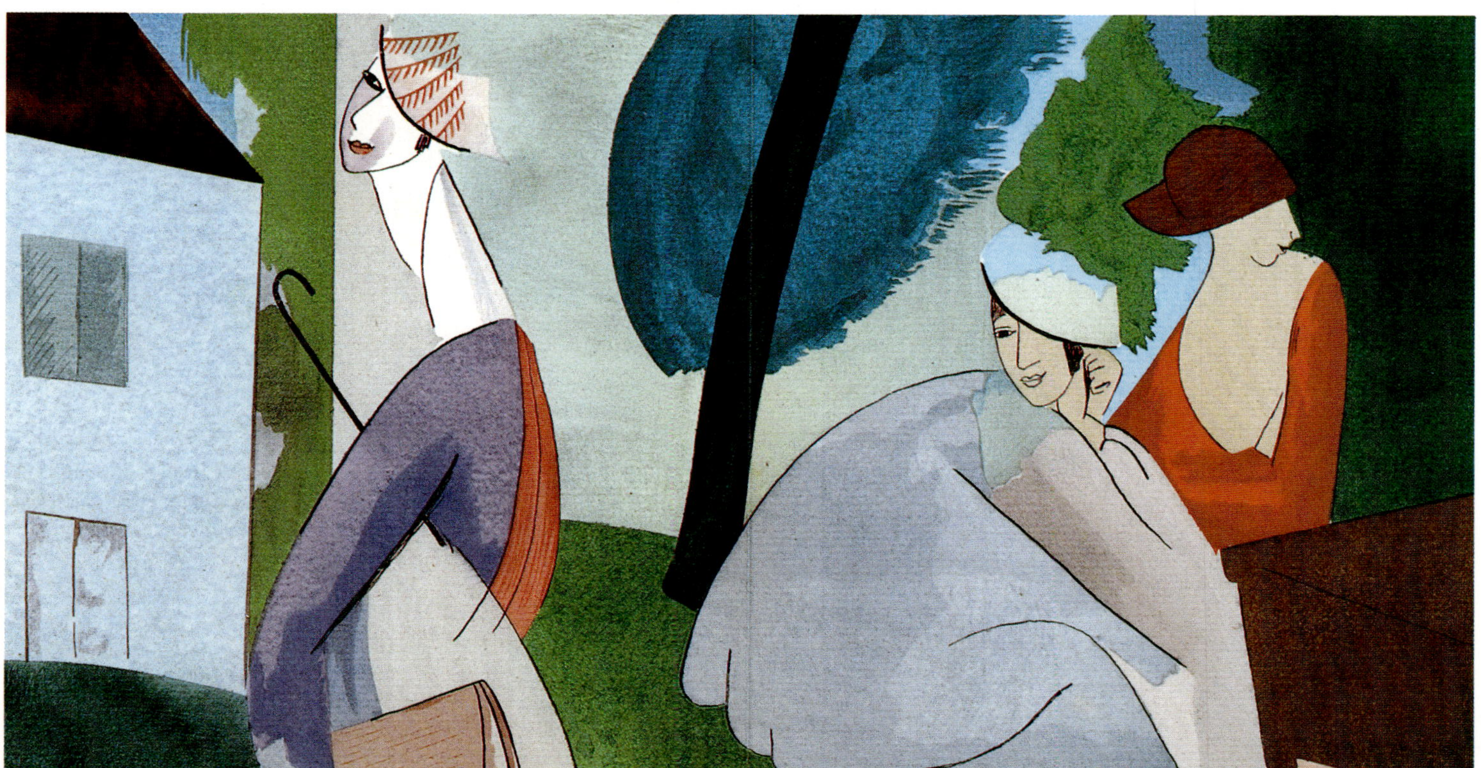

Pochoir illustration *Robes de Paul Poiret* by Boussingault, for *La Gazette du bon ton*. Paris. 1914.

At the age of eighteen, when he was tired of being an umbrella maker's apprentice, Poiret sent twelve of his sketched ideas to Madame Chéruit, owner of a small but prestigious couture house in the Place Vendôme. To his amazement and delight, she purchased all twelve. During the next few weeks he devoted his time to preparing more sketches, some influenced by an assortment of oriental exhibitions from Persia, China, Japan and India then currently being held in Paris. These he sent to Jacques Doucet who, after purchasing them and several smaller collections, invited him to become his junior tailoring assistant. Doucet also asked Poiret to design several theatrical costumes for Eleonora Duse and Sarah Bernhardt and to provide ideas for other famous actresses and demi-mondaines who were among his favoured customers.

During his stay with Doucet, Poiret totally reorganised the tailoring workrooms and rejuvenated many of Doucet's day-wear designs. He left Doucet at the end of 1900 to undertake a year's compulsory military service. Then, after working for a short period with a number of other couture houses, including the House of Worth, and privately for several leading actresses and demi-mondaines, in 1904 he opened his own couture house in the Rue Auber. Initially his designs were quite simple, almost *'Directoire'*, in appearance and, like Vionnet, he advocated abandoning the stiff whalebone corset.

In 1908 Poiret published the first of his now famous albums of designs, *Les Robes de Paul Poiret*, illustrated by one of his own young protégés, Paul Iribe; the album contained designs in both *'Directoire'* and 'oriental' styles. It was followed in 1911 by a similar album, *Les Choses de Paul Poiret*, illustrated by another young design assistant, Georges Lepape. Both of these albums were printed by Jean Saudé, using the deluxe *pochoir* process, which can involve more than thirty different stencils per illus-

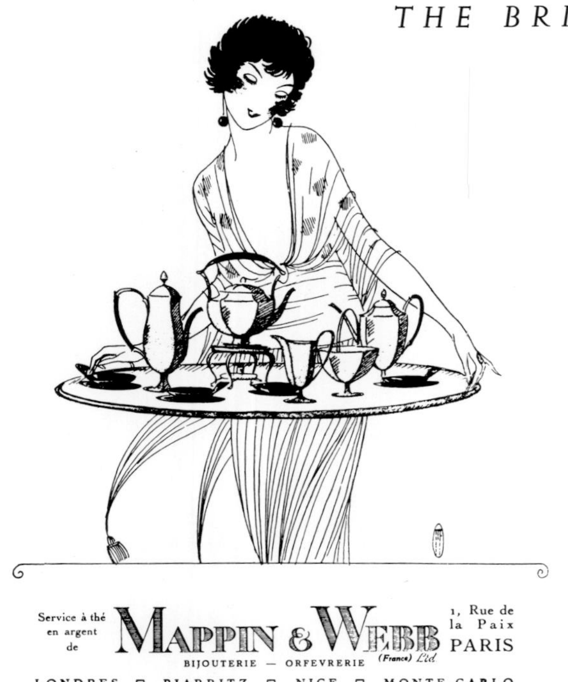

tration. These two unique albums are today regarded as landmarks in the development of both Art Deco design and Art Deco illustration.

Poiret was a great publicist and by the time his second album of designs had appeared he had become one of the most famous and influential couturiers in Paris, with a much enlarged *maison de couture* now situated in the Avenue d'Autin, plus a school of design called 'Martine' in the Faubourg Saint-Honoré. For his increasing range of commissions he employed numerous unknown artists — among them Dufy, Matisse, van Dongen, Erté, Benito, Derain and Segonzac — to design fabrics, furnishings, and an array of decorative artifacts and objets d'art. In June 1911 he created an international sensation when he introduced his new Persian-inspired pantaloons and tunic dresses at his famous One Thousand and Second Night fete: his previous employer Jean Worth described the designs as 'vulgar, wicked and ugly'; others said they were 'only fit to be worn by savages'.

Reports of the new Poiret fashions were headline news around the world, and it was reported that in Paris 'no one talks of art, literature or public affairs. All conversation is concentrated on those detestable garments'. But Poiret had caught the mood of the moment, managing to endow his designs with a magical allure and just a hint of exotic sexuality and sinfulness, which was precisely what the women of fashion wanted. American *Vogue's* Paris reporter wrote several months later, 'Excitement has raged in Paris unlike anything in my memory of gowning'.

The following year Poiret visited New York, taking with him a film of his new designs. He had planned to use the film at a lecture but it was confiscated on the grounds of obscenity by customs officials, and the *New York Herald* printed a letter from Cardinal Farley in which he warned against the temptations offered by this demon of the new lascivious fashions. 'This Evil,' he pronounced, 'constitutes a social as well as a moral danger to the Christian community for the licentious nature of its creations'. Poiret retorted by drawing attention to the 'outrageous décolletages' which the Cardinal and others of supposedly good taste and high morals approved, and declared that in his opinion it was these décolletages that were obscene because they were as unnatural as the whalebone corsets that supported the still fashionable mono-bosoms.

Poiret later wrote that at that time he

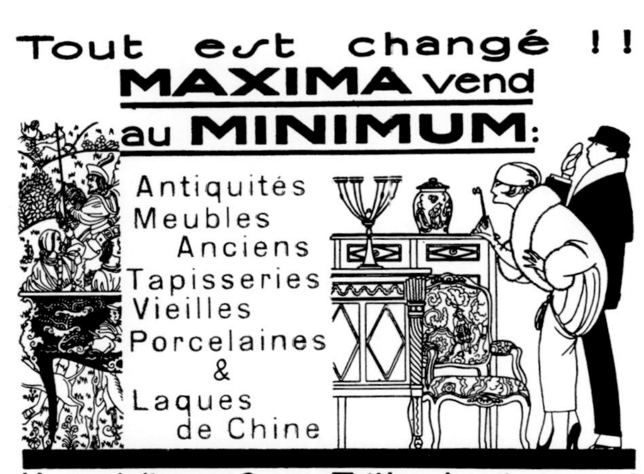

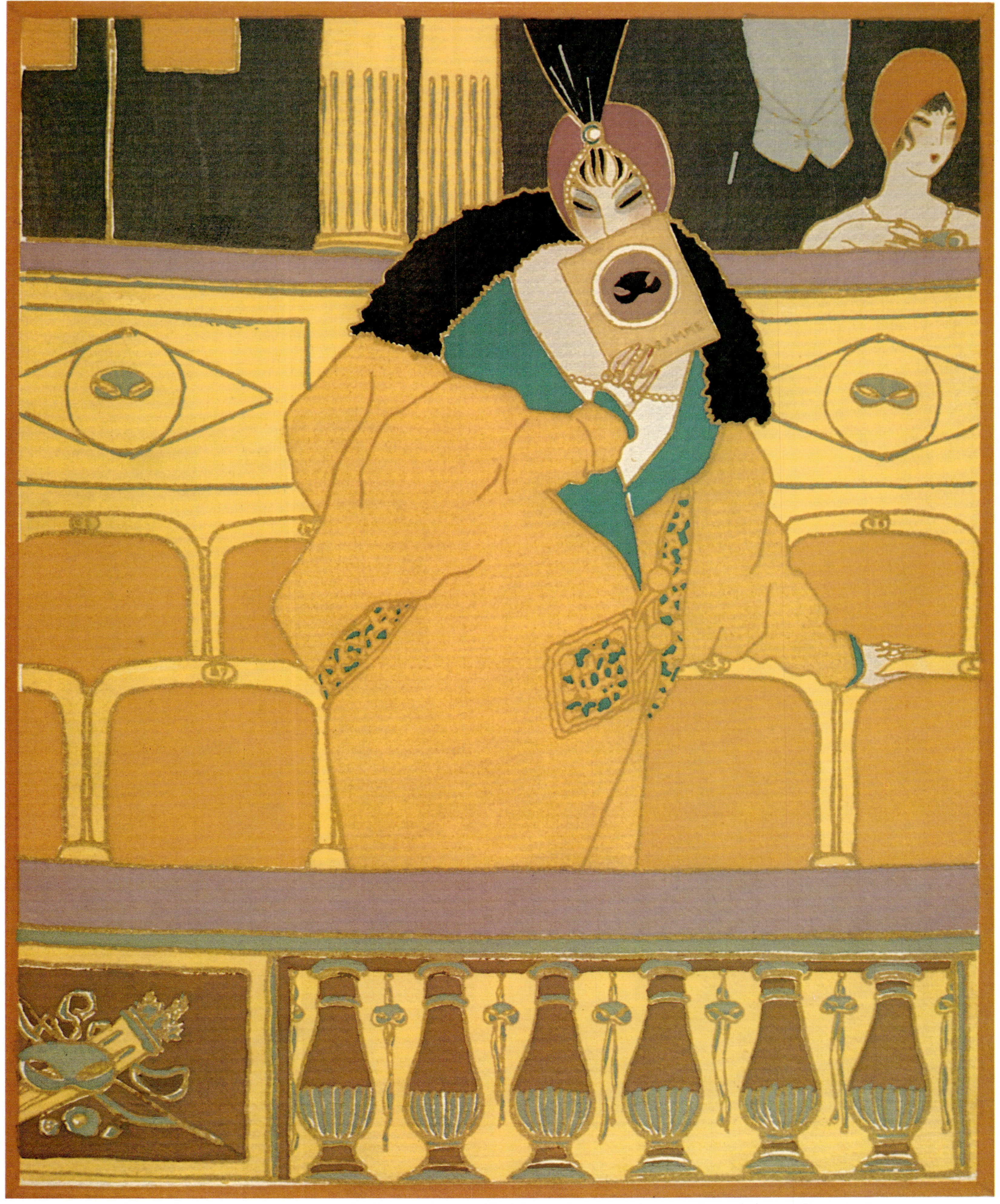

Pochoir illustration *Serais-je en avance?* by Georges Lepape (Paul Poiret theatre coat), for *La Gazette du bon ton*. Paris. 1912.

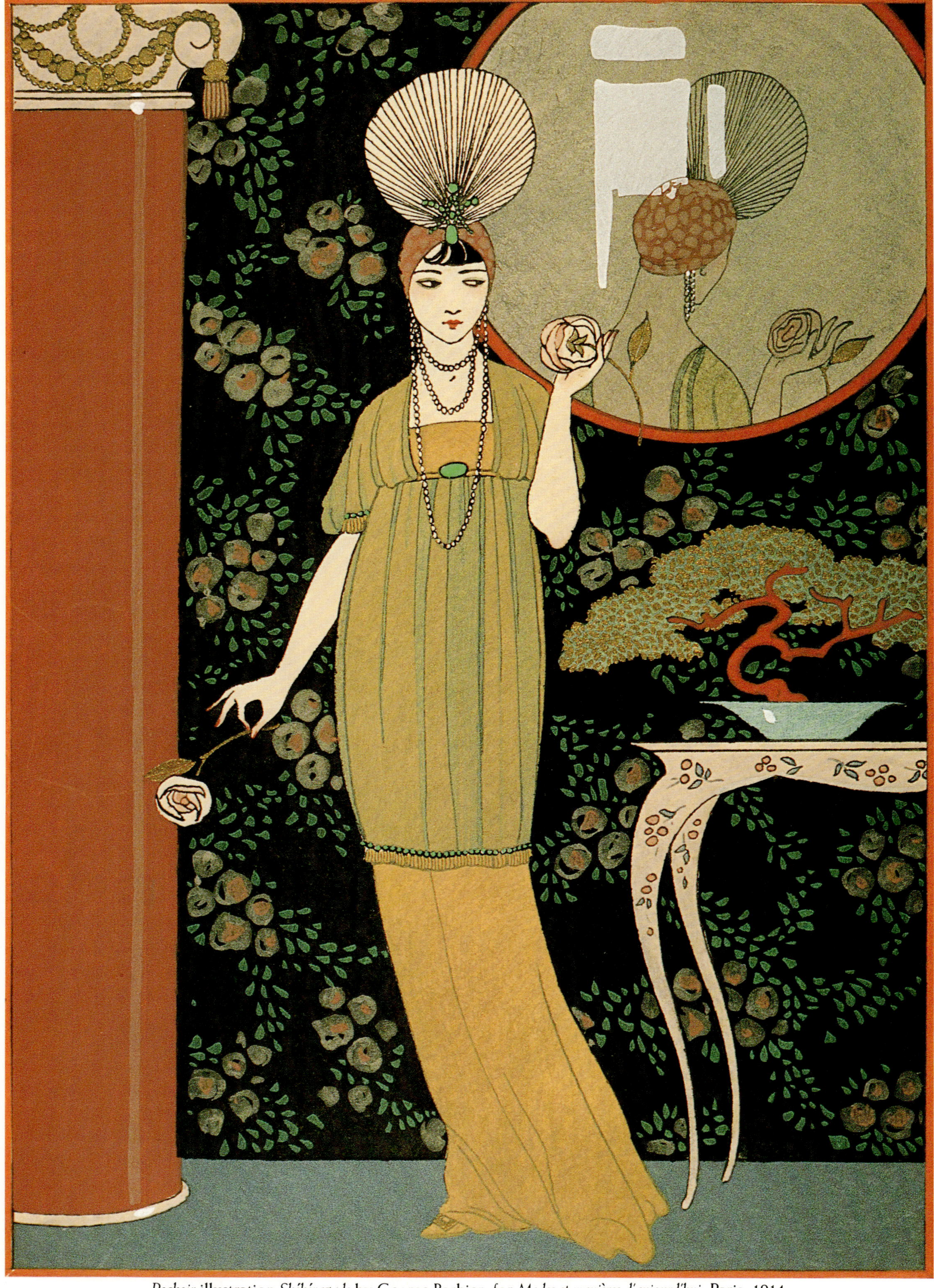

Pochoir illustration *Shéhérazade* by George Barbier, for *Modes et manières d'aujourd'hui*. Paris. 1914.

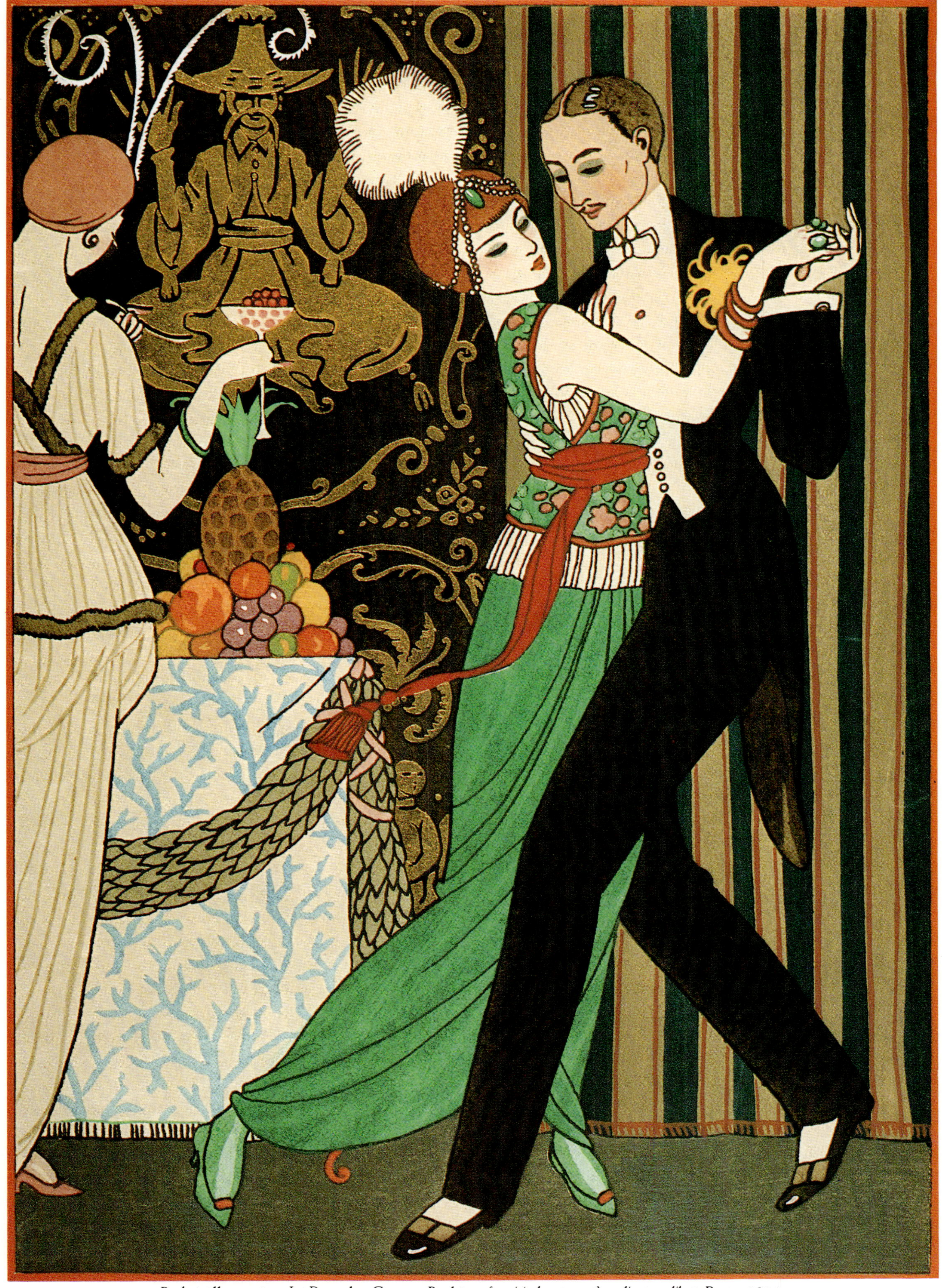

Pochoir illustration *La Dance* by George Barbier, for *Modes et manières d'aujourd'hui*. Paris. 1914.

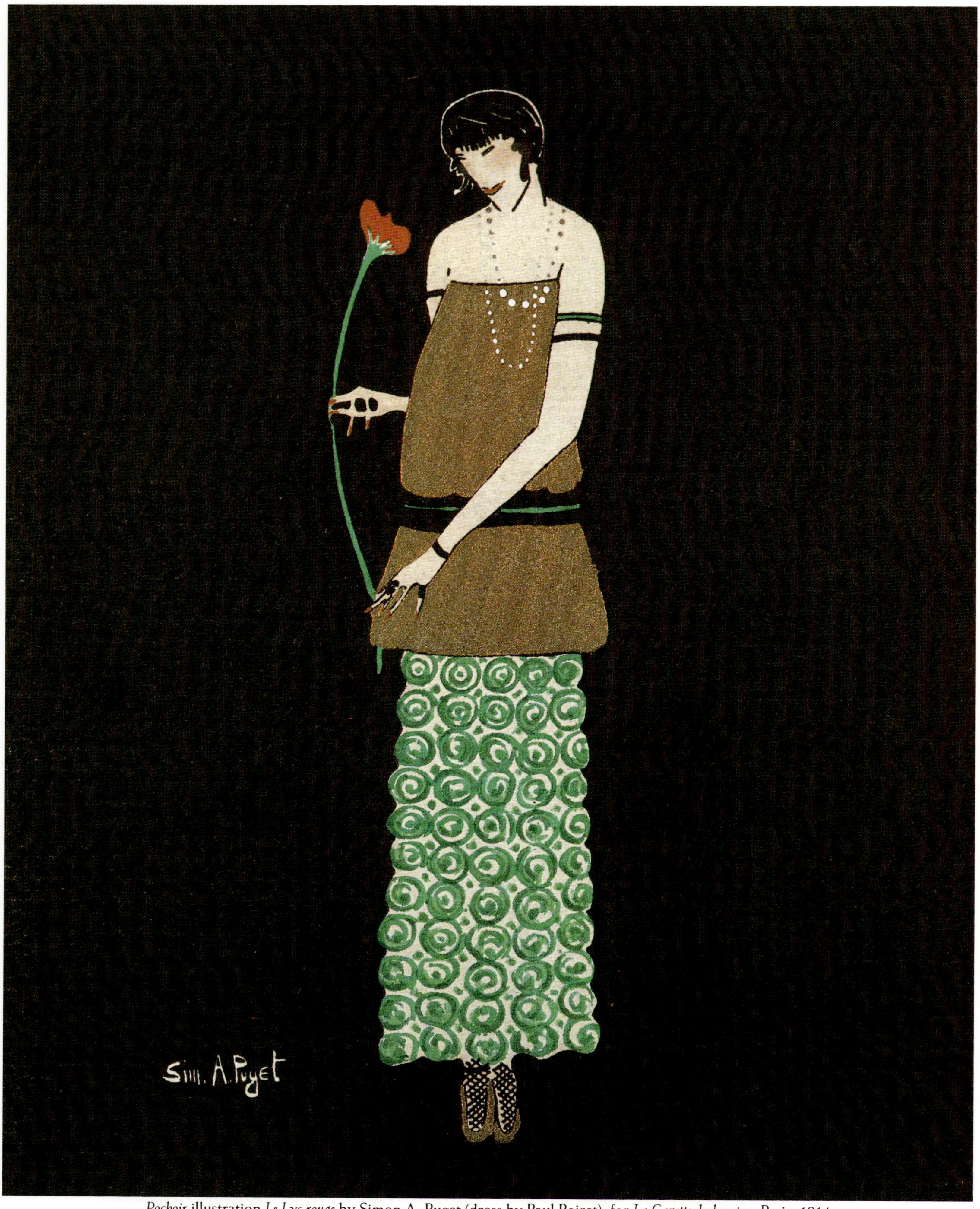

Pochoir illustration *Le Lys rouge* by Simon A. Puget (dress by Paul Poiret), for *La Gazette du bon ton*. Paris. 1914.

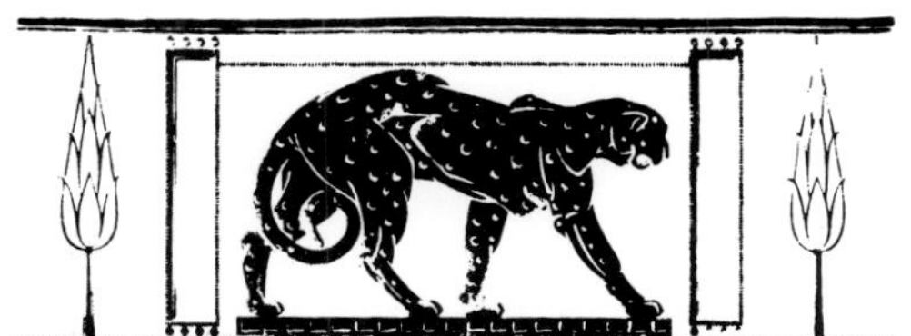

favoured the Botticelli-style bosom:
I favour small breasts that rise forth from the bodice like an enchanting testimonial to youth. Can anything be more captivating than this beauteous roundness? It is unthinkable that the breasts should be sealed up in solitary confinement in a castle fortress like the corset. And in *Vogue* he is quoted as saying,
To dress a woman is not to cover her with ornaments; it is to underscore the endowments of her body, to bring them out and stress them. It is what a woman leaves off, not what she puts on, that gives her cachet.
These were the ideas and ideals Poiret shared with Vionnet but, whereas Vionnet shunned publicity, Poiret revelled in it and his fashions continued to make headline news until the mid-1920s.

After the great Art Deco Exhibition of 1925 the style began to change and Poiret's designs appeared increasingly dated: having become totally encapsulated in his own world and despite lack of sales and diminishing publicity, he continued to produce the kinds of fashions for which he had become famous. In 1929 his couture house was forced to close, and to pay his debts he was obliged to sell his collection of paintings and objets d'art, in which were represented many famous artists of the Art Deco period — van Dongen, Braque, Modigliani, Matisse, Picasso, Benito, Rouault, Derain and Segonzac. Yet that same year he turned down an offer of US$16 000 a year to endorse the products of an American shoe company: the designs offended his aesthetic sensibility. He died fifteen years later at the age of 65, in abject poverty and a forgotten, lonely man.

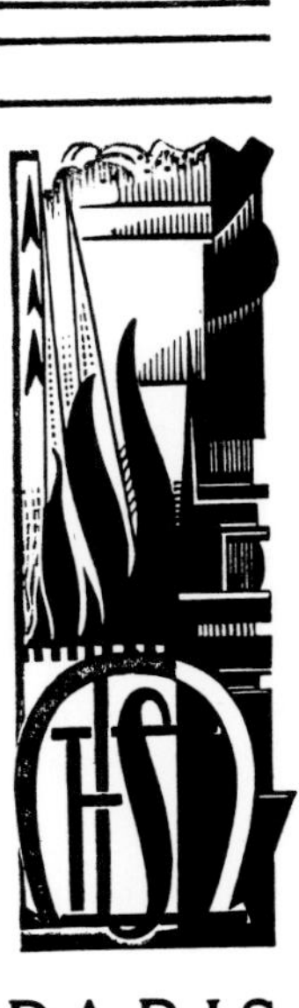

PARIS 1928

Another great couturier from the Art Deco period was Jeanne Lanvin, who, like Madeleine Vionnet, had started at the very bottom of the haute couture ladder, becoming an apprentice dressmaker at the age of twelve. She was born in Paris in 1867, the first of ten children of a Breton couple who worked as concierges. After having various jobs as an apprentice dressmaker and millinery assistant she opened her own small business, first as a milliner and then as a dressmaker in 1890. Her business prospered throughout the 1890s and by the turn of the century she had established a thriving shop in the Rue du Faubourg Saint-Honoré; by 1908 this had developed into a *maison de couture*.

Throughout the Art Deco period and until her death in 1946 Jeanne Lanvin specialised in clothes of unabashed femininity: youthful looking in soft, flowing fabrics and pretty colours. Like the styles of Vionnet and Poiret, these styles did not suit the dowagers of the period, but they did attract the attention of their wealthy daughters, the younger demi-mondaines, and many of the more fashionable actresses,

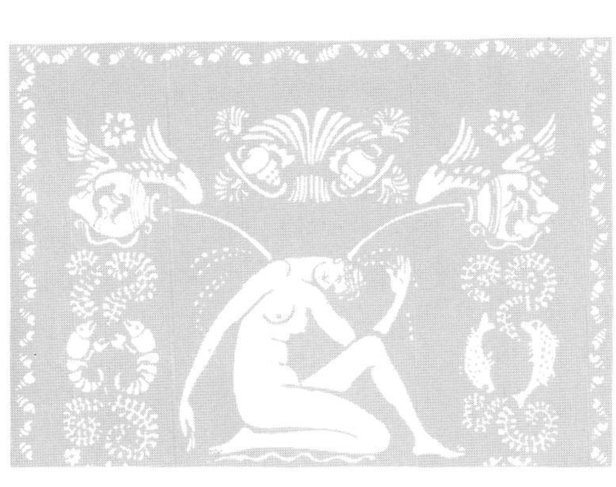

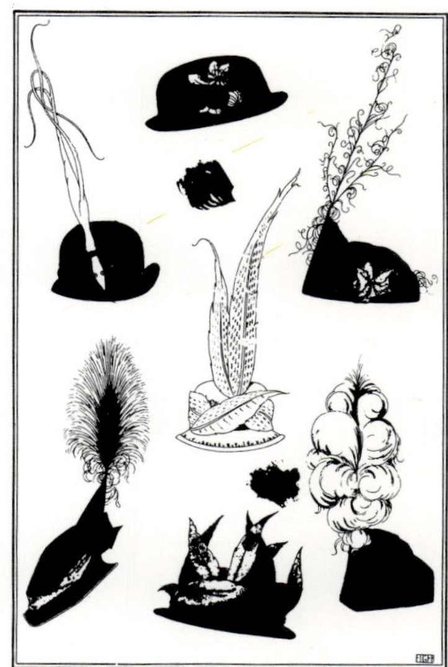

including those who were beginning to work in the growing film industry. By 1910 Lanvin was established as one of the leaders of the new group of Art Deco-inspired couturiers who were noted for producing what were regarded as revolutionary new clothes — inventing an attitude and style of dressing that has survived to this day.

These revolutionary couturiers, and the more traditional houses of Worth, Redfern, Chéruit, Paquin and Doeuillet, were still expected to promote their full range of design ideas in February and August each year, when their salons would be replete with the world's fashion elite. Business was excellent.

Each season, each of the leading houses was completely refurbished, using only the very best of the new design ideas that the multitude of talented designers and master-craftsmen could offer. This of course created great rivalry among the many famous ateliers that specialised in unique forms of glassware, furniture, ceramics, tapestries, carpets, lacquer work, metal screens, silverware, textiles, objets d'art of all sorts, and furs and jewellery.

But the couturiers and their extravagant clients had their critics. Many deplored such 'conspicuous consumption'; they regarded all new fashions in clothing, furniture and jewellery, and all forms of objet d'art as clearly demonstrating a wilful lack of prudence on the part of the haut monde who, they said, blatantly exhibited an insidious desire for something different and seemed to suffer from an almost uncontrollable urge for sybaritic indulgence. They were flaunting their wealth and privilege at the expense of the rest of Western society, which seemed to be crumbling around them.

Following the lead of Cardinal Farley, the critics became more insistent: many of the new fashions were indecent and even obscene; they offended society's moral code and religious beliefs; they were elitist and anachronistic and should never be permitted in a democratic society. Despite the critics' strident cries the new styles continued to develop and the haut monde was untroubled. Change occurred according to customer demand, not according to the complaints of moralists.

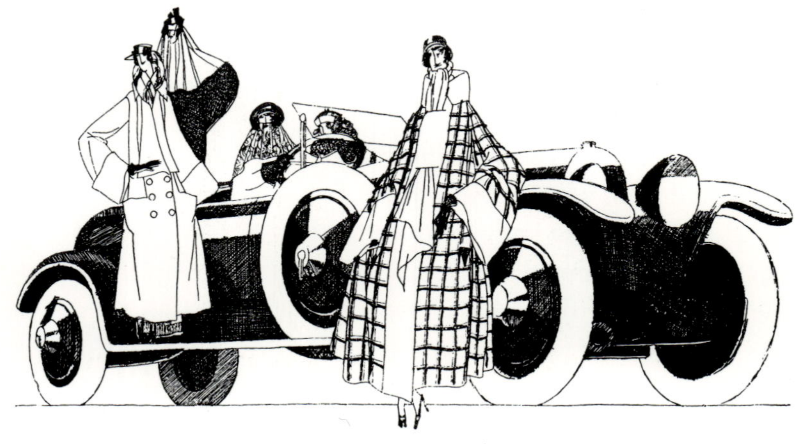

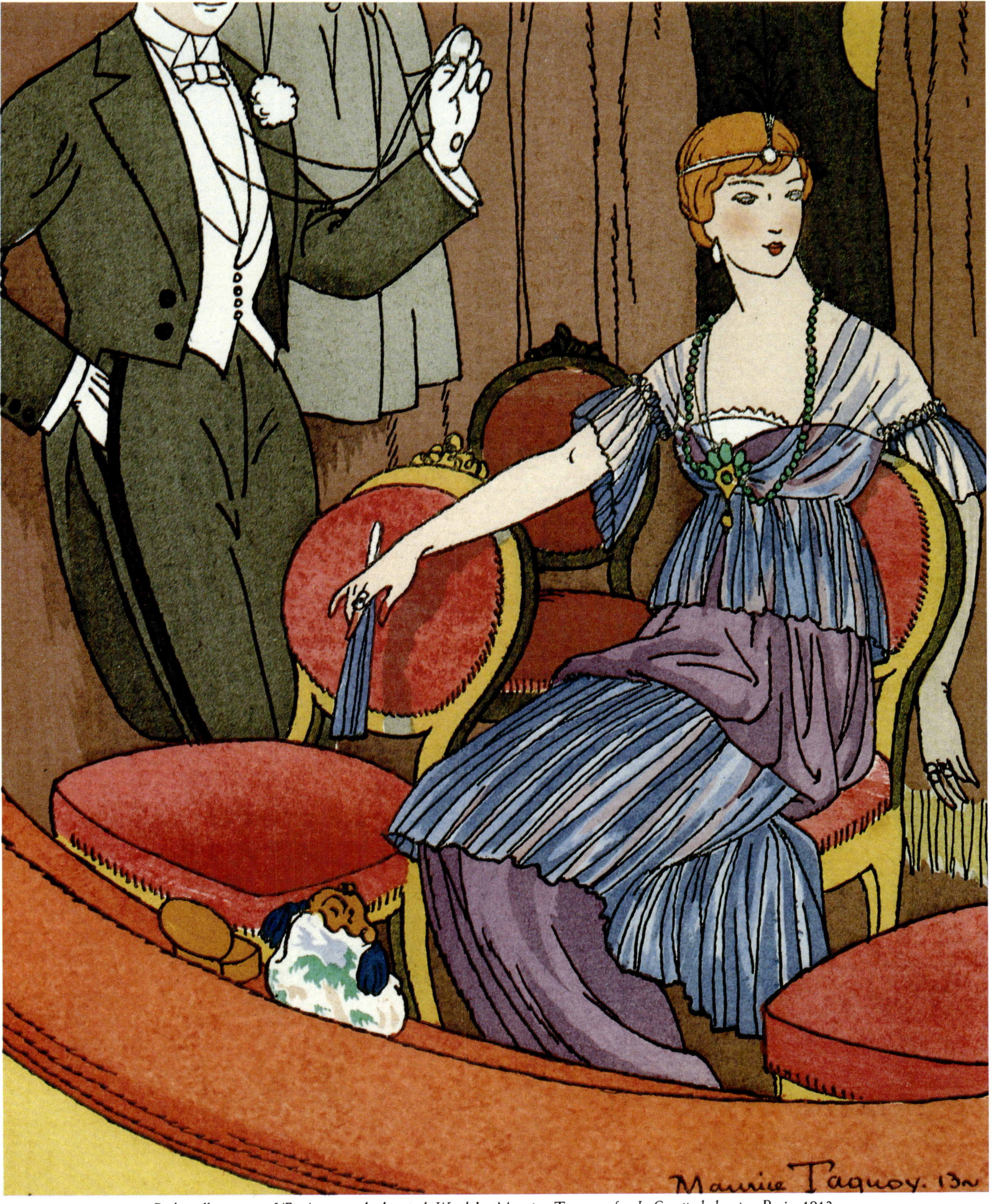

Pochoir illustration *L'Entr'acte — robe du soir de Worth* by Maurice Taquoy, for *Le Gazette du bon ton*. Paris. 1913.

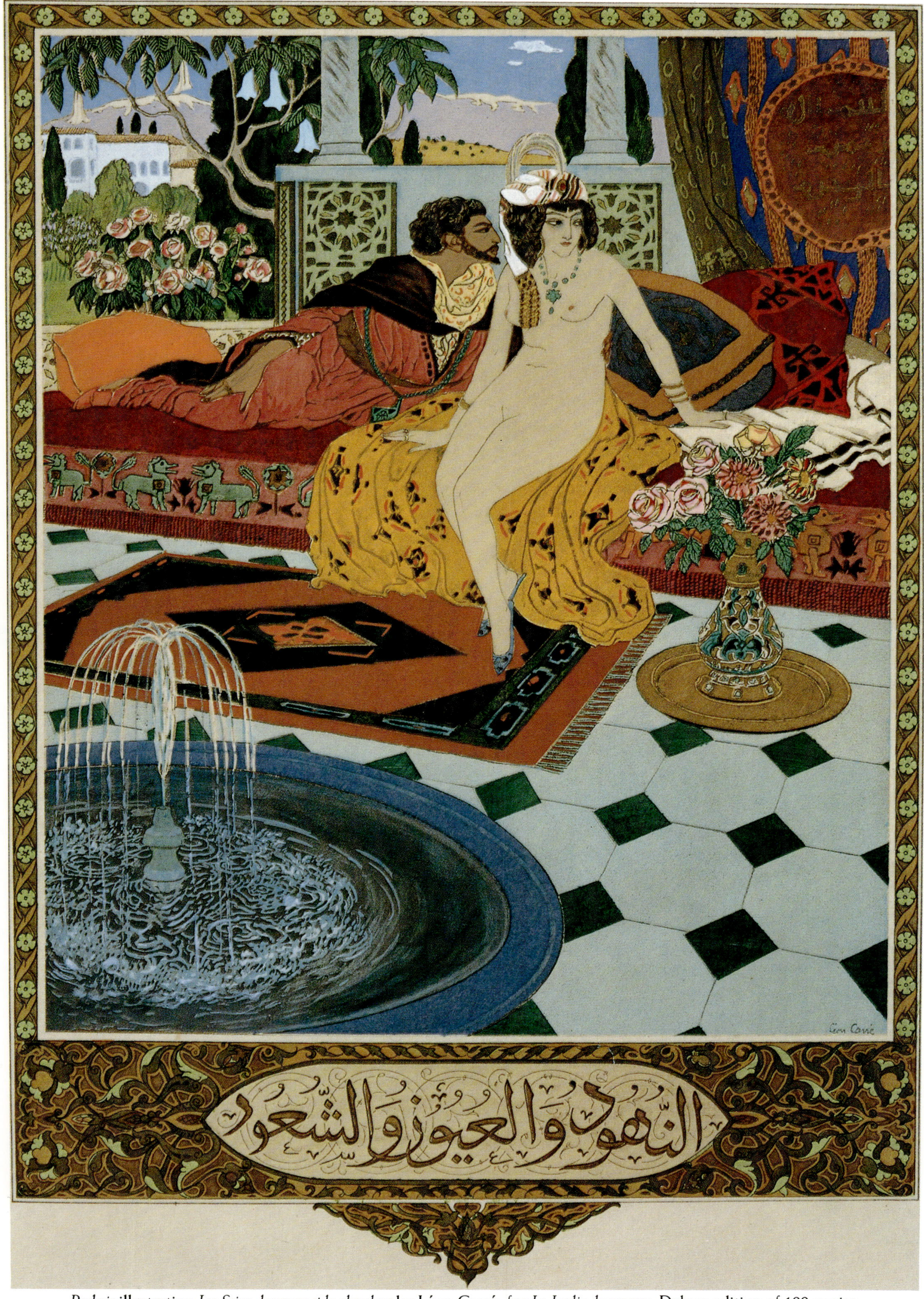

Pochoir illustration *Les Seins, les yeux et la chevelure* by Léon Carré, for *Le Jardin de caresses*. Deluxe edition of 100 copies. Published by L'Edition d'Art, H. Piazza, Paris. 1914.

The new styles of paintings — by Picasso, Matisse, Klimt, Modigliani, Braque, van Dongen, Rouault and Kandinsky — were also under attack from moralists and social critics, as were many new books, new forms of music, new styles of architecture, the new motorised transport, the development of the aeroplane, new theatrical plays, new cinema epics, and the new operas and ballets. Sergei Diaghilev's new Ballet Russe production *Schéhérazade*, with music by Rimsky-Korsakov, sets and costumes by Léon Bakst, choreography by Fokine, and featuring the dancers Ida Rubinstein and Vaslav Nijinsky, caused a sensation when it was performed for the first time at the Paris Grand Opera House in June 1910.

This extravagant and sensual production was a frenzied tale of harem jealousies and intrigue, with the notorious 'orgy' sequence in the middle of the performance being especially striking, particularly when Rubinstein and Nijinsky appeared almost nude. The clergy and professional moralists of the time were outraged; the performance was described in the press as 'undeniably barbaric' and 'unnecessarily vulgar'. But the audience was ecstatic and overwhelmed the end of the production with its roar of applause.

Russian-born entrepreneur Sergei Pavlovich Diaghilev had first visited Paris in 1906, with an exhibition of Russian paintings by Bakst, Bilibin and other contemporary and traditional artists. This had created much interest in Russian art and in 1907 he returned with the works of the contemporary Russian composers Rachmaninov, Rimsky-Korsakov, Scriabin and Glazounov, conducted by Nikisch. In 1908 he had introduced the young Russian singer Chaliapin to the Western world in Moussorgsky's opera *Boris Godounov*, which featured sets and costumes by Bilibin and Bakst. But he made his biggest impact when he returned the

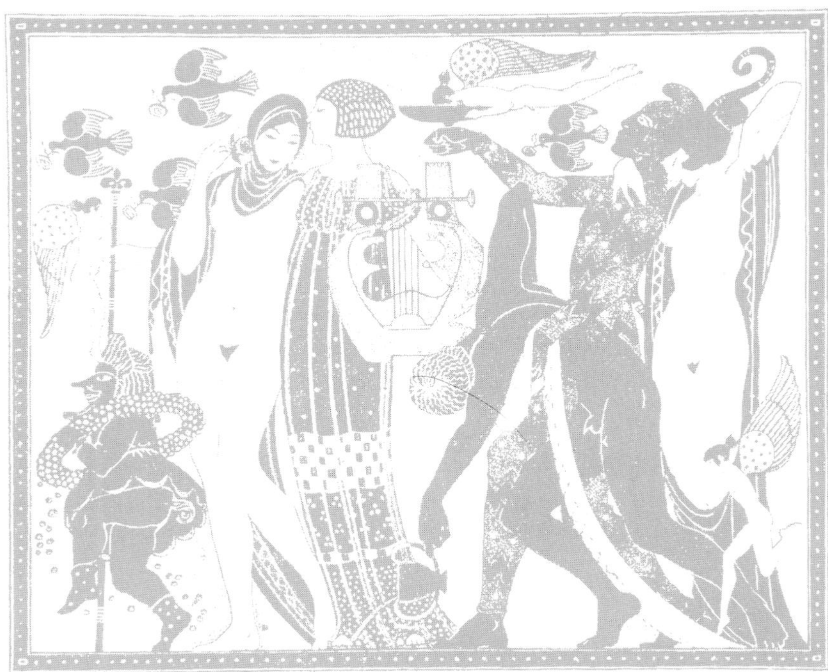

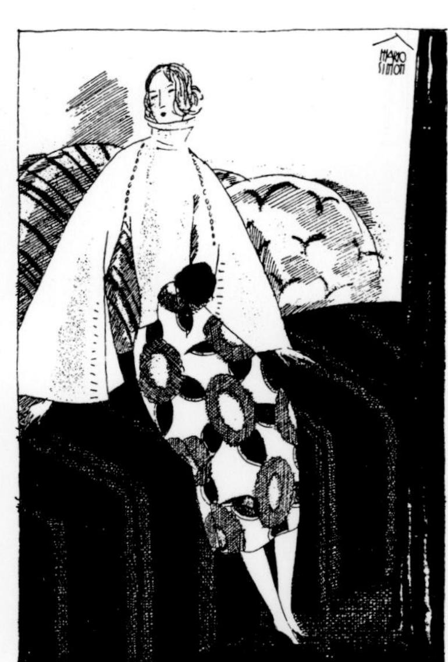

following year with his newly formed Ballet Russe, a company of dancers selected from the famous imperial dance companies of St Petersburg and Moscow — Anna Pavlova, Tamara Karsavina, Ida Rubinstein, Vaslav Nijinsky, Michel Fokine and Léonide Massine — who performed a selection of new ballets at the Théâtre du Châtelet, including *Le Pavillon d'Armide*, *The Polovtsian Dances from Prince Igor*, *Les Sylphides*, and *Cléopâtre*.

Diaghilev had also brought with him some of the Russian set and costume designers from the St Petersburg Imperial Theatre. The aesthetic sensibilities and the daring of Benois, Bakst and Korovine stunned the Paris audiences, who had never seen such colourful decor and such exotic and erotic costumes. Each production was a sensation and the Ballet Russe became the talk of Paris. Diaghilev and his company of dancers and designers returned to Paris in 1910, this time to the Grand Opera House, where they staged the new ballets *Le Carnaval*, *Giselle*, *L'Oiseau de feu*, *Les Orientales* and *Schéhérazade*; this last ballet was undoubtedly the climax of the Paris cultural season.

The production of *Schéhérazade*, with its hard, acid colours, sumptuous settings, oriental costumes, sensual dancing, and a story of lust and intrigue, acted as a catalyst in popularising the new mood of the time, finally and irrevocably breaking the ties that remained with the nineteenth century. And although the production was condemned as barbaric and vulgar, many of the intellectuals of the period saw in this vulgarity and barbarism a means of freeing themselves from a constricted and inhibited past.

The depth of social repression inherited from the nineteenth century made this cultural rebellion all the more electrifying; the Western world was swept forward by the euphoria of change. At the same time, many of the older members of Western society clung to their ideals and became increasingly horrified, and even more regressive in attitude, as they saw 'respectable' women painting their faces in the mode of the demi-mondaines, dancers and actresses, and throwing off their corsets and superfluous layers of lingerie so that they too could wear the new figure-revealing dresses. Even more horrifying, these women were demanding the right to vote, to drive a car, to smoke in public, to dance the previously forbidden tango and cakewalk, to partake in active sports wearing sports clothes that revealed their legs, and even to don one-piece bathing costumes like those in which Annette Kellerman had shocked the world just three years before, in 1907.

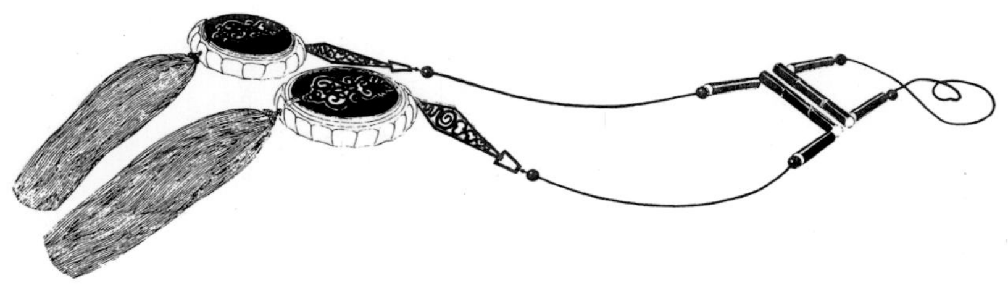

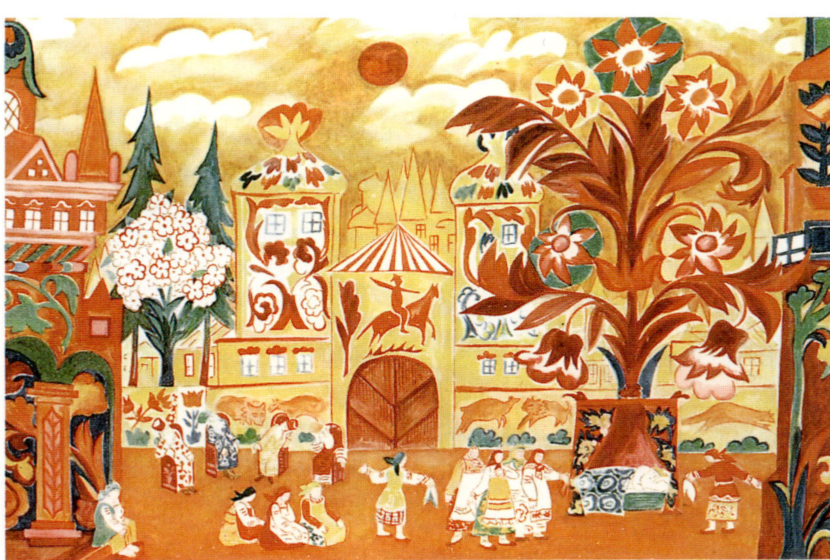

Drawing by Goncharova of a set design for the Ballet Russe production of *Le Coq d'Or*. Paris. 1914.

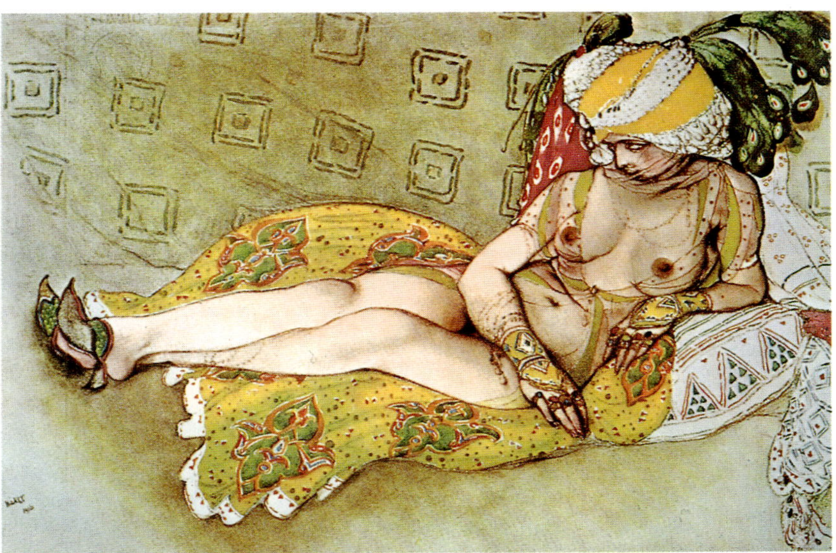

Drawing by Léon Bakst of Ida Rubinstein in the 1912 production *Schéhérazade* produced by Sergei Diaghilev, Ballet Russe theatre program. 1916.

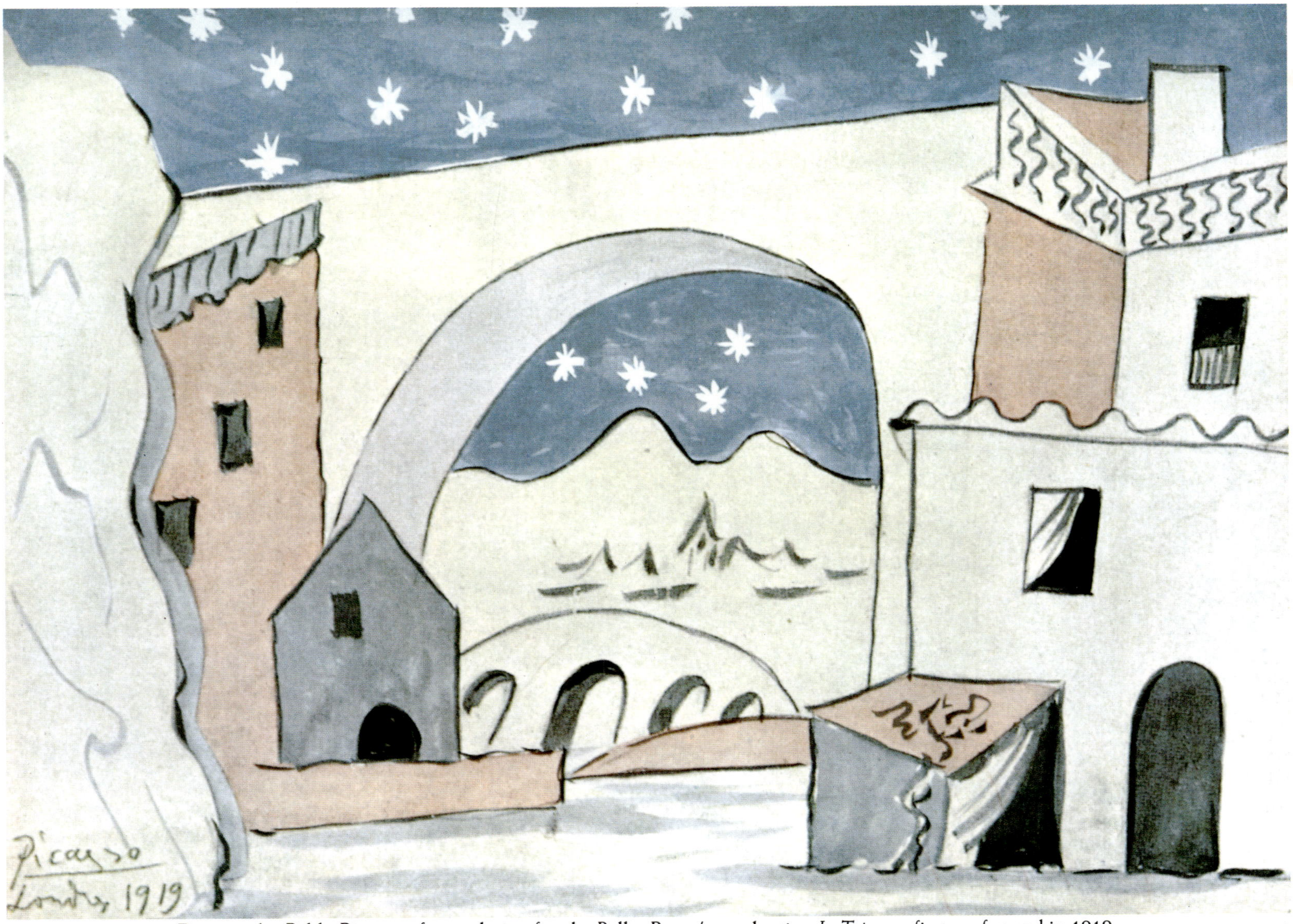

Drawing by Pablo Picasso of a set design for the Ballet Russe's production *Le Tricorne*, first performed in 1919.

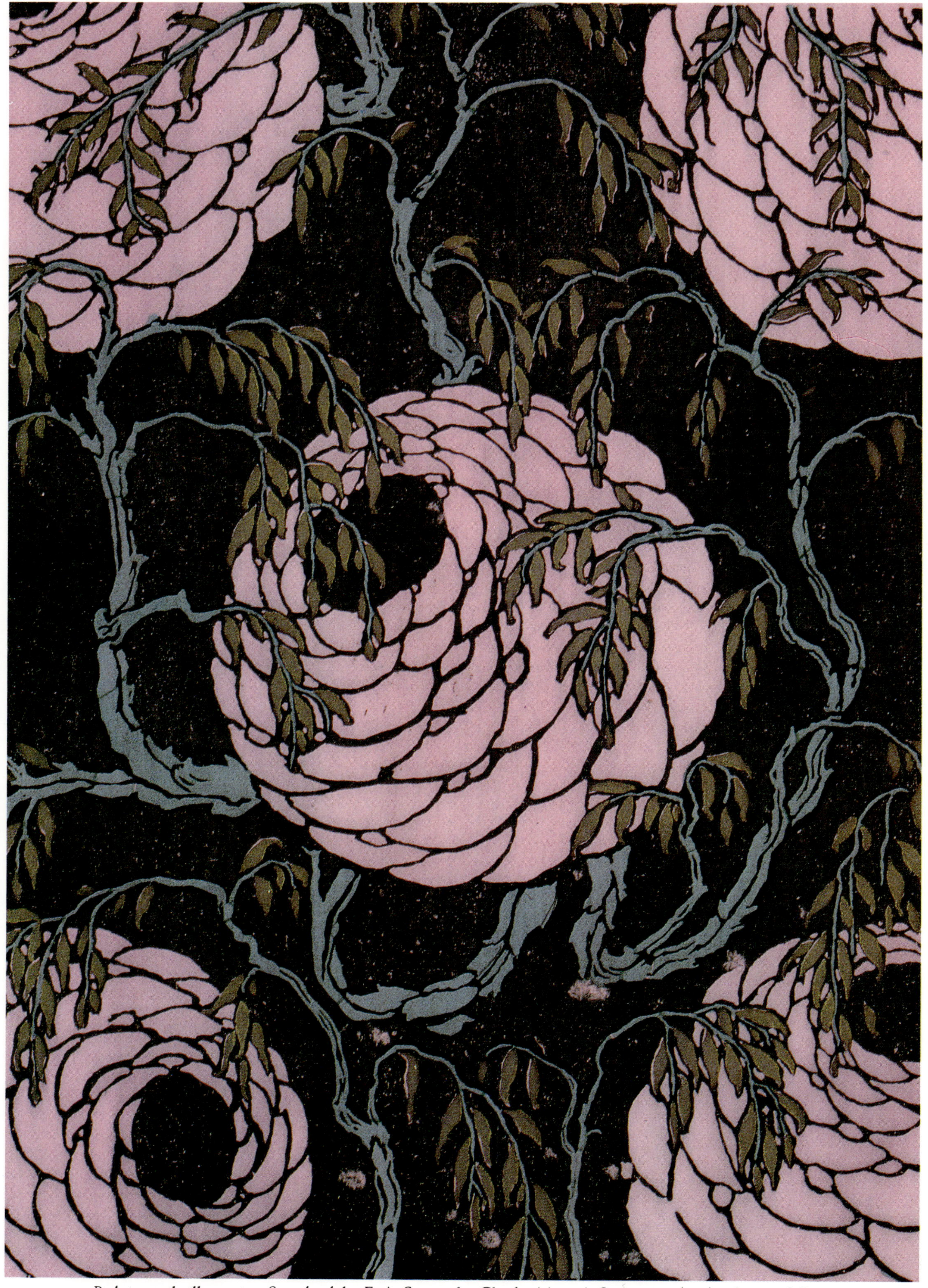

Pochoir textile illustration *Samarkande* by E. A. Seguy, for Charles Massin's *Compositions dans le goût oriental*, Paris. Circa 1914.

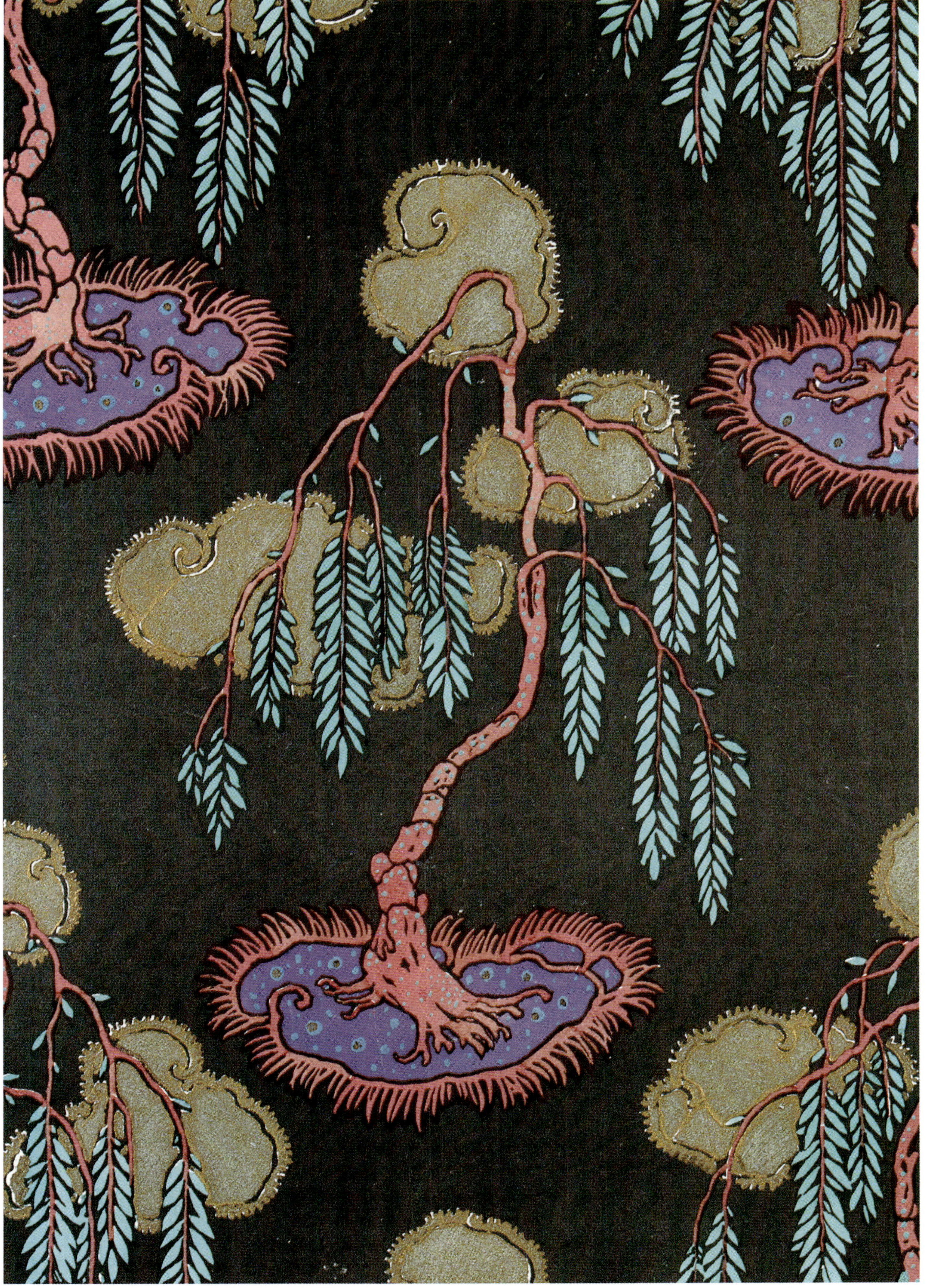

Pochoir textile illustration *Samarkande* by E. A. Seguy, for Charles Massin's *Compositions dans le goût oriental*, Paris. Circa 1914.

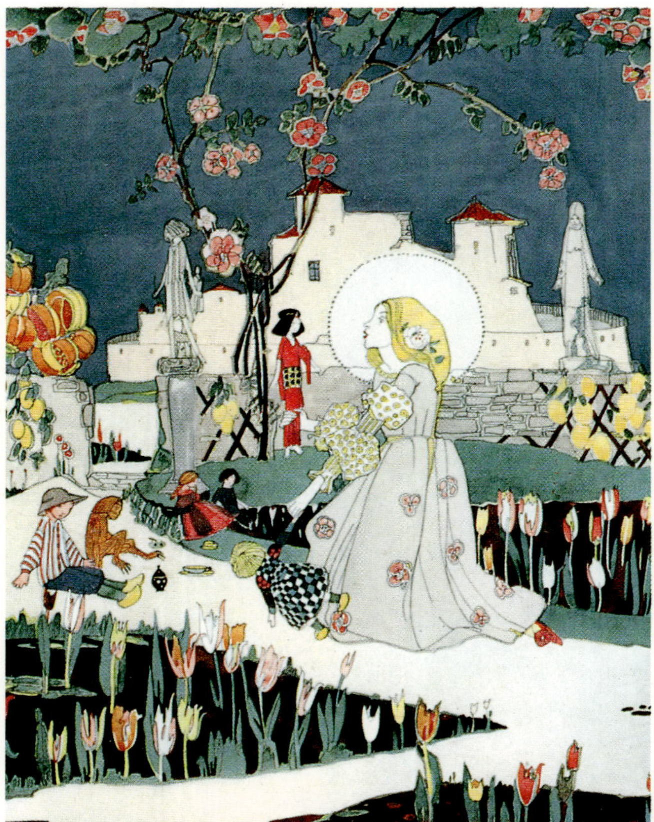

Illustration of *The Little Princess* by Jessie M. King, for *A House of Pomegranates*. Published by Methuen & Co., London. 1915.

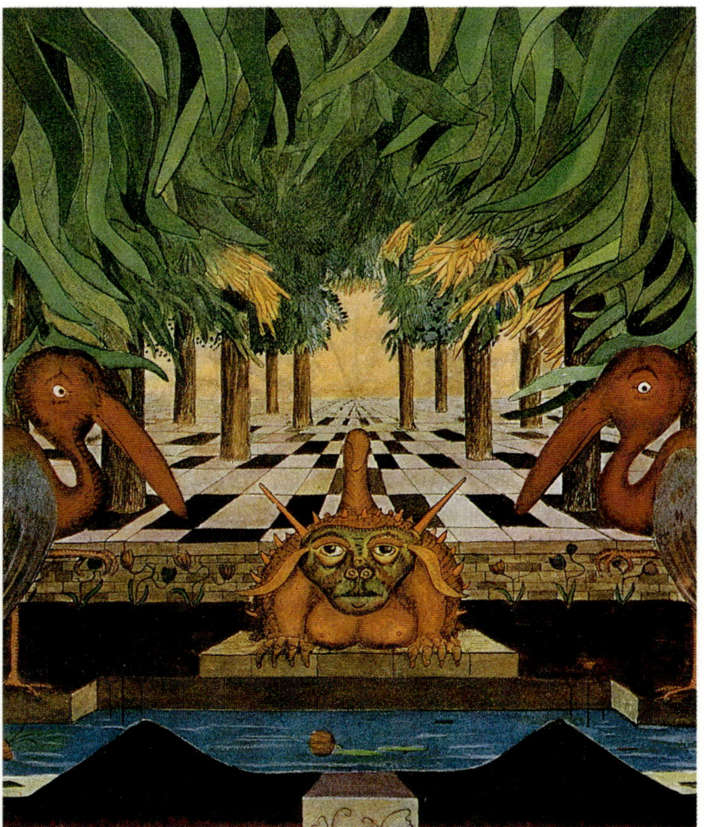

Illustration of *The Googles Garden* by V. C. Vickers, from *The Google Book*. Deluxe edition of 100 copies. Published by J. & E. Bumpus, London. 1913.

Other aspects of Western life had also been changing. Between 1908 and 1912 the film industry in North America and Europe had grown rapidly and by 1912 it had a regular weekly audience of many millions; the new films seemed to have the power to change people's ideas and ideals overnight. Cars were becoming larger, faster, and much more numerous. Aeroplanes could now fly great distances, linking major cities in a matter of hours. Trains were becoming increasingly popular, transporting large numbers of people over the vastnesses of Europe, Russia, India and parts of Africa, Canada and the United States. The electric light was now in common use in most of the industrialised countries of the Western world. The sewing machine and methods of mass production had made modern clothing available to an ever-increasing population. Ships were becoming larger and more comfortable, enabling more people to travel abroad. And each year more than 1.25 million people from the poorer, working classes were leaving Europe and parts of Great Britain in the hope of finding a better life in the United States, Canada, South Africa and Australia.

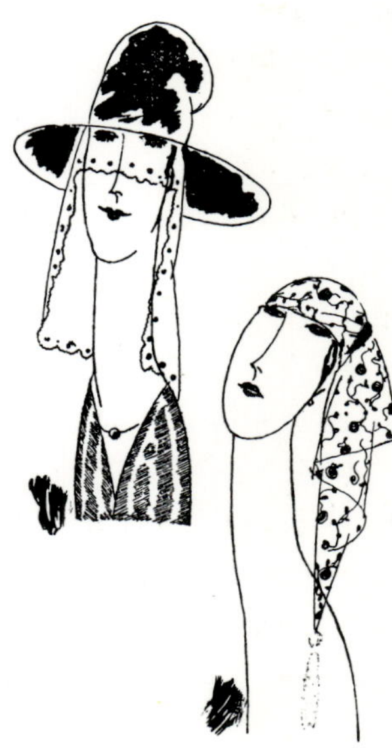

During the first decade of the century many large department stores had been built in the major cities of the Western world, to cater for the increasing spending power of the new middle classes. This in turn created an expanding market for new forms of 'middle-market' merchandise. The success or failure of these department stores depended on their ability to lure casual passers-by into the store and to make purchasers of them. This was generally achieved by large, attractive window displays that pandered

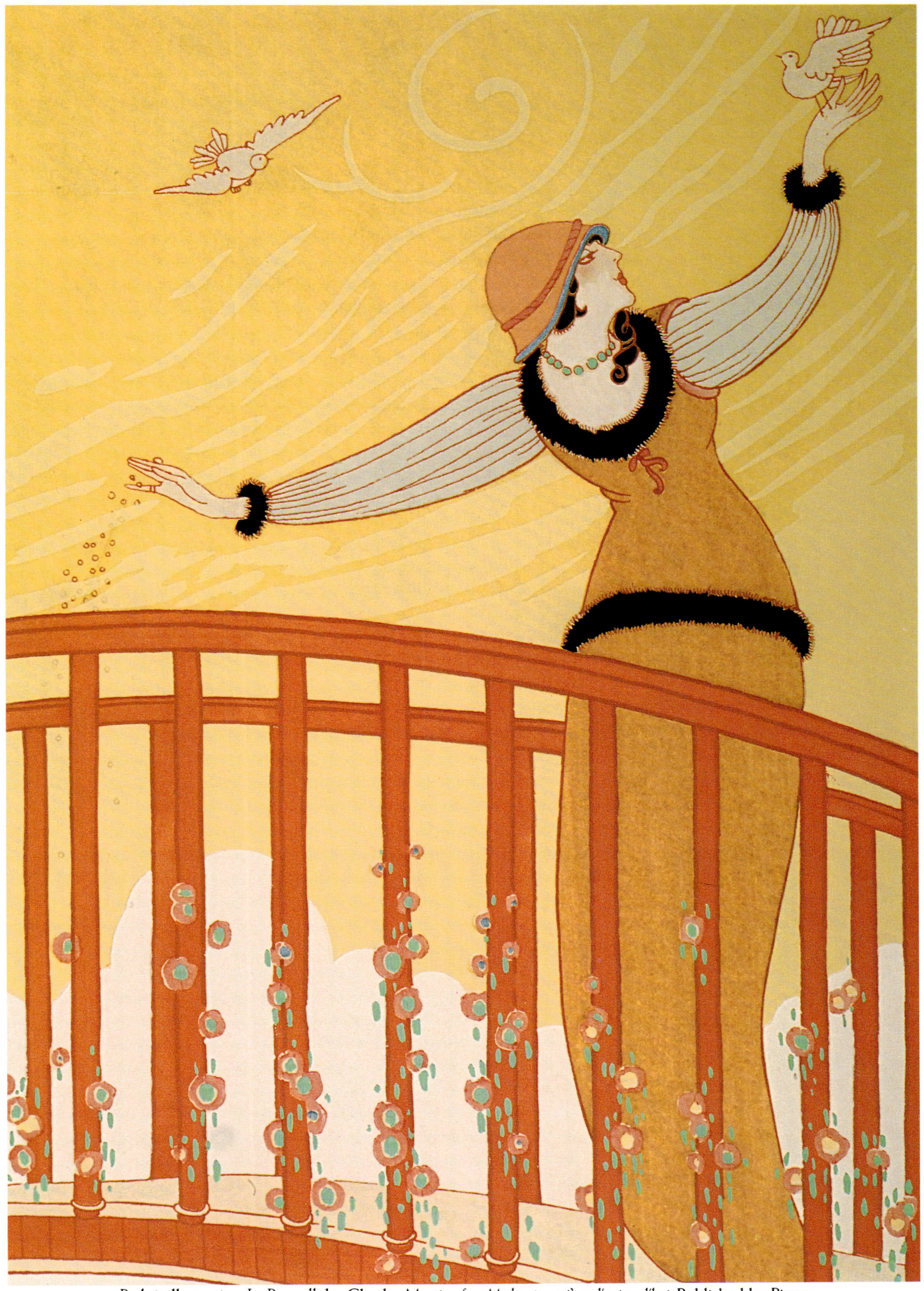

Pochoir illustration *La Passerelle* by Charles Martin, for *Modes et manières d'aujourd'hui*. Published by Pierre Corrard, Paris. 1913.

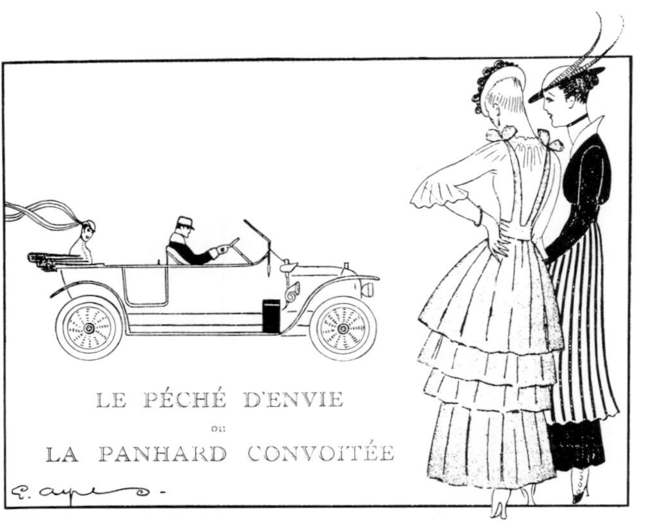

to the potential customer's whims and fantasies. The twentieth century middle-class consumer society had begun in earnest. It was to develop rapidly during the next twenty-five years, eventually offering far more opportunity for profit than the expensive and exclusive tastes of the haut monde. This fact alone was to change the design and marketing philosophy of many product designers of the 1920s and 1930s.

But before World War I very few department stores made significant inroads into the Art Deco market: members of the elite continued to purchase their clothes from the great *maisons de couture* and to satisfy many of their artistic whims at the numerous ateliers that were still specialising in their own unique forms of design. The Ateliers Modernes, run by the young furniture designer and illustrator Francis Jourdain; Clément Mère's Maison Moderne; the furniture and interior design studio of Pierre Lehalle; the carpentry workshop of the young Jacques-Emile Ruhlmann; the design studio of Paul Iribe and Pierre Legrain, who specialised in exclusive wallpapers, textiles, furniture and objets d'art; François-Louis Schmied's printing workshop, where many of the finest Art Deco books were to be printed; Jean Saudé's *pochoir* workshop, where Paul Poiret's two albums of designs had been printed; and Poiret's own Atelier Martine, where the exclusive products of the Martine school could be purchased and where commissions were undertaken by specialist designers such as Dufy, Erté, Matisse, van Dongen, Segonzac, Fauconnet and the Martine graduates — all these enterprises flourished at the hands of the haut monde.

Along with the Atelier Martine, the design studio run by Paul Iribe (the pseudonym of Paul Iribarnegary) and his assistant Pierre Legrain was regarded as one of the most experimental and influential during the early period of Art Deco. Although primarily a painter, Iribe had begun his professional career in 1907, as publisher of the satirical magazine *Le Témoin*, to which Jean Cocteau and Raoul Dufy had contributed. In 1908 he illustrated *Les Robes de Paul Poiret*, which had revolutionised both fashion and fashion illustration. Thereafter he was in constant demand as an illustrator, costume designer and interior decorator and he also undertook design commissions in furniture, textiles, wallpapers, jewellery and objets d'art. Pierre Legrain joined Iribe in 1910 and together they undertook a huge array of commissions, including the entire refurbishing of Jacques Doucet's house in the Avenue du Bois, where his unique collection of Art Deco paintings was displayed.

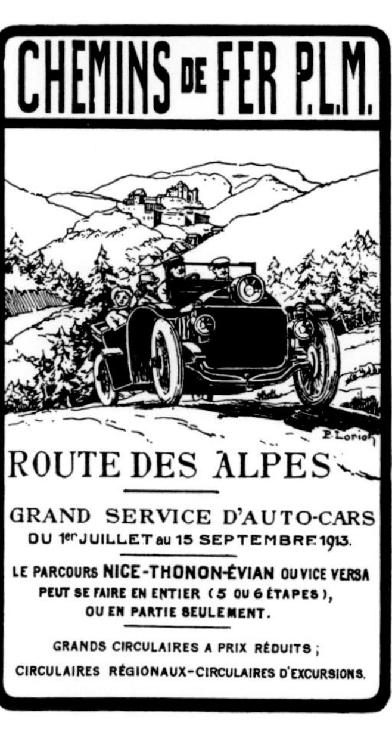

In 1919 Iribe left Paris for Hollywood, where he worked with Cecil B. DeMille and other leading directors on some of the most famous

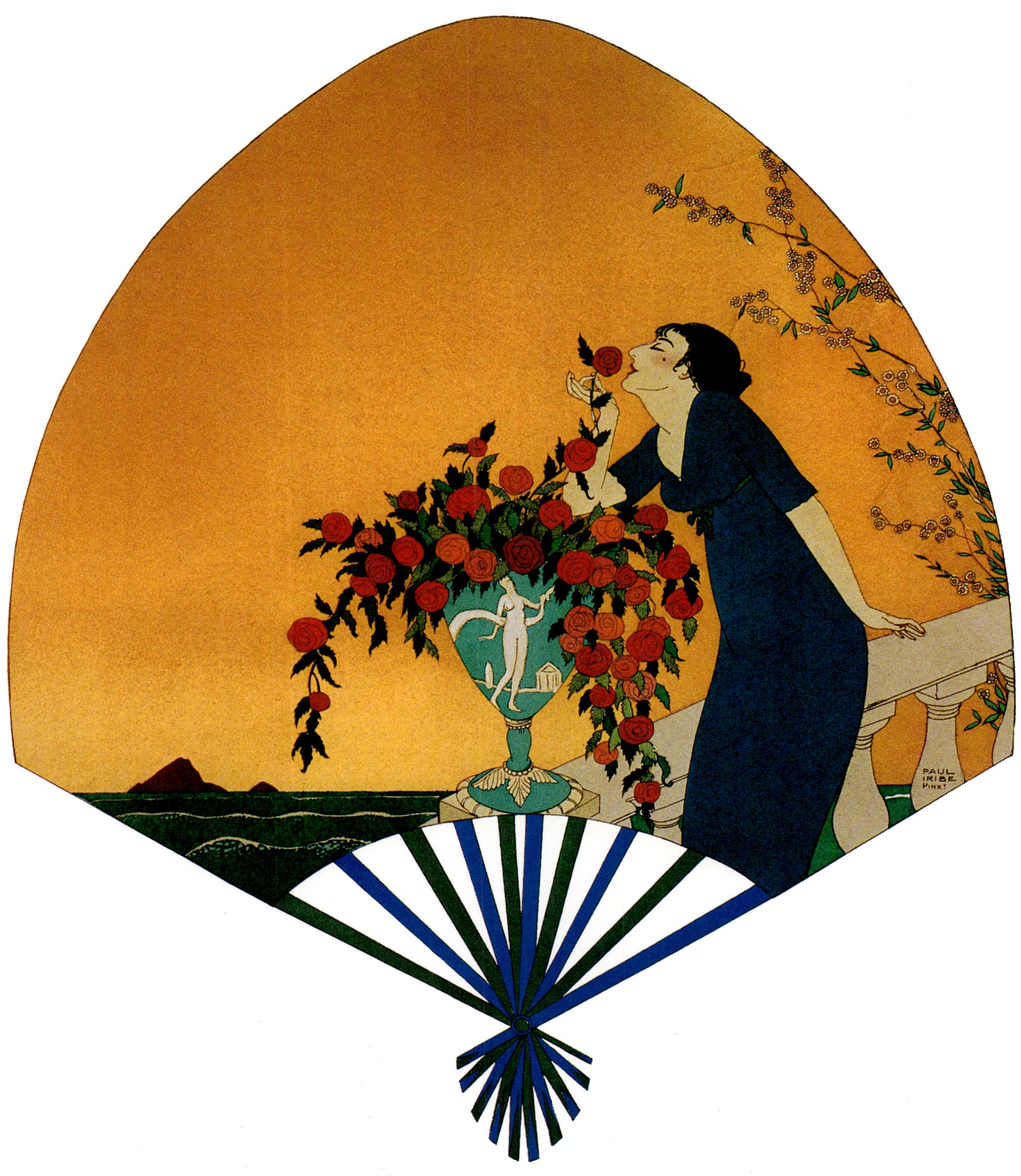

Pochoir illustration by Paul Iribe for *L'Eventail et la fourrure par Paquin*. Published for Madame Paquin, by Maquet et Cie. Paris. 1911.

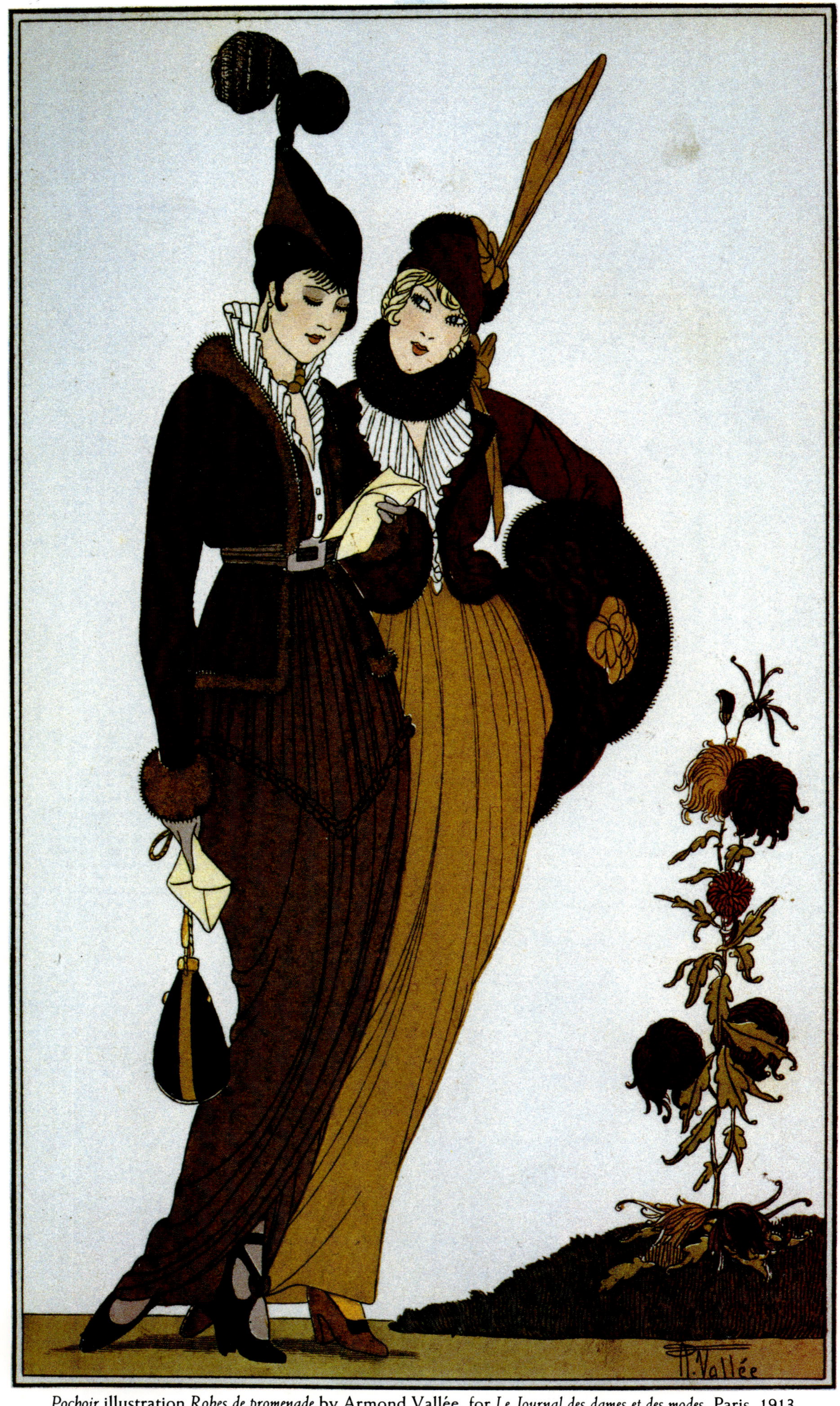

Pochoir illustration *Robes de promenade* by Armond Vallée, for *Le Journal des dames et des modes*. Paris. 1913.

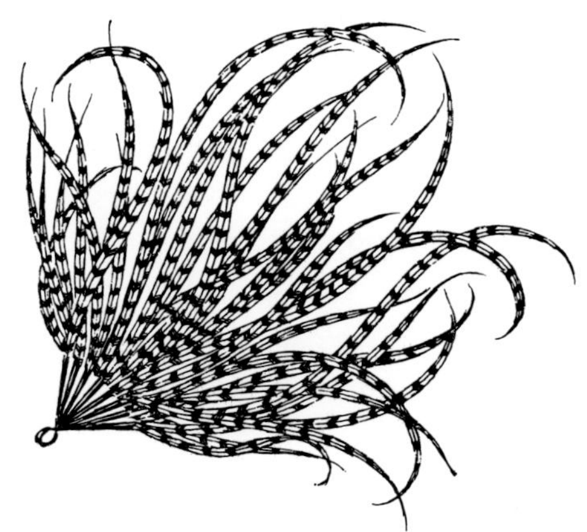

and lavish epics produced by the early film industry, the first one being *Male and Female*, which made Gloria Swanson an international star; it also popularised the glamorous Hollywood Deco style of design. Iribe continued working in Hollywood until 1930, on such films as the 1923 production of *The Ten Commandments*, *Madame Satan* and the sumptuous *Affairs of Anatal*. He returned to France in 1931 and died there four years later.

After working for several small Art Nouveau ateliers between 1900 and 1910, Clément Mère opened his own furniture workshop in Paris, specialising in the design and manufacture of highly individual items of furniture in the modern mode. These he skilfully constructed from rare woods, with inlays of marquetry, enamelled metals and carved ivory, with lacquer work, sections in stained leather or polished sharkskin called 'shagreen', which was stained to bring out the natural texture; these techniques were also combined with other forms of decorative surface treatments, giving a rich patterning to his rather simple geometric designs.

Like Mère, Pierre Lehalle had also started by making Art Nouveau furniture in the early 1900s, but by the end of the decade he was beginning to work in the modern Art Deco style. He specialised in designs made from a range of fine-figured woods to which he added inlays of mother-of-pearl, West African ivory and shagreen, with extra contrast being provided by the use of lacquer work and gilding. He also co-operated with Maurice Lucet and Alfred Levard on a number of important interior design schemes, and the three exhibited much of their work in the design exhibitions held at the Salon d'Automne and the Salon of the Société des Artistes Décorateurs, which were instrumental in establishing Art Deco as a new art form.

The painter, illustrator and designer Francis Jourdain opened his atelier in 1911, specialising in simple forms of Art Deco-style furniture that was suitable for small production runs, and in designs for fabrics, wallpapers and ceramics. By the early 1920s his business had expanded into a fully operational factory in which his furniture was produced in quantity. He also became the founder of the Union des Artistes Modernes and was a noted exhibitor in the 1925 Paris Art Deco Exhibition.

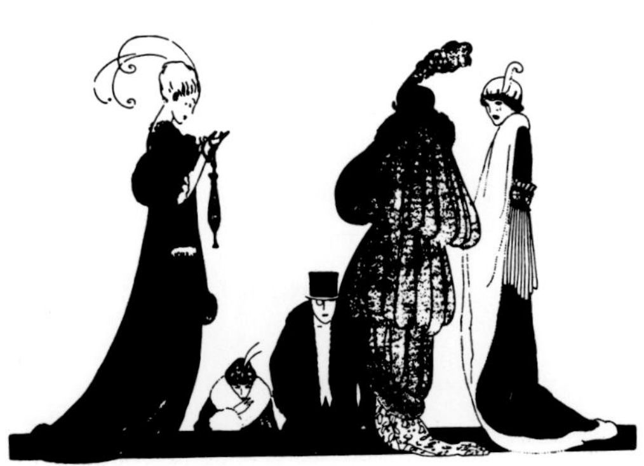

Léon Tallot began his career in Nantes

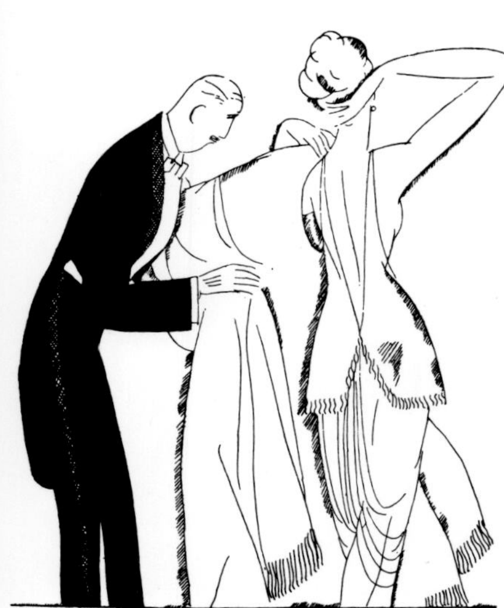

in 1893, working in several of the famous Art Nouveau ateliers of that city, including Emile Gallé's famous glass and *marqueterie sur verre* workshops, which at the time employed over three hundred craftsmen. In 1899, at the age of 25 years, Tallot was manager of Samuel Bing's Art Nouveau furniture workshop, and four years later he set up his own workshop, where he manufactured small quantities of expensive Art Nouveau furniture, carpets, fabrics and tapestries. By 1910 he was beginning to design in the modern style, his furniture shapes becoming increasingly simplified and stylised and being either lacquered or inlaid with sections of shagreen or fine leather.

Many other designers, such as Robert Bonfils, Eileen Gray and Edouard Bénédictus, were only just beginning their professional careers, whilst established designers like Henry van de Velde, Josef Hoffmann and Peter Behrens, having served their Art Nouveau and early Art Deco apprenticeships, went on to find their own unique forms of expression outside the mainstream of classifiable styles, as did painters such as Picasso, Matisse, Kandinsky and Klimt.

As the demand increased for more Art Deco products, many of the designers who had continued to work in the Art Nouveau style began to modify their designs, reducing the flowing curves and increasing the angularity of shape. Although they often did this without really changing the original design concept (thus losing any design integrity the original product may have had), their work was nevertheless eagerly accepted by customers who found the original functional aspects of Art Deco too austere and who wished to cling to some of the more sensual aspects of the past style whilst being seen to be keeping abreast of change. Other designers simply copied the ideas they had gleaned from their more successful competitors and adapted them as their own.

As more and more designers and craftsmen adopted the Art Deco style, the style began to lose its vitality and to suffer from stereotyping and lack of innovative talent. This developed into a major problem in the late 1920s, when it became increasingly clear that many products then being produced were simply 'kitsch' versions of the Art Deco style. Many art historians and authors have often confused these kitsch pieces with real Art Deco.

Fortunately, this stereotyping of kitsch-style Art Deco did not create any great difficulty in the period 1910–14, because most of those who could afford to purchase items in the new style did so from the reputable ateliers. And the glossy magazines such as *Les Modes* and *Vogue*, and the new deluxe *pochoir* albums, which by 1912 were beginning to be produced to promote the new style, featured only designs from the ateliers patronised by this elite group.

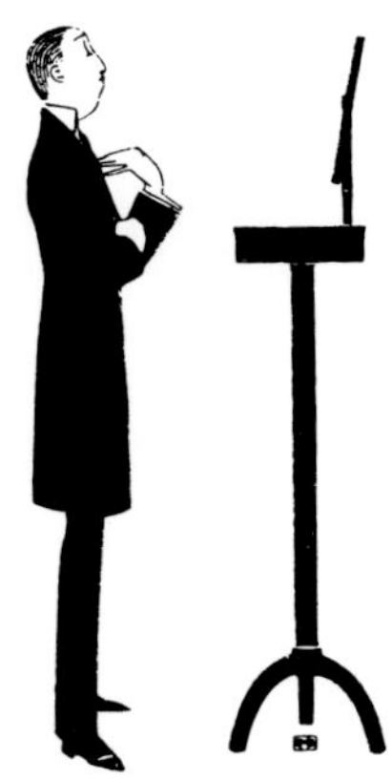

All over the Western world, the glossy magazines and new *pochoir* folders and albums proclaimed that the Art Nouveau style had finally

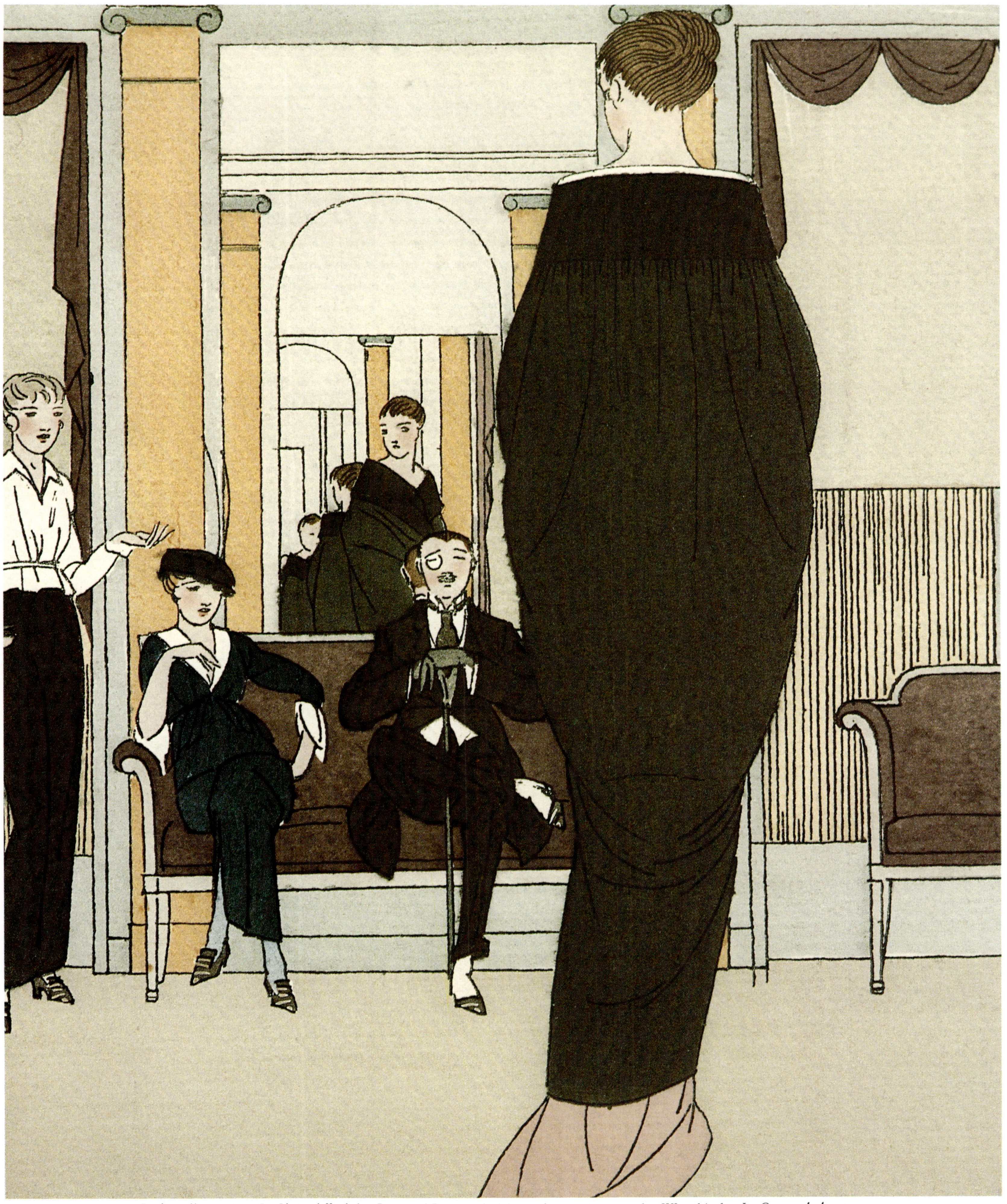

Pochoir illustration *Le Choix difficile* by Bernard Boutet de Monvel (evening coat by Worth), for *La Gazette du bon ton*. Paris. 1914.

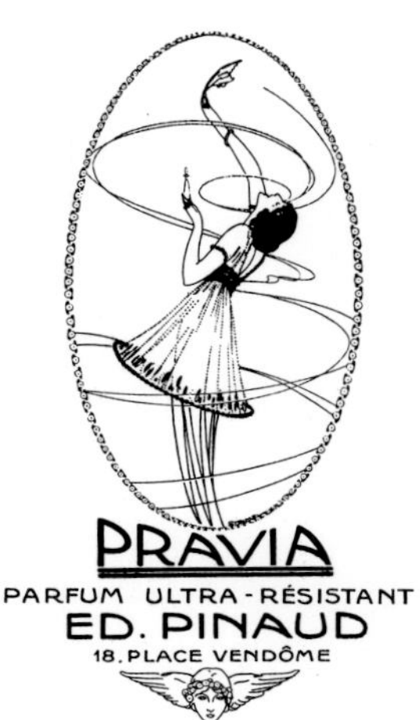

given way to this new mode of design. But, as had happened with Art Nouveau, each cultural centre began to develop its own Art Deco variations, according to its designers' own cultural interpretations of the new style. How much of the Japanese influence should be retained? How should they incorporate their own talents and traditions? How should they best use their own countries' unique resources? How much pecuniary beauty could they retain to please their local clientele, yet still be seen to be producing the sought-after new style? And how should they take into account all these considerations, and create a range of options that would enable them to sell their products for a profit?

Some designers persisted in designing within the aesthetic framework of the old Art Nouveau style: they found themselves unable, or unwilling, to adapt their skills to the new style. But after 1912 their work was regarded as anachronistic. No matter how good their products were in aesthetic terms, these designers had failed in the essential task: to be a professional innovator capable of adapting and conceiving the new artifacts that would fulfil the aesthetic dreams of tomorrow's customers. This requirement for innovation and anticipation became even more crucial as the century progressed.

Within the Art Deco movement itself, argument about the direction of the style continued. Design theorists and supporters of the vernacular tradition discussed aesthetic functionalism and the ideas put forward by William Morris in the 1880s, that good design should always be 'honest, simple and useful'. They dwelt on Jean-Jacques Rousseau's proposition that all forms of decoration were 'only in the interests of the artists, the lords, and the very rich' and that what motivated them in such matters was 'for their own self interest and their vanity, which they satisfied by setting up the cult of the difficult and the expensive'. They argued about the beliefs of Adam Smith and Henry Home, who had proposed that 'utility is one of the principal sources of beauty', and they remembered Thorstein Veblen's comments about 'conspicuous consumption' and 'pecuniary beauty'.

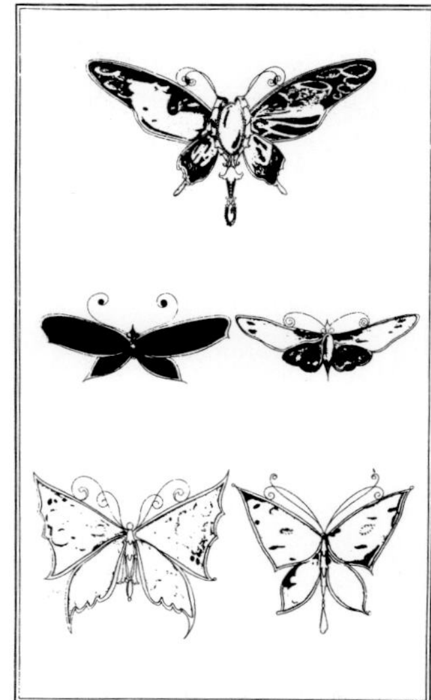

But, despite what was being said and what had been discussed, by 1912 it had become very obvious that the rationale for the current mode went far beyond the notions of the functionalists: Art Deco had become a style greatly influenced by the new aesthetic dream, and this transcended the previous European tradition.

This aesthetic dream had in fact been kindled by the numerous exhibitions of Japanese and other oriental works of art that the new group of designers and their customers had witnessed during their youth. Now it was their wish that the craft skills of the new design style be elevated to equal those of the oriental master-craftsmen whose work they had so admired and who in their own countries were greatly respected. These new designers were no longer prepared to accept the blinkered European

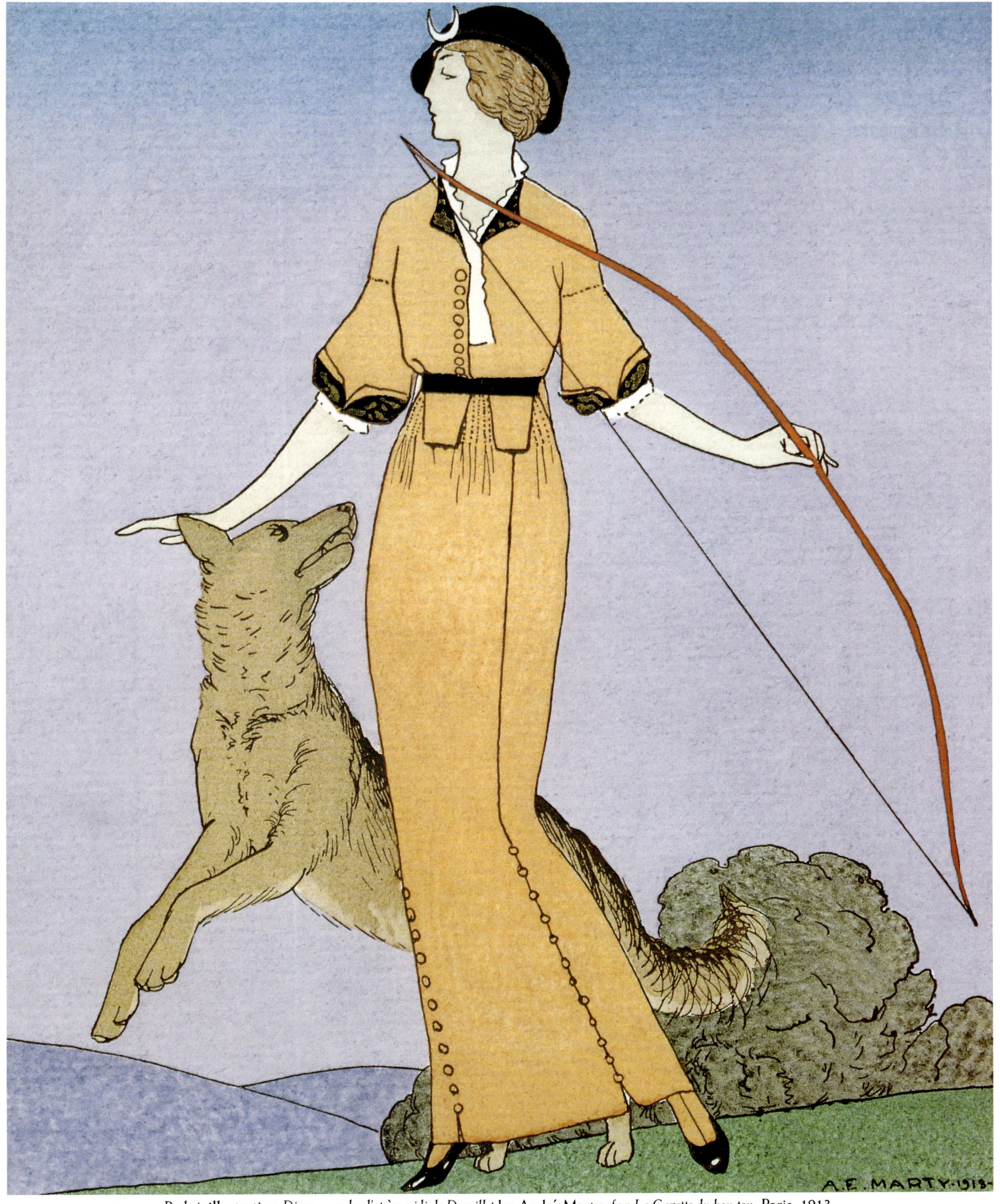

Pochoir illustration *Diane — robe d'après-midi de Doeuillet* by André Marty, for *La Gazette du bon ton*. Paris. 1913.

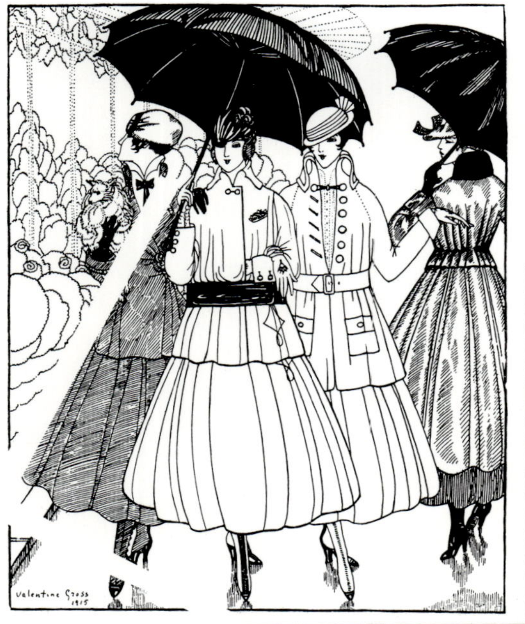

tradition that design was a secondary art, and they set out to prove that they were artists in their own right: their products just happened to be a piece of furniture, a lacquered vase, an enamelled screen, a beaded dress or a bronze statue.

This new generation of designers and craftsmen began to produce a new range of designs, and to change and experiment with other ideas and methods. The Art Deco style gradually took on a new mode of expression. It developed its own unique visual language, its own aesthetic logic, and its own exclusive badge of splendour and luxury, eventually becoming in many ways far removed from the aestheticism of its oriental origins. But the belief in superb craftsmanship and artistic integrity remained, almost sacrosanct, until the late 1920s, when financial crisis loomed over all commercial and artistic activity. This crisis was, of course, triggered by the collapse of the American stock market in October 1929, when many of the wealthy elite of the Western world found their fortunes had disappeared.

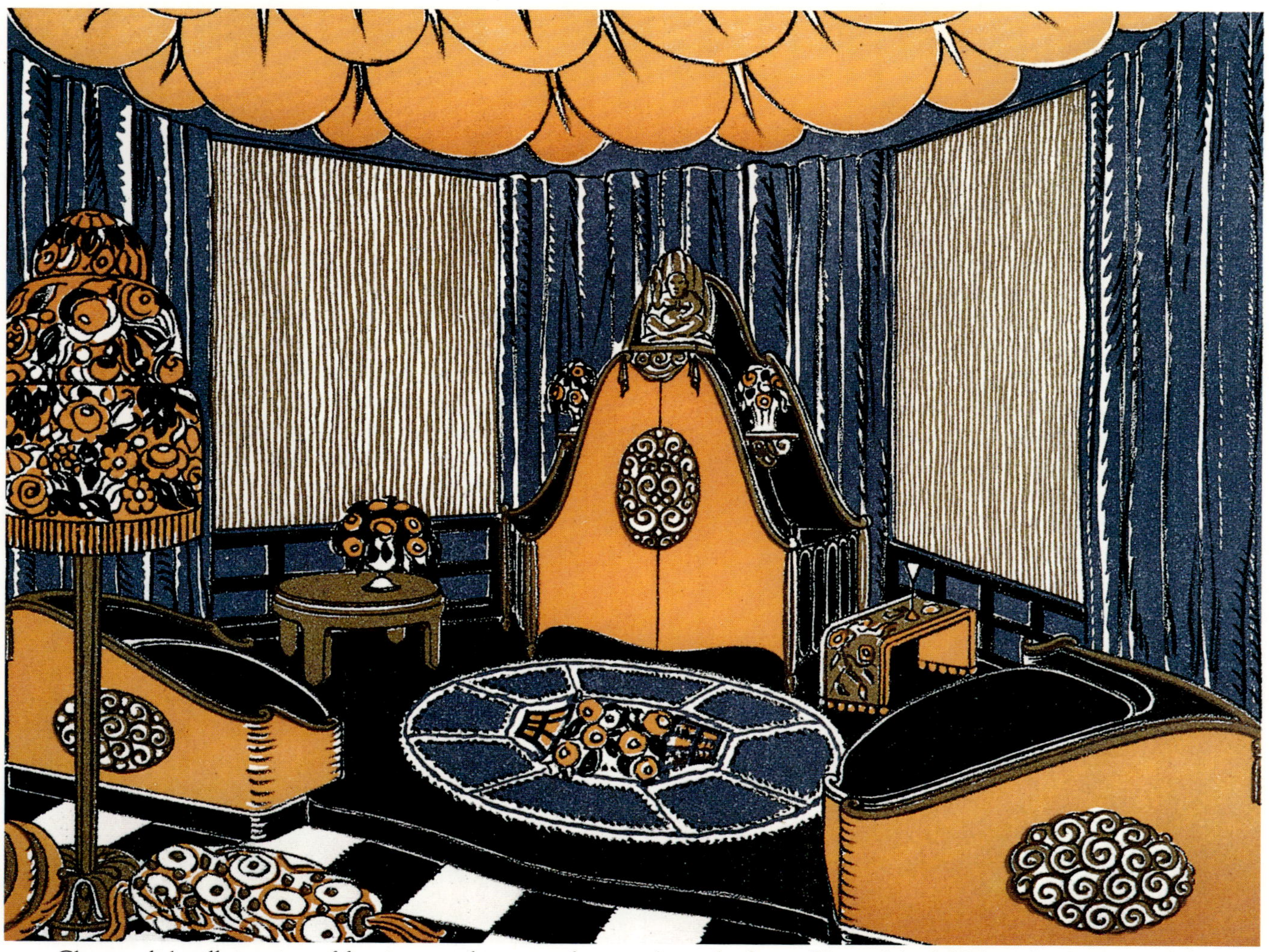

Chromo-litho illustration of furniture and interior design scheme by Louis Süe and André Mare, for *La Gazette du bon ton*. Paris. 1920.

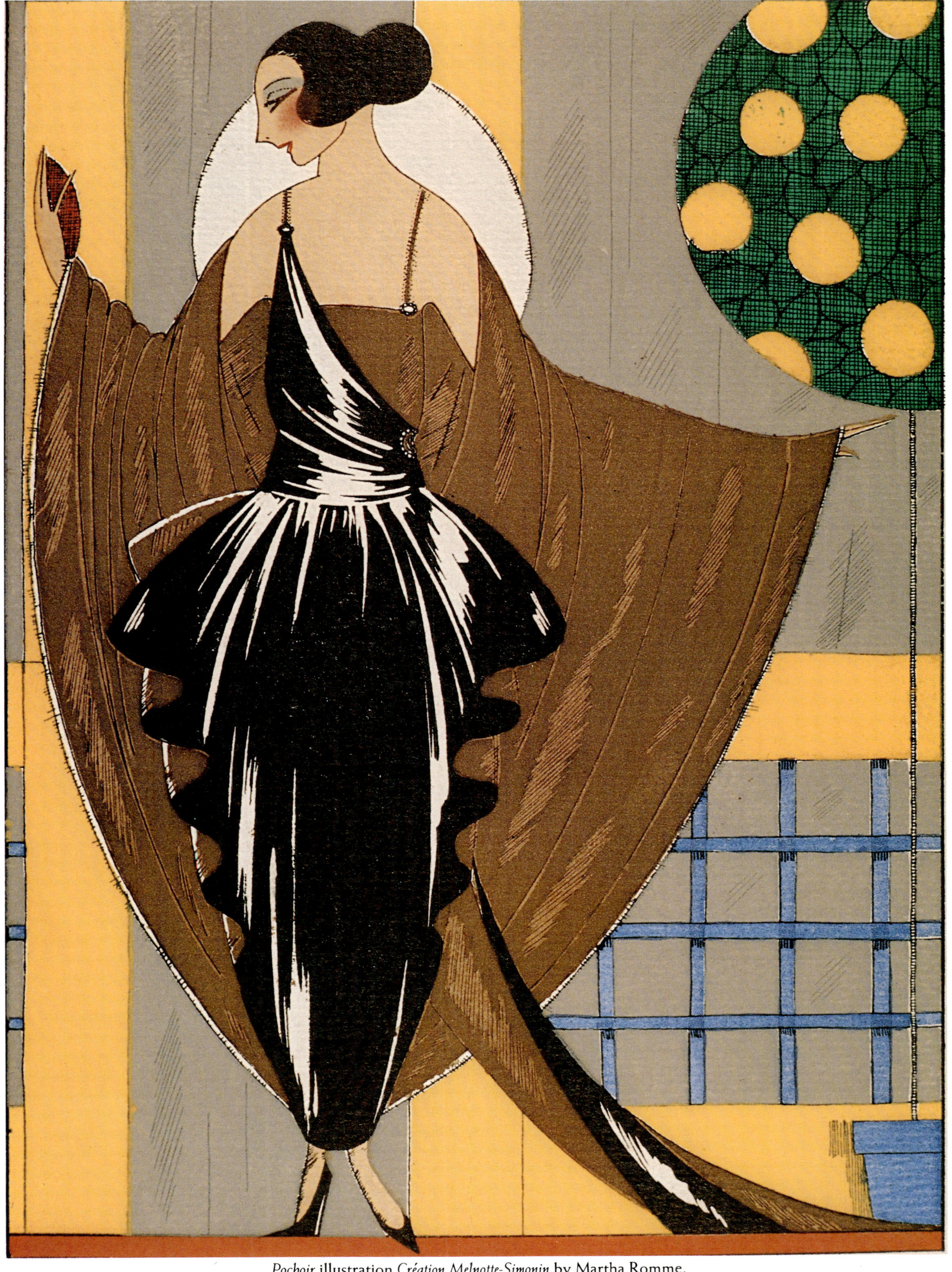

Pochoir illustration *Création Melnotte-Simonin* by Martha Romme.

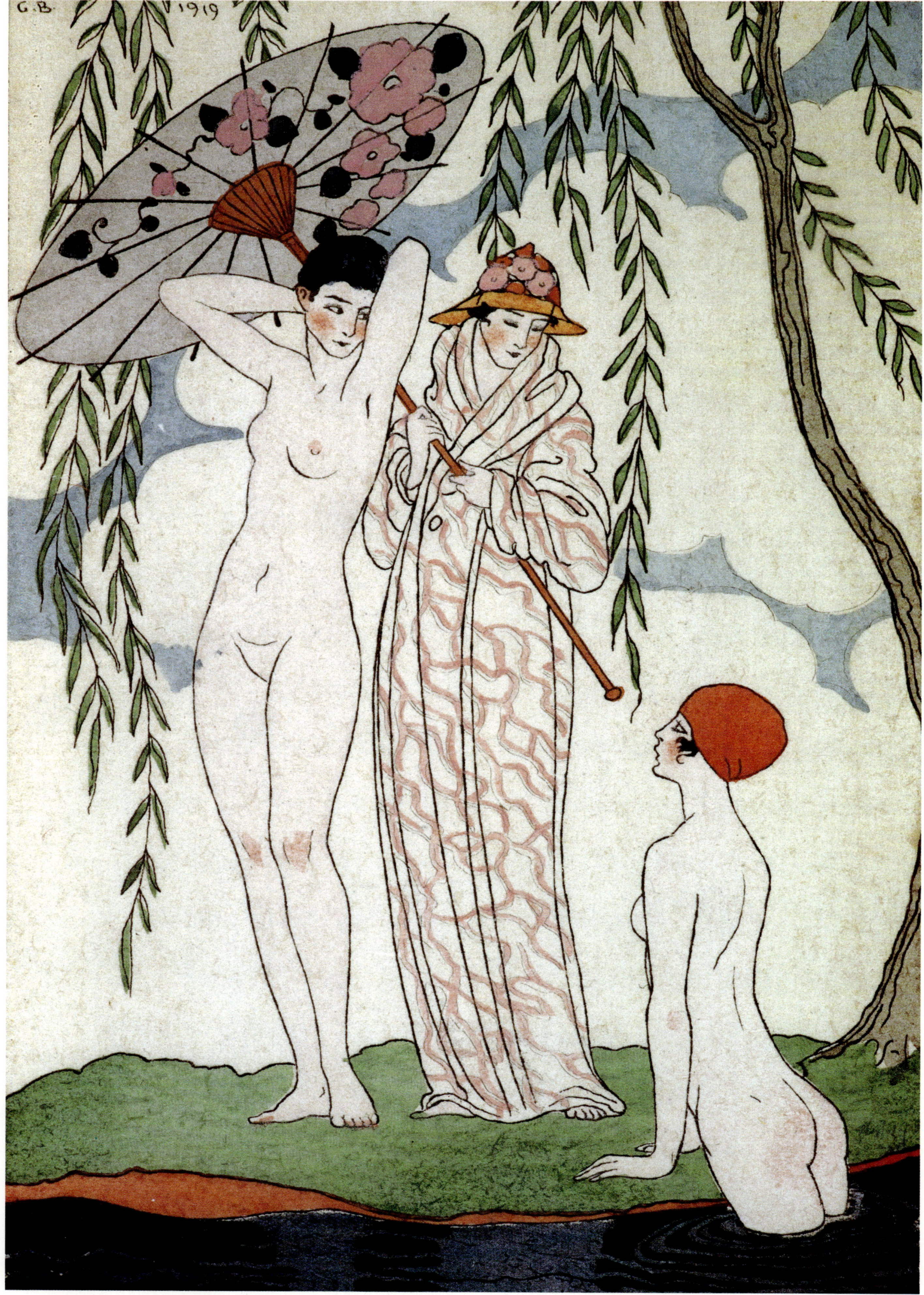

Pochoir illustration *L'Eté* by George Barbier, for *La Guirlande des mois*. Paris. 1919.

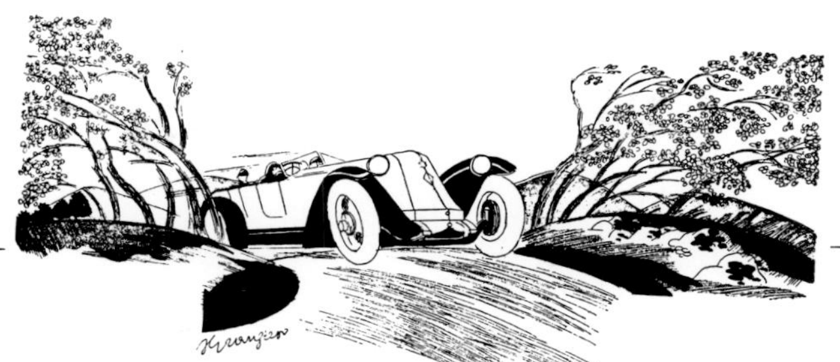

THE ARTISTS AND THE IMAGE M·A·K·E·R·S

The unique style of the early forms of Art Deco was promoted throughout the Western world by a number of illustrated deluxe magazines, albums, portfolios, books and periodicals; these publications both reflected and influenced the rapid changes that were taking place in the design of furniture, textiles, carpets, glassware, jewellery, ceramics, women's clothing, and a huge variety of other fashionable artifacts and objets d'art. The publications also contained articles about other aspects of fashionable life — recent developments in theatre, painting, music, motor cars, cinema, exhibitions, dance, and so on.

The main attraction of these exclusive publications was undoubtedly their new-style Art Deco illustrations, designed by leading avant-garde artists of the period. Their inventive and resplendent images brilliantly captured the essence of the changing times. They were not straightforward line-by-line pictorial representations of designs produced by the great couture houses and ateliers, as had been the case with similar forms of commercial illustration during the nineteenth century: the new photographic images that were the feature of prestigious glossy magazines such as *Les Modes* were already doing that job admirably.

Instead, each illustration was conceived by the individual artist as his own idiosyncratic interpretation of a design — an attempt to capture the spirit of the design rather than its surface detail. And although some of the resulting images may appear a little strange, or even bizarre today, they were nevertheless an individual statement that endowed twentieth century commercial illustration with a previously unknown artistic integrity. Fortunately, we are still able to savour the unique flavour of that era through these highly individual Art Deco images.

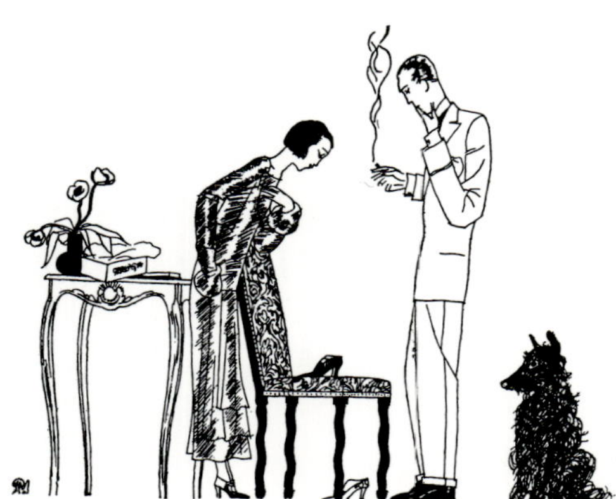

During the preceding 100 years fashionable illustration had slowly degenerated under the influence of artists of mediocre talent who had generally depicted the visual aspects of the fashionable life of the haut monde, and the design styles they chose, merely in order to display their excessive wealth and consumption, rather than to emphasise style and beauty. Even Daumier, Forain and Toulouse-Lautrec, who were among the more fashion-conscious visual commentators of the nineteenth century, preferred satire and caricature. But by 1910 fashion illustration and promotional graphics had undergone a dramatic change, and these commercial forms of image-making were becoming acceptable as legitimate art forms, attracting the skills and energies of artists such as Paul Iribe, George Barbier, Léon Bakst, Erté, Pablo Picasso, Sonia Delaunay, Georges Lepape and Etienne Drian, who applied their energy, skill and fastidiousness to capture the very essence of these new design styles.

Such an influential collaboration between the visual arts and the trappings of fashionable life had not occurred in Western modes of illustration since the eighteenth century, when painters such as Antoine Watteau and Claude-Louis Desrais had been commissioned to illustrate contemporary publications such as *La Galerie des modes*, *Les Costumes français*, and *Le Magasin des modes nouvelles*. After 1910, however, this form of image-making took on a totally new character.

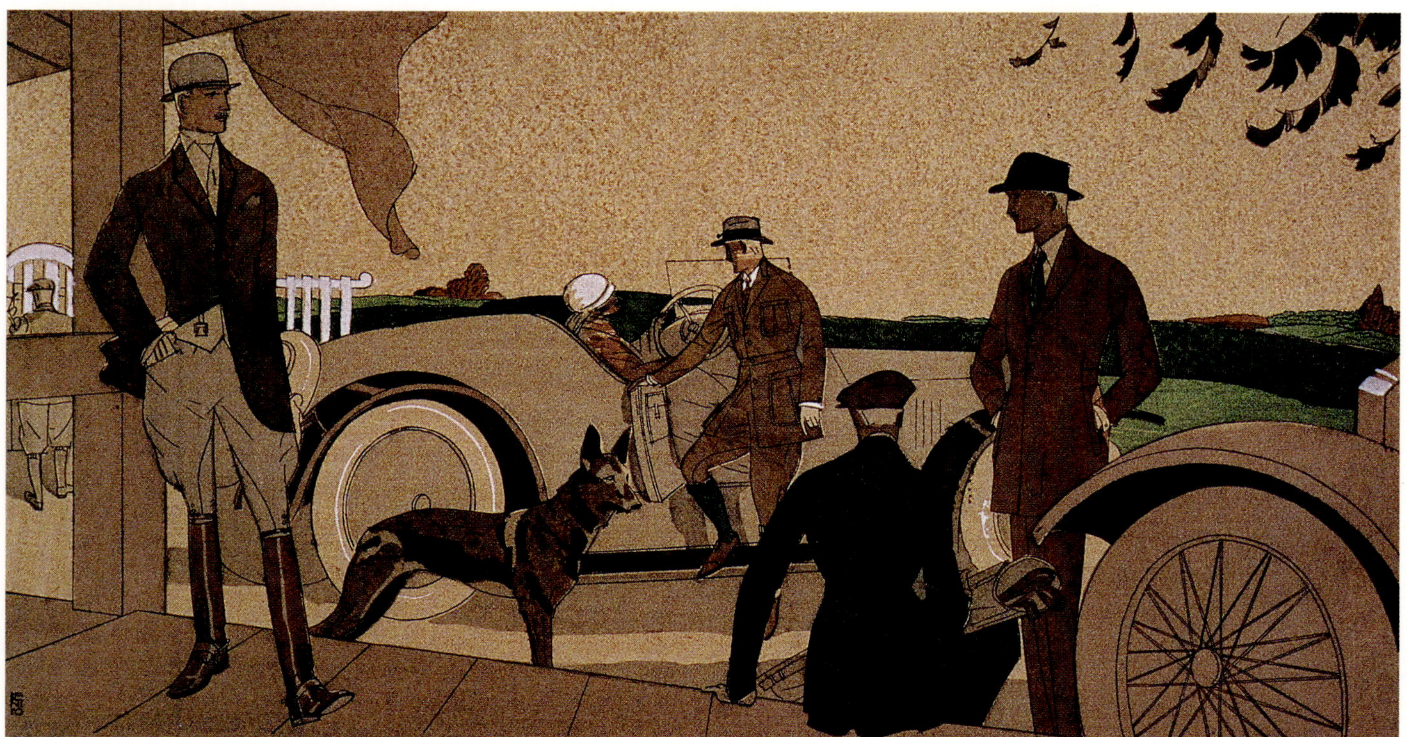

Pochoir illustration *A La Boulie* by Benito *(costumes de sports de Géo. Harrison, bottes de Coquillot)*, for *L'Homme élégant*. Paris. 1920

New forms of illustration were also developing in Great Britain and the United States. Artists of the calibre of Kay Nielsen, W. Heath Robinson, Harry Clarke, Maxfield Parrish, Arthur Rackham, Edmund Dulac, Jessie M. King, George Wolf Plank, Helen Dryden and Willy Pogany were following in the footsteps of Walter Crane, Aubrey Beardsley and Kate Greenaway by supplying illustrations for magazines, books and advertisements of all descriptions. Unfortunately, this has led many art historians and social commentators to claim that these artists were motivated solely by monetary reward and that, since their work was intended only to decorate a book or to seduce a prospective purchaser of a product, they automatically forfeit the right to be regarded as legitimate artists. Such historians and commentators have also argued that all forms of commercialisation destroy the soul of artistic creativity.

At first, this anti-commerical stance might seem to contain some truth, particularly if one contemplates today's multitudinous commercial images, many of which seem to lack any form of aesthetic sensibility or, for that matter, any redeeming quality. But if one looks more closely it becomes apparent that such a sweeping condemnation is not entirely true,

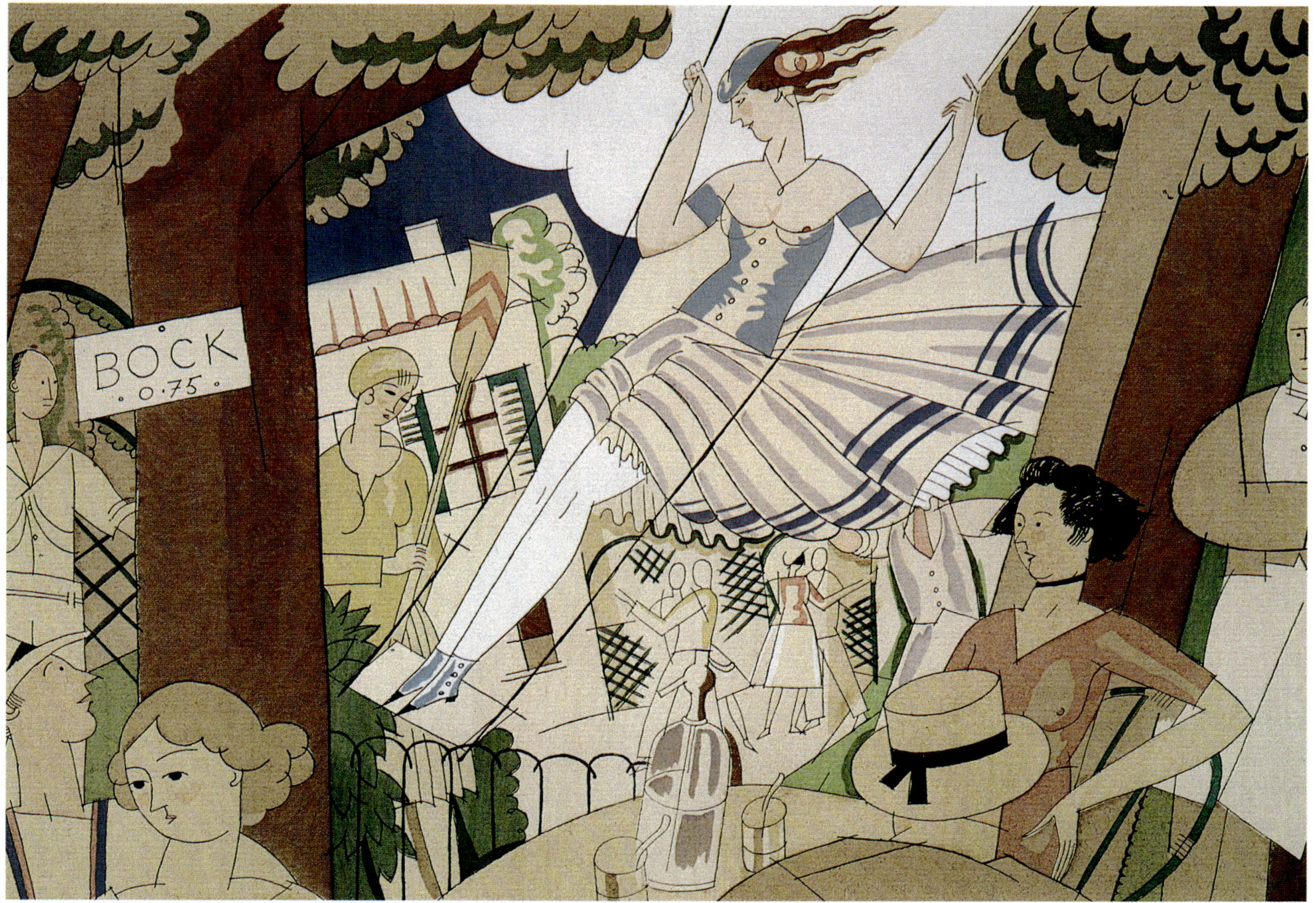

Pochoir illustration *La Balançoire* by Charles Martin, for *Sports et divertissements*, with music by Erik Satie. Deluxe edition of 225 copies. Lucien Vogel, Paris. 1920.

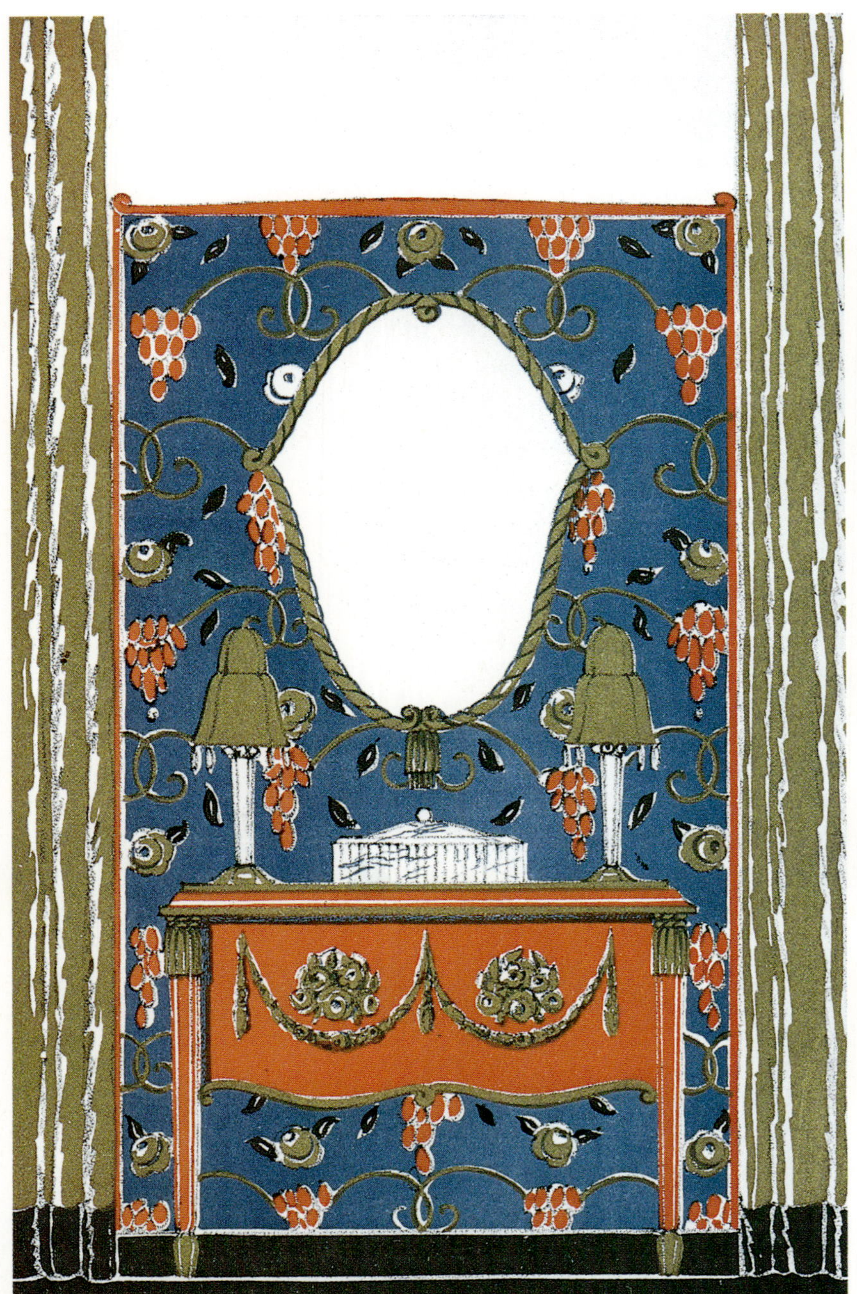

Chromo-litho illustration of furniture and interior design scheme by Louis Süe and André Mare, for *La Gazette du bon ton*. Paris. 1920.

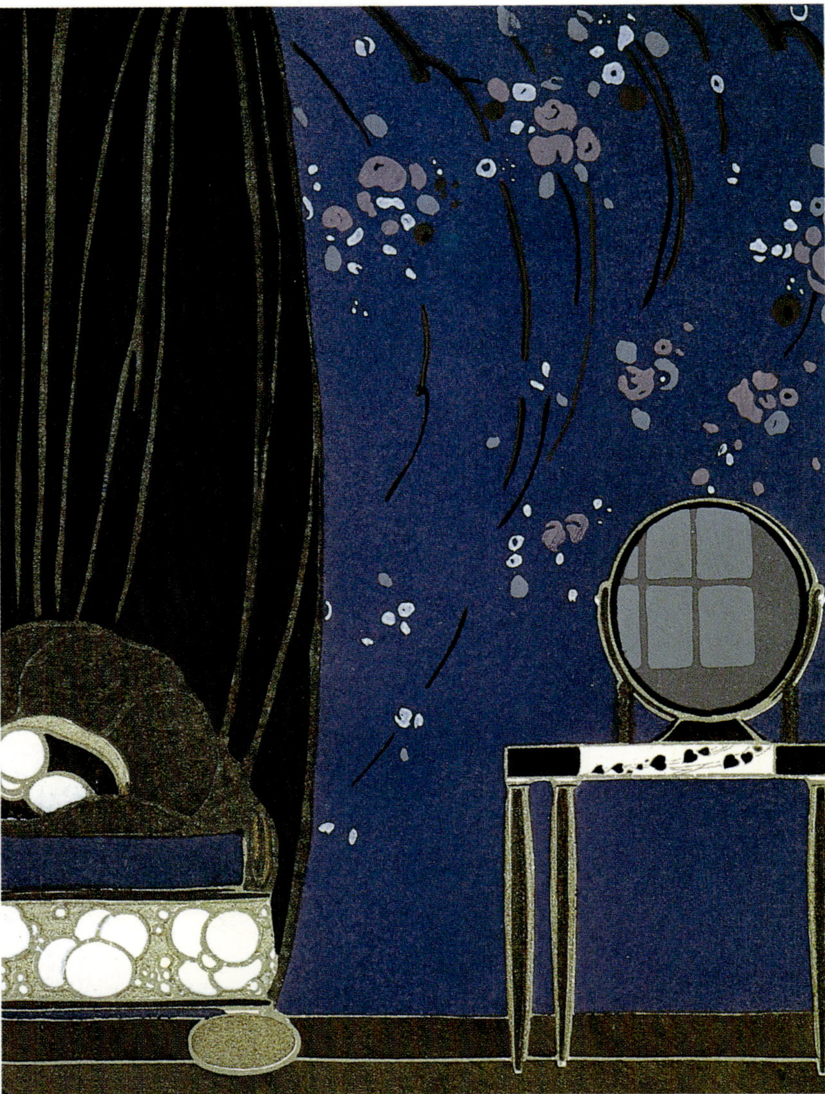

Pochoir illustration *Chez Fernande Cabanel* by M. Dufet, for *Les Feuillets d'art*. Paris. 1921.

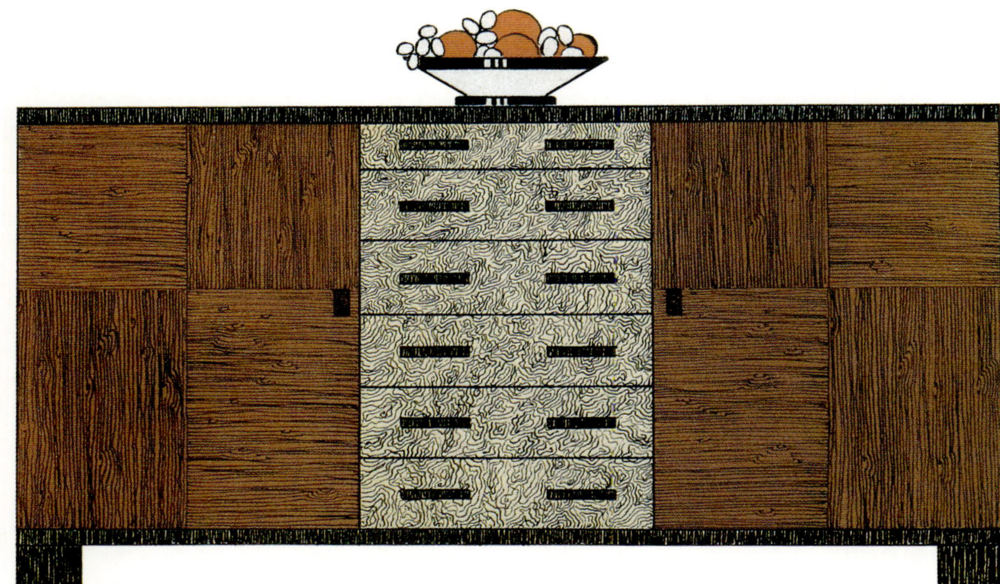

Illustration of furniture by Francis Jourdain. Printed in *pochoir* by Jean Saudé for *Répertoire du goût moderne*. Published by Editions Albert Lévy, Paris. 1928.

and that in our highly commercialised consumer society there are in fact visual images of aesthetic merit, just as there are modern products of design merit. It is simply that the mass of contemporary images and products tends to numb our sensibilities and confuse our aesthetic vision.

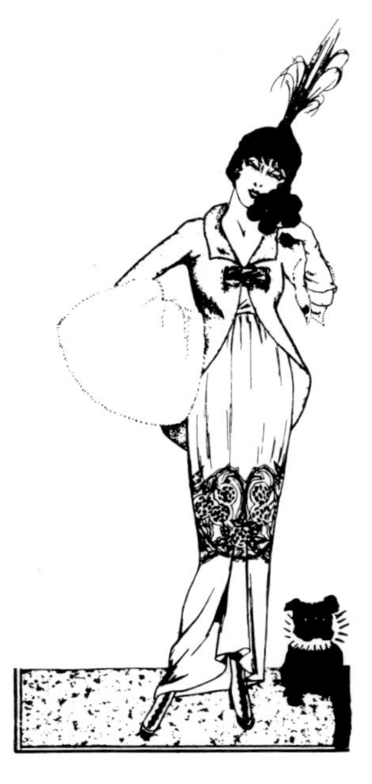

In Europe, ever since medieval times most forms of artistic endeavour were closely linked with monetary reward. Particularly noteworthy is the Italian Renaissance, when artists such as Cellini, Bramante, da Vinci, Uccello, Raphael, and Michelangelo were all paid for their services. This was also true for most artists of that period and later, among them Shakespeare and his contemporaries, and the painters Goya, Velasquez, van Dyke, Titian, and Ingres, whose sole means of survival had rested on their ability to create entertaining plays or pleasing images for which their patrons were willing to pay.

Furthermore, it is worth noting that even today monetary reward does not necessarily imply menial work. On the contrary, monetary reward often forces the artist to be more inventive in the face of open competition with his contemporaries. This was certainly the case during the Art Deco period. And, although the Art Deco artists were commissioned to undertake specific illustrative work for the various publications, their styles of image-making, and indeed often the contents of their illustrations, were not dictated to them by editors or art directors, as happens today. Each artist was encouraged to develop his own particular style and to interpret each commission as he saw fit. The very essence of the new mode was sought, so that the resulting image would appeal to the customers, both intellectually and visually.

These illustrators were the visual commentators of their time; it was their task to display and highlight the characteristics that today make the Art Deco era unique. And although their illustrations differed vastly in terms of conception, style and imagery — compare the fantasy of Leon Carré with the brisk, sketchy style of Charles Martin or the unabashed eroticism of Jean Dulac — they nevertheless act as an essential visual antidote to the mechanically produced photographic images featured in the glossy magazines of the time. They also add piquancy to the verbal images created by the contemporary novelists and playwrights, capturing and preserving the creative verve of this distinctive age.

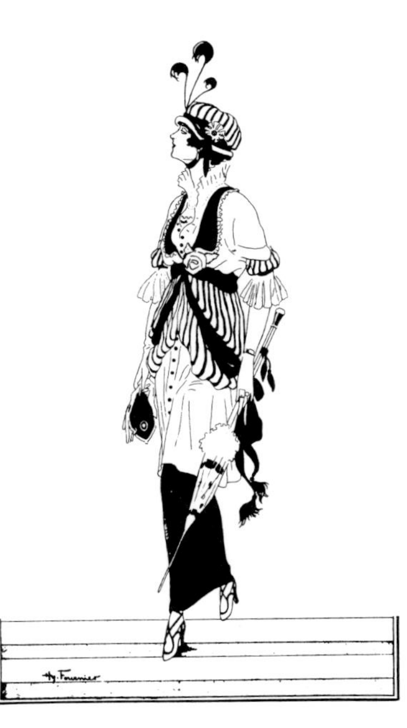

The very best of these new-style Art Deco illustrations were printed by the *pochoir* method of hand colouring, which, by means of accurately cut stencils, enabled the skilful hand colourist to reproduce the exact colours and textures of the artist's original painting. The most famous publications to include these *pochoir* illustrations were limited-edition deluxe books, albums, portfolios and magazines such as *Sports et divertissements, Répertoire du goût moderne, Samarkande, Nous deux, Conte de Tsar Saltan, La Gazette du bon ton, Le Jardin des caresses, Le Bonheur du jour, Modes et manières d'aujourd'hui, Le Goût du jour* and *La Guirlande d'art et de la littérature.*

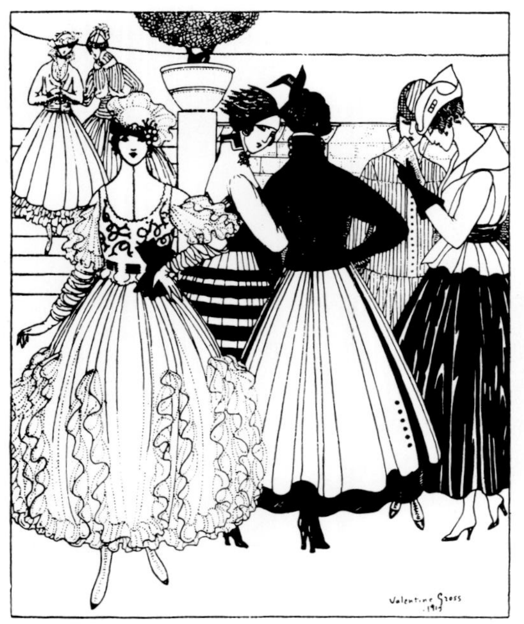

Several young French printmakers had developed the *pochoir* technique of hand colouring in Paris in the late nineteenth century. They took as their guide the Japanese art of fabric stencilling, and they sought to revitalise the art of book illustration, which at the time was suffering from monochromatic uniformity resulting from the then current obsession with photomechanical printing techniques. *Pochoir*, with its adroit use of actual pigments applied by hand through finely cut stencils, was an artistic revelation.

The use of hand-coloured stencilling was not new: in Europe, it had been used for centuries to decorate walls and furniture, to colour tarot cards during the Middle Ages, and to print seventeenth century wallpapers; early American settlers had also used stencils to decorate pieces of furniture and the inside walls of their houses, and for the production of small signs and notices; for hundreds of years Buddhist monks had applied images of their Enlightened One to the walls of their shrines through simple stencils cut from waxed card; and Fijians had used stencils cut from dried banana leaves to apply decorative patterns to their bark cloth for many generations.

A number of French hand-colouring workshops that specialised in printing fashion magazines in the mid-nineteenth century had used the stencil technique to colour some of the more intricate areas of the complicated fashion plates of the time and to accurately reproduce the embroidery diagrams that were a regular feature of these monthly publications. By the mid-1880s the number of French workrooms producing such magazines for the world market had increased dramatically, and so had the size of many of the hand-coloured fashion plates — some measured as much as 75 × 60 centimetres and contained up to twenty-five individual figures. Most of the colouring was done by a team of children working at a long trestle table, each child applying one area of colour before passing the illustration on so that the next area of colour could be applied. When the illustration reached the end of the table the final touches of colour were added by a *pochoirist* using a finely cut stencil.

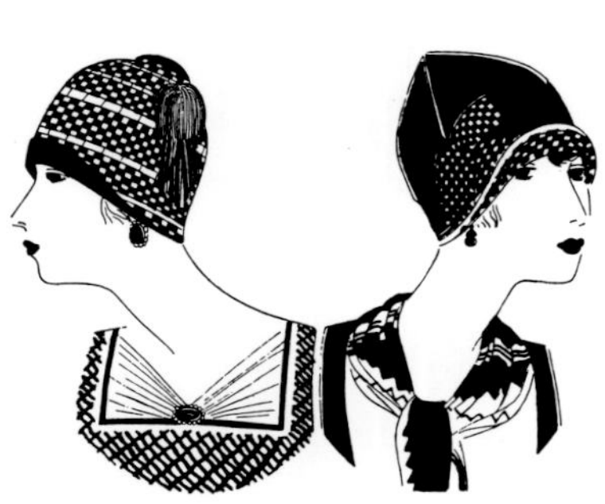

Although the colouring of such fashion plates was often very crude, and the registration of the final stencilling generally poor because of the speed required to maintain the flow of production, the method did provide a training ground for many of the later

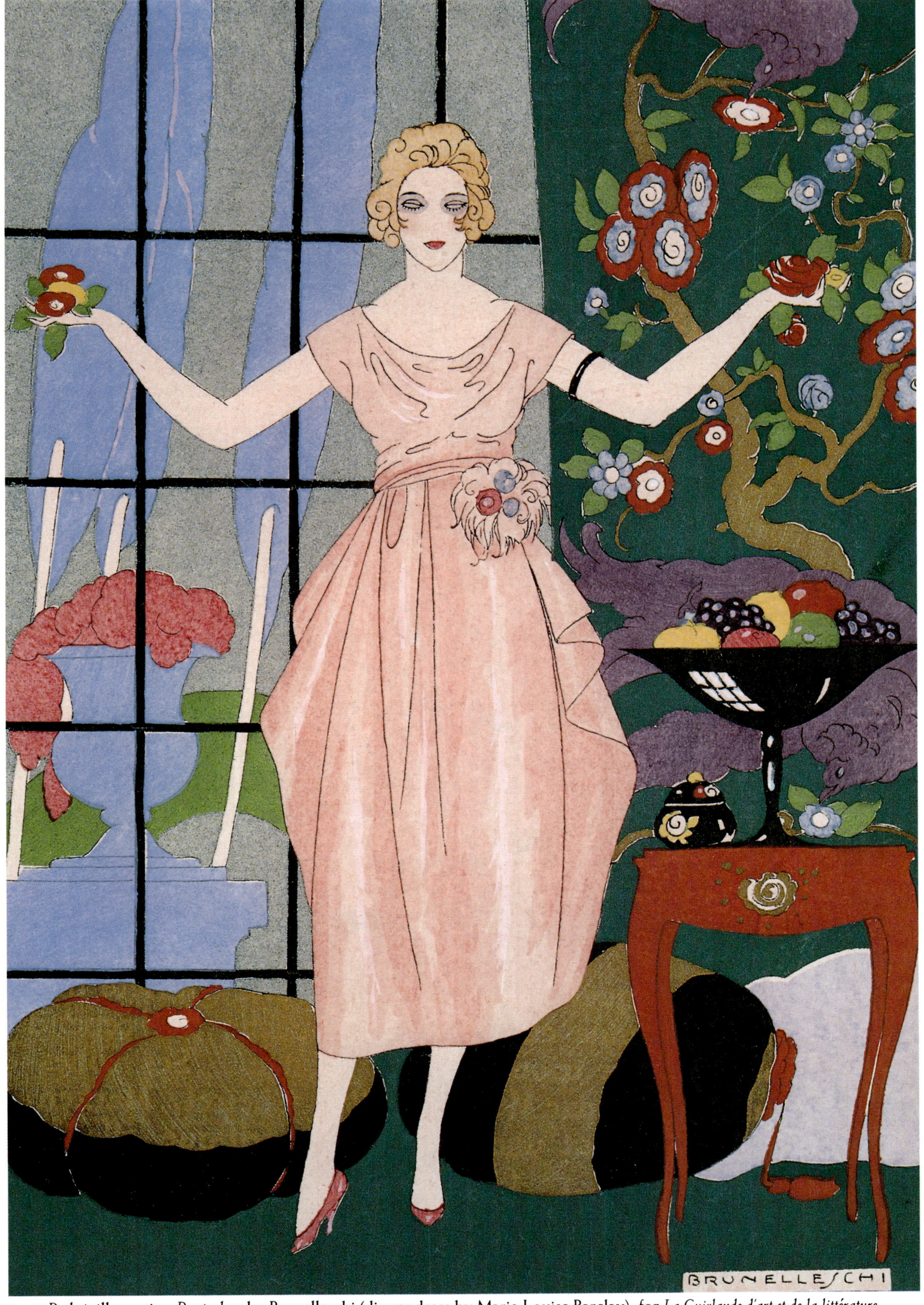

Pochoir illustration *Pompadour* by Brunelleschi (dinner dress by Marie-Louise Barclay), for *La Guirlande d'art et de la littérature.* Paris. 1919.

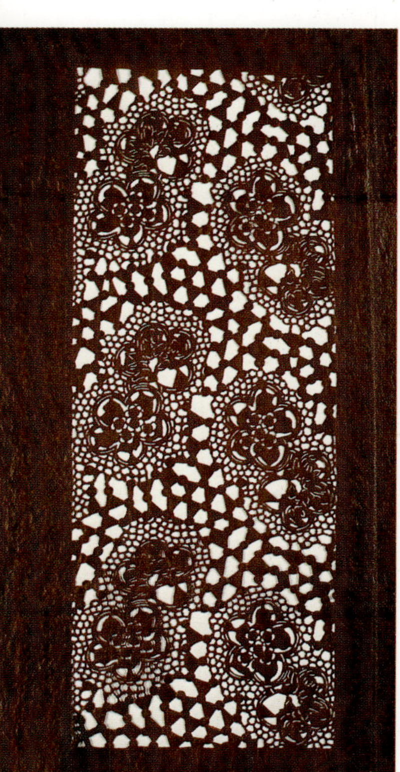

A Japanese waxed paper stencil for printing silk kimono fabrics. Early nineteenth century.

Art Deco *pochoirists*. Undoubtedly the exhibitions of Japanese stencil-printed textiles, held in Paris during the 1880s and 1890s, had helped to renew interest in the art of *pochoir* printing. In addition, in the early 1890s several books had been published on the Japanese art of *ukiyo-e* print-making and the technique of stencil-cutting, and the young *pochoirists* were at last able to improve their art by following the Japanese techniques for cutting beautifully incised stencils and arranging their blocks of colour in the *ukiyo-e* tradition.

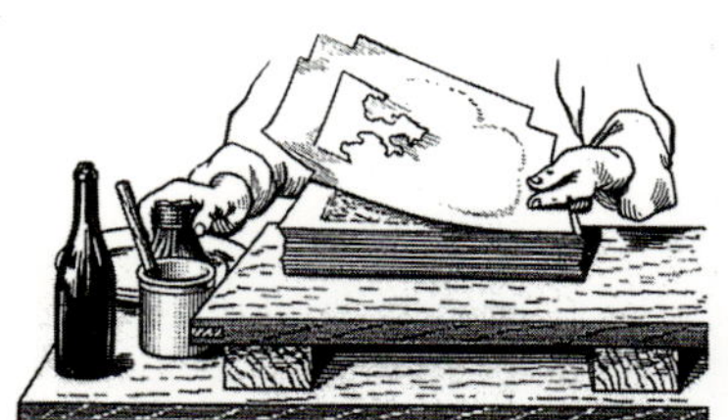

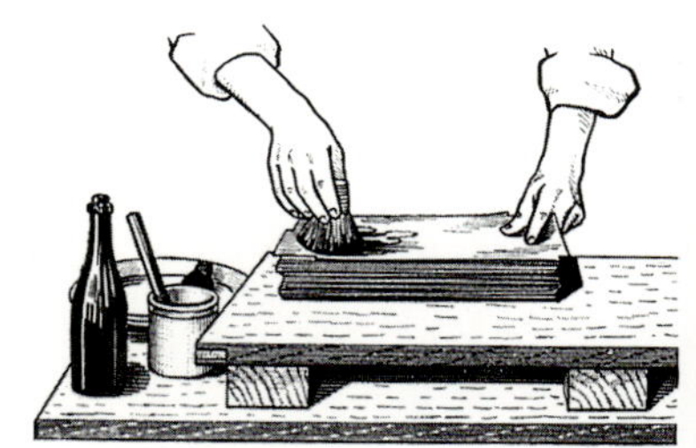

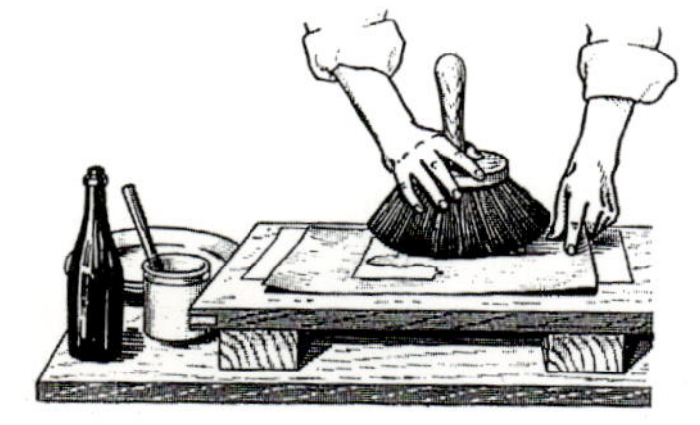

Jean Saudé, the great exponent of *pochoir* printing in the 1920s, was a trainee printmaker and colourist at Greningaire et Fils in the early 1890s and worked with Eugène Grasset and M. P. Verneuil on the first Art Nouveau portfolio of designs, *La Plante et ses applications ornementales*, which was published in 1895. He also studied the methods used by Japanese textile printers to achieve the astonishingly intricate and colourful fabrics used in their traditional kimonos — these he had seen at the great Paris Exhibition in 1889 and at the small exhibitions that proliferated in the early 1890s.

The Japanese had been printing such fabrics since the fourteenth century but it was during the Edo period (1615–1868) that the art had reached its peak. Saudé was lucky to be able to inspect some of the Japanese stencils from this period, and discovered that some areas of the stencil had been cut with a thin knife pointed like a needle and razor sharp, some were cut with the punch-like blades, and some areas were covered with dozens of incisions of infinitely fine lines: some stencils had as many as 750 cuts within a 4 centimetre square. Other stencils used for printing large designs had only the slightest filigree of stencil remaining, held together with single strands of human hair stretched between the filigree sections.

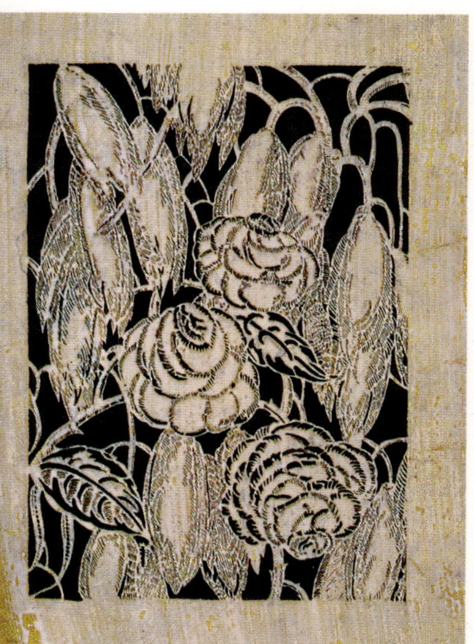

Thin copper stencil from *Traité d'enluminure d'art au pochoir* by Jean Saudé. Paris. 1925.

From these observations and the experience gained by working on the Grasset album of 1895, Saudé began developing his own technique, which he later detailed in his *Traité d'enluminure d'art au pochoir*, published in 1925. In their foreword and introduction to this monumental work Antoine Bourdelle and Georges Goursat wrote that they had witnessed how, by dedication and skill, Saudé could recreate even the most complex of illustrations:

The least nuances, the delicate shades, the washes and the running of the water-colours, the white reserves, even the repainting and corrections, down to the very subtlest values, the entire image is carried out with a perfection that creates a total illusion of the original. One can even feel the original brush-strokes.

And Edouard Bénédictus added in a note to the foreword that it was to

. . . the ingenuity and talent of M. Saudé that we owe our knowledge of certain kinds of new art, which without his pochoir process might have remained unknown to us because they were unreproduceable by any other process.

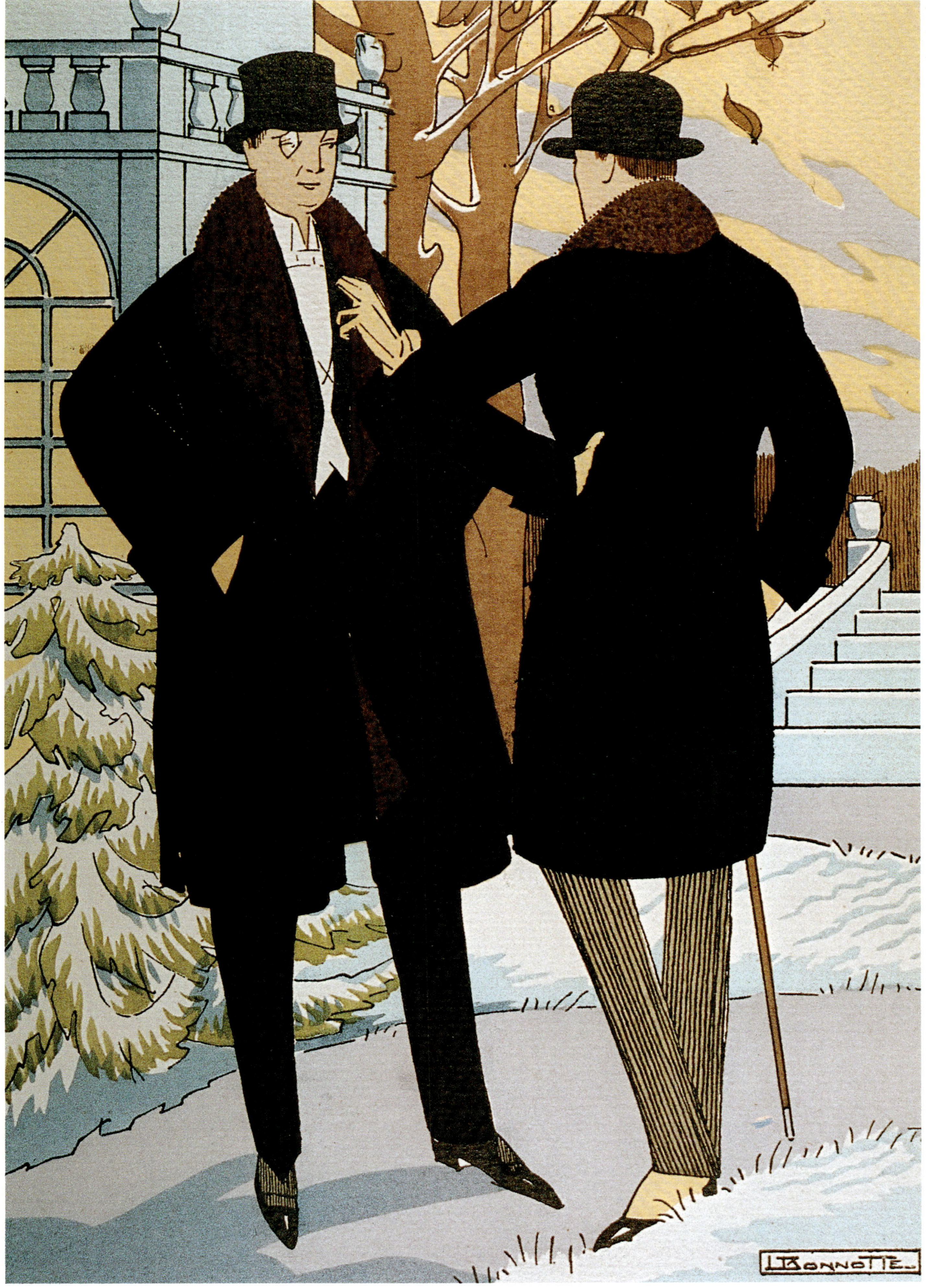

Pochoir illustration *Voici l'hiver* by L. Bonnotte, for *La Guirlande d'art et de la littérature*. Paris. 1919.

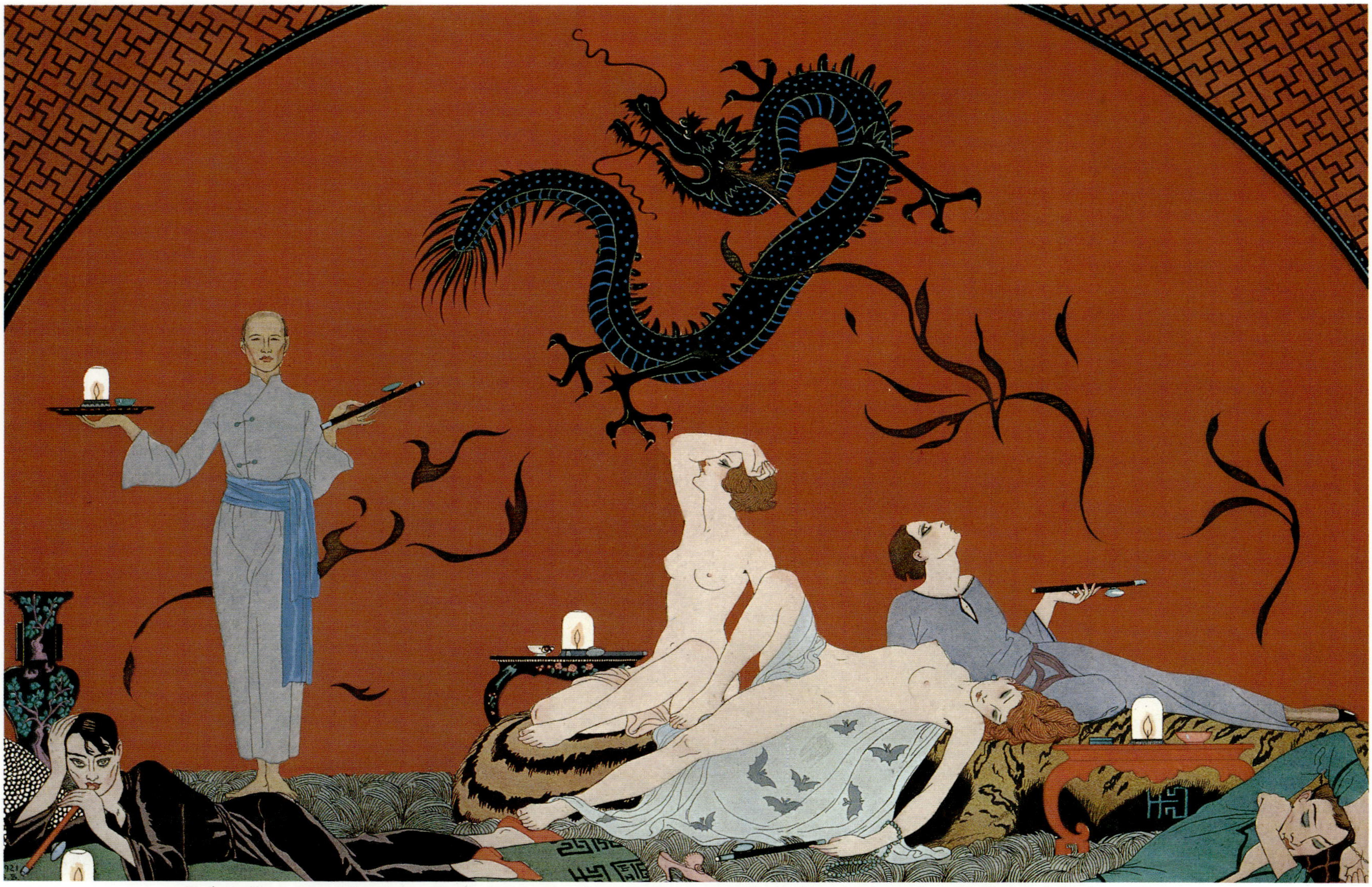

Pochoir illustration *Chez la marchande de pavots* by George Barbier, for *Le Bonheur du jour ou les grâces à la mode*. Deluxe edition, Chez Meynial, Paris. 1924.

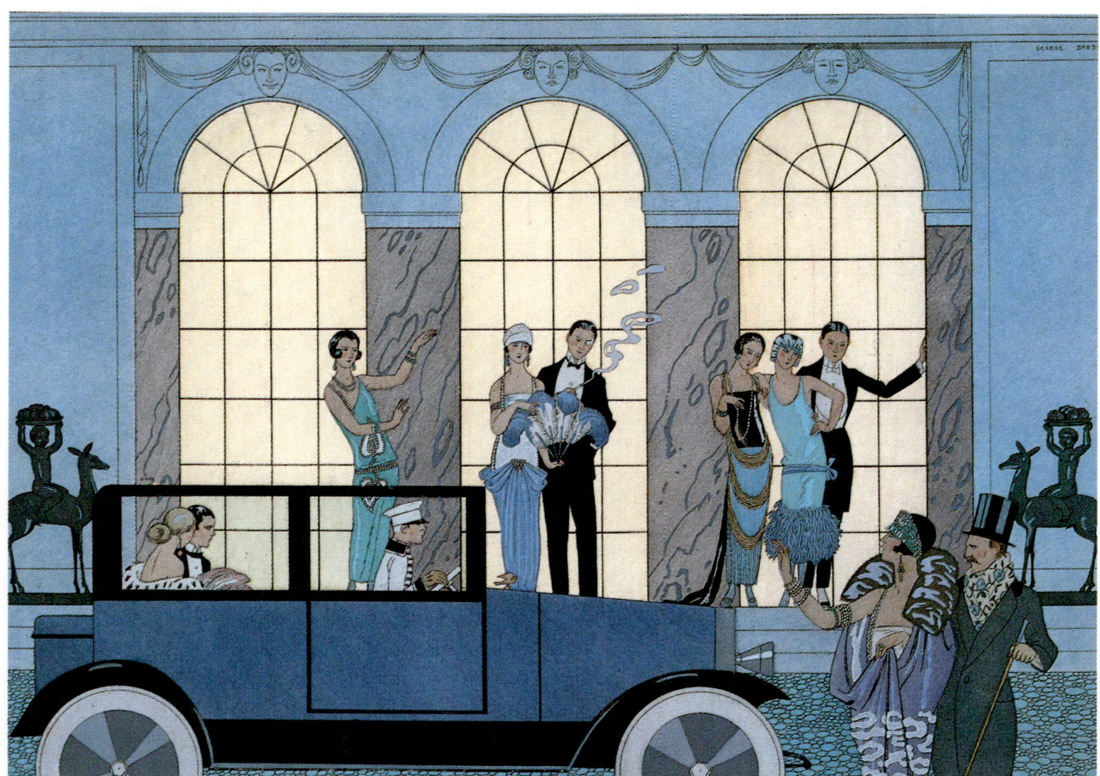

Pochoir illustration *Au Revoir* by George Barbier, for *Le Bonheur du jour ou les grâces à la mode*. Deluxe edition, Chez Meynial, Paris. 1924.

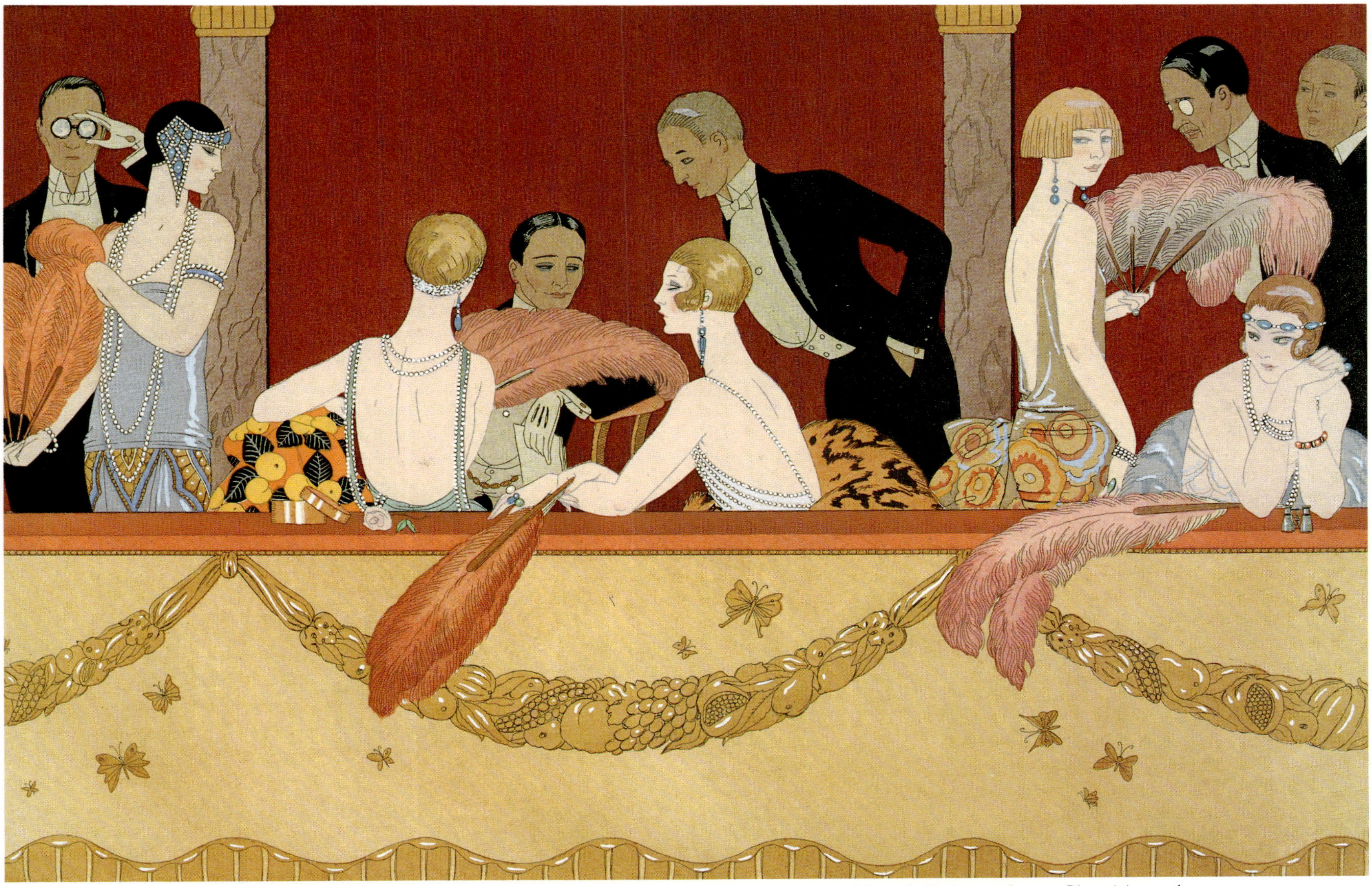

Pochoir illustration *Eventails* by George Barbier, for *Le Bonheur du jour ou les grâces à la mode*. Deluxe edition, Chez Meynial, Paris. 1924.

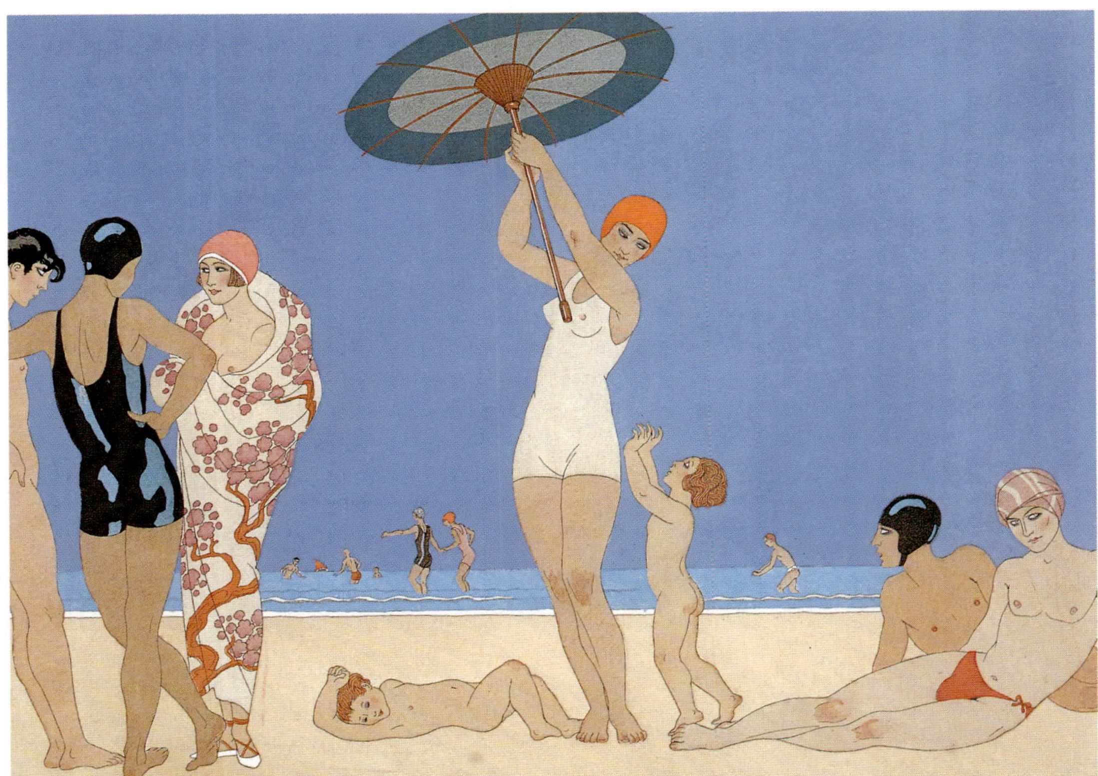

Pochoir illustration *Au Lido* by George Barbier, for *Le Bonheur du jour ou les grâces à la mode*. Deluxe edition, Chez Meynial, Paris. 1924

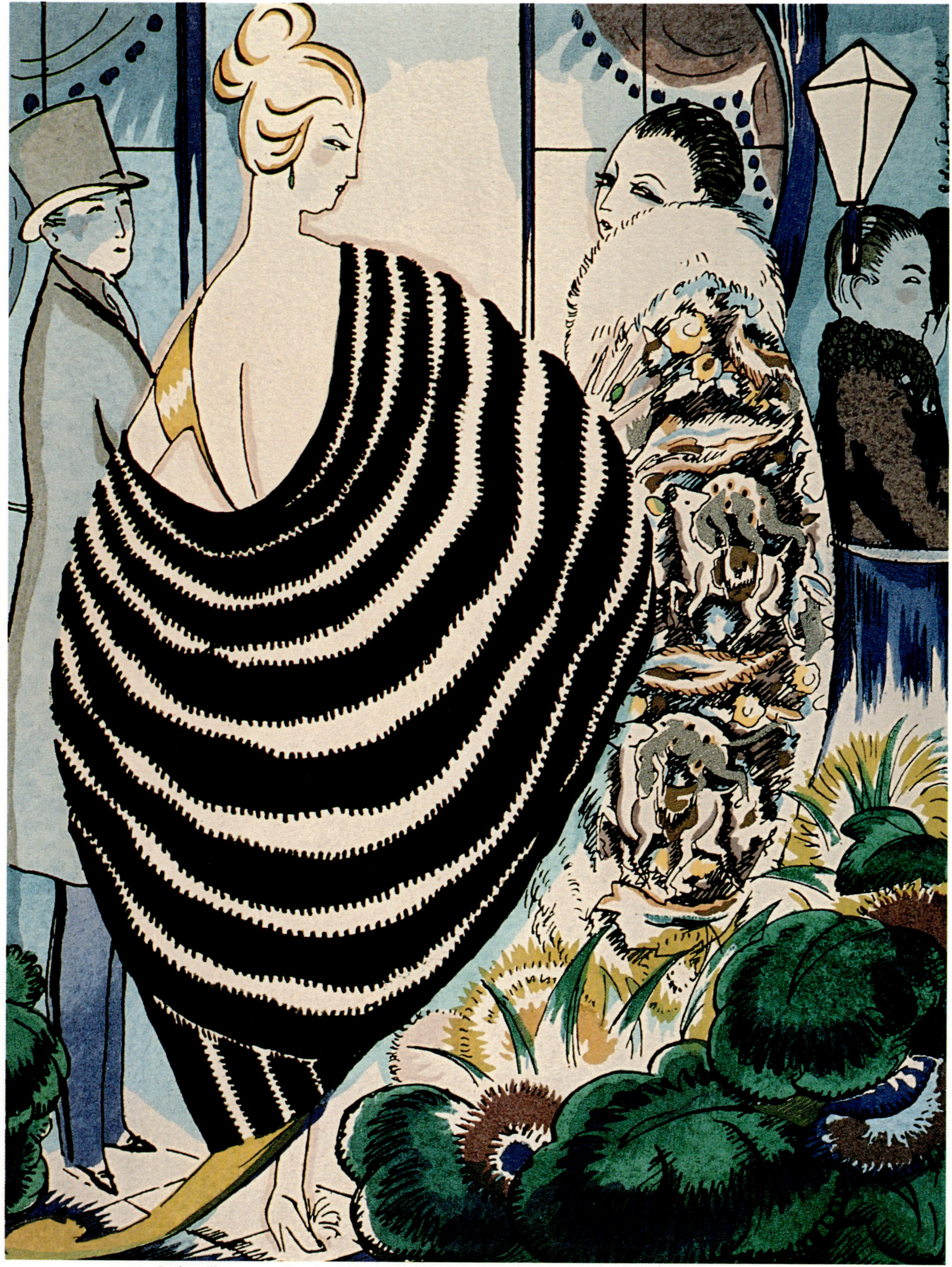

Pochoir illustration *Vers la danse* by Robert Bonfils, for *Modes et manières d'aujourd'hui*. Paris. 1920.

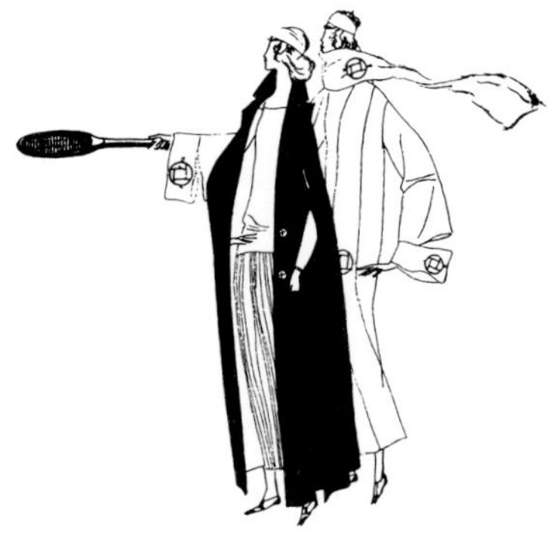

In the text of his treatise Saudé explained that in the making of a *pochoir* print three major steps are involved, each demanding a good eye and meticulous craftsmanship. First, the original illustration is analysed and broken down into its constituent parts. The underlying drawing is then translated into a wood engraving, an etching, or a lithoprint. Then each colour area is analysed in order that its own accurately cut stencil may be made, normally from a sheet of very fine zinc or copper or from thin oiled card, depending on the result required, the size of the stencil and the expected print run. The next step is to accurately cut the stencil, scrupulously following the outline and the subtle detailing of each colour. If there is a slight variation in the colour this may require three separate stencils, which can be cut to graduate the colour during the printing process. In the final step, the original colours are matched to the printer's selection of opaque, translucent or transparent colours and then a base is used to achieve the correct viscosity. The order of printing and the method of applying the chosen colours are then determined. The colours can be applied with a soft, medium, medium-hard, or stiff brush, or with a soft or textured sponge, and they may then be partly removed with blotting paper to obtain a variegated effect.

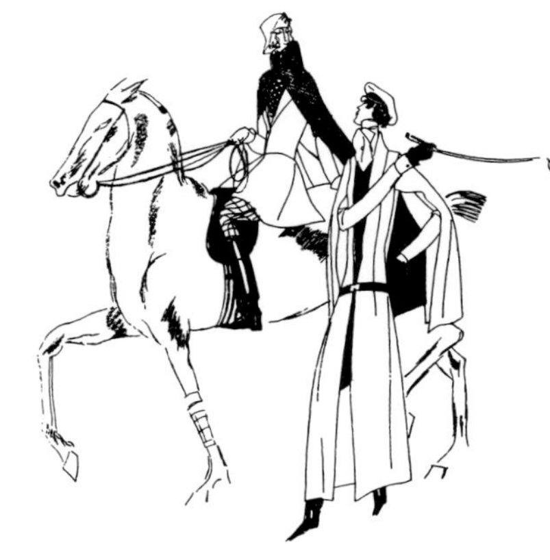

Trial prints are made in order to test the accuracy of the stencils over the background drawing, with the strong colours being printed first and the lighter ones overlapping them by a fraction of a centimetre, so that a 'backgrounding line' appears only where it is required to match the original effect of the artist's illustration. At this stage the artist is asked to approve the *pochoir* print; his signature is added only after all the necessary adjustments have been made. The agreed number of *pochoir* prints is then made — generally between 150 and 350 for a deluxe portfolio or book such as Barbier's *Le Bonheur du jour*, or up to 1250 for the deluxe magazine *Le Journal des dames et des modes*. Each print of each separate issue involves up to thirty-two stencils. Thus, if a deluxe portfolio or album contained twenty such prints and each required twenty-five stencils, just one album would involve 500 stencils in order to accurately reproduce one exact facsimile of the artist's original work; this then had to be repeated 250 or more times to achieve the total print run.

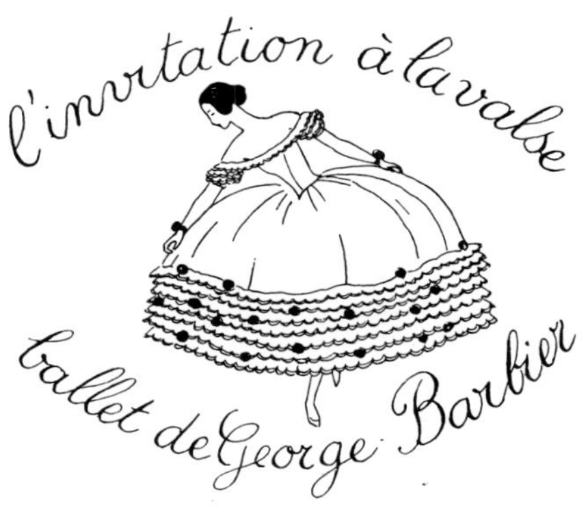

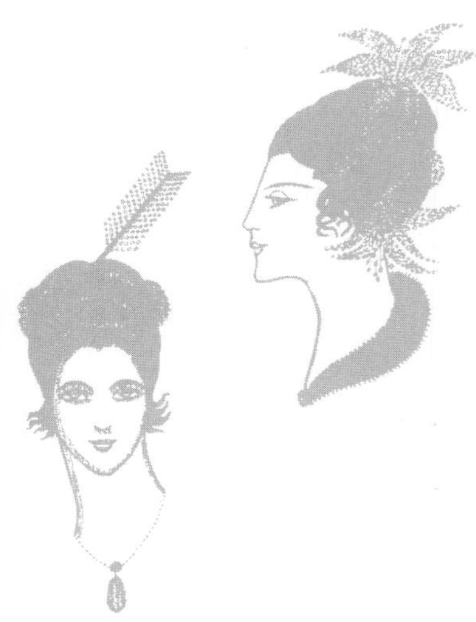

Although originally inspired by the intricacy and printing methods of the Edo textile printers, Saudé was also fascinated by the pictorial qualities of the *ukiyo-e* woodcut prints, as were many of the artists and illustrators of the period. These prints had created much interest when they were exhibited and many painters and designers worked directly from their own collections, purchased from importers such as Samuel Bing in Paris and Arthur Lasenby Liberty in London.

The *ukiyo-e* print was believed to have originated in the thirteenth century, reaching its aesthetic peak between the seventeenth and mid-nineteenth centuries, during the Edo period. At that time Japan was ruled by feudal warlords — the Tokugawa Shogunate — and the city of Kyoto was the centre of government. In the city of Edo (Tokyo), there was a rising merchant class, growing in wealth but not in political power. The ruling Shogunate deemed it unworthy to be a merchant or tradesman and recognised only priests and samurai as worthy of prestige and social position, so the merchants and tradesmen were, in effect, limited to the pursuit of physical or material pleasures as outlets for their newly acquired wealth.

The kabuki theatre and Yoshiwara, the brothel district of Edo, played an important part in their lives. In order to understand the aesthetic appeal of the *ukiyo-e* prints (which translates as 'picture of the floating world', a derisory reference to the floating, transitory pleasures of life) one must remember the transient pleasures of the Yoshiwara district of Edo and the kabuki theatre, both of which became the inspiration of the majority of *ukiyo-e* prints and from which the style developed its unique qualities.

Kabuki theatrical presentation traditionally combined the arts of drama, dance, song and music, all delivered with broad, exaggerated gestures that used mime, stylised facial expressions and elaborate costumes. The plays were well known, often lasting an entire day, and they were repeated over and over. Kabuki theatre was restricted to male actors, and certain families specialised in the female roles, often portraying specific characters for many generations, in much the same tradition as that of commedia dell'arte of Italy and the medieval theatre in England. *Ukiyo-e* prints were used to advertise the various productions of the kabuki theatre; the more famous actors were also often the illustrative subject for the entrepreneurial printmaker who wished to sell his work directly to the public.

The relationship between the *ukiyo-e* printmakers and the Yoshiwara district was similar: the various speciality houses of the brothel district used these prints as advertising material, and individual studies of famous courtesans were sold direct to the public. But, whereas the kabuki portraits were depictions of specific actors, the Yoshiwara pictures rarely centred on the features of an individual courtesan. They were more likely

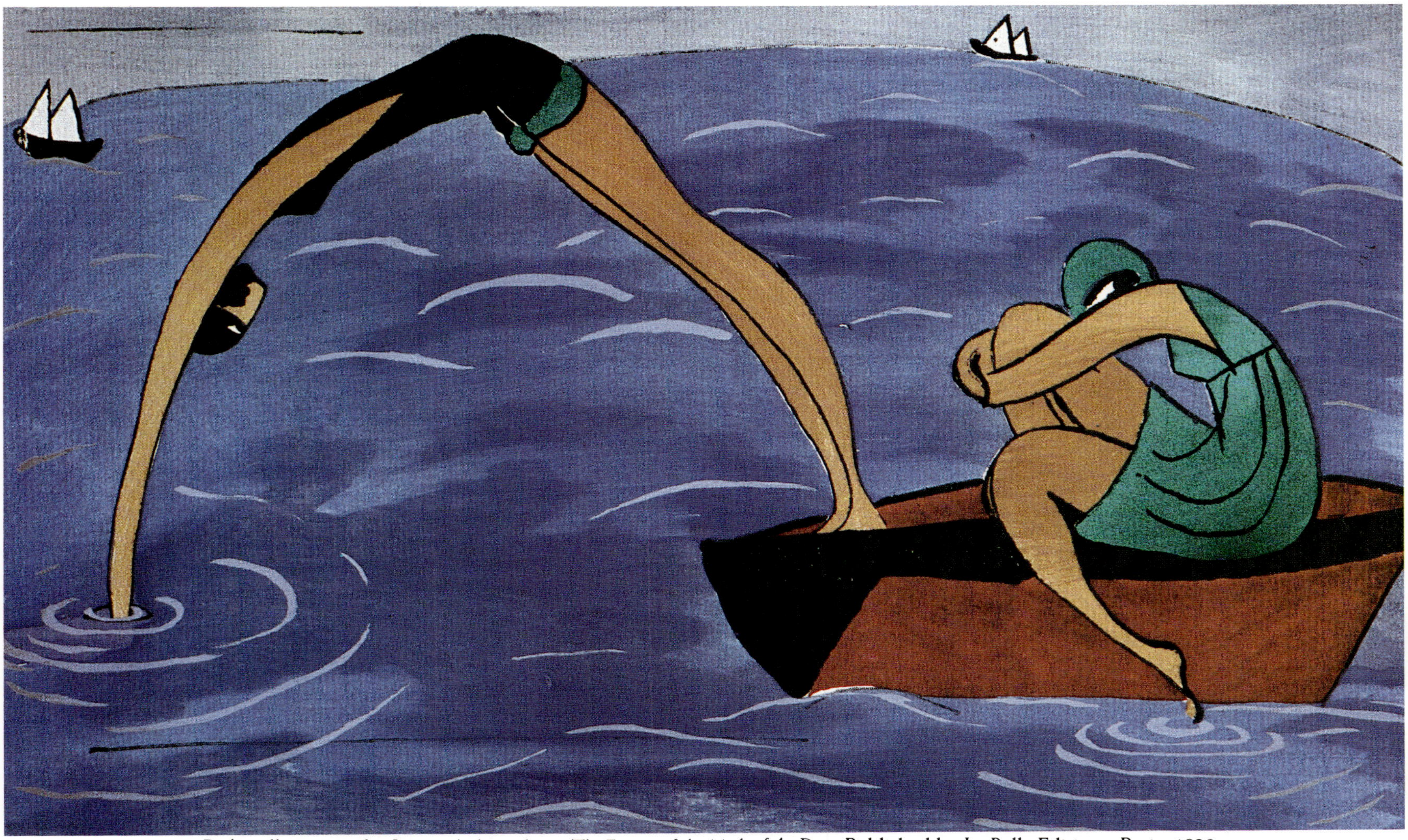

Pochoir illustration by Janine Aghion from *The Essence of the Mode of the Day*. Published by La Belle Editions, Paris. 1920.

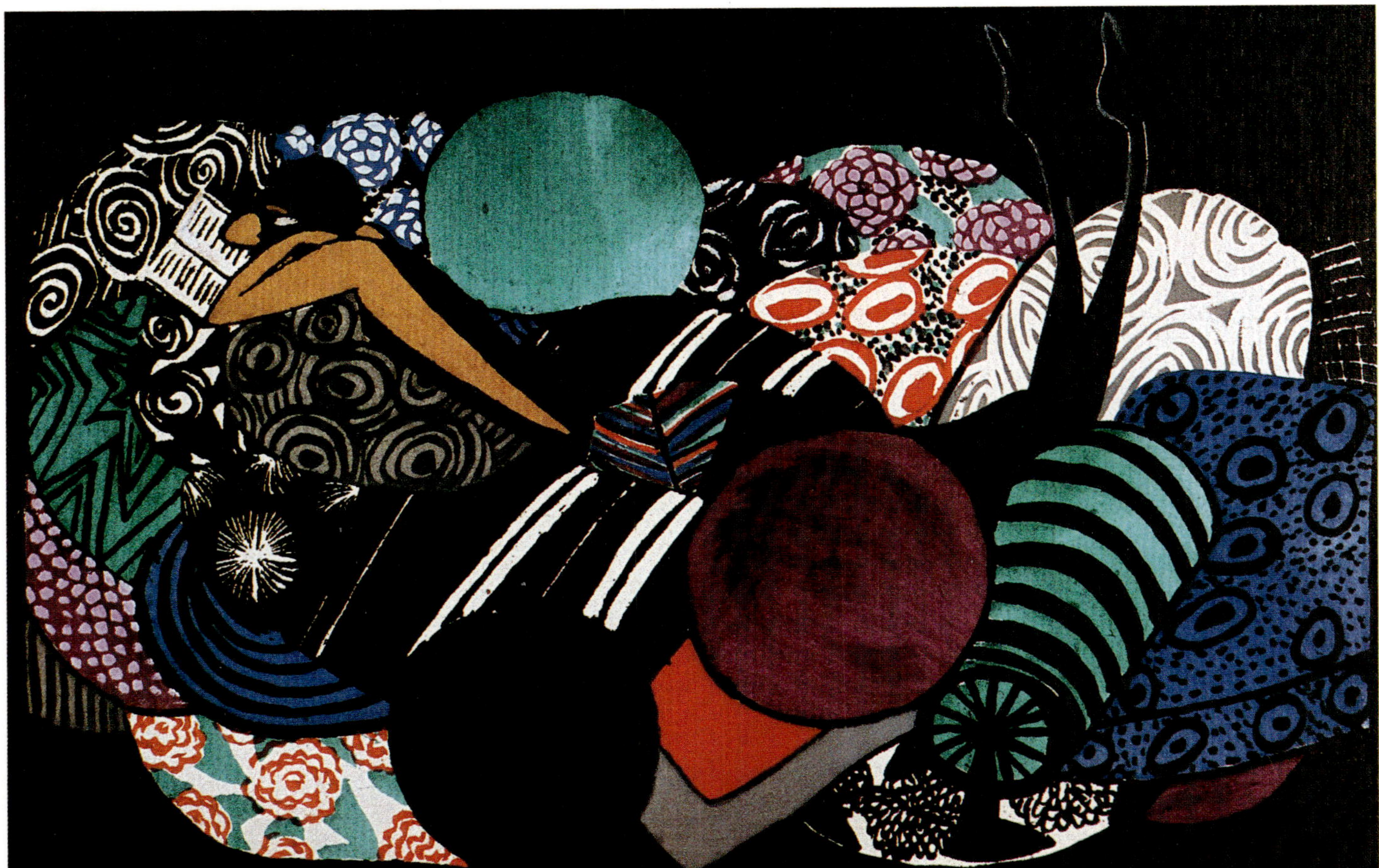

Pochoir illustration by Janine Aghion from *The Essence of the Mode of the Day*. Published by La Belle Editions, Paris. 1920.

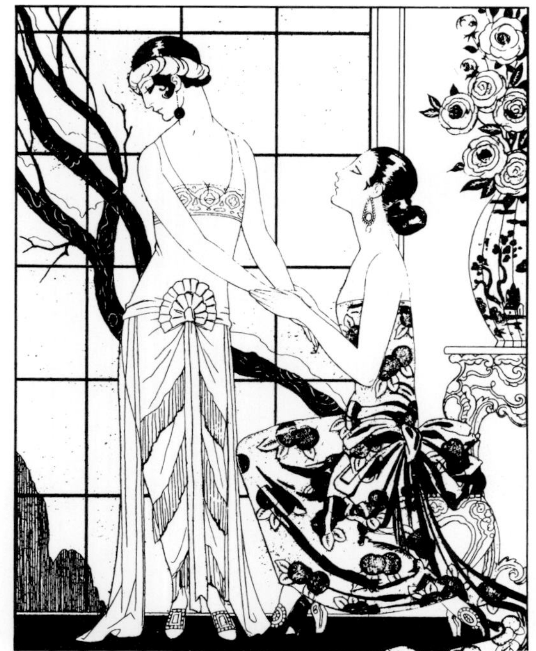

to be glorifications of the intricately patterned kimonos and idealised representations of the more obvious feminine physical attributes. The prints are often delicate and charming, yet they can also be surprisingly intimate and erotic.

Originally, the Edo *ukiyo-e* print was an outline woodcut print that was then coloured by hand, sometimes with the aid of a stencil. During the eighteenth century, however, as more and more aspects of the life and scenic beauty of Japan were being depicted, the prints began to be made in colour, using up to five woodcut blocks for the printing. The polychrome prints are in fact correctly called *nishiki-e*, or brocade paintings, and it was mainly these brocade paintings that were studied by Saudé and his contemporaries. The images of Harunobu, Shunsho, Hokusai, Kiyongo, Ultamora, Sharaku and Hiroshige were greatly admired.

Saudé was not the only *pochoirist* working in Paris in the early 1900s. Greningaire et Fils, where Saudé had been a trainee, was still very active, and the company's name appears on many fine books and albums, as do the names Ranson et Fils, E. Charpentier, M. Beaufumé, Phillippe Renouard, Gustave Raynal, (the *pochoirist* responsible for the Art Noveau album *Le Meuble au XXme siècle*), Charles Massim (responsible for the Seguy's *Samarkande* album), Tolmer et Cie (who printed the rare album of fur designs by Edy Legrand), and Vangirard et Cie (who printed the fine *pochoir* colours over the artists' own engraved prints in *Le Journal des dames et des modes*, which first appeared in June 1912).

Le Journal des dames et des modes was founded by Jacques de Nouvion and it was the first regularly published deluxe limited-edition fashion magazine to contain quality *pochoir* prints of the latest fashions as conceived by the *grands couturiers* and drawn by the leading artists of the period. It was available by subscription direct from the publishers, and seventy-nine editions were published between June 1912 and August 1914. The print run was limited to 1250 numbered copies, the first twelve being printed on cream Japon paper and the remainder on handmade linen paper. Copies were mailed direct to subscribers in London, New York, Rome, St Petersburg, Rio, Buenos Aires and Berlin.

This publication was originally conceived as a twentieth century version of the famous eighteenth century fashion publication of the same name, which was started by Pierre La Mésangère, a former priest and a professor of philosophy. The first edition of the original publication appeared in 1797, just as fashionable Parisian life was beginning to recover after the bloody revolution. In the introduction to his new edition, Jacques de Nouvion paid tribute to his predecessor and to the

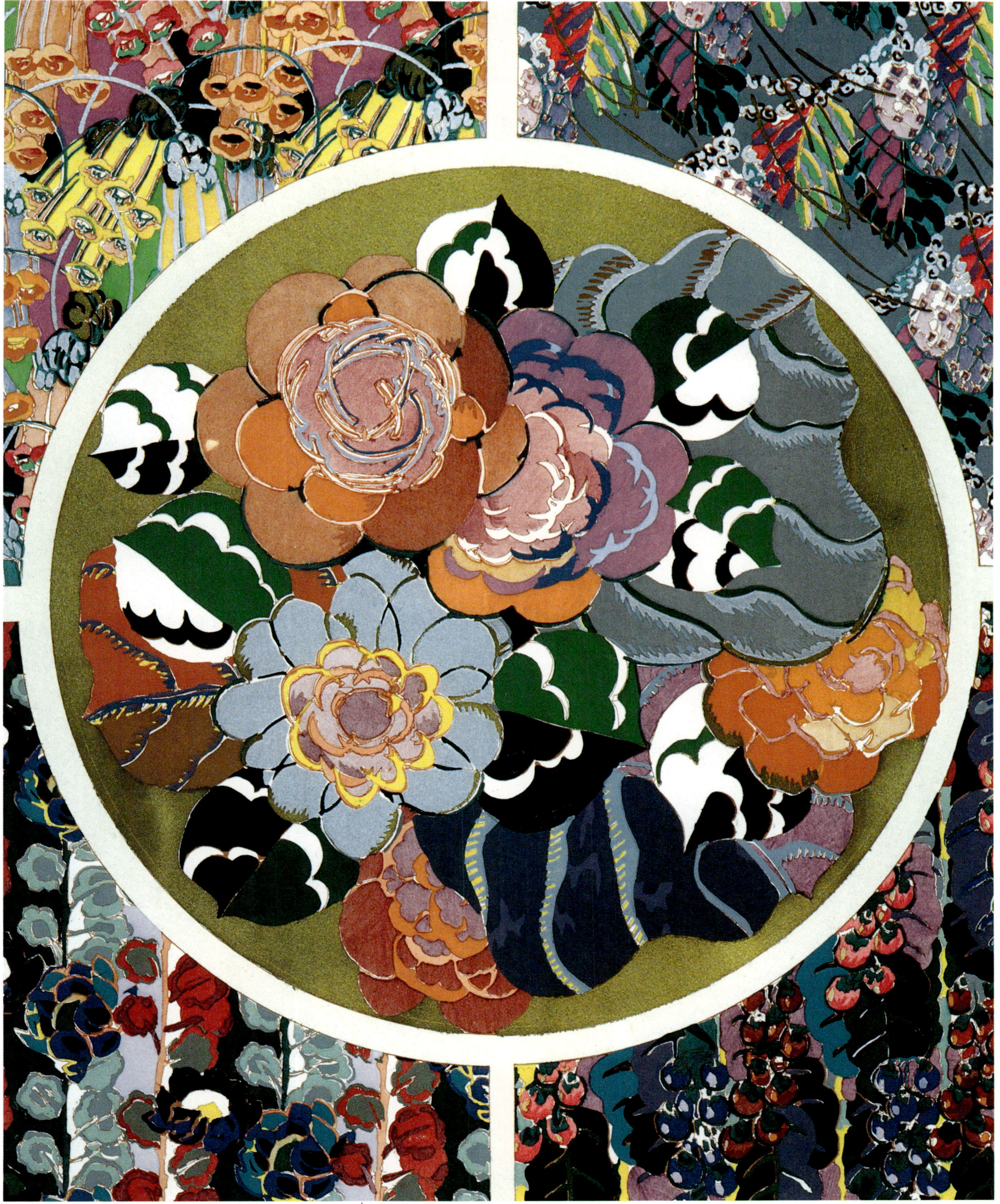

Pochoir textile design *Variations* by Edouard Bénédictus. Printed by Jean Saudé for Editions Albert Lévy, Paris. 1924.

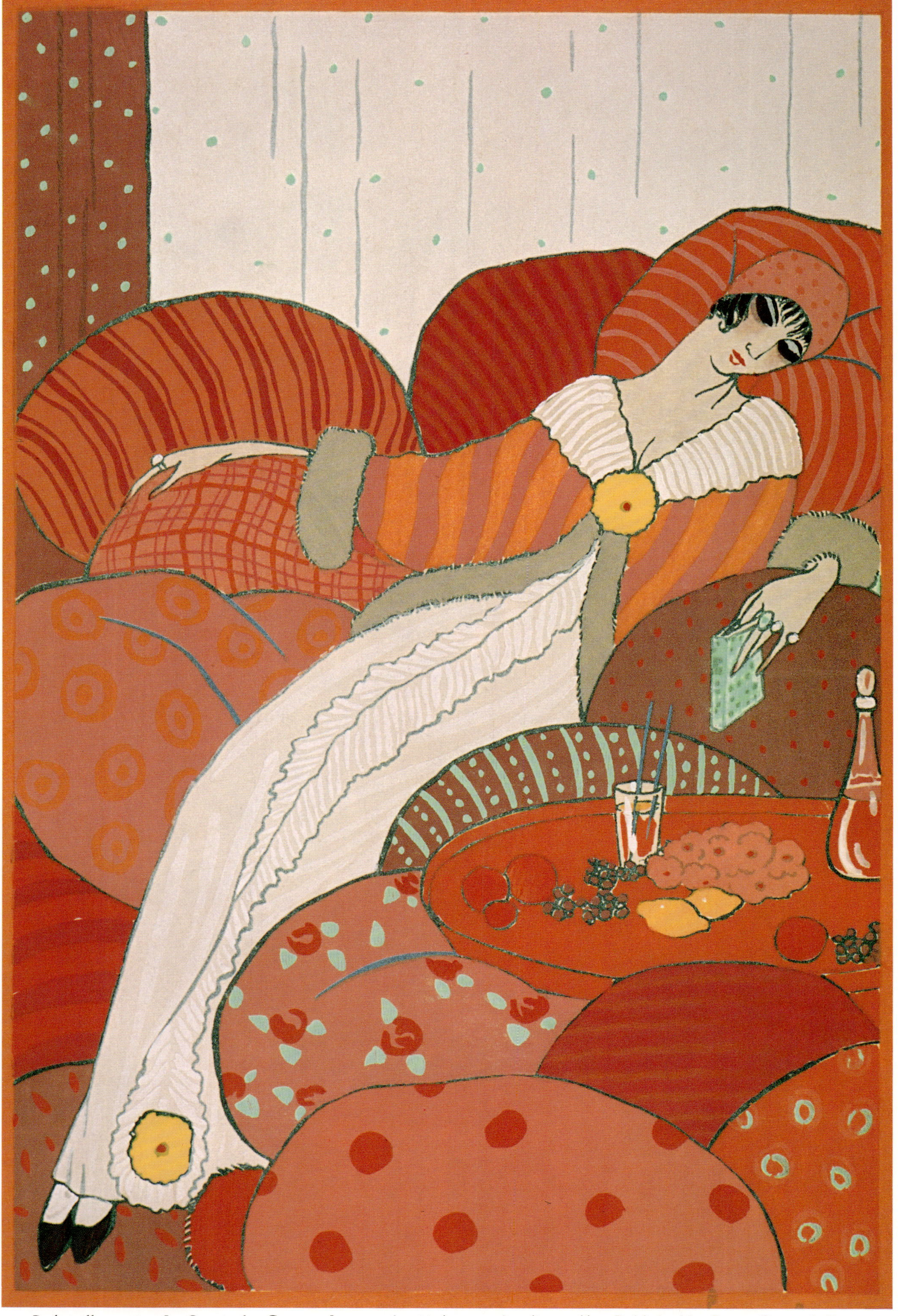

Pochoir illustration *Les Coussins* by Georges Lepape, for *Modes et manières d'aujourd'hui*. Published by Pierre Corrard, Paris. 1912.

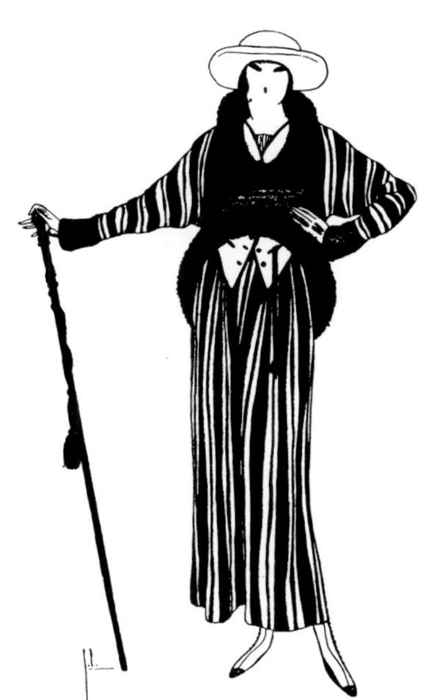

diaphanous Greek-style fashions that were then the rage in Paris and London; a facsimile fashion plate of an original design of that period was enclosed with the first issue, along with two contemporary fashion plates and eight pages of text covering numerous points of interest to the haut monde.

Le Journal des dames et des modes was followed in November 1912 by the first edition of *La Gazette du bon ton*, which was founded by Lucien Vogel and his wife Cosette, with the aid of seven leading couturiers of the early Art Deco period — Chéruit, Doeuillet, Doucet, Paquin, Poiret, Redfern and Worth — who reserved for this publication their most important trend-setting fashions. These new fashions were drawn by a group of artists who were to become known as the 'Beaux Brummels of the Brush' — Francesco Javier Gosé, Bernard Boutet de Monvel, André Marty, Georges Lepape, Pierre Brissaud, Jacques Drésa, Charles Martin and George Barbier. Their distinctive work appeared regularly in the *Gazette* and, in company with Etienne Drian, Guy Arnoux, Umberto Brunelleschi, Robert Dammy, Erté, Jean-Louis Boussingault, Maurice Taquoy, Léon Bonnotte and Léon Bakst, they set the visual style of the magazine.

The first annual edition of the luxurious album *Modes et manières d'aujourd'hui*, containing twelve sumptuous illustrations by Georges Lepape, also appeared in 1912, founded by Pierre Corrard and printed by Marquet et Cie. The *pochoir* colouring was done by Saudé, who had also been responsible for printing the two Paul Poiret albums, *Les Robes de Paul Poiret* in 1908 and *Les Choses de Paul Poiret* in 1911. Saudé had also printed the *pochoirs* for the 1911 Paquin album *L'Eventail et la fourrure*, which featured drawings by Iribe and Barbier. Like *Le Journal des dames et des modes* and *La Gazette du bon ton*, the special deluxe albums were intended as showcases for the newest fashions; they combined the luxury of beautiful materials and superb craftsmanship with an artistic excellence that even the most fastidious connoisseur could not fail to appreciate.

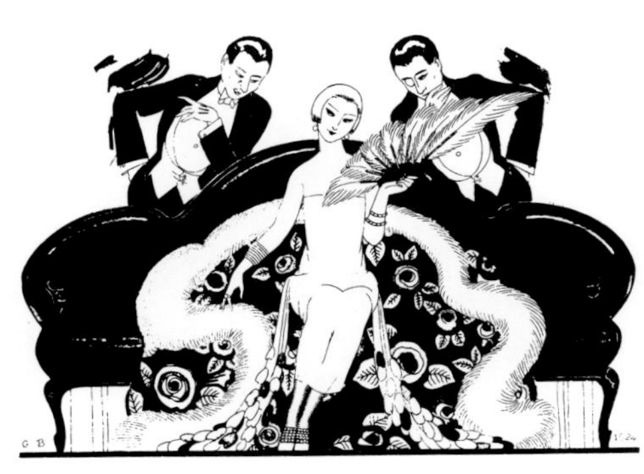

It is obvious from the introduction to these publications, and those that were to follow during the next few years — *Luxe de Paris, Le Goût du jour, La Guirlande d'art et de la littérature, Les Feuillets d'art, La Guirlande des mois, Falbalas et fanfreluches, Les Douze Mois de l'année*, and many others — that they were not just fashion magazines as we understand the term today: they were what Monsieur Valotaire described in a 1930 edition of *The*

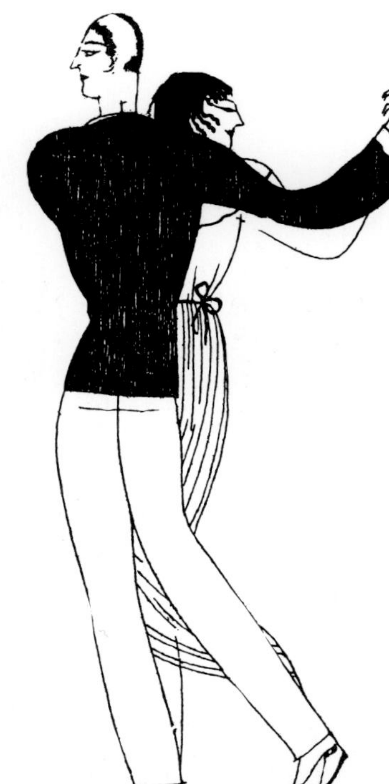

Studio Magazine as 'a monument to the taste of the age'.

In the period 1912–1914 it was generally acknowledged that, although the couturiers of the Rue de la Paix were the creators of the individual fashion styles, it was the illustrators who were the true inventors of the new Art Deco mode of fashionable design. It was they who invented new images that permeated the imaginations of the haut monde and made them long for even more new ideas. As an editorial in *La Gazette du bon ton* stated at the time, 'Artists today are in part the inventors of fashion; what doesn't fashion owe to Iribe, who introduced to it simplicity of line and an oriental flavour, or to Drian, or Bakst? . . .' And in another article the editor asked,

Are we on the threshold of a twentieth century Renaissance, in the sense that we are putting into our daily service and using for the adornment of everyday life the brains and inventions of the geniuses of our day? Artists are proud to contribute to the beautifying of all objects of luxury — what we see, what we touch, what we wear . . . Lalique has provided the fair sex with jewellery such as has not been seen since the great days of Florence, and men like Bakst, Barbier, Marty, Iribe, Drian and Delvaille have been proud to design the clothes worn by fashionable women . . .

The article continued by drawing the readers' attention to the eight to ten *pochoir* illustrations that were included in each issue of the *Gazette*, explaining that there would be 'no confusion of tints inevitable in photographic reproduction; each picture is coloured exactly the same way as the artist's original — a real picture, not a mere reflection of a lifeless mannequin . . .' It concluded with the statement, 'This is an expensive publication, expensive to produce and expensive in its aim to be the true mirror of all that is smartest and most elegant in the social life of our day'.

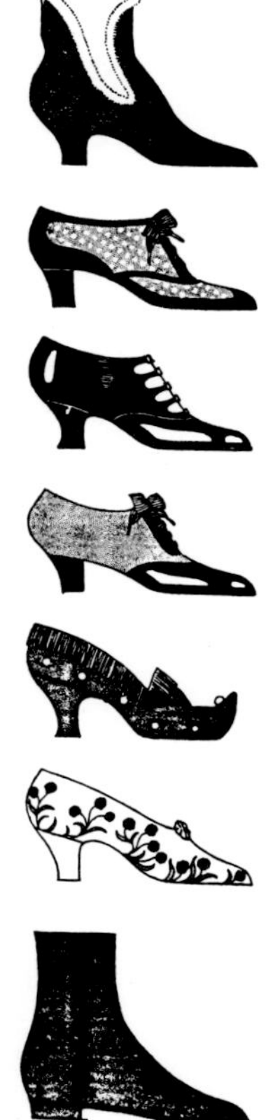

The idea behind the *Gazette*, as well as the *Journal des dames* and many other publications, was to 'revive the tradition of fashionable journalism of the eighteenth century, in order to forget the events and absurdities of the nineteenth'. Numerous editorials made reference to the illustrations of Antoine Watteau, Leclerc, Gabriel de Saint-Aubin, Desrais, Defraine, Vernet, and the work of publisher Pierre La Mésangère, but being well aware that they were living in the twentieth century and not the eighteenth they did not attempt to simply copy the style of those earlier publications. Instead, they declared, 'A new age and new methods of production demand new publications', to which *La Gazette du bon ton* added,

Today the entire world is interested in the new forms of design. Painters everywhere are collaborating with designers, and the visual pleasure of a woman's appearance is no longer judged inferior to the other arts. . . It is our intention to gather together in these pages the true spirit of this age, scattered as it is in the Bois, the theatre, the races, the restaurants, and at the fetes — capturing it alive and preserving it in all its freshness and glory.

In addition to the *pochoir* illustrations such publications contained

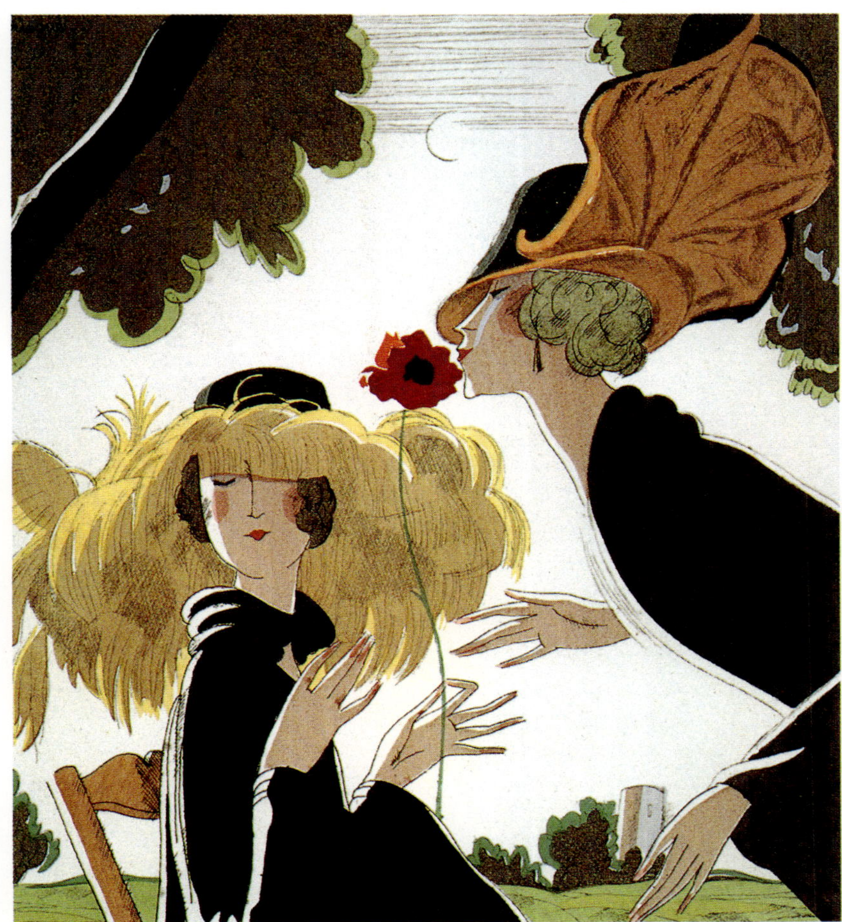

Pochoir illustration *Les Cinq Sens* by Pierre Mourgue *(chapeaux de Camille Roger)* for *La Gazette du bon ton*. Paris. 1922.

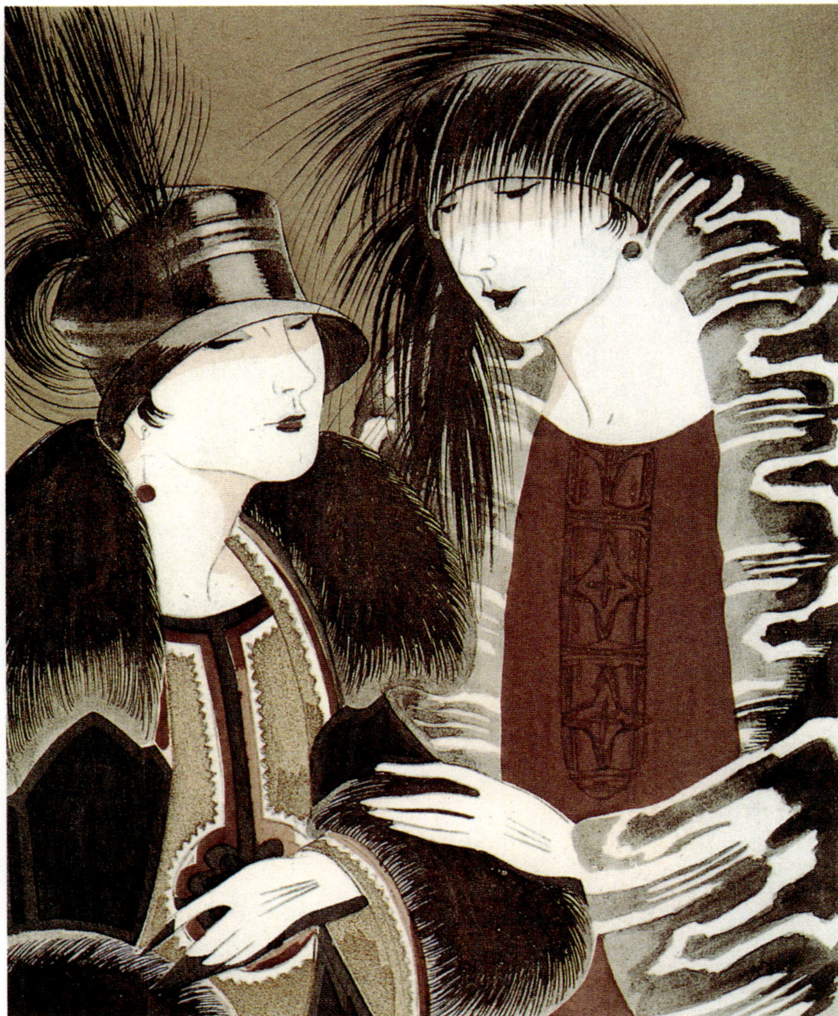

Pochoir illustration *Unterhaltung* by Zeichnung von Offterdinger, for *Der Styl*. Published by Otto von Holten, Berlin. 1923.

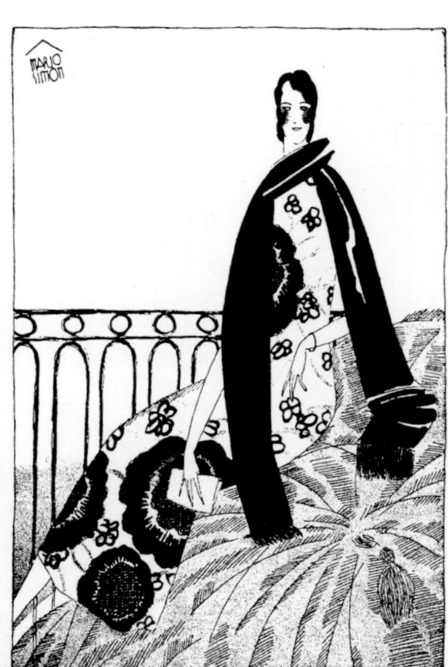

articles by many of the diligent and witty *littérateurs* of the time, among them Jean Cocteau, André de Fouquières, Henri Duvernois, Marcel Boulanger, René Blum, the novelists Anatole France, Marcel Proust and Paul Margueritte, the poet Fernand Gregh, the dramatists Pierre Véber and Henri Lavendan, and the composer Erik Satie, who wrote on a wide variety of subjects. Their fascinating range of narrative styles was fitting complement for the range of illustrative styles.

The illustrators, like the writers, were a very varied group of people who had travelled from all over Europe in order to live and work in Paris. Umberto Brunelleschi, for instance, was born in Montemurlo in Tuscany in 1879 and, after completing his studies in Florence, he moved in 1900 to Paris where he became well known as a printer, book illustrator and costume designer. Between 1912–14 and 1919–21 he regularly contributed to several of the prestigious fashion publications, and then he embarked on a career as a set and costume designer for the Folies Bergère, the Casino de Paris, the Châtelet, and for several shows at the Roxy Theatre, New York, and various theatres in Italy and Germany. He was also the artistic director of *La Guirlande d'art et de la littérature*.

Francisco Javier Gosé was born in the Spanish town of Lerida in 1876 and after studying in Barcelona he travelled to Paris, where he established a small studio in 1901. His early illustrations appeared regularly in such magazines as *Le Rire*, *L'Assiette au beurre* and *Simplicissimus* before he began working for both the *Journal des dames* and the *Gazette*. Ill-health forced Gosé to return to Spain in 1914, and he died there one year later.

The French illustrator Pierre Brissaud was born in Paris in 1885. He studied painting, illustration and engraving at the Ecole des Beaux Arts and from 1910 onwards he supplied an increasing number of illustrations for deluxe-edition books, popular magazines and exclusive fashion publications. Brissaud's close associate Bernard Boutet de Monvel was also born in Paris in 1885. After studying painting and engraving with Luc-Olivier Merson and Jean Dampt he became an illustrator for *Le Rire*, *La Vie parisienne* and *L'Assiette au beurre*. Later, at the suggestion of Paul Poiret, for whom he had designed a range of menswear, he became one of the early contributors to *La Gazette du bon ton*, and subsequently *Harpers Bazaar*.

Georges Lepape was an important illustrator of the Art Deco period. He was born in Paris in 1887 and, after studying painting with Laurencin and Braque at the Academy Hubert, he enrolled at the Ecole des Beaux Arts to further his studies in portraiture. In 1910 he was commissioned to undertake illustrative and design work for Paul Poiret, and the ensuing album — *Les Choses de Paul Poiret* — launched him as an illustrator. A steady flow of commissions followed. In 1912, twelve of his illustrations were published in the first edition of *Modes et manières d'aujourd'hui* and he commenced his long collaboration with Lucien Vogel and *La Gazette du bon ton*.

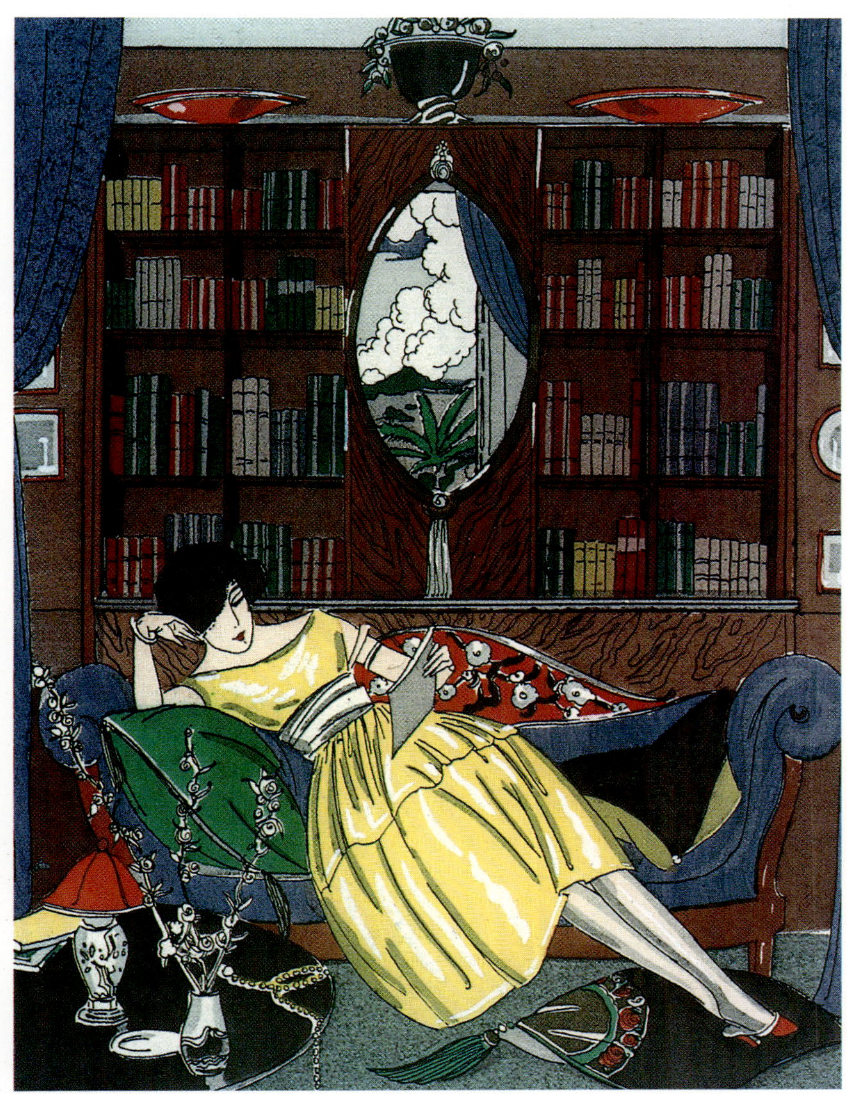

Pochoir illustration *Pour rêver un peu* by M. Cito, for *La Guirlande d'art et de la littérature*. Paris. 1920.

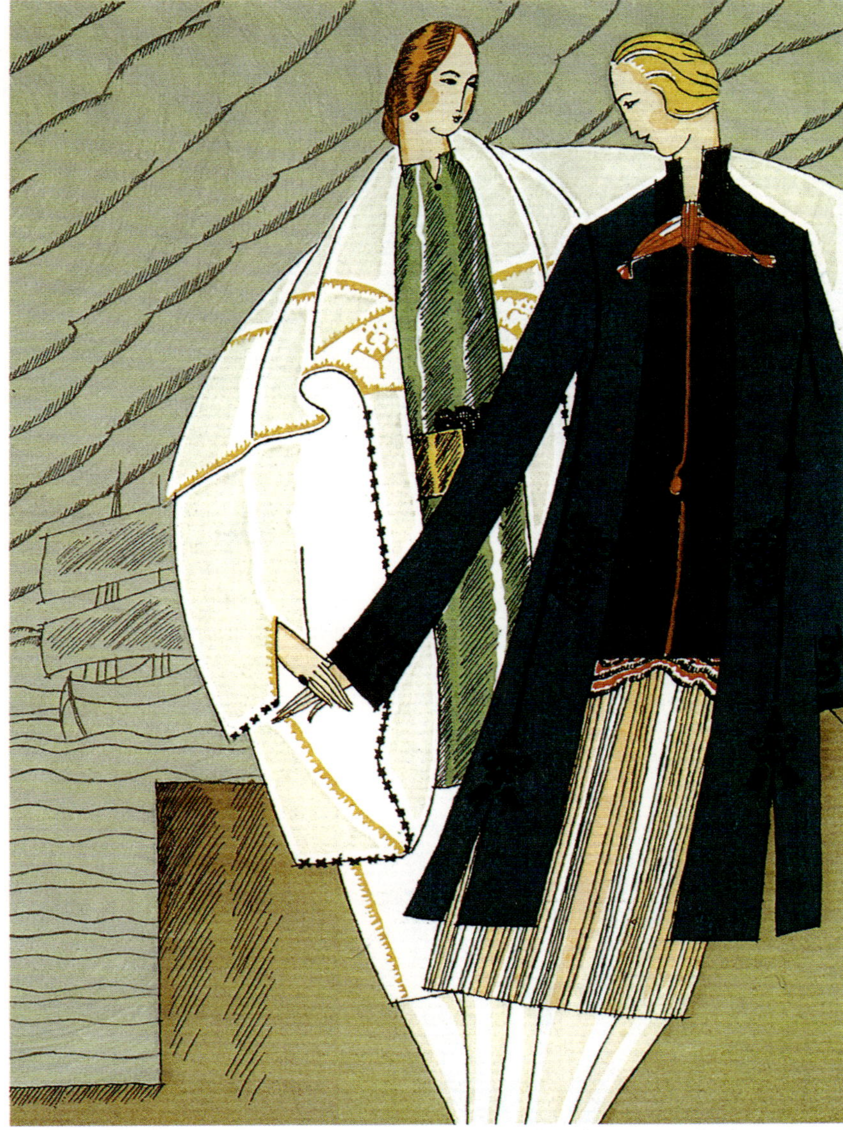

Pochoir illustration *Manteaux inspirés des costumes tchécoslovaques* by L'Hom, for *La Gazette du bon ton*. Paris. 1920.

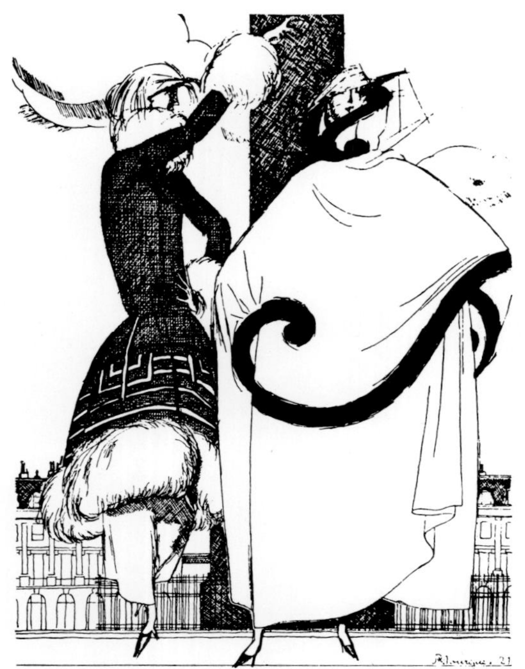

Lepape also designed fabrics, theatrical sets and costumes, covers for *Vogue* and numerous book illustrations. His career spanned over thirty-five years, and today he is regarded as one of the great illustrators of the Art Deco period.

But the most prolific and arguably the greatest illustrator of the period was George Barbier, whose work appeared regularly in *La Gazette du bon ton, Le Journal des dames et des modes et manières d'aujourd'hui, Les Feuillets d'art, La Guirlande d'art et de la littérature, Falbalas et Fanfreluches* and *La Guirlande des mois.* Born in Nantes in 1882, Barbier spent two years (1908–10) in the studio of Jean-Paul Laurens at the Ecole des Beaux Arts in Paris; here he developed a love of Greek antiquity, which he later combined with an erotic sophistication and oriental colours and detail. For Barbier, a sense of luxury of detail tinged with an erotic decadence was a serious business and most of his illustrations remain uncorrupted by any redeeming social values. Barbier also worked on a surprisingly large number of deluxe books and portfolios, among them the famous *Le Bonheur du jour ou les grâces; Le Chanson de Bilitis,* Pierre Louys' celebrated lesbian novel, in collaboration with the Swiss wood engraver and printer François-Louis Schmied; *Nijinski,* published by La Belle Editions; the 1914 edition of *Modes et manières;* five editions each of *Falbalas et Fanfreluches* and *La Guirlande des mois;* and *Personnages de comédie,* again in collaboration with Schmied.

As well as being an engraver and printer for such books as *Le Chanson de Bilitis* and *Personnages de comédie,* François-Louis Schmied was one of the most interesting book illustrators of the time: his books *Daphne, La Création* and *Le Cantique des cantiques* are considered three of the greatest illustrative achievements of the Art Deco period. Schmied was born in Geneva in 1873. He studied wood-engraving at the local Ecole des Arts Industriels where he met Jean Dunand, who was studying sculpture and later became the great master of Art Deco lacquer work and enamelling. The two men became close friends and design collaborators. Schmied moved to Paris in 1895, eking out a living as an illustrator and wood engraver. In 1910 he received his first important commission, to engrave and print Paul Jouve's illustrations for a deluxe edition of *Le Livre de la jungle,* with text by Rudyard Kipling. This was followed by numerous other book commissions and, being a man of many talents, he also undertook set designs for the Théâtre Pigalle, tapestries for the weavers Gobelins,

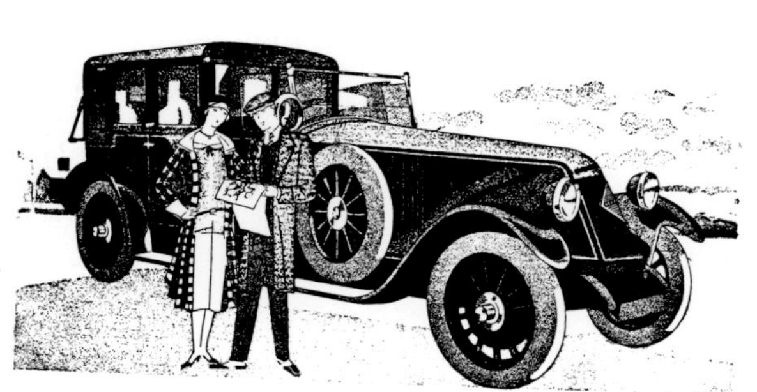

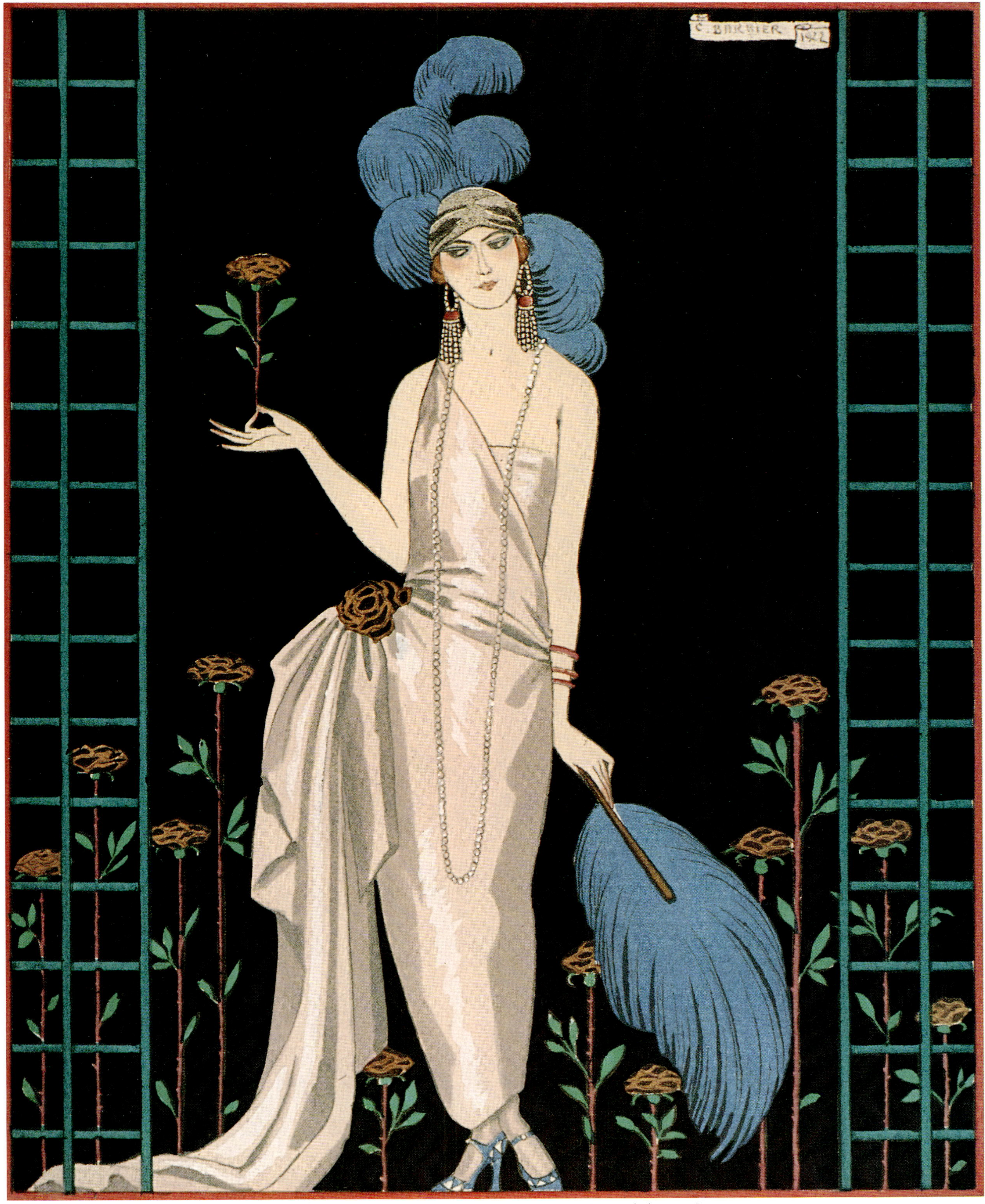

Pochoir illustration *La Roseraie* by George Barbier, for *La Gazette du bon ton*. Paris. 1922.

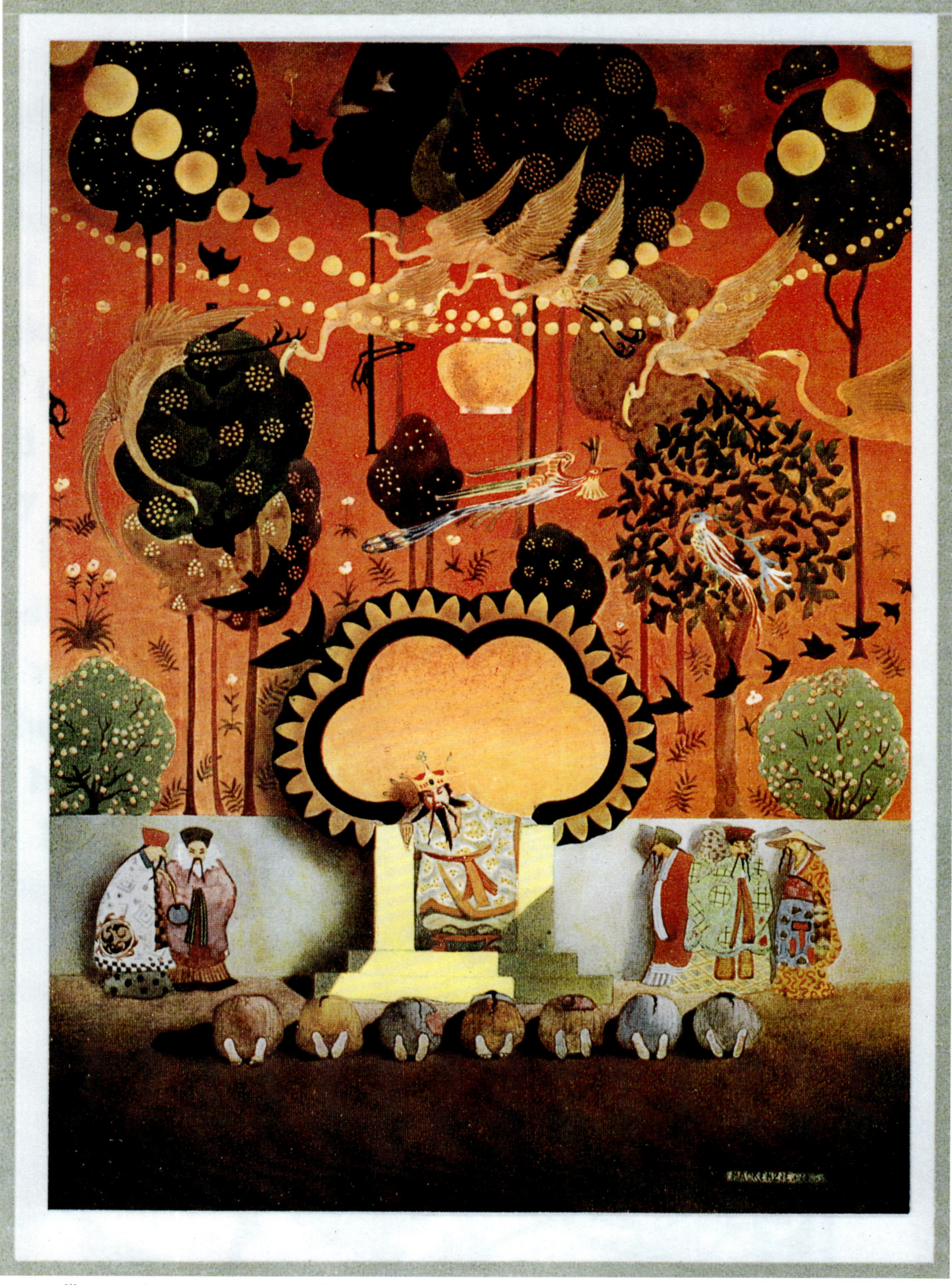

Illustration by T. MacKenzie for *Aladdin and his Wonderful Lamp* by Arthur Ransome. Deluxe signed edition of 250 copies. Published by Nisbet & Co., London. 1919.

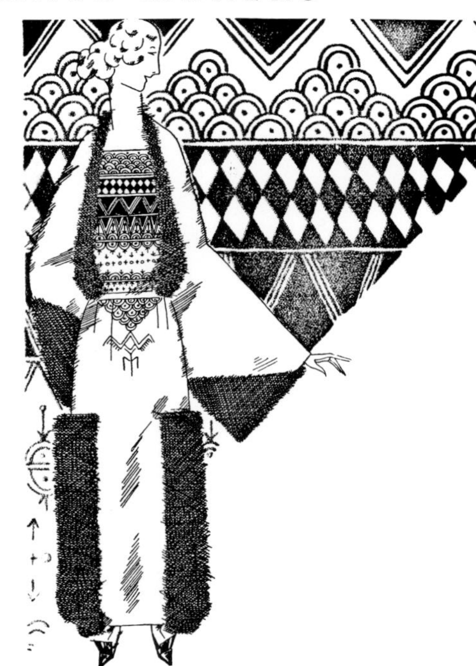

and towards the end of his career he designed several decorative panels for the luxury French liner *Normandie.*

The Russian designer and illustrator Lev Samoilovich Rosenberg — better known by his adopted name Léon Bakst — was born in St Petersburg in 1868 and, after completing a course of academic art studies at the local School for the Advancement of the Arts, he went to Paris to complete his studies in painting. It was whilst in Paris that he adopted his grandmother's maiden name 'Bakst'. On his return to St Petersburg in 1895 Bakst was appointed an official painter to the imperial family, a post he held until 1899 when Prince Volkonsky, director of the Imperial Theatre, introduced him to Sergei Diaghilev, who was at that time the artistic director of the theatre. Prince Volkonsky's idea was to get Bakst to collaborate with another young Russian designer, Ivan Bilibin, on a Diaghilev production to be staged at the Imperial Theatre. Diaghilev, Bakst and Bilibin collaborated successfully on several productions at the Theatre, and both Bakst and Bilibin became regular contributors to Diaghilev's *World of Art* journal.

In 1909 Bakst travelled to Paris with Diaghilev and the Ballet Russe. He designed the sets and costumes for *Cléopâtre* and the outstandingly successful *Schéhérazade* — the luxury and sensuality of his designs became landmarks in the development of the early Art Deco style. He continued to design for the Ballet Russe until his death in 1922, shortly after he had finished work on *The Sleeping Princess*. Between 1910 and 1914 he had also worked for the couturier Madame Paquin and contributed illustrations to both *La Gazette du bon ton* and *Le Journal des dames et des modes*.

Léon Bakst's early collaborator Ivan Bilibin was born in 1876 in Tarkhovka, a small town near St Petersburg, and he studied painting with Bakst in St Petersburg. He then travelled throughout Europe for several years, studying and painting, and on his return he worked on various productions for the Imperial Theatre and the Bolshoi Theatre in Moscow, and on illustrations for several books of Russian folk tales, including *Conte de Tsar Saltan* and *The Tales of the Golden Cockerel.*

In 1906 Diaghilev had exhibited a number of Bilibin's paintings in the Exhibition of Russian Art in Paris, alongside those of Bakst and others. He then commissioned Bilibin to design the sets and costumes for Moussorgsky's opera *Boris Godounov*, which Diaghilev produced with great success at the Paris Grand Opera House in 1908. Bilibin, with Bakst, Benois and Korovin, was then commissioned to design the sets and costumes for the forthcoming season of the Ballet Russe, which was staged in Paris in 1909. Unlike the other designers, however, Bilibin did not travel to Paris; instead, he took up an appointment as an art teacher at the St Petersburg School for the Advancement of the Arts. He continued to design sets and costumes for the Imperial and the Bolshoi Theatres until they were closed by the revolution of 1915.

One of Bilibin's protégés in St Petersburg was the only son of a wealthy admiral in the Russian Navy: Romain de Tirtoff who was destined to become the famous illustrator and designer Erté (in French his initials are pronounced 'air tay'). Erté was born in St Petersburg in 1892 and, although a somewhat frail and shy child, he nevertheless enjoyed the elegance of fashionable and artistic life in St Petersburg. In 1900 he had travelled through Europe with his parents, visiting, among other things, the Great Paris Exhibition. This, he later said in his autobiography, endowed him with a great love for Paris, and when Paul Poiret visited St Petersburg in 1910 Erté finally determined that he would travel to Paris to become a fashion designer. After studying drawing for a short time in 1911 he boarded the Paris train, little realising that within a year he would be working as a designer for Poiret, designing theatrical costumes that were soon to rival those he had seen as a child at the St Petersburg Imperial Theatre.

In the 1920s Erté also became known as a designer of scanty costumes made of sequins and feathers for the Folies Bergère, and as a designer of the covers of *Harpers Bazaar*. His drawings are now avidly collected. At their best, they recall the serenity of a Russian icon, the lithe figures dressed in a fantasy of feathers and pearls set against a background of oriental splendour, the brightly coloured gouaches overlaid in gold, silver and bronze, and the flat linear language complemented by intricate geometric patterning.

Many other illustrators, designers and craftsmen came to Paris at the beginning of the Art Deco period — they came from Italy, the United States, England, Ireland, Poland, Denmark, Austria, Hungary, Spain, and many other countries to work alongside the great artists and craftsmen of this golden age, whose energies and talents were beginning to change the way people talked, looked, dressed and thought.

But on 28 June 1914 people around the world were assailed by the news that the Austrian Archduke Franz Ferdinand and his Consort had been assassinated at Sarajevo. War clouds began to gather over Europe, threatening the Western way of life. On 3 August war was declared between the major European nations, ending the artistic migration and the further development of the Art Deco style of design.

During the next four years and three months of bloody conflict the great couture houses, publishing companies and ateliers struggled against continual shortages of raw materials and manpower. Many of the artists, designers and master-craftsmen were called upon to undertake much grimmer tasks than the design or illustration of Art Deco artifacts.

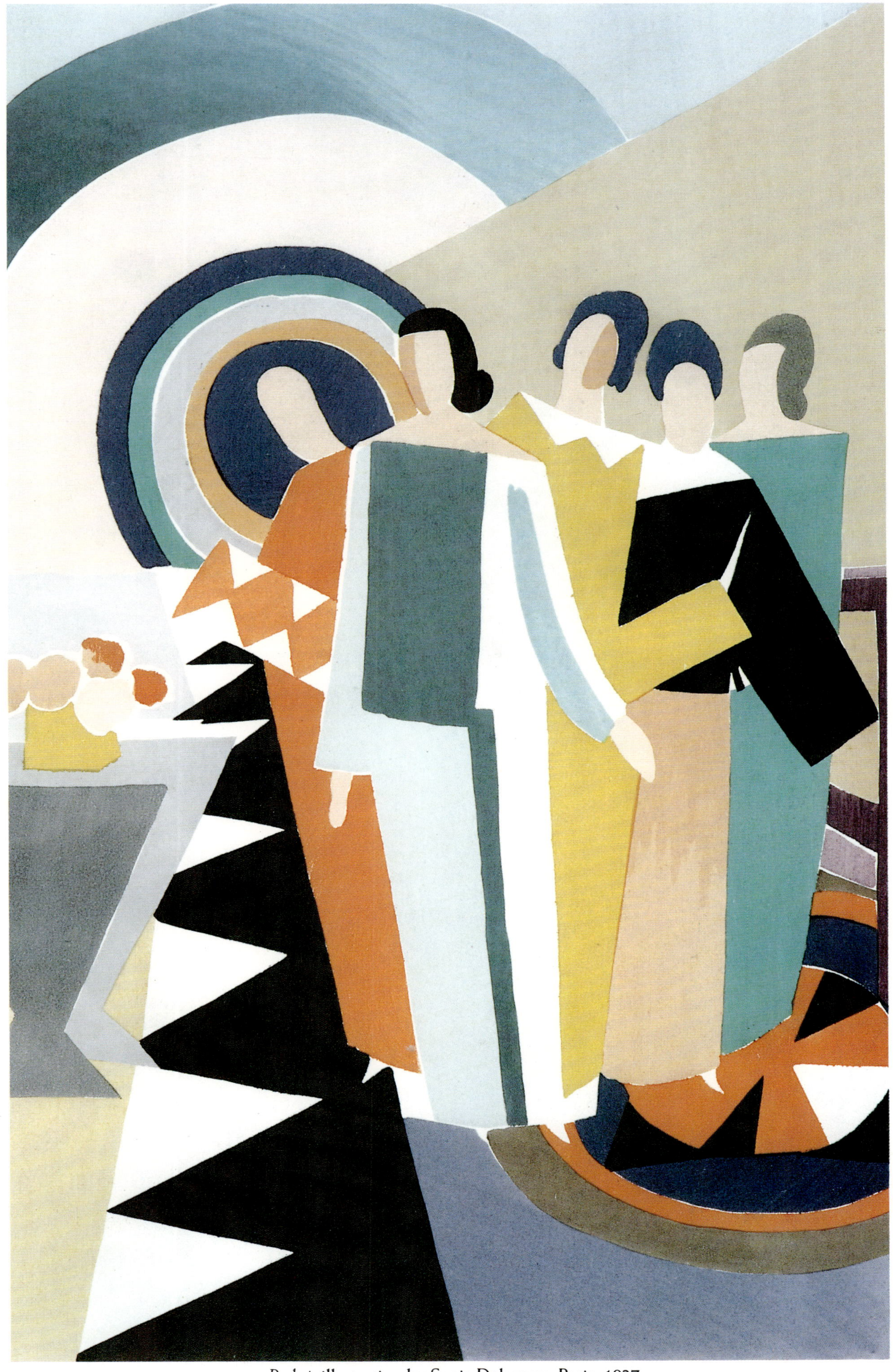

Pochoir illustration by Sonia Delaunay. Paris. 1927.

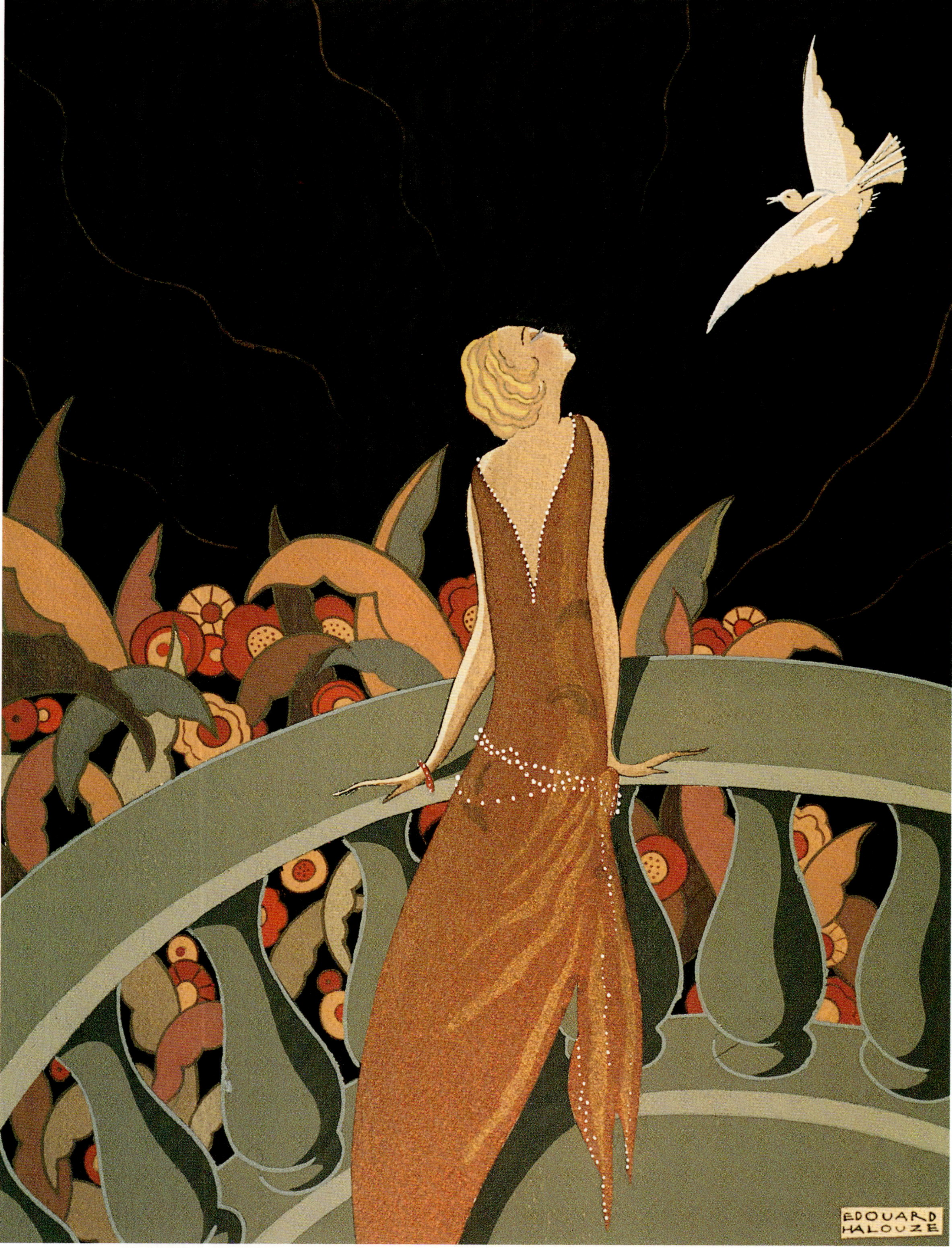

Pochoir illustration *Le Messager* by Halouzé. Printed by Jean Saudé for his *Traité d'enluminure d'art au pochoir*.
Published by Editions de L'Ibis, Paris. 1925.

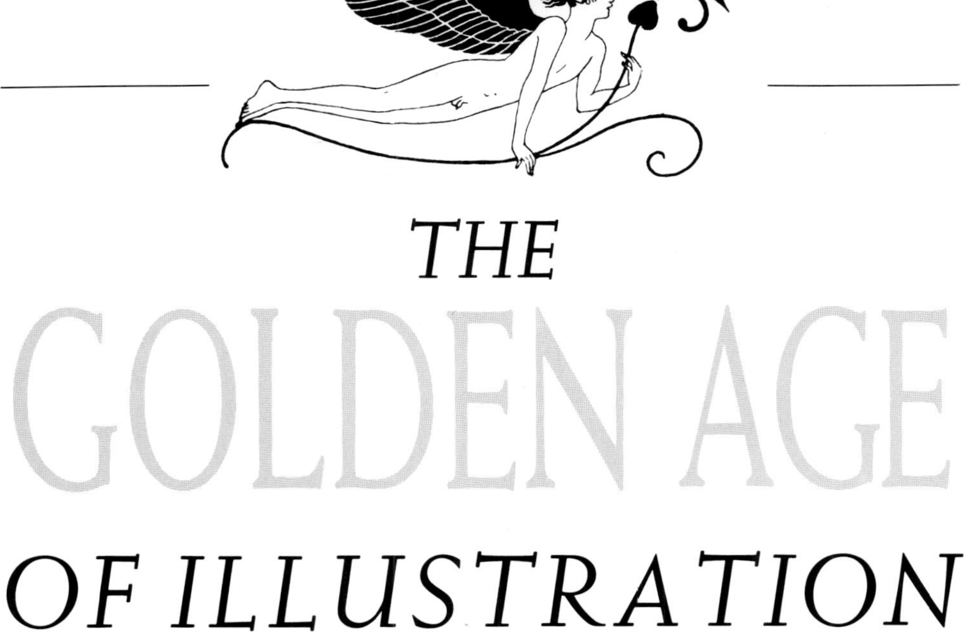

THE GOLDEN AGE OF ILLUSTRATION

The Armistice was signed in 1918: the war to end all wars had at last come to an end. Once again, the European nations were at peace and life was returning to its normal pace. The fashionable life of the wealthy elite began to regain its momentum as the new decade approached. But to the members of the pre-war haut monde, who had travelled their world enjoying luxury and leisure, life no longer seemed to follow the tradition of unquestioned authority and privilege.

In fact, the war changed many aspects of Western life, for all levels of society: the way people thought, the way they looked, the way they lived. The change was especially vivid for the younger generation, for it was they who had been most involved in the mechanics of the war. The young women, liberated from work in the hospitals and munitions factories, were painting their faces, raising their hemlines, and bobbing their hair so as to look like one of their favourite movie stars: Mae Murray, Blanche Sweet or the vampish Theda Bara — these women had made an enormous impression on the young generation during the drab wartime years. The young men, on the other hand, freed at last from the bloody conflict itself, kicked up their heels. Together, men and women began to dance to the rhythm of jazz, played by the newly arrived American Negro musicians.

Jazz music is believed to have originated in New Orleans during the latter part of the nineteenth century. According to most authorities, it developed and flourished in the well-organised red-light district of that city. There, the Negro slaves who had been freed after the American Civil War, especially those who were either physically attractive or had some musical talent, found sporadic employment entertaining visitors to

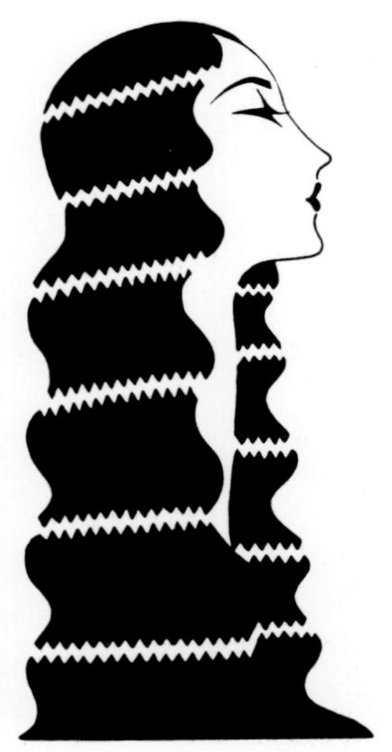

the madams' 'sporting houses'. The musicians also accompanied various street parades and carnivals, and provided the music for revivalist meetings, funerals and numerous other local events.

This New Orleans jazz music was originally improvised, and it was largely based on rhythms inherited from a distant, almost forgotten African culture; it was tempered by the sorrow and pain of generations of slavery and the exhilaration that came with the freedom resulting from the end of the Civil War. Thus, jazz could be readily adapted to express the desolation of the 'blues' or the hectic exuberance and gaiety of the newly invented cakewalk and ragtime.

Although originally confined to the brothel district of New Orleans, where the term 'jazz' originated — *jasz* meaning sexual intercourse in Creole — jazz had gradually spread via the paddle-steamers of the Mississippi to St Louis, and then to Chicago and New York, where it was adapted to express local needs and conditions. Thence it travelled to Europe when the American troops arrived in 1917.

After hostilities ceased in Europe many ex-army jazz musicians found their way to Paris, a city comparatively free of colour prejudice. And by the early 1920s the ex-army musicians had been joined by an increasing number of well-known jazz exponents, flocking to Paris to play in the night clubs and dance halls. White musicians had also begun to adopt the new idiom, and composers such as Stravinsky and Hindemith began incorporating jazz rhythms into their work to express the mood of the post-war era. This added a gloss of cultural acceptability to what was then still considered a slightly risqué mode of musical expression.

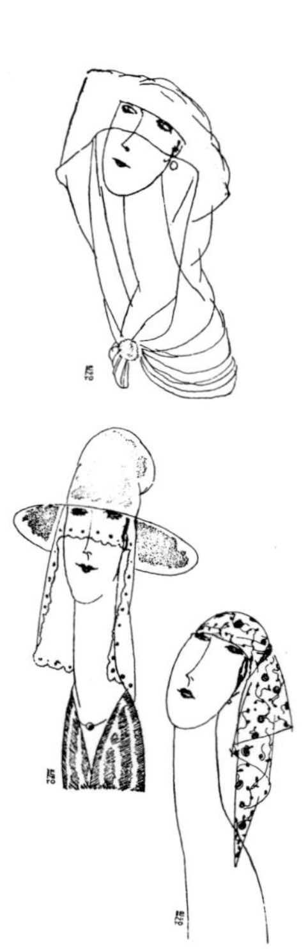

Most Europeans were exhausted both physically and mentally by the war, and many were near to bankruptcy. The sense of relief that the grim struggle for supremacy in Europe had ended mingled with bewilderment at the realisation that there would be no returning to the tranquil days of the pre-war era. The entire social structure of the Western world was changing.

The French, English and American delegates at Versailles were largely responsible for drawing up the new map of Western Europe, and they had all agreed that it was essential to make the countries bordering Soviet Russia as large and strong as possible in order to resist the westward march of communism. Their fear of the spread of communism was strengthened when the Bolsheviks seized power in Hungary for a few months in the summer of 1919 and there were similar attempted uprisings in Germany and elsewhere. But by June 1920 the last treaty had been signed, reparations agreed, and the last boundary line drawn.

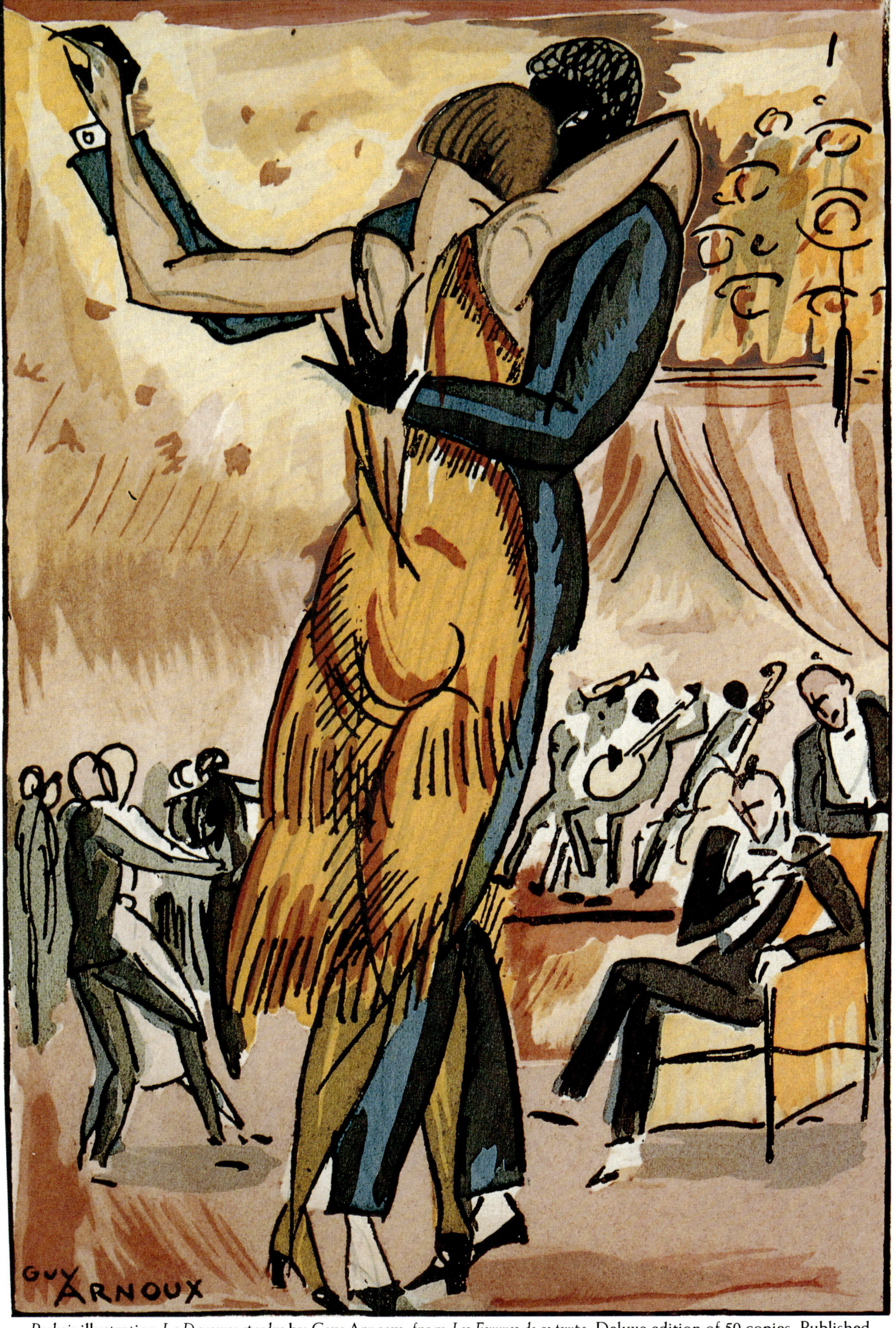

Pochoir illustration *La Danseuse eperdue* by Guy Arnoux, from *Les Femmes de ce temps*. Deluxe edition of 50 copies. Published by Chez Devanbez, Paris. 1920.

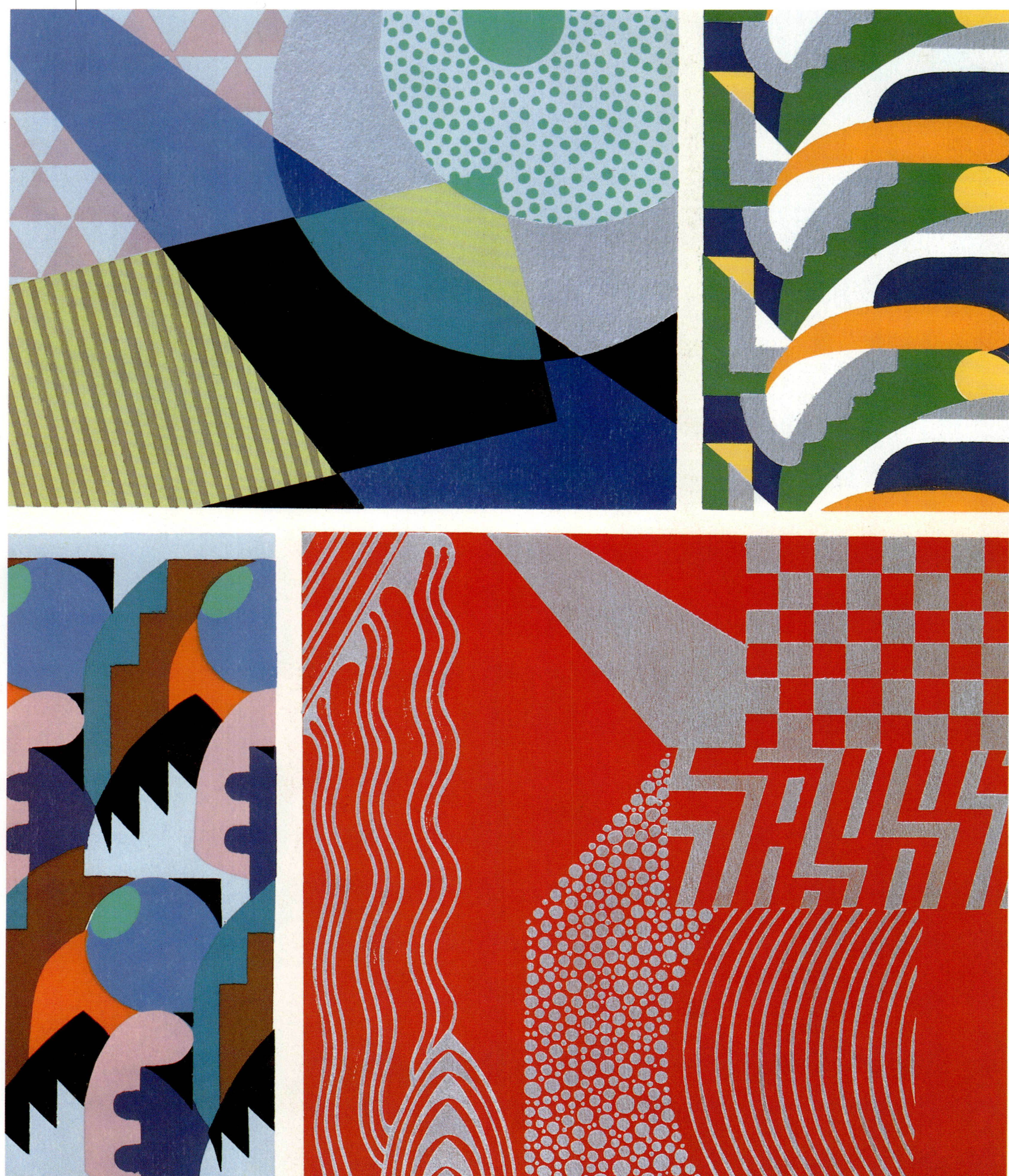

Designs from *Kaleidoscope* by M. P. Verneuil. Printed in *pochoir* by Jean Saudé for Editions Albert Lévy, Paris. 1926.

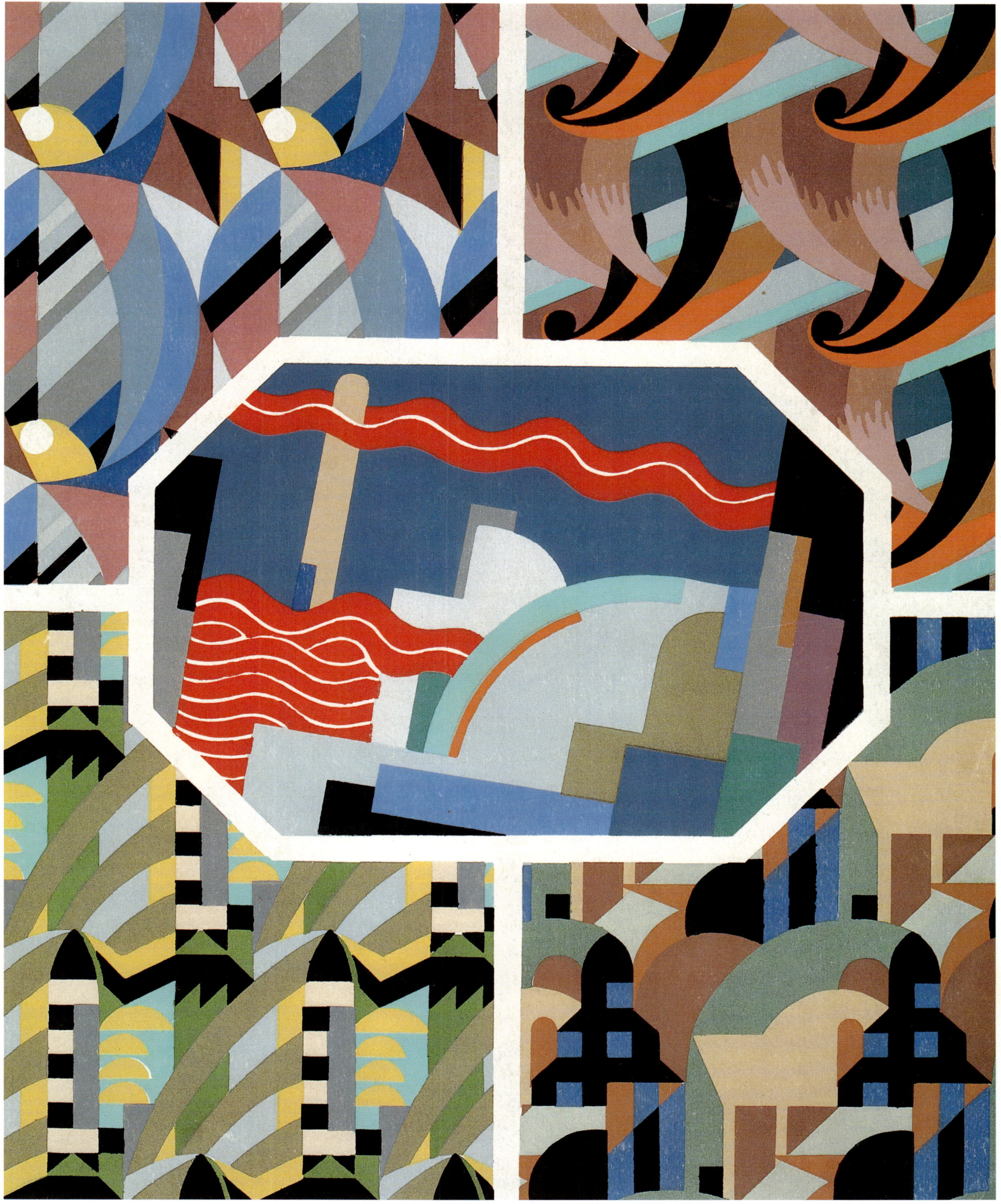

Designs from *Kaleidoscope* by M. P. Verneuil. Printed in *pochoir* by Jean Saudé for Editions Albert Lévy, Paris. 1926.

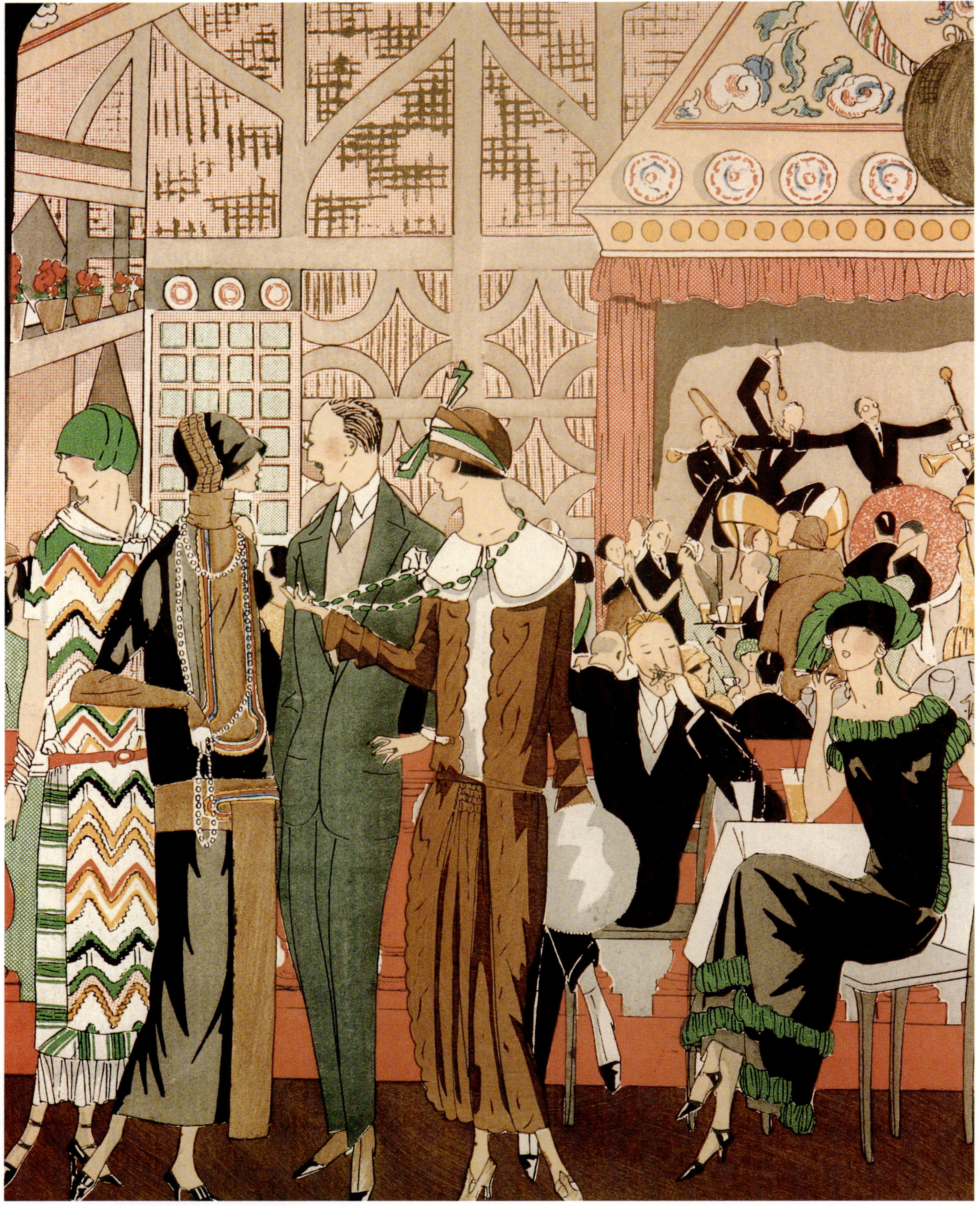

Pochoir over chromo-litho illustration *Seen at the Acacias* (designs by Jean Patou and Drecoll), for *Art-Goût-Beauté: Feuillets de l'élégance féminine*. Paris. 1922.

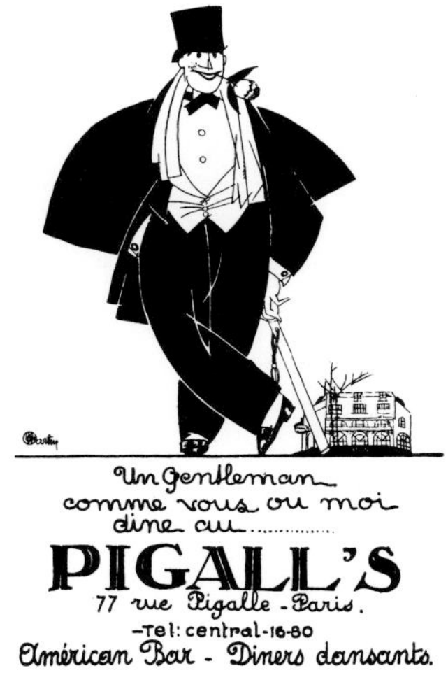

The terms of recompense that the Allies demanded of the defeated nations, and the re-allocation of national boundaries had, however, given rise to unease throughout central Europe: people began to realise that much of the enormous sacrifice of life that had taken place between August 1914 and November 1918 may well have been in vain since many of the European nations still did not trust one another and still coveted parts of each other's territory. Unfortunately, this unease and envy continued to rumble for another two decades, until September 1939, when yet another 'war to end all wars' began with the German invasion of Poland.

But in 1920 all this unrest and envy could be temporarily forgotten in the frantic gaiety for which the Negro jazz music had provided the initial release, and which designers, illustrators, film makers, and a wide variety of other entertainers in America and Western Europe quickly followed.

On the social scene, the remaining members of Europe's pre-war haut monde were joined by almost 10 000 new American millionaires, people who had supplied the European nations with weapons and other needs of war. There was also a surprising number of French, German and British people who had profited from the conflict. This new group was referred to as the 'nouveau riche'.

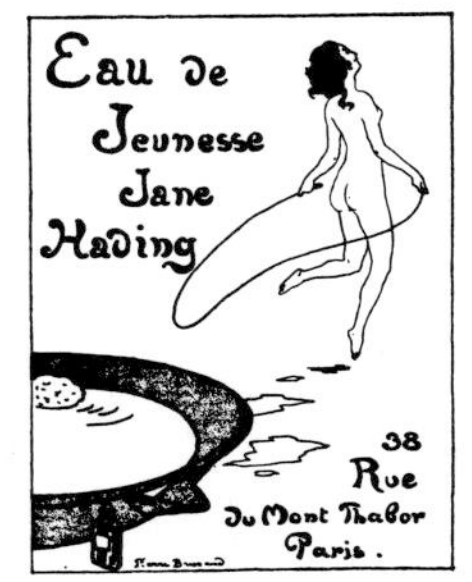

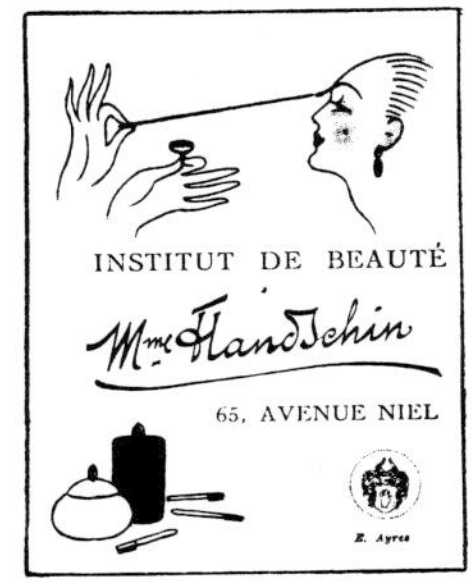

The combination of the pre-war haut monde and the nouveau riche was further enlivened by the addition of a mix of international authors, playwrights, artists and composers who were now accepted as part of the world of wealth and high fashion, and by an influx of entertainers. In England it became the mode for young actresses, dancers, and the like, to marry older peers: Gertie Millan became the Countess of Dudley, Bea Lillie became Lady Peel, and the dancer June ended up as Lady Inverclyde. The American heiress Thelma Morgan — twin sister of Gloria Vanderbilt — became Lady Furness, and other American heiresses were quickly snapped up by European and British aristocrats whose power and influence were waning. All this provided London and Paris with a new vitality, and supplied the couturiers and craftsmen with a new clientele.

At the beginning of the 1920s the traffic of ideas between the United States and Europe was opening up as never before: a steady stream of new music, films, and entertainers flowed eastward from New York to enliven the war-weary Europeans; the latest Paris fashions, Art Deco artifacts and objets d'art, antiques, and so on, were shipped westward to add a touch of European culture to the New World. Everywhere society strove to be bright and youthful, although the brazen manners and habits of the 'bright young things', as the younger generation was generally referred to, shocked and often outraged the older generation — the letter columns of many publications were full of their complaints. Nevertheless, the new young generation of the early 1920s was rightfully beginning to exercise

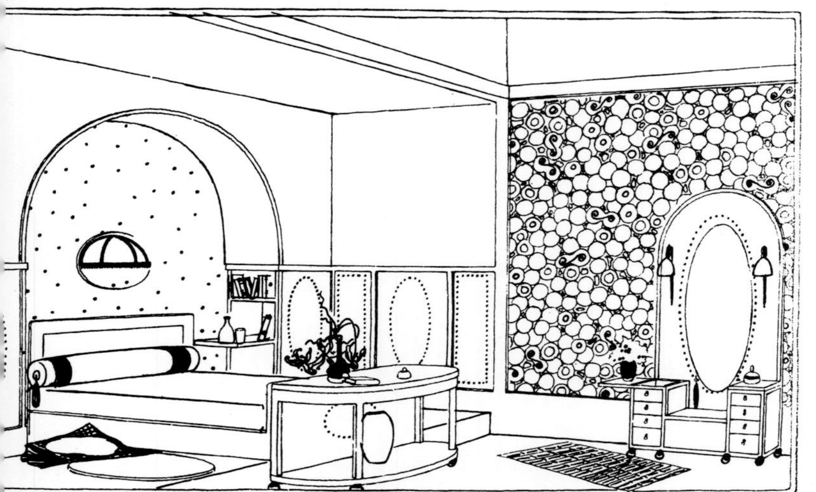

its freedom. This was going to be a decade of emancipation.

After the war most women had the vote, although in England it was limited to women over 30 years, and in 1919 the American-born Lady Astor became the first woman to be elected to the British House of Commons. Several of the famous universities began to admit female undergraduates, and the opening of the first birth-control clinics brought many women the hope of sexual freedom — although pioneers Marie Stopes and Margaret Sanger were lambasted by the British and American press, moralists, clergy and magistrates for their 'beastly, filthy, and immoral messages of free love and debauchery'.

In the United States prohibition had been introduced, denying both men and women the right to drink intoxicating liquor in public, although it was still available in the numerous speak-easies that operated in most cities. The war years had brought enormous prosperity to much of the United States: the annual trading surplus with Europe had risen from $690 million in 1913-14 to over $3000 million by the end of the war.

During the war, European nations had expanded their trade with their scattered colonial territories, and this activity was now turning towards exploitation of all sorts of rare and exotic natural materials that designers were seeking to use in their products in new and unexpected combinations. Their creativity was given an extra boost by technological advances that had occurred as a result of the war effort. By the early 1920s, for example, a wide range of new materials such as cellulose acetate, plastics and chromium-plated nickel alloy had been developed and these materials were being used by the experimental designers.

This was the social and economic climate in which the new group of European and American designers, artists, illustrators and craftsmen found themselves as they began to settle down to their work.

In Germany, the carnage of the war and the economic collapse facing the manufacturing industries gave rise to the establishment of the design principles of the Bauhaus, led by Walter Gropius and his group of teachers and technicians at the Weimar School of Art. With the painters Kandinsky and Paul Klee, and a number of designer–craftsmen, Gropius was beginning to evolve a theory of modern design based on the new technology. It was to be entirely functional in concept and free from any kind of decoration, and its aesthetic appeal was to rely solely on the

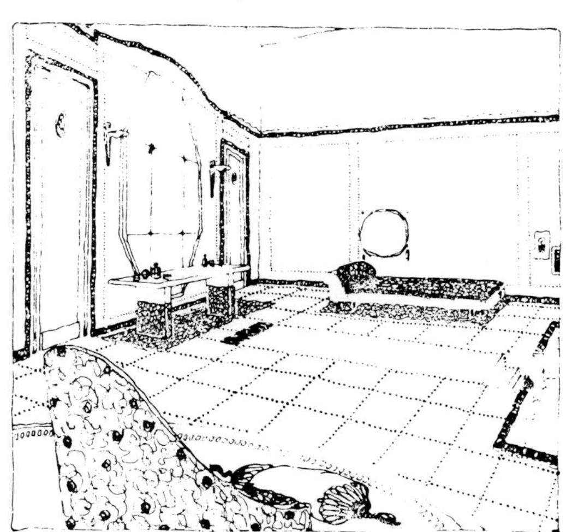

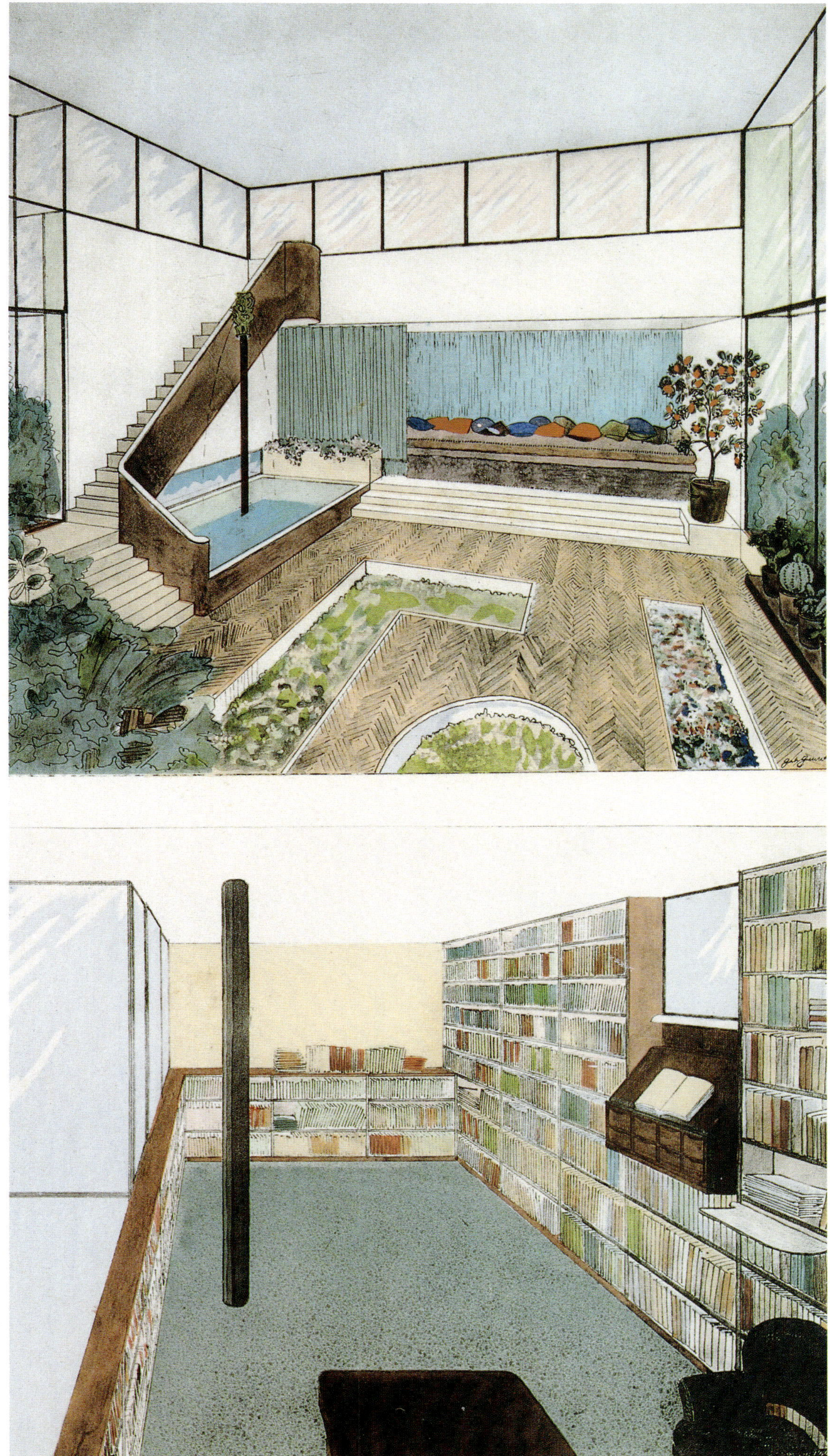

Illustration *Salon et terrasse* by Gabriel Guernékian. Printed in *pochoir* by Jean Saudé for *Répertoire du goût moderne*. Published by Editions Albert Lévy, Paris. 1928.

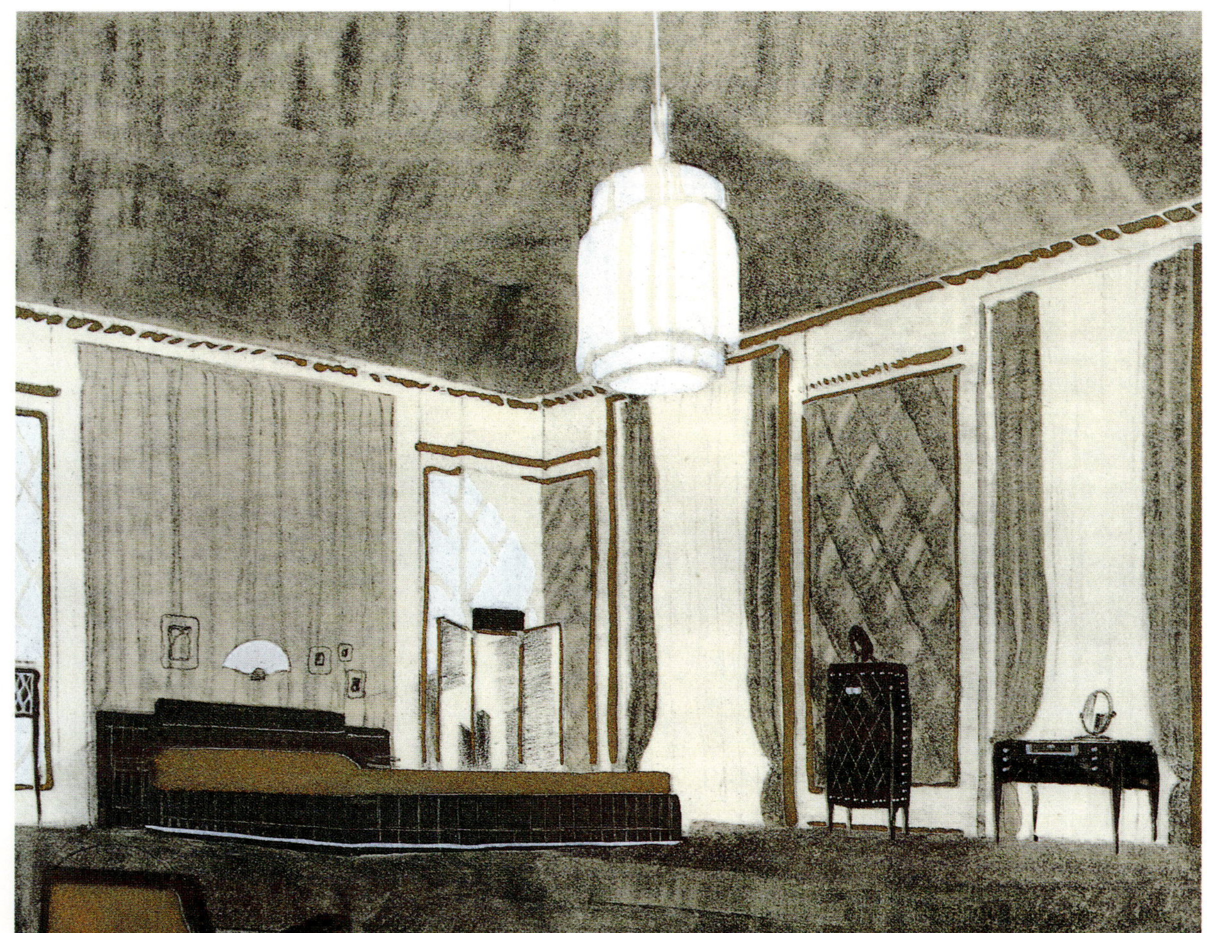

Illustration *Chambre* by J. Ruhlman. Printed in *pochoir* by Jean Saudé for *Répertoire du goût moderne*. Published by Editions Albert Lévy, Paris. 1928.

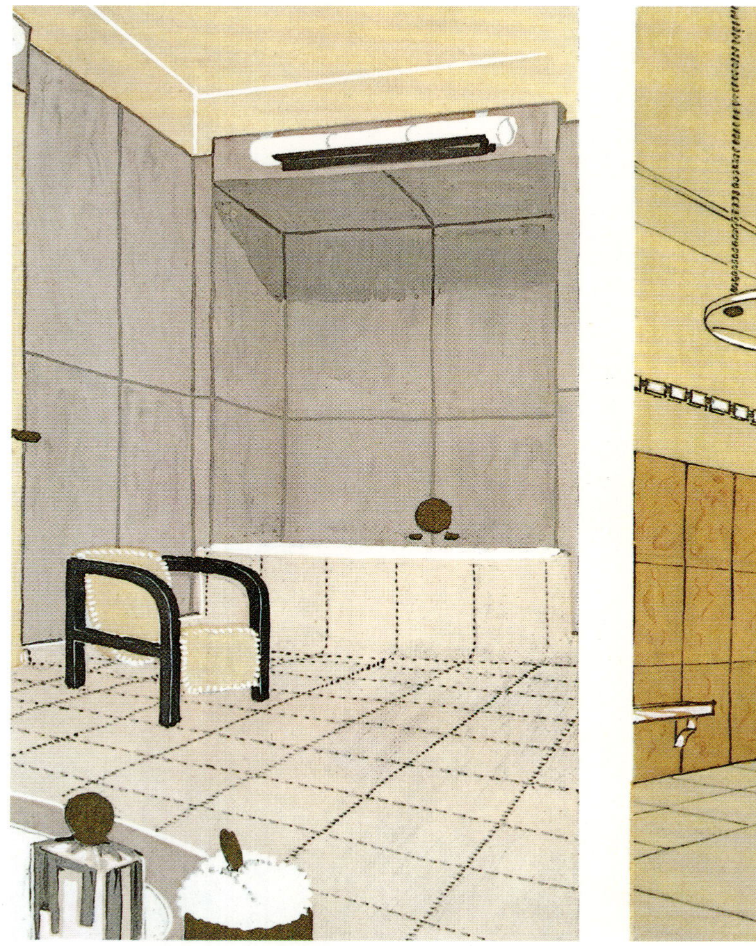

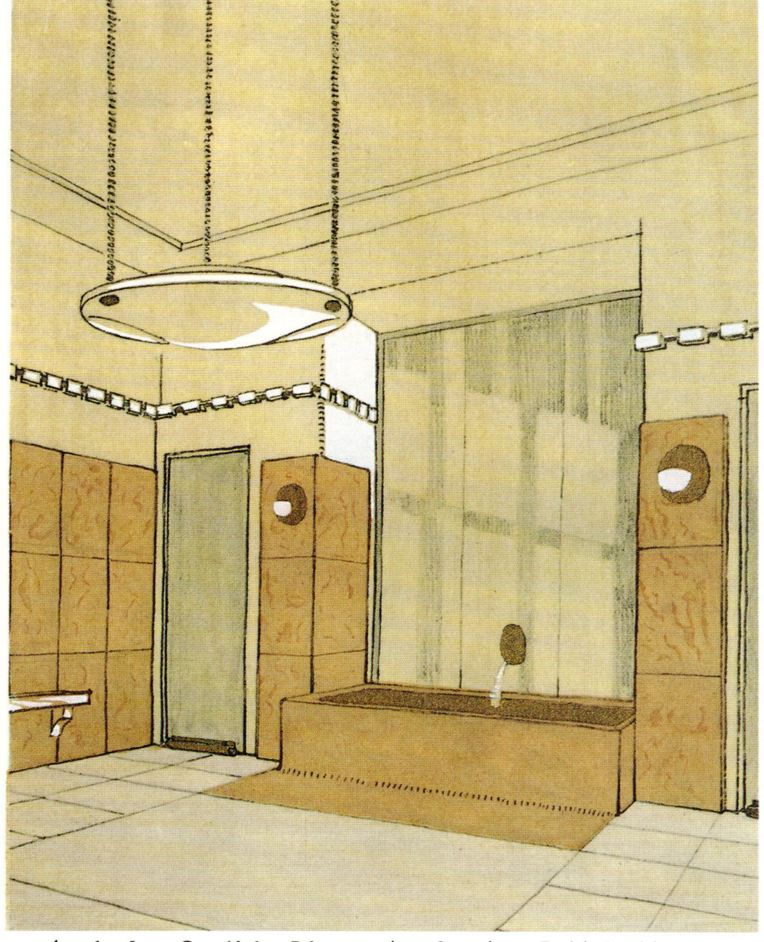

Illustration *Salles de bains* by J. Ruhlmann. Printed in *pochoir* by Jean Saudé for *Répertoire du goût moderne*. Published by Editions Albert Lévy, Paris. 1928.

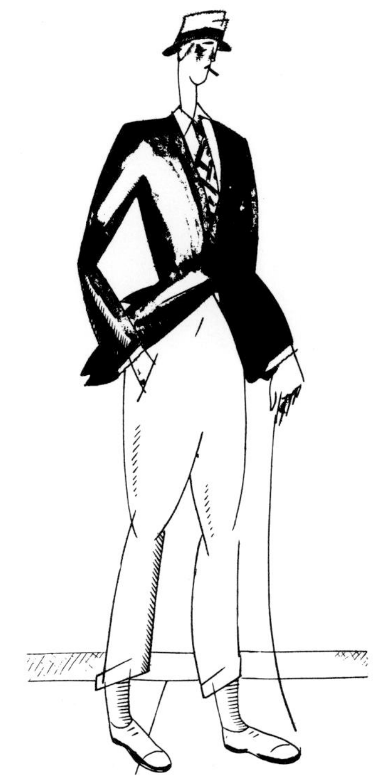

perceived relationship between the balance and proportion of its component parts, and their relationship to the intended function. The concept was similar to that originally articulated by Adam Smith in 1759, when he proclaimed that 'utility is one of the principal sources of beauty', and by Henry Homes, who contended in 1761 that a manufactured artifact 'void of intrinsic beauty appears beautiful from its utility'. These principles had been adapted by various functional and proto-modern designers in the late 1890s and the first Art Deco designers early in the twentieth century. But, whereas the designers of the 1890s and early 1900s had tried to achieve their ideals by using the traditional methods of hand craftsmanship that had so bedevilled the British Arts and Crafts Movement, making their products far too expensive for the average consumer, Gropius and his contemporaries proposed that their aims could only be achieved by modern technology and the recent advances in mass-production methods.

The theories evolved at the Bauhaus, with their emphasis on *Sachlichkeit* (meaning 'matter-of-factness', attention to function and practicality), started the German search for an austere, rational mode of design and new methods of production that would be based upon materials of minimal cost and free of all forms of ornamentation. This became essential for Germany's continued survival as a manufacturing nation, and the designers devoted themselves to it with great determination.

In France, on the other hand, manufacturing industries had been completely destroyed during the German invasion and much of the machinery had been looted and converted into armaments. The French were therefore unable to concentrate on mass-produced products. Fortunately, though, the luxury trades, which by tradition were situated mainly in Paris, remained virtually untouched, and it became economically imperative to expand the emphasis on luxury and extravagance. French designers and manufacturers decided to present themselves to the world as well-equipped producers of a new range of luxurious and extravagant merchandise, and the major Paris fashion houses and ateliers became the principal suppliers of these offerings. But these offerings could not be the same as those offered to the haut monde in pre-war days: the changing times had created a new aesthetic dream, one that reflected the ideas and lifestyle of the nouveau riche.

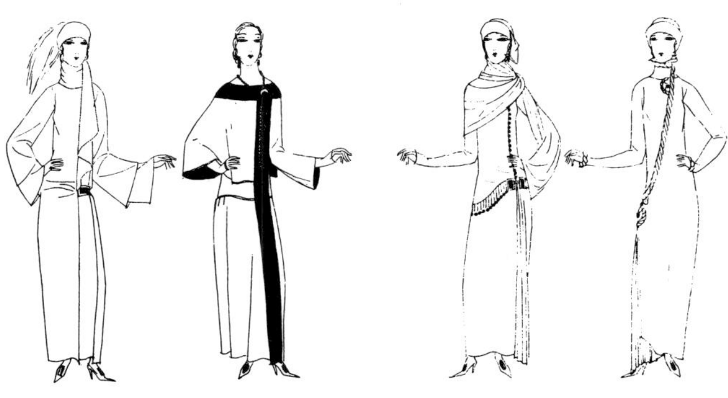

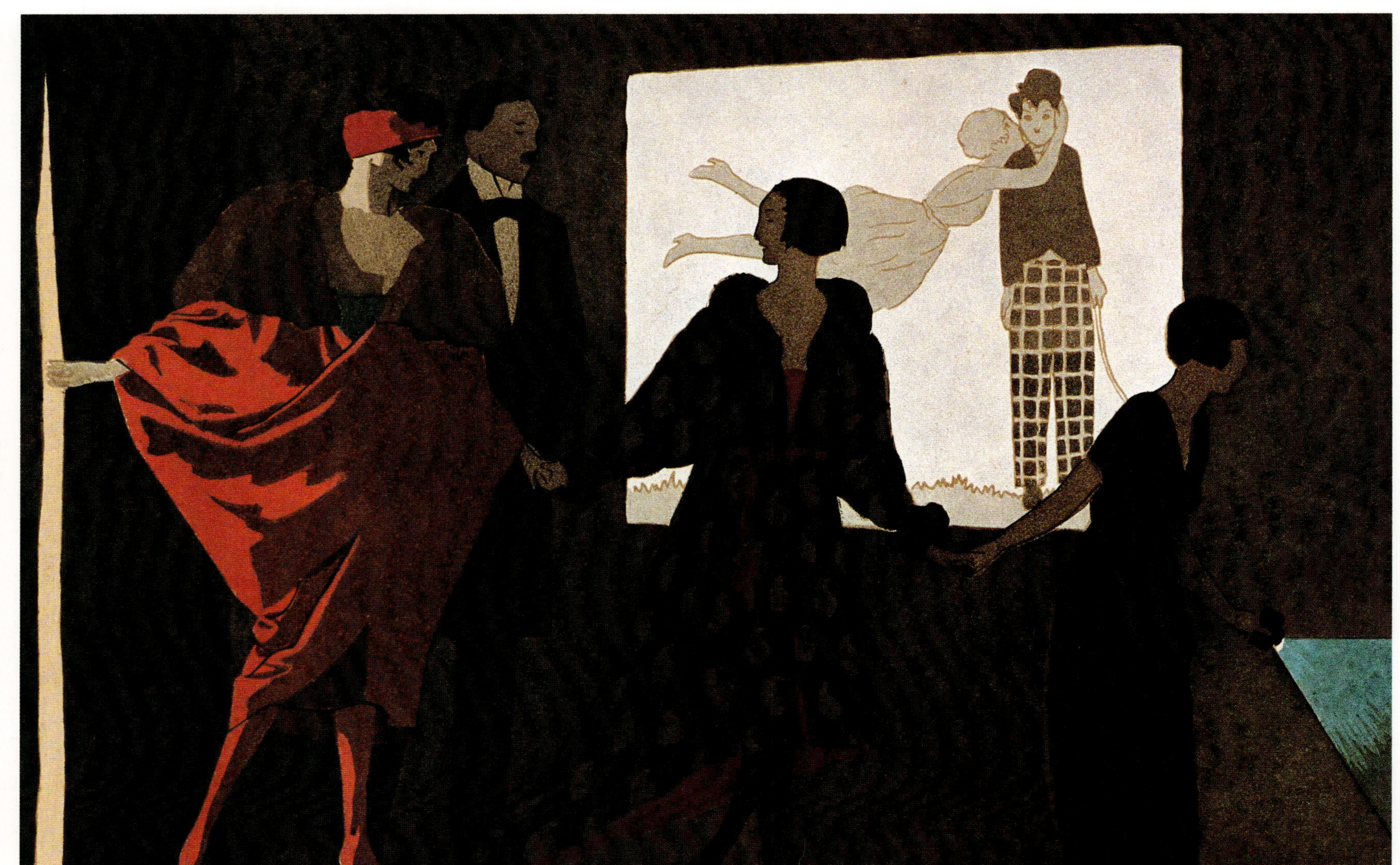

Pochoir illustration *Le Ciné* by André Marty, for *Modes et manières d'aujourd'hui*. Pierre Corrard, Paris. 1921.

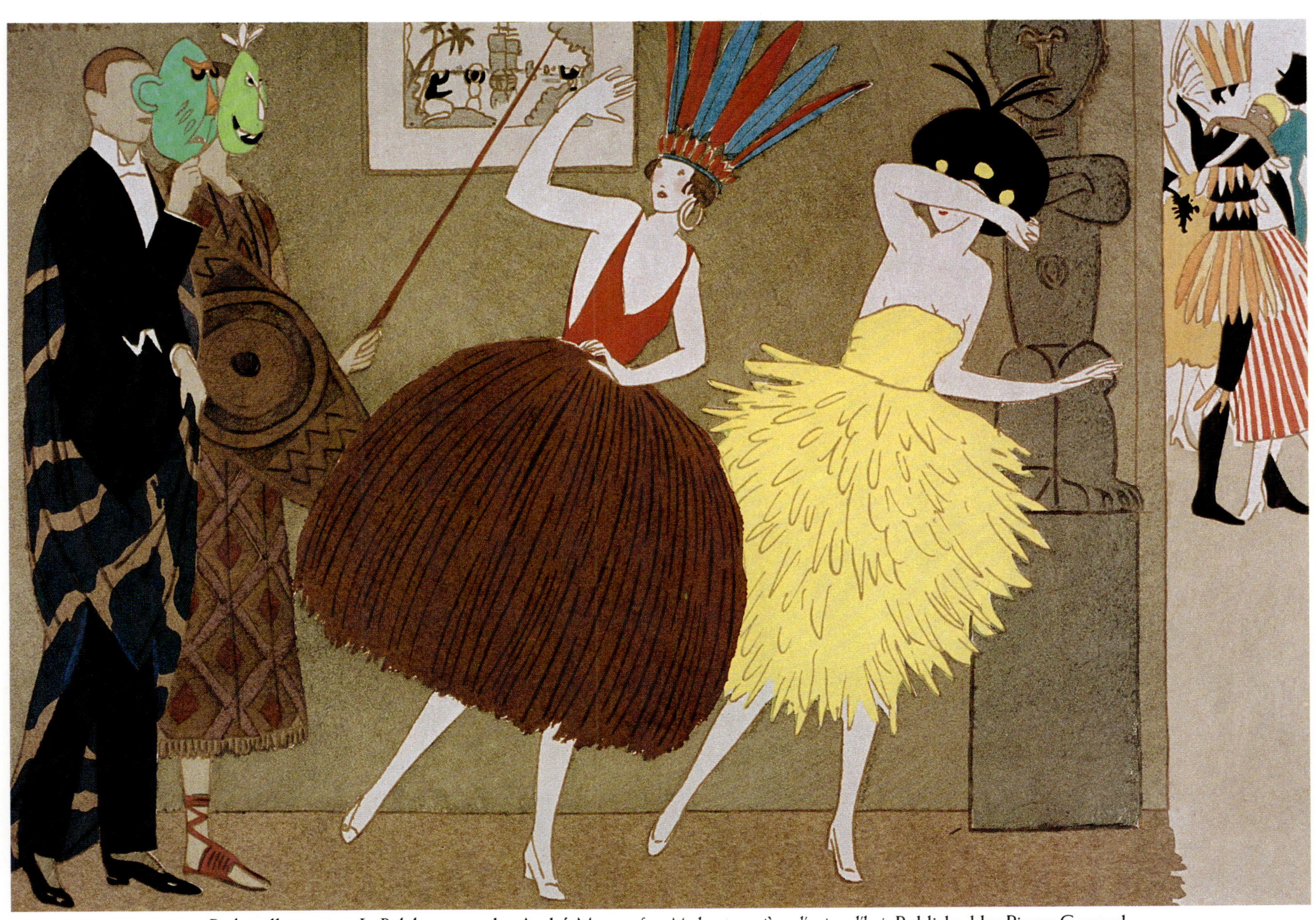

Pochoir illustration *Le Bal de sauvages* by André Marty, for *Modes et manières d'aujourd'hui*. Published by Pierre Corrard, Paris. 1921.

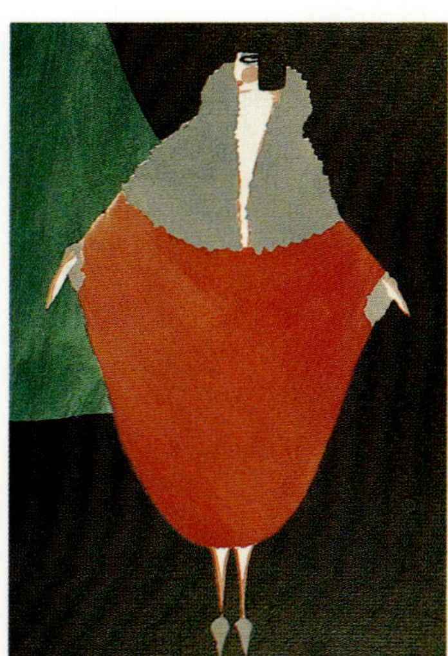

Pochoir illustration by Janine Aghion from *The Essence of the Mode of the Day*. Published by La Belle Editions, Paris. 1920.

The ideas, aspirations, lifestyles and dreams of this new generation of customers became the motivating force in the design styles produced by the couturiers, designers and master-craftsmen of 1920 — in fact, they had begun working towards a new mode of visual expression as soon as the wartime restrictions had been relaxed at the end of 1918. Although still within the general province of the pre-war Art Deco style, the new modes required a different vocabulary of visual ideas, based upon the concepts of exclusivity, modernity, extravagance and luxury. The designers pursued these goals single-mindedly.

Although not quite as aesthetically refined as the earlier Art Deco designs, the new designs were nevertheless full of vigour and inventiveness. And they possessed one feature that was especially striking, and which above all else differentiated them from many earlier works: the obvious avoidance of the pretty. The Art Deco pieces of the early 1920s were smart, elegant, stylish and luxurious — sometimes to the point of being brash — but they were never pretty. Prettiness was now considered the prerogative of the 'proletariat', who eagerly accepted it as a flow-on from the earlier Art Nouveau style and failed to understand the appeal of the new Art Deco designs. This, of course, helped to maintain the exclusiveness of the new style.

An embryonic version of this new 1920s Art Deco style had first appeared in the summer of 1915 when, in the midst of war, the Paris couturiers who had not been called upon to perform essential war work, decided to hold an exhibition of their latest wartime fashions at the 1915 San Francisco Panama Pacific International Exposition, to help boost French finances by increasing overseas demand for their fashionable merchandise. To promote this exhibition and the new wartime fashions, the publishers of *La Gazette du bon ton*, who had closed down their promotional activities in August 1914, produced a special deluxe edition containing twelve sumptuous *pochoir* illustrations by Drian, Lepape and Barbier, who had been released from their wartime duties to undertake the task. One month after the publication of this edition in June 1915, a facsimile edition was published by Condé Nast (the publishers of *Vogue*), using coloured litho plates instead of the *pochoirs*, and including the only photographs ever used in any of these luxurious publications. The editors of the *Gazette* proudly stated,

Although a part of French soil is yet in the hands of the invaders, Paris remains as ever the Paris of good taste and fashion. Therefore, in spite of the glorious trials of war, and in order that Paris may retain her accustomed rank in every 'Exposition', the following great and justly renowned dressmakers have sent to San Francisco their latest and most stylish creations — Beer; Callot; Chéruit; Doeuillet; Doucet; Jenny; Jeanne Lanvin; Martial et Armand; Paquin; Premet; Worth.

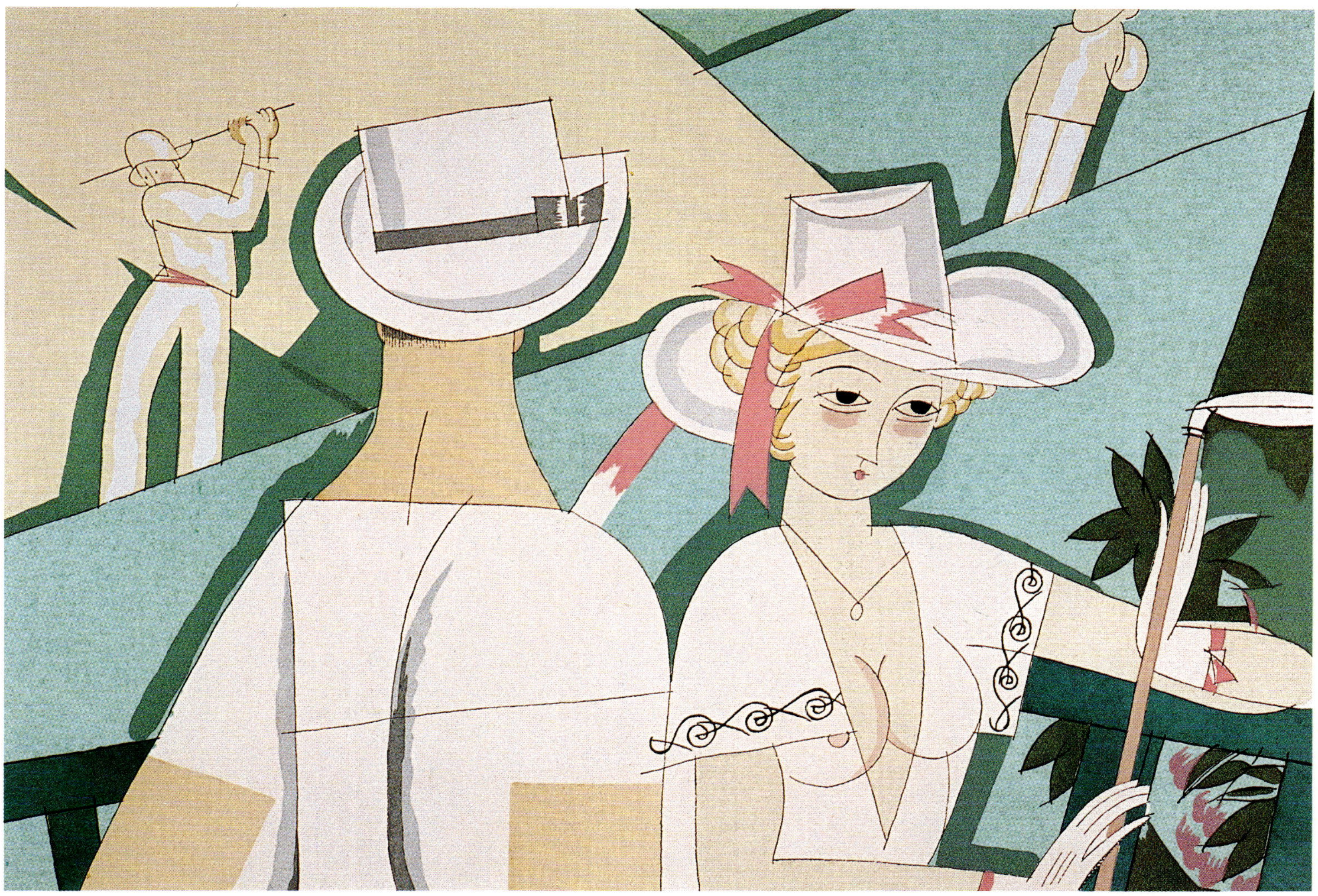

Pochoir illustration *Le Golf* by Charles Martin, for *Sports et divertissements*. Deluxe edition of 225 copies. Published by Lucien Vogel, Paris. 1920.

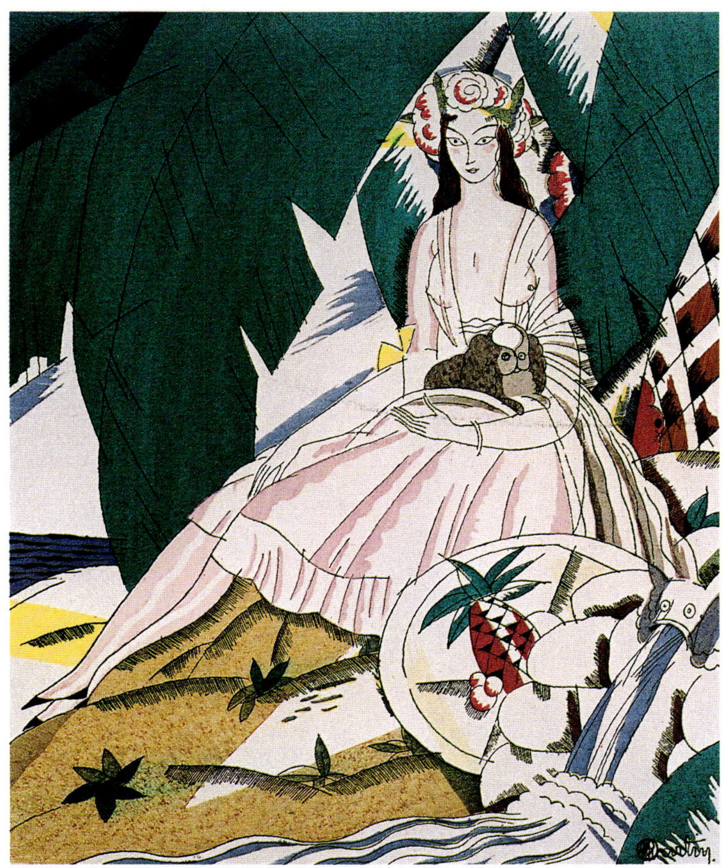

Pochoir illustration *La Belle Torquatienne* by Charles Martin, for *La Gazette du bon ton*. Paris. 1920.

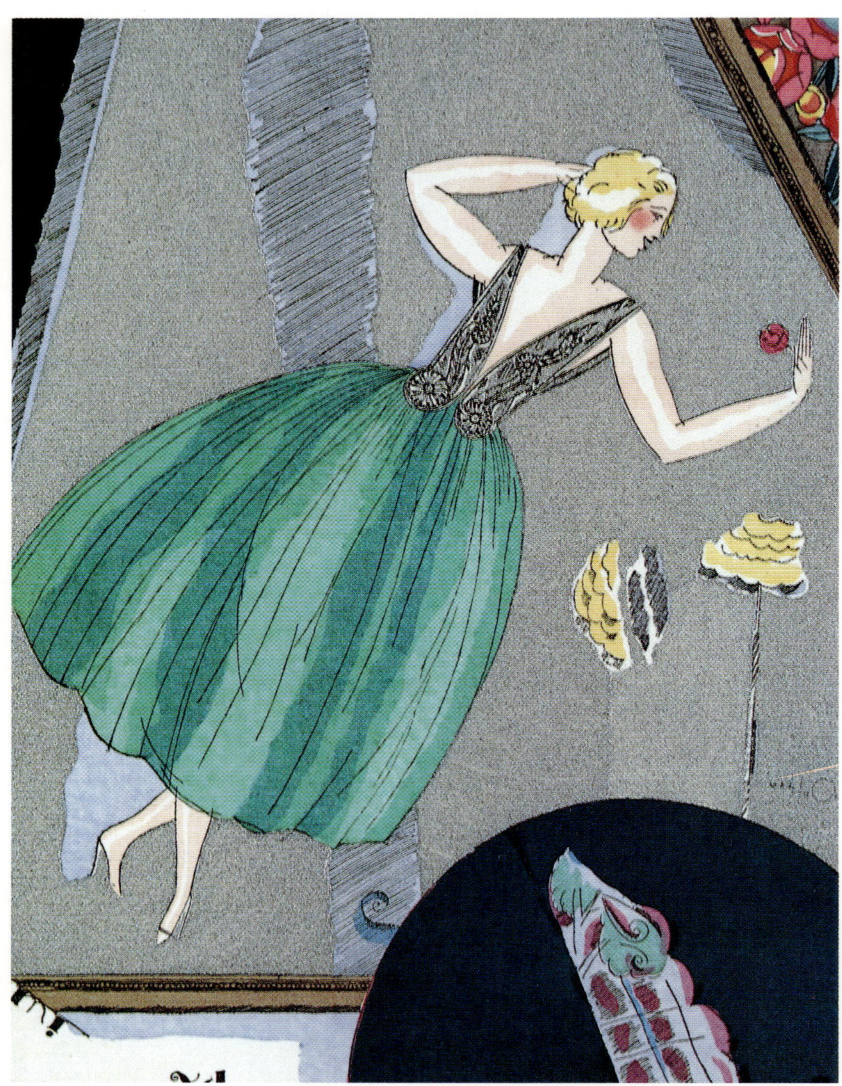

Pochoir illustration *Mirage* by Mario Simon (*robe du soir* by Paul Poiret), for *La Gazette du bon ton*. Paris. 1920.

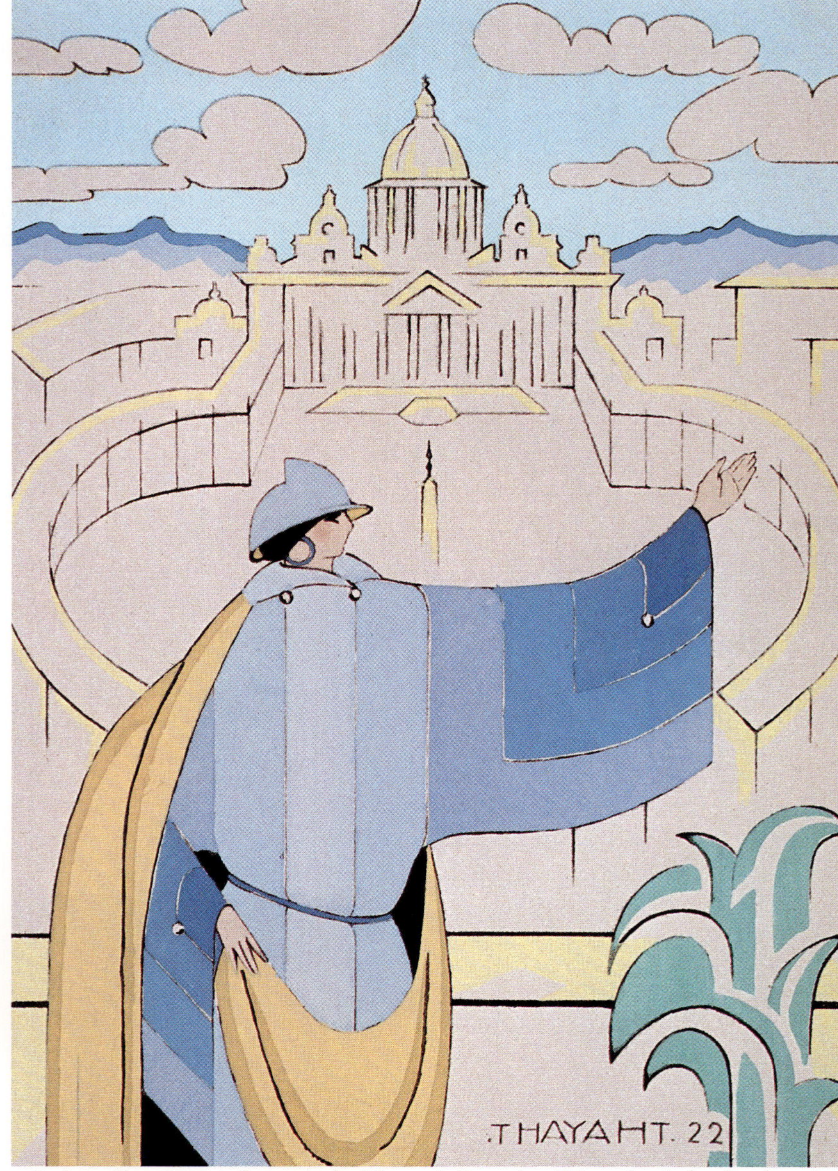

Pochoir illustration *Souvenir de Pâques à Rome* by Thayaht (*robe d'après-midi* by Madeleine Vionnet), for *La Gazette du bon ton*. Paris. 1922

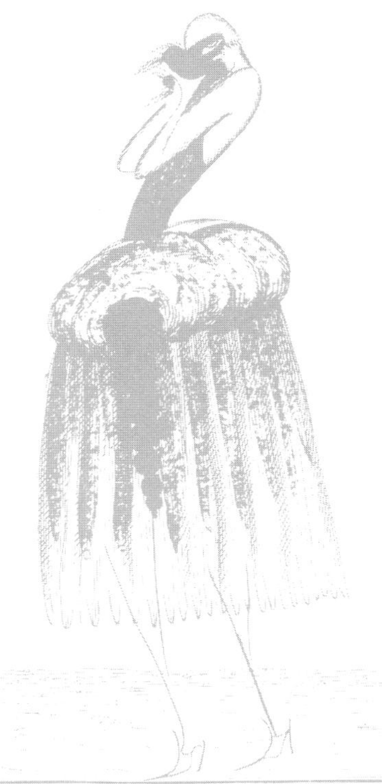

(Vionnet had closed her couture house for the duration of the war so that she could devote her energies to the war effort, and Poiret had joined the army as a military tailor.)

In August 1915 Lucien Vogel launched a new deluxe magazine, *Le Style parisien*, aimed at the American market and intended to further boost the export of the new French fashions. And at the beginning of 1919 two new fashion magazines containing high quality *pochoir* illustrations in the Art Deco style were initiated by the French designers: *La Guirlande d'art et de la littérature*, under the guiding hand of Umberto Brunelleschi and limited to 800 copies per monthly issue, and *Les Feuillets d'art*, Lucien Vogel's new venture. Vogel's *La Gazette du bon ton* also reappeared as a regular monthly magazine in February 1920, sponsored by the couture houses of Chéruit, Doeuillet, Doucet, Lanvin, Poiret, Worth, Paquin and Redfern; a little later it was expanded to include the houses of Beer, Martial et Armand, Madeleine Vionnet, Camille Rogers, the milliner Martha Collot, the menswear designers Lus et Bèfre, Kriegck and Larsen, the jeweller Cartier, the car manufacturer Renault, and the fabric merchants Bianchini and Ducharne.

Another deluxe fashion magazine appeared at the beginning of 1920: *Le Goût du jour* was limited to 1400 numbered copies, and a new group of illustrators was also introduced, among them Raoul Dufy, Edouard Halouze, Martha Romme, Edouardo Bénito, Fernand Siméon, Mario Simon, José Zinoview, Marcelle Pichon, Robert Bonfils, Thayaht, Jean-Emile Laboureur, Charles Guérin, Jean Dulac, Gabriel Daragnes and Janine Aghion. A number of the pre-war artists also continued as regular contributors: illustrations by George Barbier, André Marty, Charles Martin and Georges Lepape were regularly featured. The changing mood of the post-war times was reflected in the new emphasis being given in the text to contemporary lifestyles, travel, the theatre and music. Articles on such subjects as *'Le Jazz americain'* and *'Le Mouvement moderniste'* took precedence over the promotion of the luxury elements of the new Art Deco design style.

Lucien Vogel also started a glossy magazine, *Le Jardin des modes*, to rival the American-owned publications *Vogue* and *Harpers Bazaar*, which had begun to use many of Vogel's original artists for their covers, notably Georges Lepape for *Vogue* and Erté for *Harpers Bazaar*. Vogel also published a number of limited-edition deluxe books, one of which — *Sports et divertissements* — was illustrated in the Cubist style by Charles Martin.

The changing times were also reflected in the new visual language used by many of the other illustrators. Their stylised drawings often defied the laws of traditional perspective; some of them were deliberate attempts to outrage middle-class sensibilities; others had developed a simplicity of flat linear patterning that was then offset by an intricacy of decoration; still others utilised broad areas of bright colouring overlaid

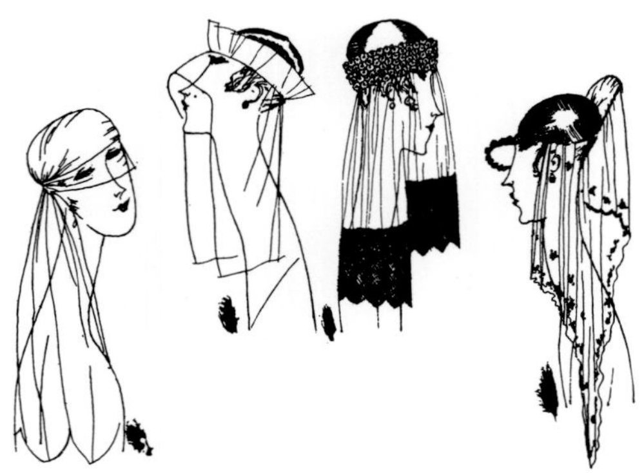

with metallic pigments such as bronze, gold silver and copper on a very simplified two-dimensional illustration.

But most of the illustrative styles remained obviously influenced by the Japanese *ukiyo-e* prints of the eighteenth and early nineteenth centuries, and by earlier Chinese calligraphic pictures, with their absence of centralised perspective and traditional receding planes, their asymmetrical compositioning, often with diagonal interest, and with a powerful visual tension created by the juxtaposition of flat textured surfaces and bright colours in the foreground. Some illustrators of the early 1920s added interest to their illustrations with a mixture of horizontal and vertical patterns that were cut off at the edge of the picture, giving the effect that they were floating and thereby achieving a detached viewpoint that heightened the intensity of the design. Other illustrators chose to use a particular pose or gesture to subtly add an almost imperceptible touch of eroticism or a risqué piquance to an otherwise straightforward rendering.

Following the lessons of the *ukiyo-e* artists, the illustrators articulated their figures to portray a particular mood, heightening this mood by the use of colour and patterning and with just a few bold linear strokes to stimulate the observer's interest. Sometimes they gave the middle-ground figures the same emphasis as those in the foreground, with each figure being isolated like a statue on a floating stage — frozen yet mobile, exemplifying the *ukiyo-e* mood of the kabuki theatre. Other illustrators appear to have been guided by the teachings of Su Tung-po, the eleventh century Chinese poet who had written about the powers of memory when illustrating from nature:

Before you paint the bamboo you must first of all imagine how it looks to you in your mind. Only then take up your brush, concentrate your attention and keep what you want to represent clearly before your mind's eye. Go to work with a will and make speed with your brush. Select only what you have perceived, for just as the bird of prey swoops when it has seen the hare, so your eyes must fasten on its object. If you hesitate for only an instant it will be too late.

This method of direct but imaginative drawing, as distinct from the line-by-line rendering typical of so many previous European styles, became an important addition to the illustrator's armoury in the 1920s. It was to develop even further and become a major influence in the 1930s when adopted by the illustrators Eric, R. B. Willaumez, René Bouché and Marcel Vertès.

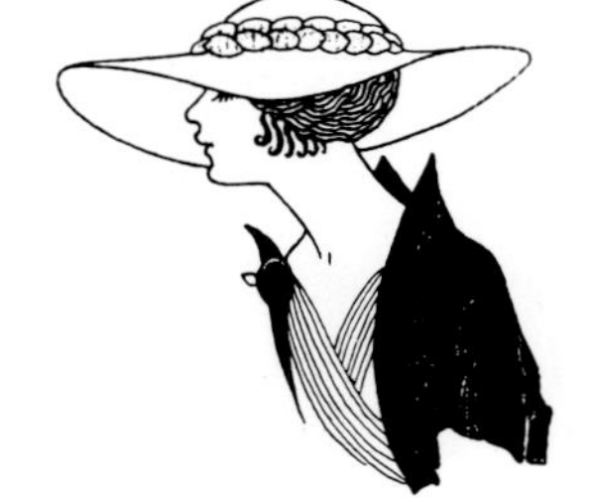

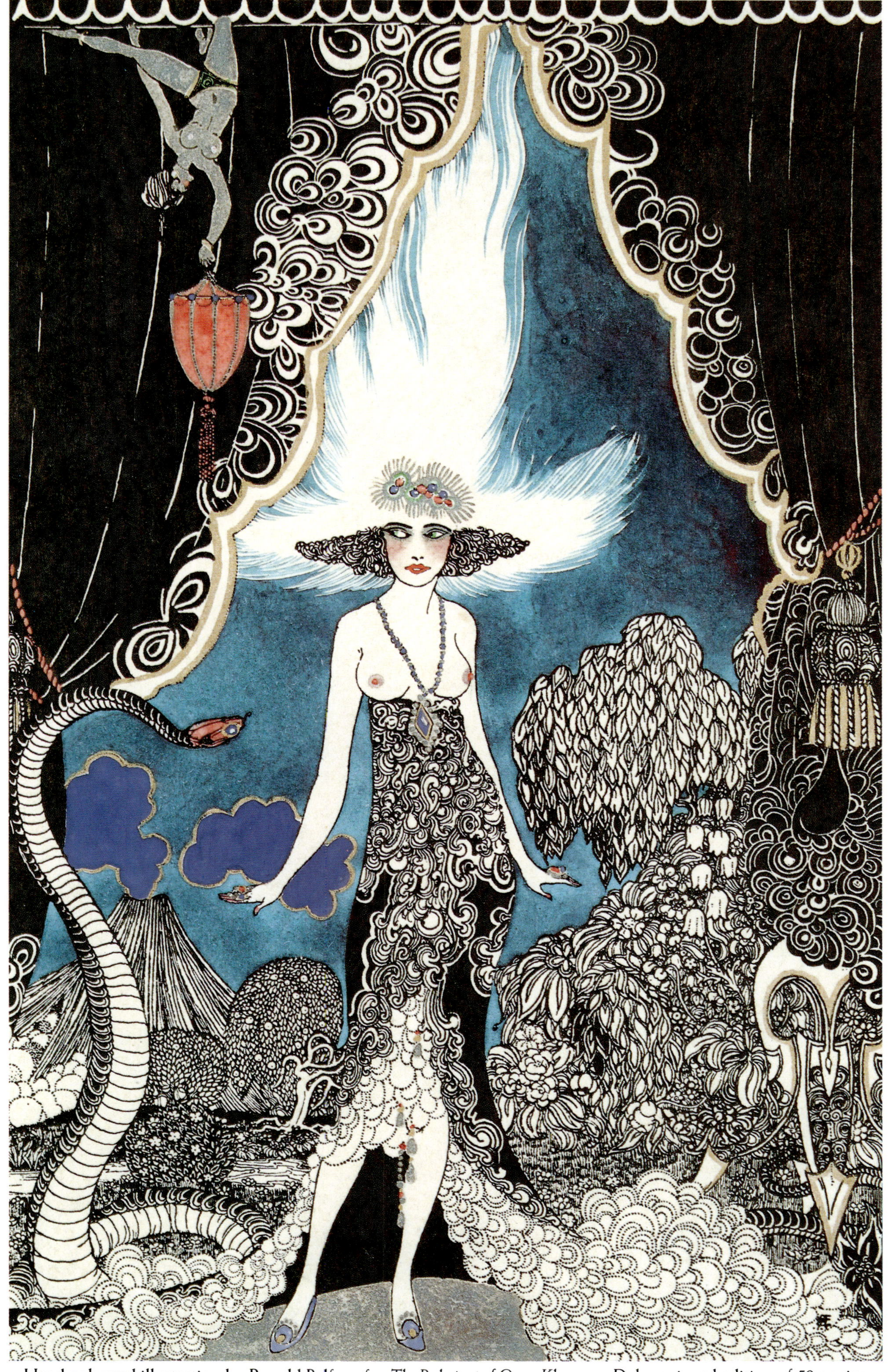

Hand-coloured illustration by Ronald Balfour for *The Rubaiyat of Omar Khayyam*. Deluxe signed edition of 50 copies. Published by Constable & Co. Ltd., London. 1920.

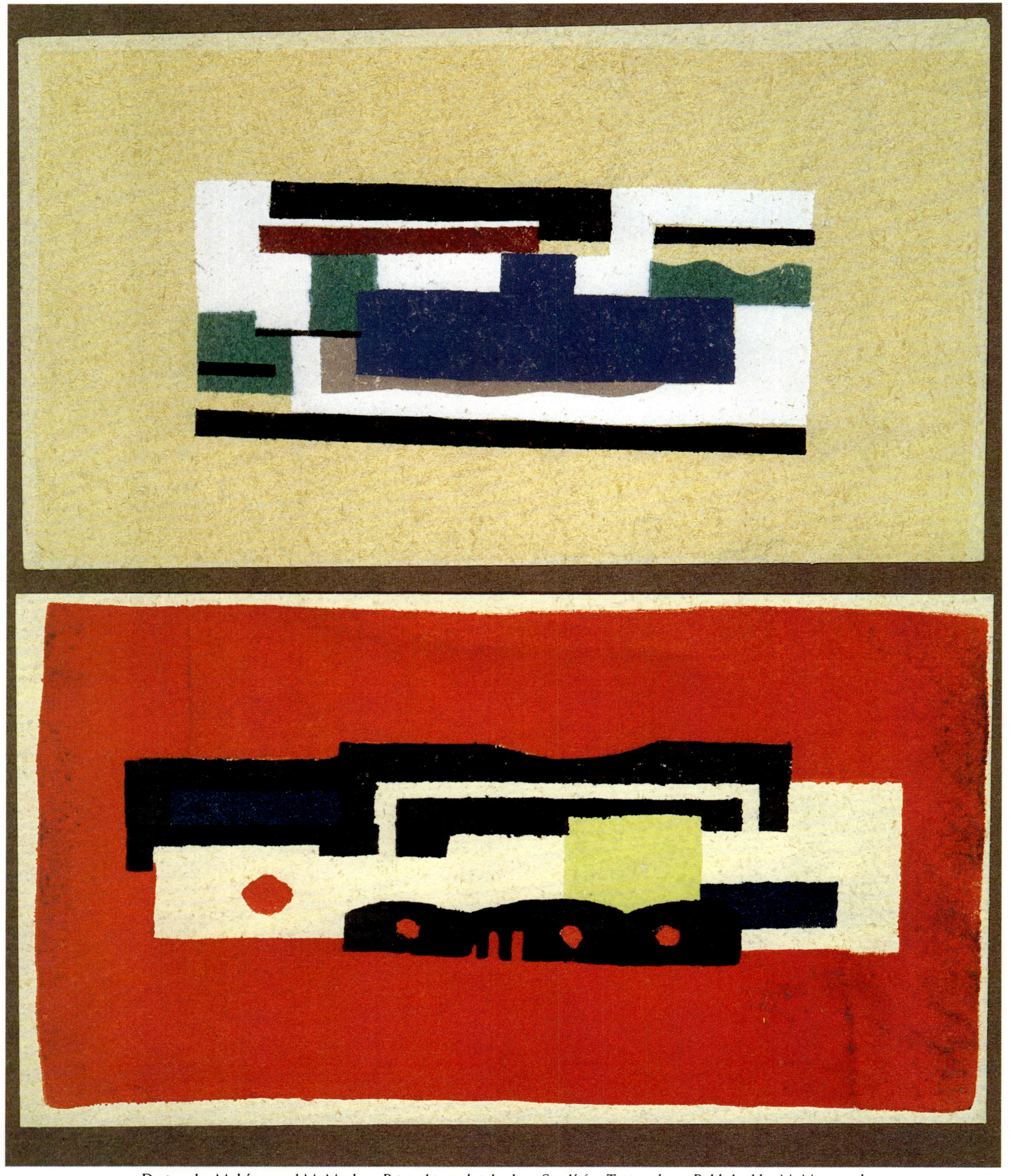

Designs by M. Léger and M. Myrbor. Printed in *pochoir* by Jean Saudé for *Tapis modernes*. Published by M. Matet and H. Ernst, Paris. 1926.

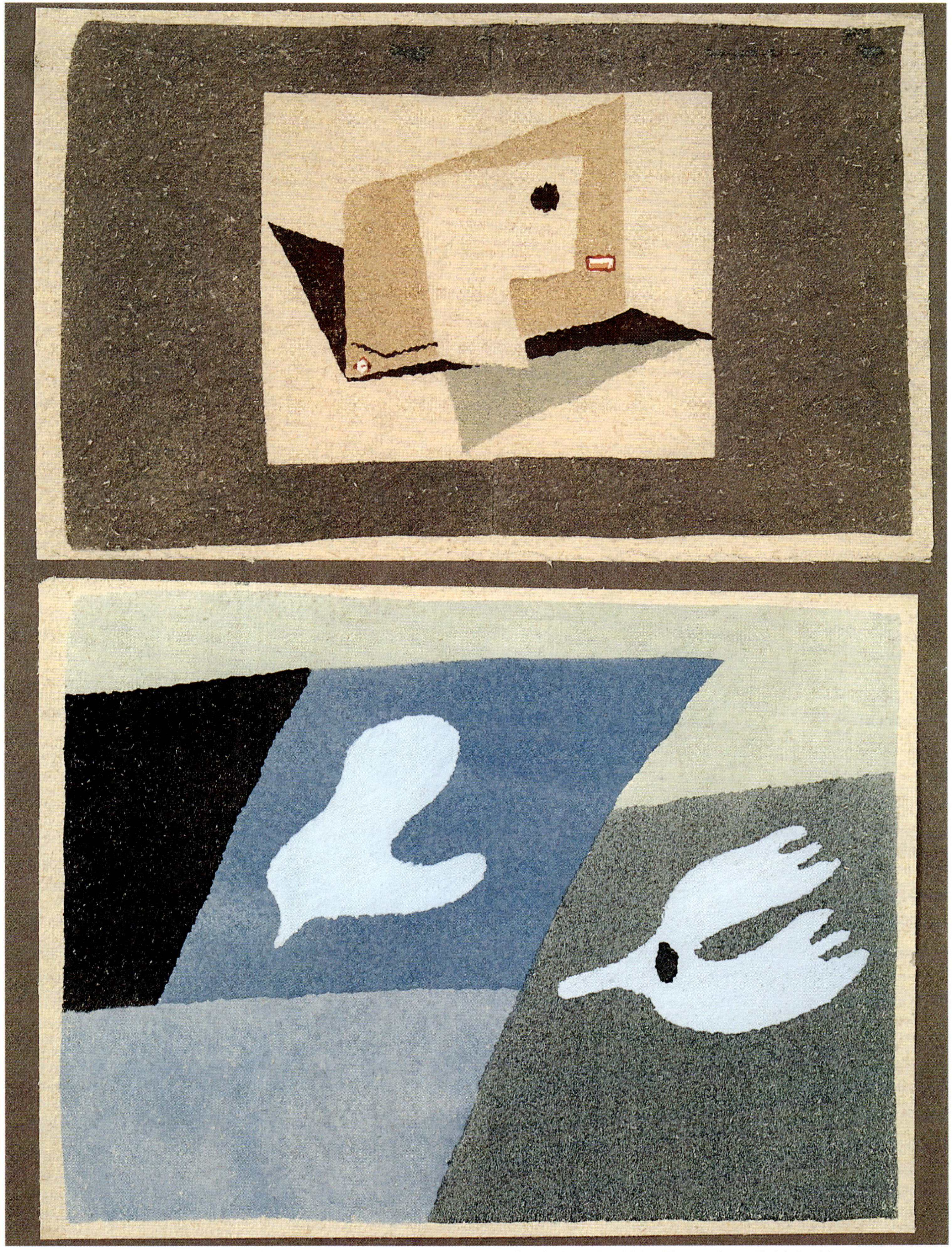

Carpet designs by Pablo Picasso and Jean Arp. Printed in *pochoir* by Jean Saudé for *Tapis modernes*. Published by M. Matet and H. Ernst, Paris. 1926.

In fact, by the 1920s the illustrators had finally thrown away the European dictatorship of naturalistic illusionism and, instead of employing the single perspective obtained from a fixed viewpoint, they created their illusions by directing the observer's eye towards the distant or middle ground. This they did by arranging foreground objects that were so close to the observer that they had to be cut off at the edges of the picture to form a kind of frame. The distinct swing away from the imitative photographic style of drawing allowed the illustrators to use their skill to perform a valuable mediating role, bringing to a wider public the latest developments in Art Deco design and haute couture, and enabling the public to more readily accept these styles.

Moreover, the inventiveness of these artists in composing the right style and setting for each of their *pochoir* illustrations had a distinct influence on subsequent Art Deco design, affecting not only the couturiers (who by their nature were always ready to pick up the latest nuances and variations), but also the designers of furniture, textiles, carpets, ceramics, and all manner of other items. This interaction between designers, couturiers, illustrators and artists had in fact been a two-way affair since the experimental forms of Art Deco of the early 1900s, when the Fauves and Cubists introduced an oriental influence gleaned from the *ukiyo-e* prints. This accustomed the public to accepting a new mode of visual expression, and in turn encouraged many painters and sculptors to experiment with other non-European styles, thus increasing the momentum of change.

New techniques of photography were also beginning to have an effect on the illustrative styles featured in the deluxe magazines, portfolios and books of the 1920s. Baron Gayne de Meyer and Edward Steichen had both developed their own distinctive methods of creating attractive photographic images for magazine reproduction, using staged studio settings and original lighting techniques. The three French brothers Jules, Louis and Henri Seeberger, on the other hand, were specialising in outdoor photography without the aid of special lighting, recording the daily happenings at fashionable sporting events and ritzy resorts where the elegant women and their wealthy consorts gathered to be photographed for the weekly society magazines.

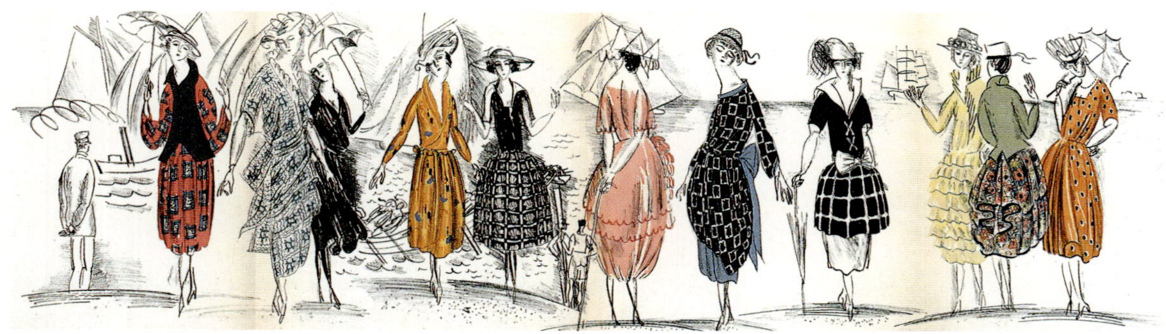

Chromo-litho illustration *Robes pour l'été 1920* by Raoul Dufy, for Bianchini Férier and *La Gazette du bon ton*. Paris. 1920.

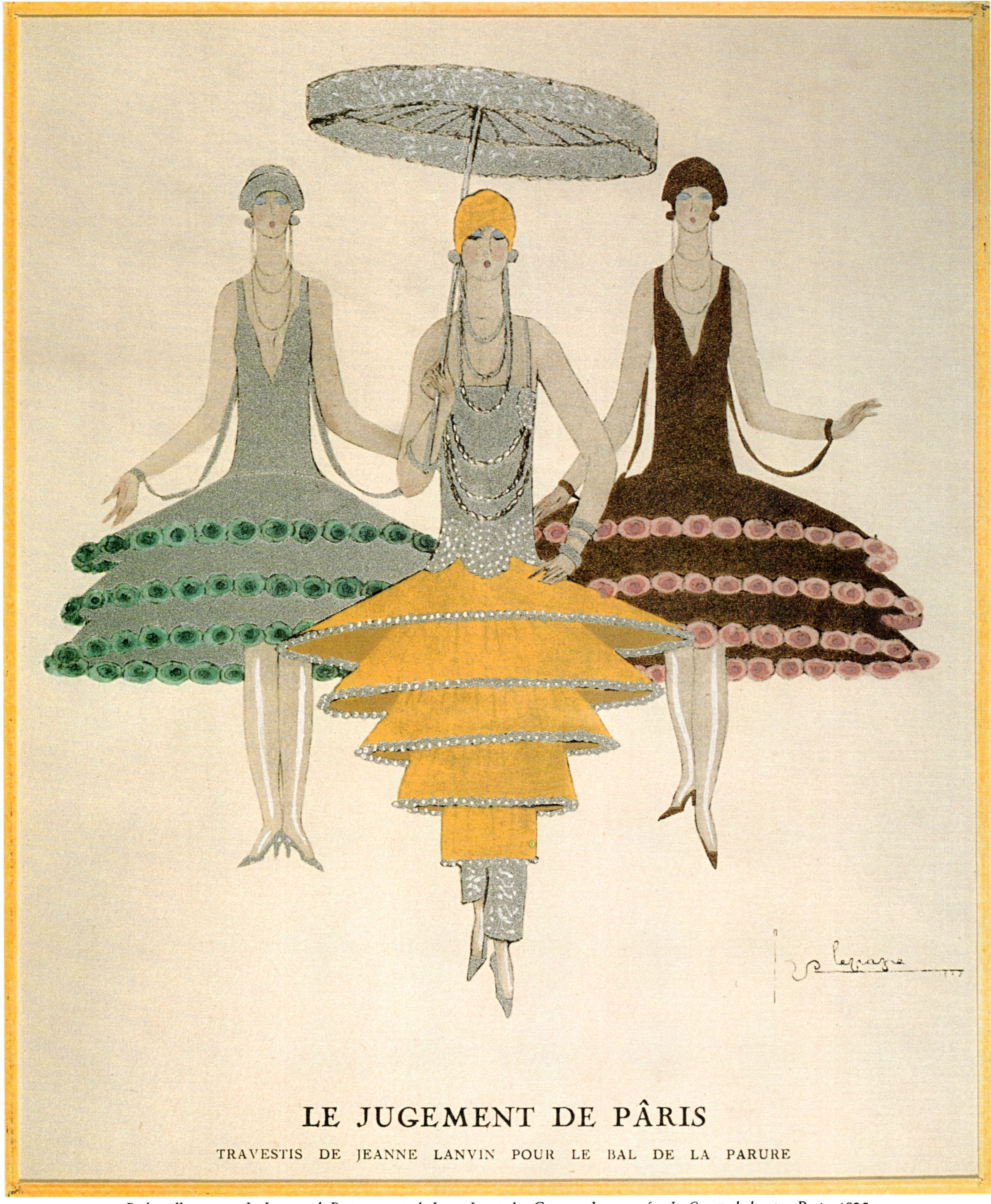

Pochoir illustration *Le Jugement de Paris: travestis de Jeanne Lanvin* by Georges Lepape, for *La Gazette du bon ton*. Paris. 1925.

Other photographers specialised in advertising photography, creating images of the latest glass pieces, jewellery or ceramics, and a few were creating images of an erotic nature. Erotic photography was not new in France; the open sale of such images had encouraged a number of authors to publish limited-edition copies of their erotic novels, many of which were illustrated with witty and amusing illustrations that today are collectors' items. Among the more notable publications were *Nous deux*, published in two volumes in 1925 as a limited edition of 295 copies with illustrations by Jean Dulac; Pierre Louy's erotic lesbian novel *Le Chanson de Bilitis*, illustrated by George Barbier and limited to 133 copies; *Mémoires d'une chanteuse*, with a preface by Helpey (the pseudonym of Louis Perceau) and limited to 240 copies; and *Lettres à la Présidente et galanteries poétiques*, by Louis Perceau.

The early 1920s produced a noticeable change in attitudes toward sex. There were many reasons for this. Four years of war had accustomed men to living mainly with other men. Younger women had become accustomed to doing without men at all; they had found a great deal of independence in working; and there was more accessibility of information about birth-control methods. Sexuality was being exploited in the cinema in such films as Cecil B. DeMille's *Male and Female* and *Forbidden Fruit* and almost weekly sex scandals and reports of licentiousness emanated from Hollywood. The feminine form was openly displayed at the Ziegfeld Follies and numerous nude shows were also a major attraction in Paris. The fact that homosexual relationships were still illegal, and therefore risqué, novel and fashionable, made all sorts of love affairs and sexual liaisons, including lesbianism and certain forms of incest, unusually prevalent, and even socially acceptable, during the early 1920s.

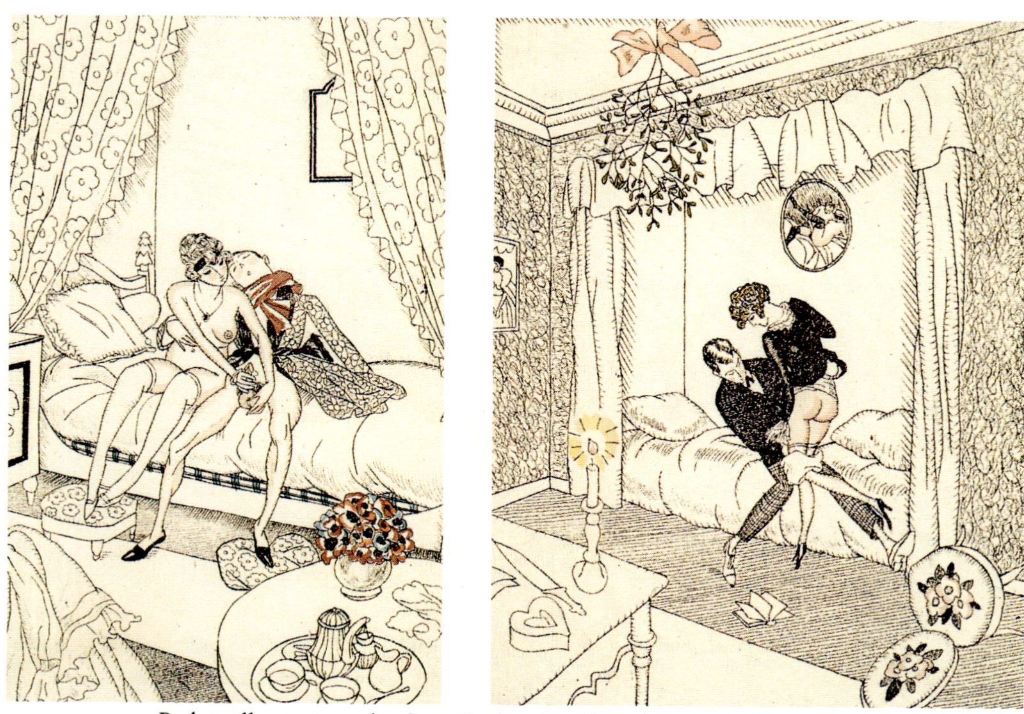

Pochoir illustrations by Jean Dulac for *Nous deux* by Nelly et Jean. Deluxe edition of 295 copies. Paris, 1925.

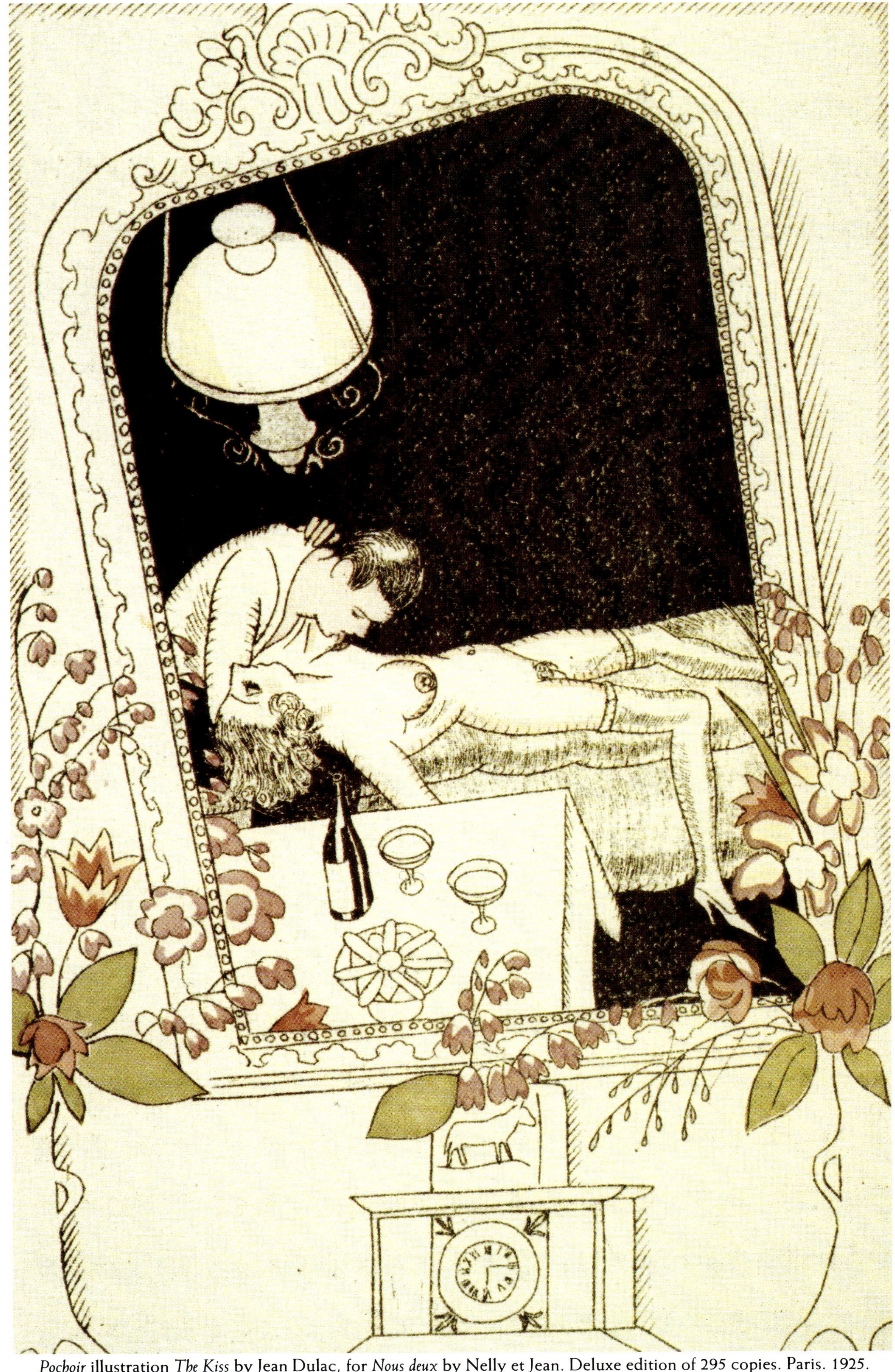

Pochoir illustration *The Kiss* by Jean Dulac, for *Nous deux* by Nelly et Jean. Deluxe edition of 295 copies. Paris. 1925.

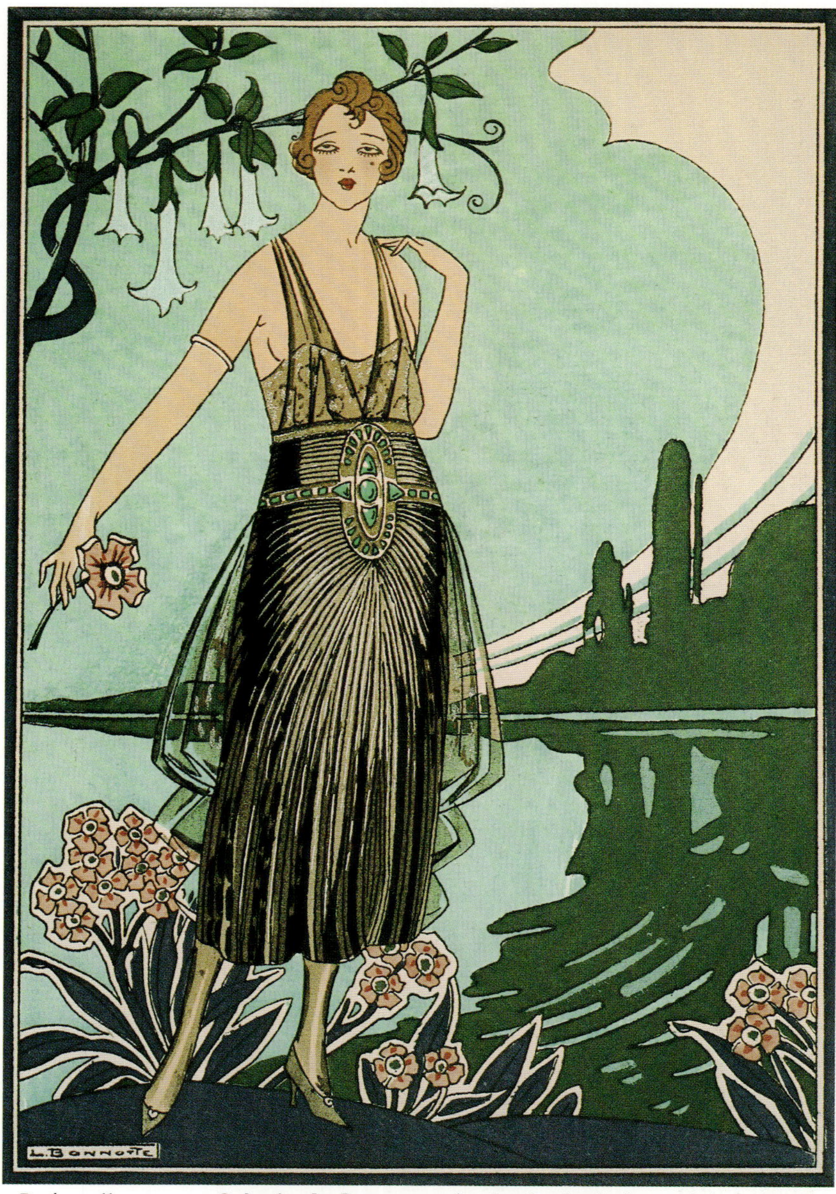

Pochoir illustration *Sirène* by L. Bonnotte, for *La Guirlande d'art et de la littérature*. Paris. 1920.

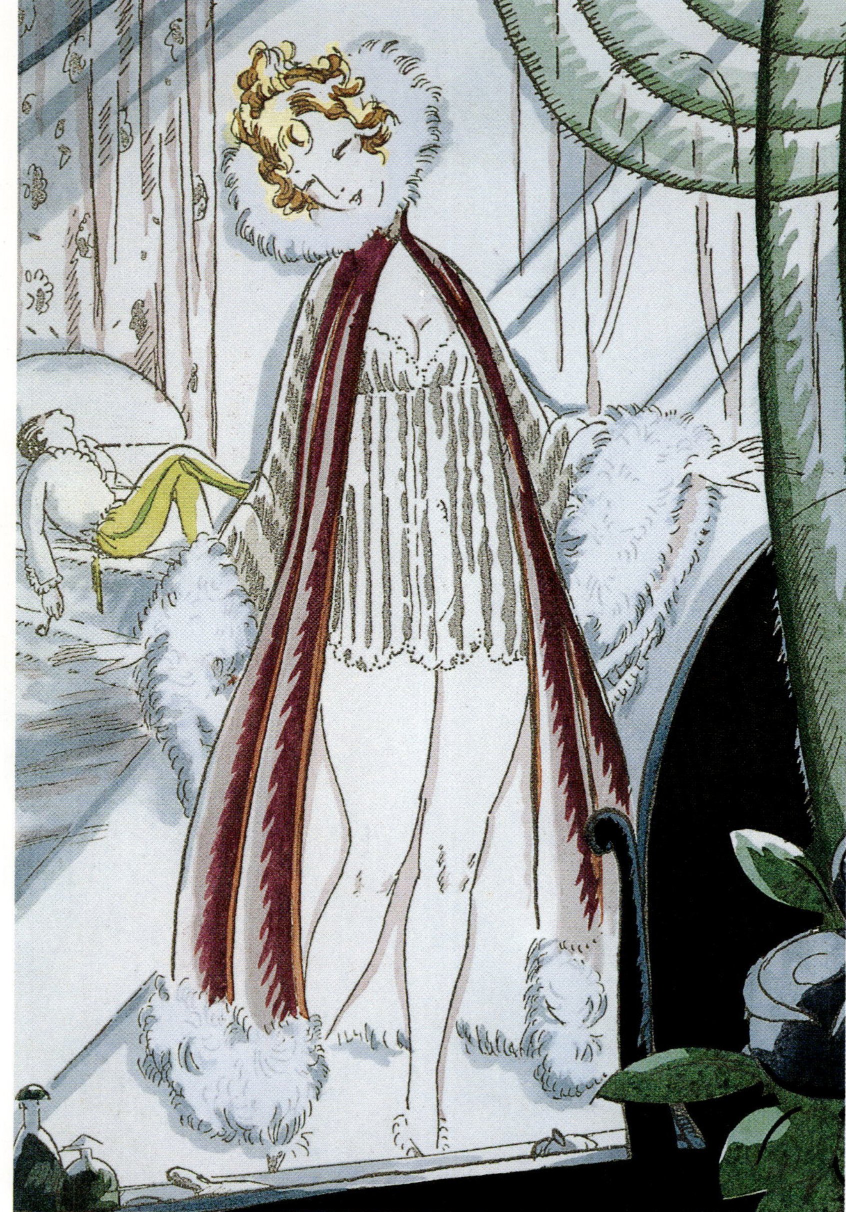

Pochoir illustration *La Robe d'amour* by Robert Bonfils, for *Modes et manières d'aujourd'hui*. Paris. 1922.

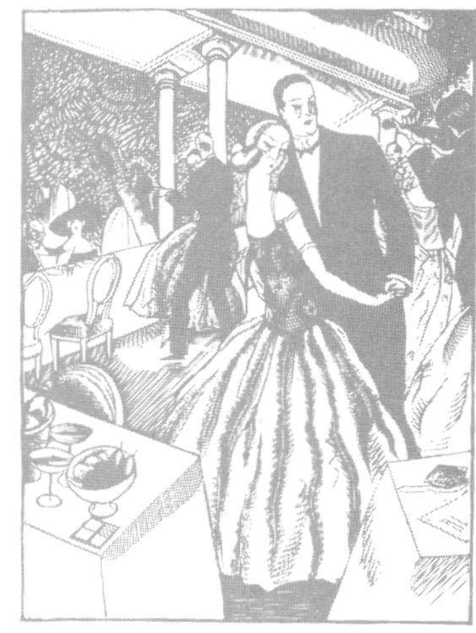

Fashions, of course, reflected this relaxed attitude in various ways: see-through dresses were introduced; delicate decorative lingerie was worn, often with the intention that it be glimpsed under the ever shortening skirts; wide-legged French knickers with a buttoned crotch became fashionable; topless bathing suits were introduced for wear on exclusive Riviera beaches or remote South Sea islands; the use of facial make-up simulated the look of sexual arousal; mannish, tailored suits, often with trousers, were worn by avant-garde actresses and society hostesses; and phallic and other erotic symbols were used in textile designs and promotional drawings.

Today, of course, we are accustomed to these types of fashionable apparel and the sexual connotations of much of the advertising we hear and see. It seems strange that pretty lingerie, for instance, or the use of lipstick and rouge should be thought of as indecent. But decorative underclothing and facial make-up were relatively new in the 1920s, and many of the older generation regarded such apparel and decoration as fit only for courtesans, divorcees, and 'scarlet' women — women of easy virtue who wore scarlet lipstick as a mark of their trade. It may surprise readers to learn that the lips redden quite naturally during sexual arousal: they become engorged with blood, mimicking the change that is taking place in the genitalia; this is why the wearing of lipstick is sexually appealing. It may also surprise readers that the wearing of any form of bifurcated underclothing on the lower parts of the female body, under the traditional flannel and linen petticoats, had been a hotly debated moral issue throughout most of the nineteenth century, the clergy and many moralists condemning such garments as being against the laws of God.

The wearing of perfume also horrified many of the older generation. Magazine and newspaper reports spoke of 'the creeping influence of mass-produced Hollywood glamour' and letters of complaint were regularly published. It would seem that many people of the early 1920s supported the notion that perfumes and facial make-up were 'the work of the devil', as was proposed in the mid-eighteenth century when an attempt was made in the British House of Commons to forbid 'all women of whatever rank or profession, whether virgin, maid or widow, to seduce and betray into matrimony any of her Majesty's subjects by scent, paint, powder or any other form of artifice', under penalty of fine or imprisonment.

But despite the attacks of the moralists, religious leaders, and many of the older generation — who attacked everything from the 'licentiousness' of the new styles of dancing and the depravity of the works of artists such as Picasso and Modigliani and the avant-garde writers to the loathsome motor car and the corrupting radio — the deluxe publications continued to feature such topics, with interesting editorials and articles and eye-catching illustrations.

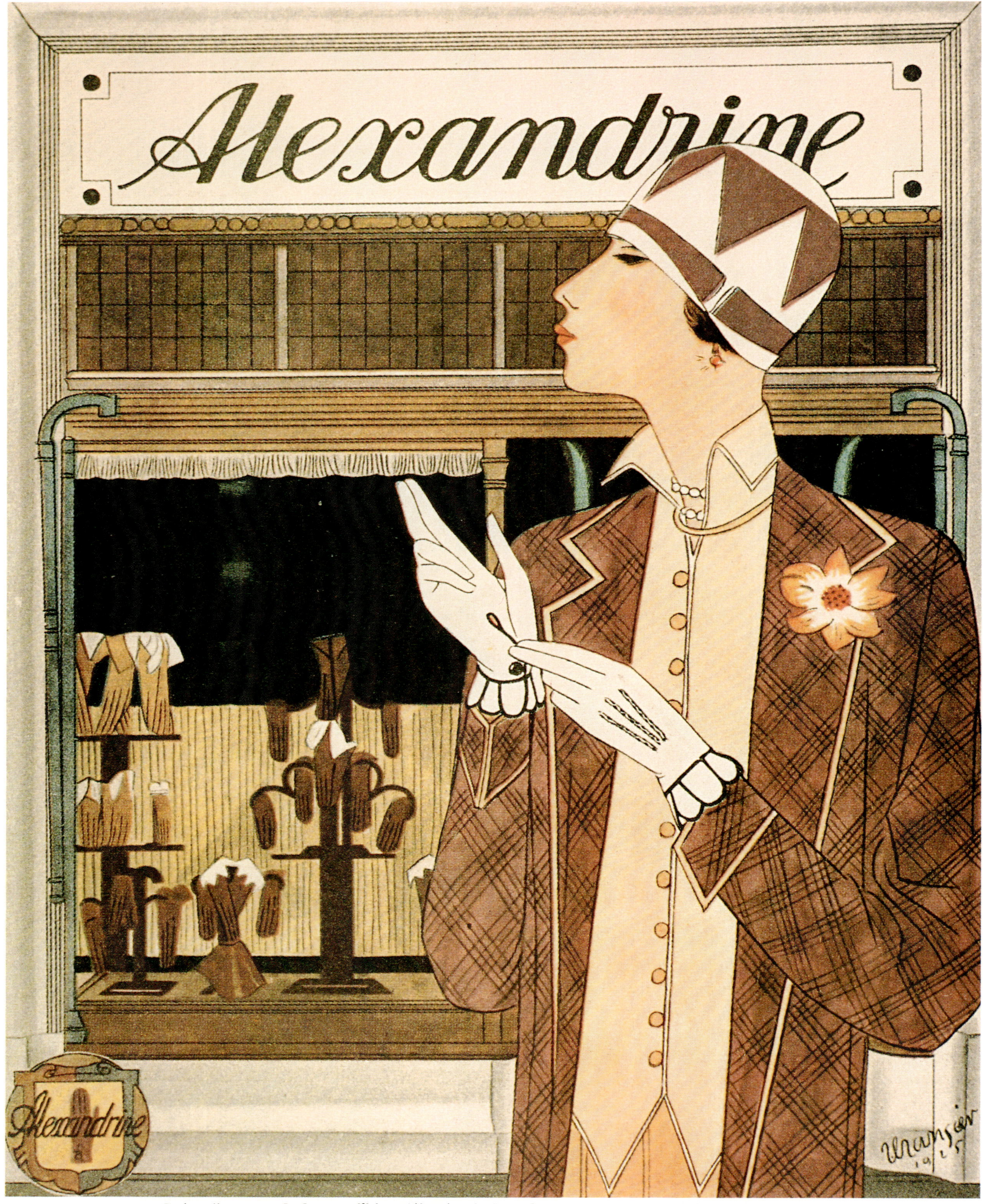

Pochoir illustration *Le Gantier préféré par Aléxandrine* by Jean Grangier, for *La Gazette du bon ton*. Paris. 1925.

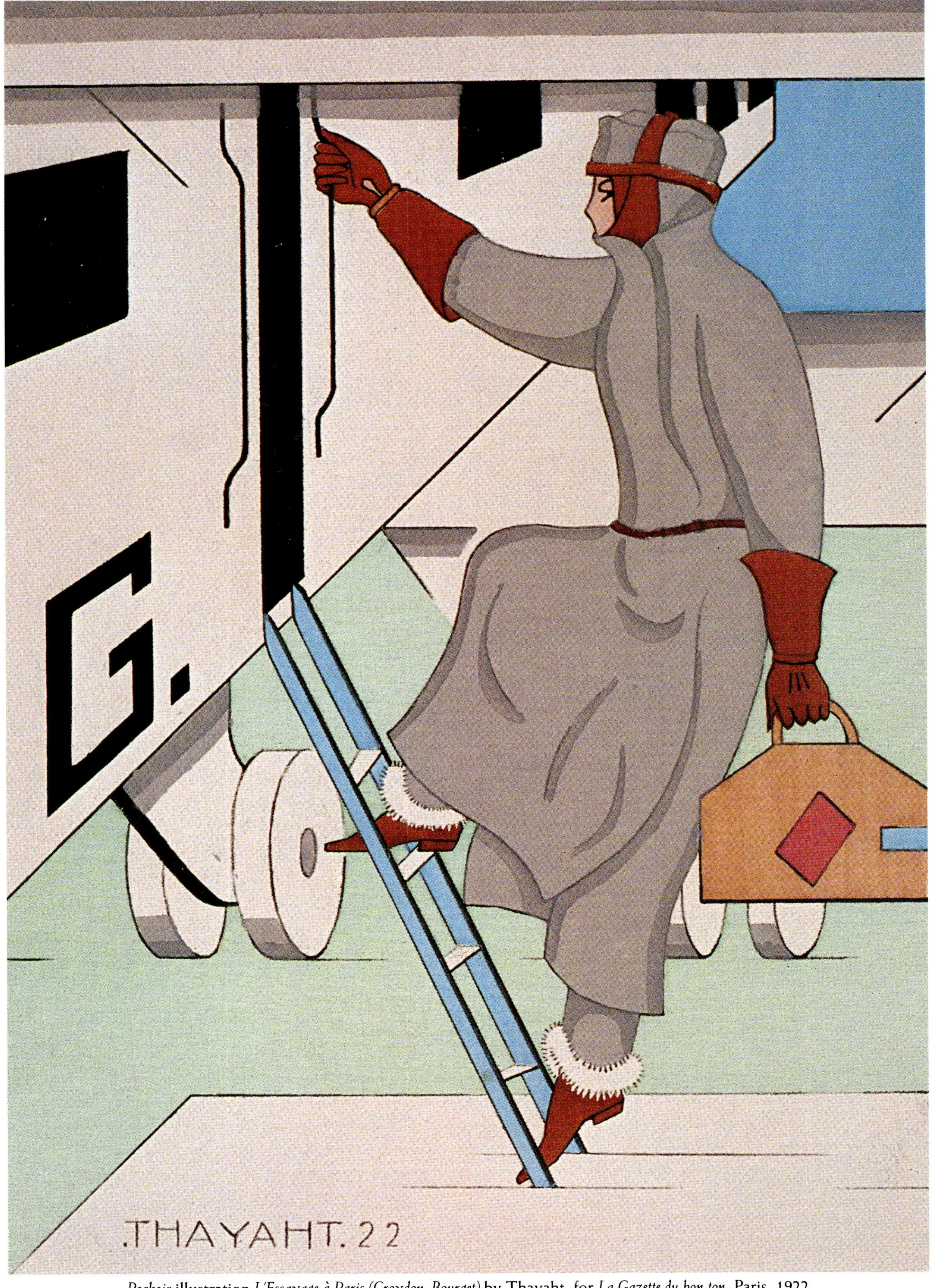

Pochoir illustration *L'Essayage à Paris (Croydon–Bourget)* by Thayaht, for *La Gazette du bon ton*. Paris. 1922.

The couturiers of the 1920s catered for the changes taking place by producing a wide range of fashionable styles within the currently accepted mode, and the illustrators worked hard to produce images that conveyed the new ideas, needs and aspirations of the society in which they lived and worked.

Such images were, in fact, the medium best suited to catch and preserve the flavour of the era: the skilled artists and illustrators were contemporary commentators, and it is through their eyes and depictive skills that we are best able to savour the time. Many of the illustrations are purely fanciful; others are more straightforward and factual; still others are ironic, bizarre, eccentric or grossly exaggerated. Collectively, though, they bring visual balance to the written commentary of that golden age, enabling us to come to terms with a particular period in our history and to enjoy the wide range of visual images that seems to expose the very essence of Art Deco.

As for the individual images themselves, the actual method of reproducing them by the labour-intensive *pochoir* process had also undergone a number of changes as the skilled *pochoirists* continued to experiment with different methods. Serigraphy, a form of fine silk-screen printing, had been introduced for many of the larger areas of flat colouring. Colours applied *à la poupée* were also used — several colours are applied directly onto the engraved copper plate used to print the drawn outline of the illustration, enabling the colours to be printed simultaneously with the drawing and producing a flat, wash-like effect. Colour lithography was in use, too, and many of the more complex background illustrations were now being mechanically printed by the photogravure process, particularly for the larger print runs of *La Gazette du bon ton*, which in 1925 was selling between 2000 and 2500 copies each month.

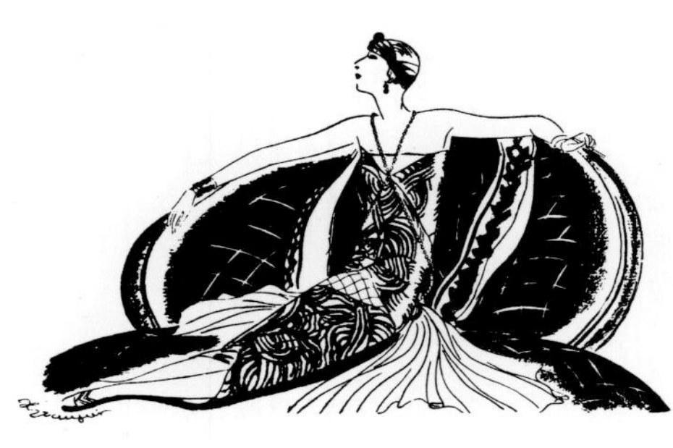

For the large print runs of the *Gazette*, fewer *pochoir* colours were being used. The number of illustrative plates included with each issue had been reduced to between four and six and these were supplemented by additional coloured litho *croquis* of designs from special ateliers; examples are the Raoul Dufy *croquis* for Bianchini Férier, and the Ruhlmann *croquis* of interiors. Many of the in-text vignettes, which had previously been highlighted with *pochoir* colouring, were now being coloured by mechanical means, whilst the text was being written under the direction of Jean Labusquière, Lucien Vogel having departed at the end of 1922 to concentrate on his new venture, *Le Jardin des modes*, which together with the *Gazette* had been taken over by the Condé Nast organisation.

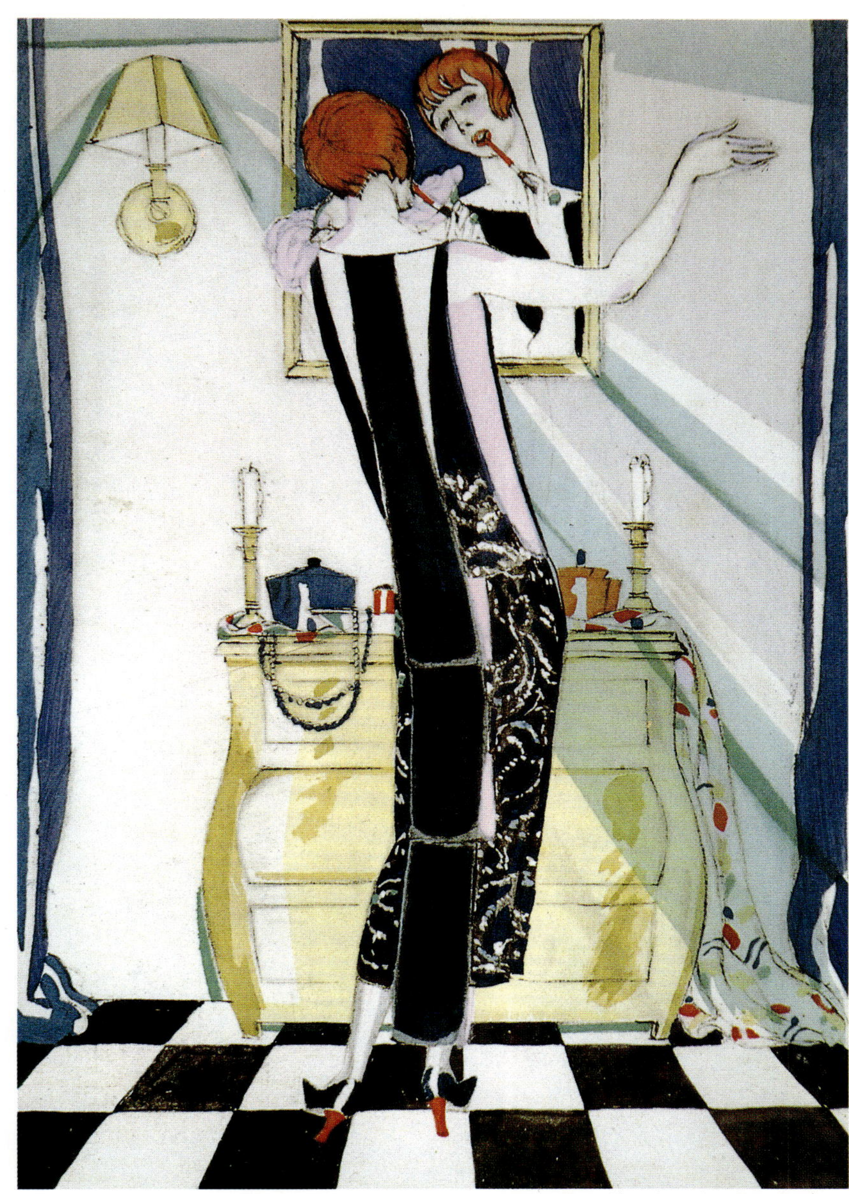

Pochoir illustration *Rote Lippen* by Zeichnung von Friedlander, for *Der Styl*. Published by Otto van Holten, Berlin. 1924.

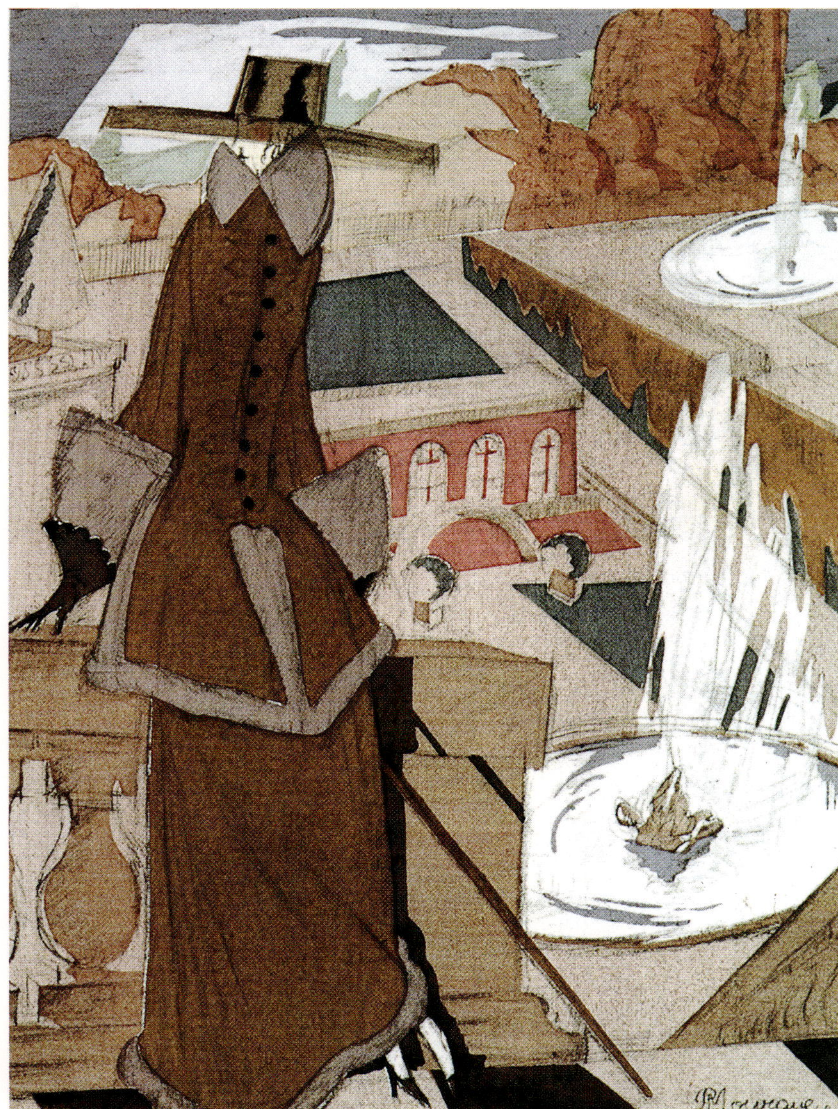

Pochoir illustration *La Petite Mademoiselle* by Pierre Mourgue, for *La Gazette du bon ton*. Paris. 1924.

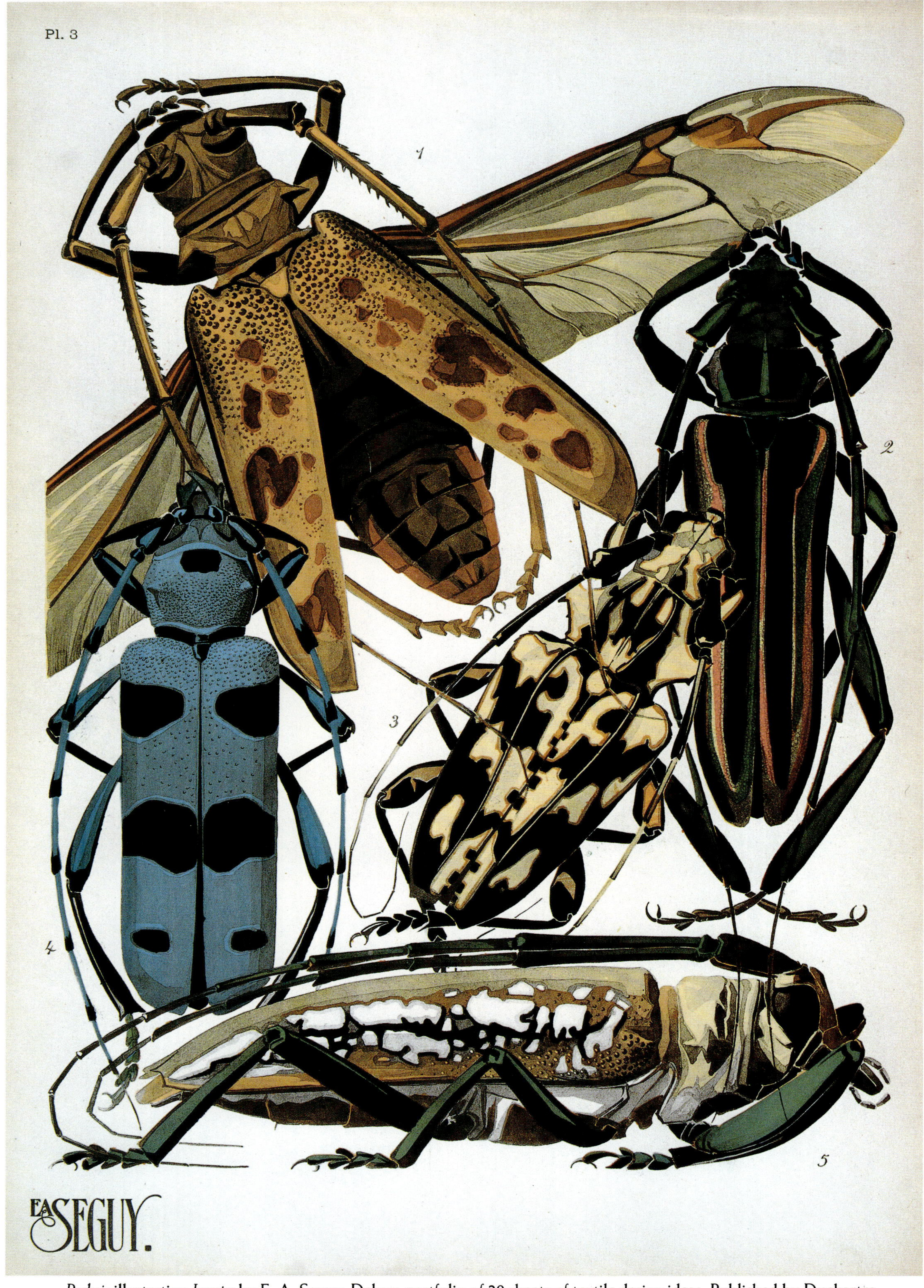

Pochoir illustration *Insectes* by E. A. Seguy. Deluxe portfolio of 20 sheets of textile design ideas. Published by Duchartre et Van Buggenhoudt, Paris. 1924.

Numerous portfolios and albums of designs and a variety of illustrated deluxe-edition books were also being published by Vogel and others, using a wide range of printing techniques in order to achieve the particular visual effect desired by the illustrator. For instance, *La Dernière Lettre persane* featured twelve stylish illustrations by Edouardo Bénito from designs by Paul Poiret for Fourrures Max and was printed in gold leaf, highlighted with *pochoir* colouring, with the black and embossed detailing being printed by woodcuts. In Janine Aghion's illustrations for *Grains de poivre* the background black areas were printed from woodblocks, then highlighted in silver and colours by using an adaptation of the *pochoir* process developed by Jacoub et Cie. Jean Dulac's erotic illustrations for *Nous deux* utilised copperplate engravings tastefully highlighted in *pochoir* by La Belle Editions; Pushkin's *Conte de Tsar Saltan* was illustrated by Natalia Goncharova and printed entirely in *pochoir*, with set-in letterpress text printed by Bertrand Guégan. Barbier's illustrations for *Le Bonheur du jour ou les graces à la mode*, published by Chez Meynial, had colours applied *à la poupée* and was then overprinted in *pochoir* by Jean Saudé. Edouard Seguy's sumptuous portfolio of textile designs, *Insectes*, was printed in rich multicoloured *pochoir* over a photogravure background. The new deluxe fashion magazine *Art–Goût–Beauté*, which first appeared in 1922, combined *pochoir*, coloured wood engravings, photography, lithography and photogravure modes of printing to give great variety to the visual images.

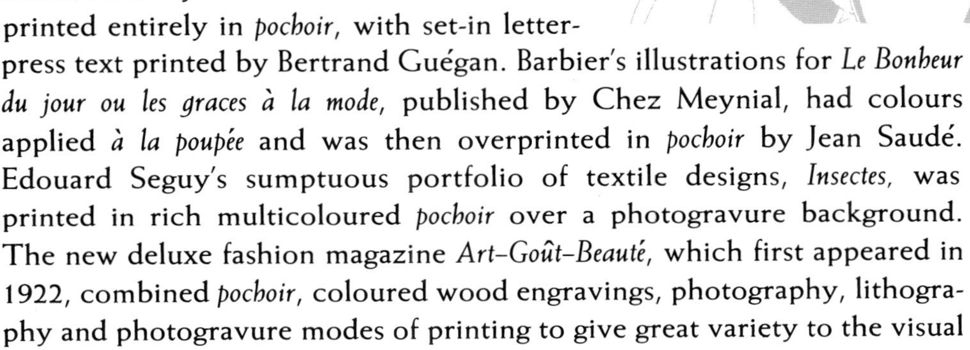

François-Louis Schmied was, of course, still printing deluxe-edition books using his unique coloured wood engravings, whilst in England and America attempts were being made to capture some of the aesthetic excellence of the French printing techniques. Notably successful were Ronald Balfour's and W. S. Sefton's (under her pseudonym 'Fish') rival editions of the *Rubaiyat of Omar Khayyam*; Alastair's *The Sphinx*; Michel Sevier's *Tales of Igor*; and the deluxe signed vellum-bound editions printed on handmade paper with tipped-in chromotypogravure illustrations such as *The Kingdom of the Pearl* illustrated by Edmund Dulac, *Aladdin* illustrated by Mackenzie, *English Fairy Tales* illustrated by Arthur Rackham, and *The Ship that Sailed to Mars* illustrated by William Timkin. Numerous other illustrators, such as Jessie M. King, W. Heath Robinson, John Austin, Kay Nielsen, and Willy Pogany, also contributed to bringing this golden age of illustration to a fitting climax.

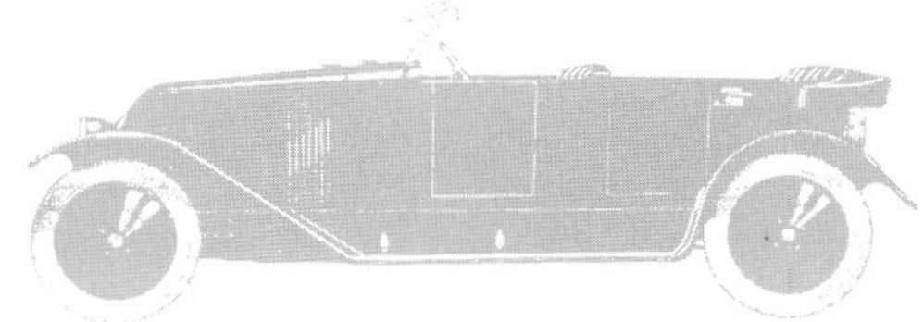

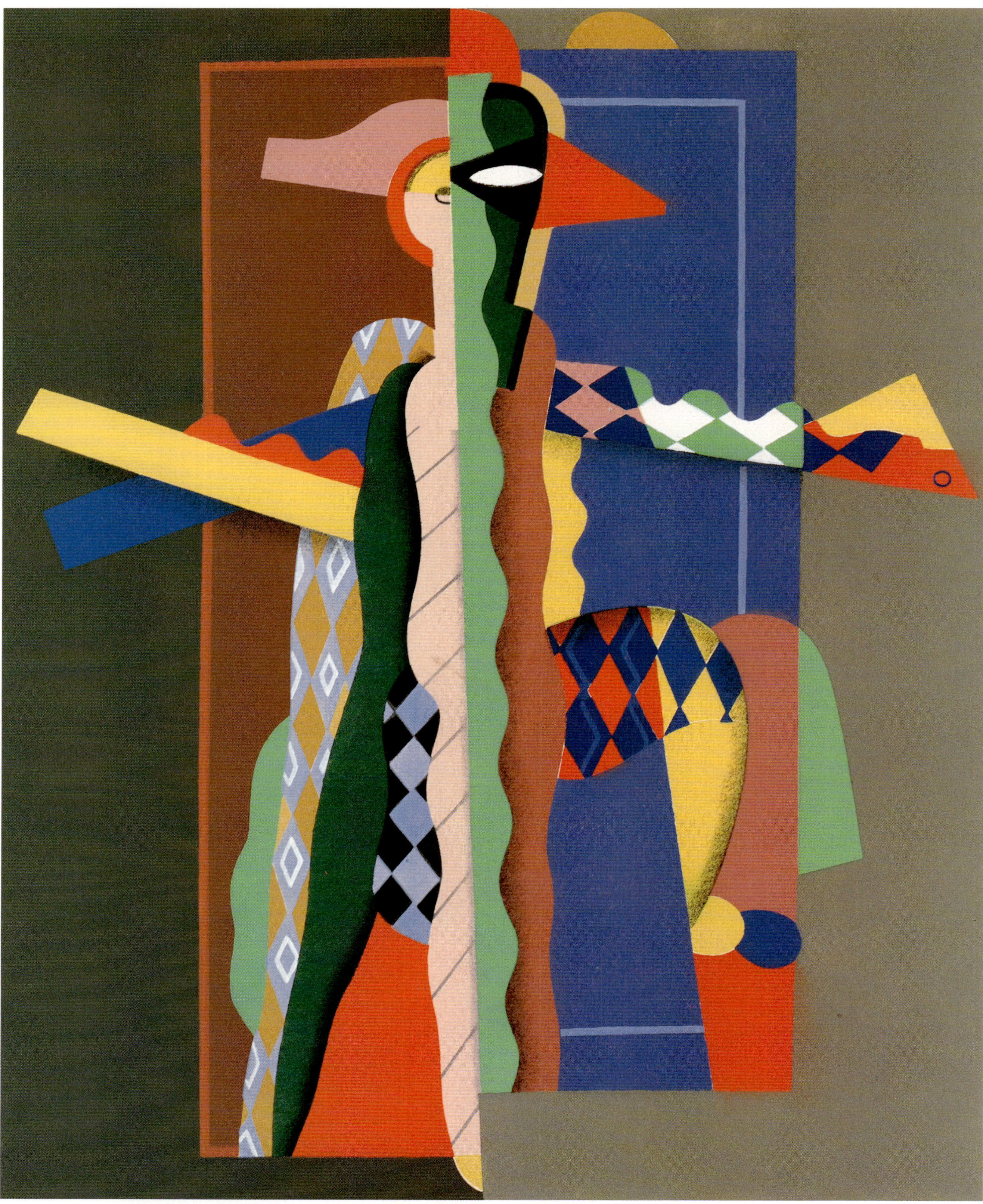

Collection of designs *Décors et couleurs* by Georges Valmier. Printed in *pochoir* by Jean Saudé for Editions Albert Lévy, Paris. 1929.

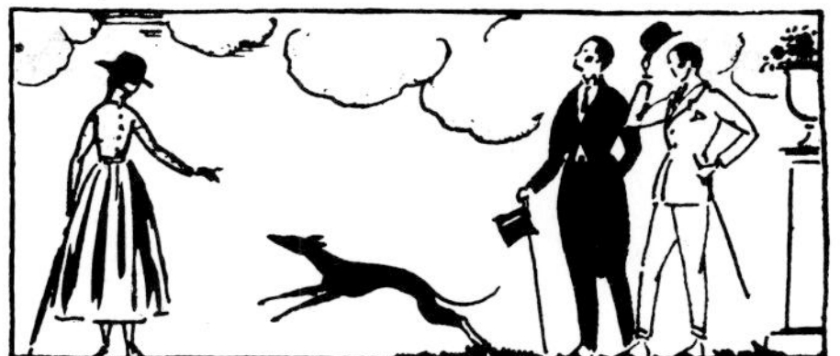

THE CHANGING IDEALS OF ART DECO

The Paris Exposition Universelle, held in 1900 to herald the arrival of the new century and to proclaim French superiority in the fashionable and decorative arts, had been a triumph for the protagonists of the Art Nouveau style of design — a celebration of the free-flowing forms and curvilinear shapes of the great designers and illustrators of the period. Now, just twenty-five years later, another great exhibition was being held in Paris: L'Exposition Internationale des Arts Décoratifs et Industriels Modernes was to celebrate the arrival of the second quarter of the twentieth century. But this time there was not a free-flowing curve in sight, for a great many things had changed. The opulence of the Belle Epoque had long since been forsaken; there had been great industrial expansion throughout the Western world; transportation over land and sea and in the air was now faster and cheaper; the world's major cities were much larger; and four years of bitter conflict had left their mark on almost every aspect of Western life.

A different society had become established during the twenty-five years that had elapsed, and its members had new ideas about most of the things that affected them. They had new political beliefs, new means of transportation, new ambitions, a new style of architecture; they listened to a new kind of music and watched new kinds of entertainments; and they had developed a new mode of design to fulfil their aesthetic dreams. This was the golden age of Art Deco, a style of design that had swept away the curves and pastels of Art Nouveau, just as Art Nouveau had swept away the opulence of the Belle Epoque. The new generation of designers had established a visual language of clear, acid colours and angular shapes, and this became the feature of the 1925 Paris Exhibition.

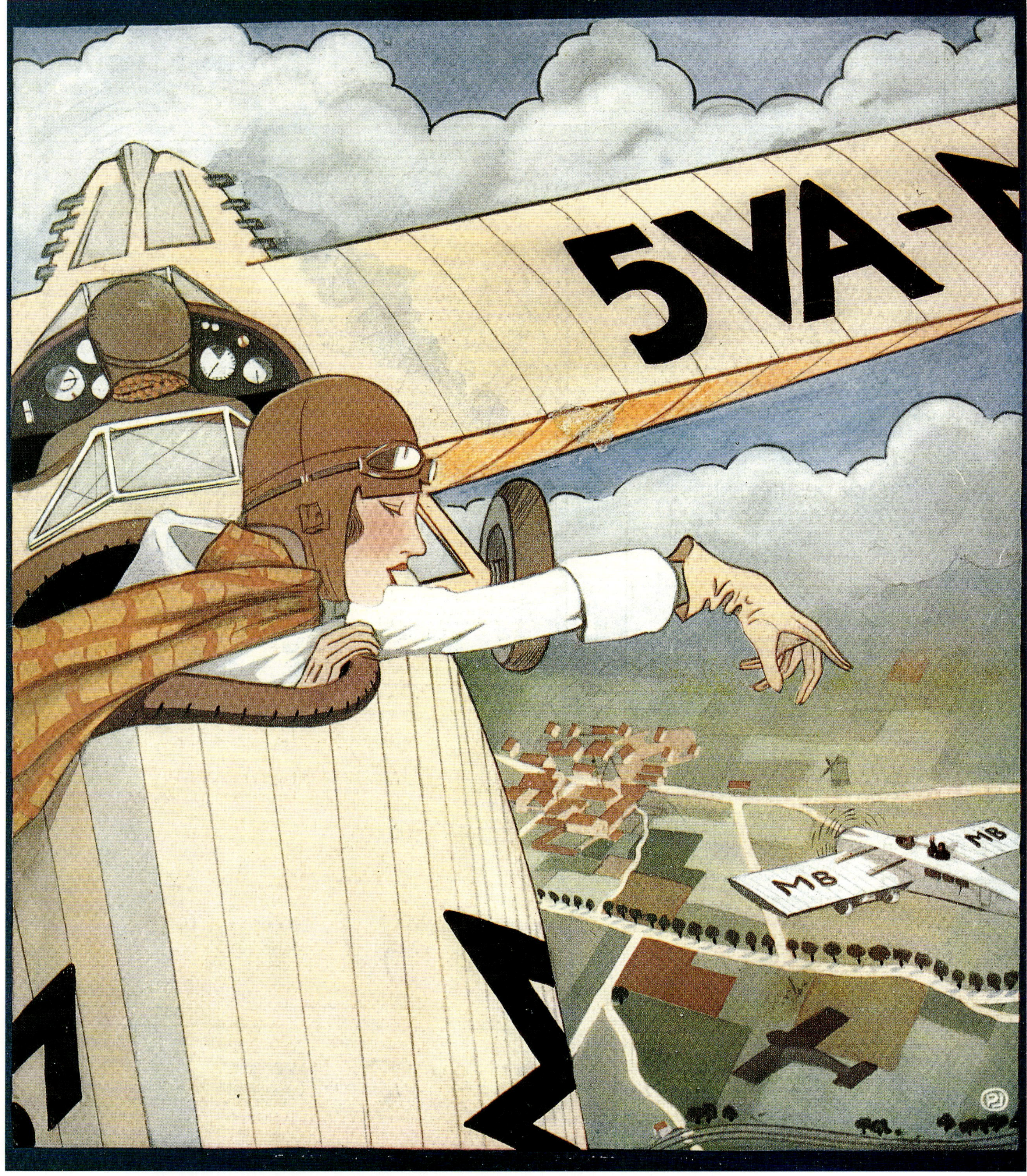

Cover illustration by P. Jiguet, for *La Femme chic*, Paris. 1928.

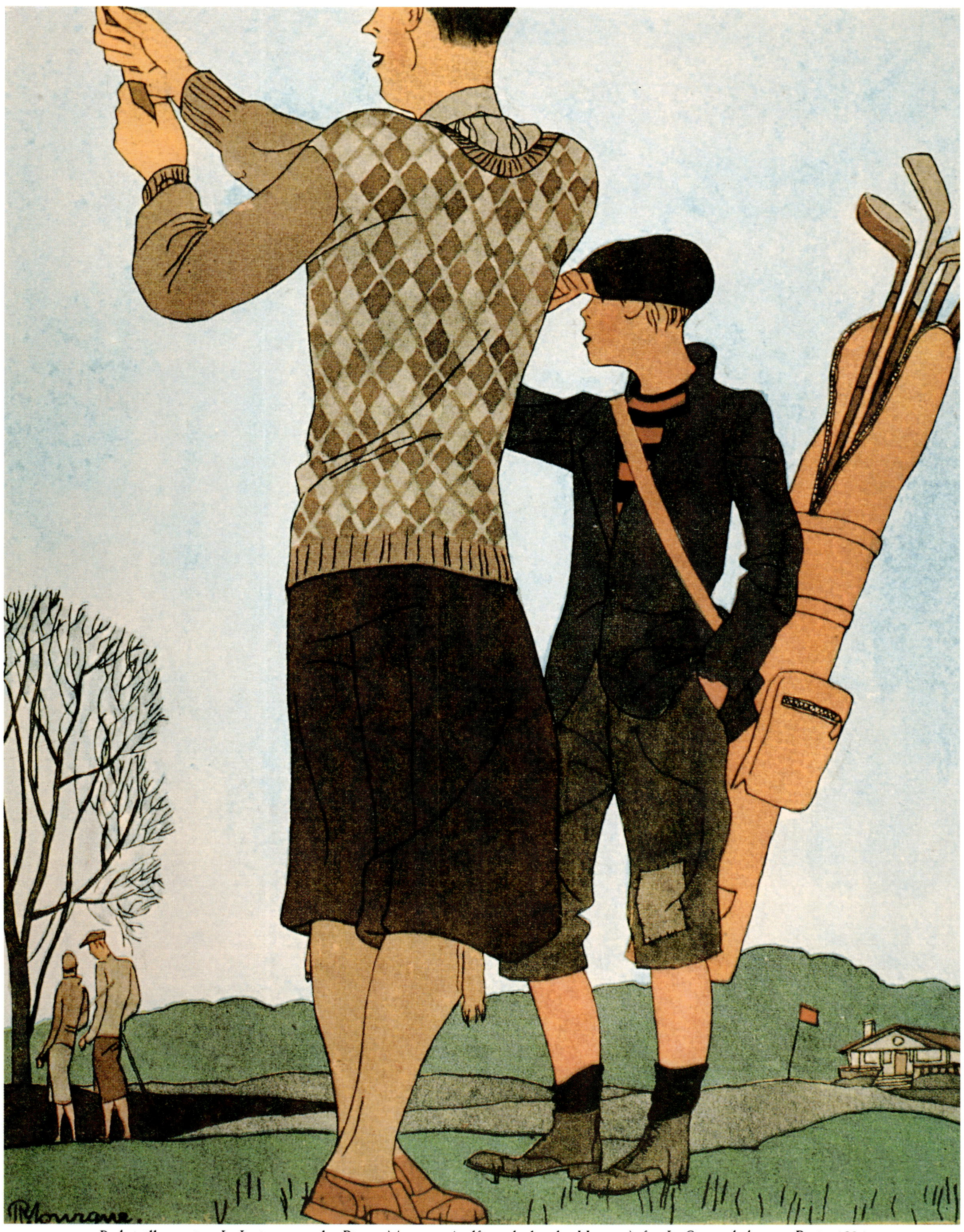

Pochoir illustration *Le Jeu interrompu* by Pierre Mourgue (golfing clothes by Hermes), for *La Gazette du bon ton*. Paris. 1924.

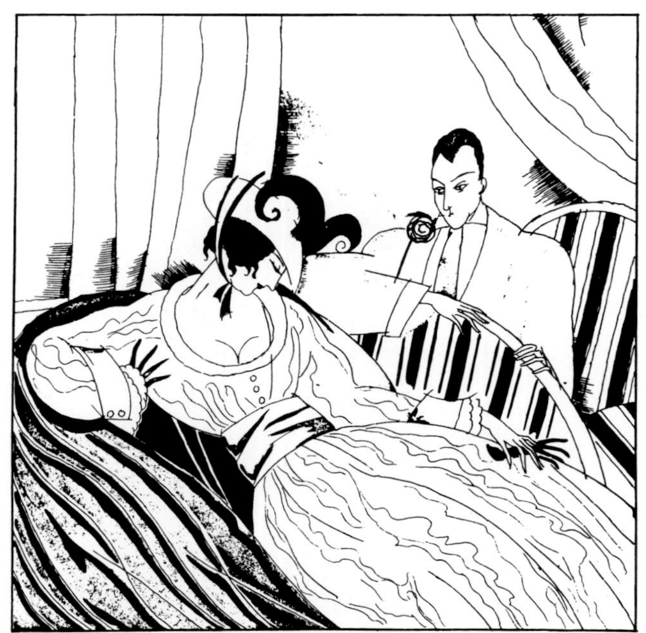

The original Art Deco style had developed out of ideas taken from nineteenth century proto-modern designers such as Christopher Dresser and Michael Thonet, from the theories of William Morris, Walter Crane, and members of the British Arts and Crafts Movement and the earlier industrial philosophers, and from the aestheticism of Japanese master-craftsmen. The individual contributions of Henry van de Velde, Josef Hoffmann, Peter Behrens and Charles Rennie Mackintosh, the colours of the Fauves, the visual impact of Léon Bakst and Diaghilev's Ballet Russe made further contributions, as did the revolutionary dress styles of Madeleine Vionnet and Paul Poiret, and the writings of Havelock Ellis and Sigmund Freud. All these innovators helped to rid Western society of the overbearing and outdated mores, morals and merchandise of the nineteenth century.

The great designers of the new mode — Jean Dunand, Jacques-Emile Ruhlmann, René Lalique, François-Louis Schmied, Francis Jourdain, Jean Luce, Pierre Legrain, Eileen Gray, Süe et Mare, and others — decided that, in order to achieve a consistent aesthetic standard in their products, only natural materials of the finest quality should be used. The designs were also to be original in concept and made with the skill of the finest craftsmen available. The end product was exclusive, luxurious and expensive, and it was sold to wealthy collectors from all over the world.

Jean Dunand, for instance, noted for his fine lacquer work, had studied under the Japanese master Sougawara and had then applied this ancient art to create his own designs which, when complete, were far from oriental in inspiration. René Lalique, on the other hand, who had originally been an Art Nouveau jeweller, had by 1925 created a new career in glassware, producing glass objects of every description, from large glass panels for architectural use to tiny scent bottles; each piece was individually made, hand finished, and often sandblasted to create geometric or stylised patterns.

Pierre Legrain started his professional career as a furniture and interior designer with Paul Iribe, and he had worked on redesigning Jacques Doucet's house in the Avenue du Bois. Doucet had then commissioned him to design some modern-style bookbindings, even though he had never before done such work. Nevertheless, he set about his task, using materials he had used in his furniture work — rare woods, shagreen, ivory and mother-of-pearl — which he applied in geometric shapes, criss-crossed with gold tooling. The work was a success and, with Doucet's encouragement and help, Legrain began to specialise in bookbinding designs, using a number of professional bookbinders, notably René Kieffer, to carry out his unusual ideas. By 1925 the talents of Legrain and Kieffer had evolved a very distinctive style: it created much interest at the 1925 Exhibition and their work was highly prized by discerning collectors.

Like Jean Dunand, Eileen Gray had studied the intricacies of traditional Japanese lacquer work with Sougawara, and early in her career she designed and made some exceptionally fine pieces of lacquered furniture for discerning customers such as Madeleine Vionnet. She then studied carpet weaving and furniture design and by the early 1920s she had opened her own interior design gallery, specialising in expensive furniture, lacquer work, carpets and small objets d'art. Although she was a noted exhibitor in the 1925 Exhibition and received many valuable commissions from all over the world, the following year she turned to designing tubular steel furniture and her interiors became increasingly abstract — 'more in time with the times', she said. By 1930 she had closed her gallery to concentrate on architecture and steel furniture, and she continued to do so until her death in 1976 at the age of ninety-seven.

Süe et Mare was a partnership formed in 1919 between Louis Süe and André Mare, both of whom had originally been painters but had also designed furniture and textiles from about 1910. With a small group of specialist designers they established a thriving interior design studio that was considered very *outré* and somewhat theatrical, characterised by works with gilded surface patterning and intricate forms of decoration that called for very detailed and skilful attention. Their pavilion, the Musée des Arts Contemporains, was a great success in the 1925 Exhibition; their South American clients particularly admired the updated Art Deco versions of the Louis-Philippe gilded style. Süe et Mare sold their business in 1928 and both returned to painting.

Jacques-Emile Ruhlmann was the son of a prosperous builder and as an apprentice in his father's firm he specialised in carpentry and built-in

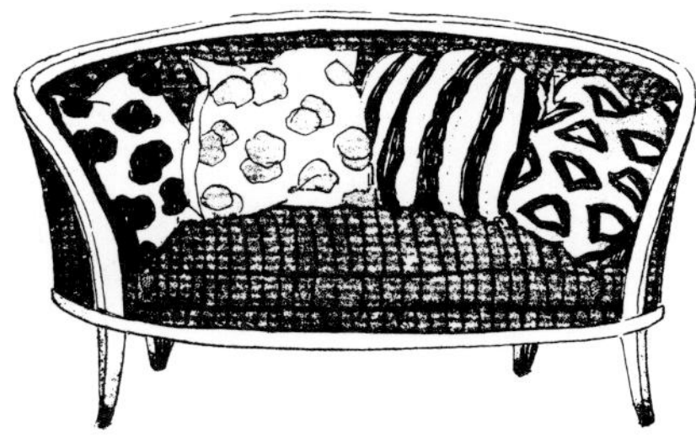

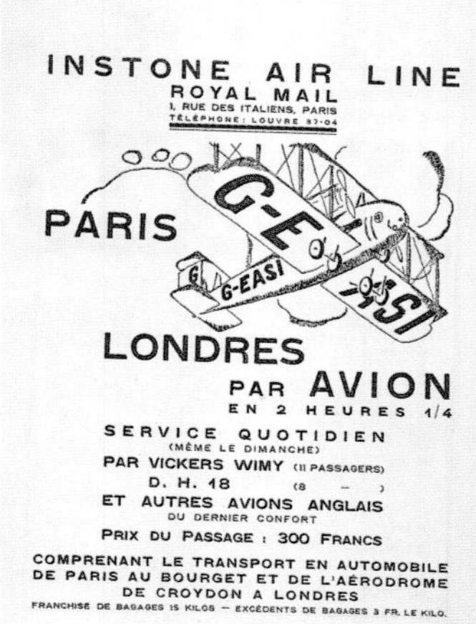

furniture. When his father died in 1920 he took over the business and began to concentrate on built-in furniture, adding a range of designs and opening an interior design section. By 1923 his name had become associated with expensive, well-made furniture using rare woods inlaid with ivory, shagreen and fine leathers. But it is the 1925 Exhibition and his spectacular display intended for 'rich collectors' for which Ruhlmann is best remembered. From that time his name became synonymous with comfort, luxury, and superb styling, and he resolutely undertook to win over the world's rich clientele by using only the most exotic materials — amboyna, Macassar ebony, burr walnut, ormolu, shagreen, tortoise shell, ivory, rare metals and the finest lacquer work.

Like the Exhibition of 1900, the Paris Exhibition of 1925 was situated in the very heart of Paris, spanning the Seine from the Port Alexandre III to the Port de L'Alma. The Alexandre III bridge, which had been specially designed and constructed for the 1900 Exhibition and was embellished in true *fin de siècle* style, was ingeniously altered by Maurice Dufrêne, who turned it into a shopping precinct rather like the Ponte Vecchio in Florence. This is where avant-garde designer Sonia Delaunay and many other specialists who were not included in the main pavilions had their shops and displays.

The 1925 Paris Exhibition had been originally planned to take place in 1915, to demonstrate French leadership in twentieth century design, but it had been postponed because of the war. It was then re-scheduled for 1921, and finally 1925, when it was decided to expand its compass to include manufactured products of original design and entirely modern in concept. All nations were invited to participate and the Exhibition was the first major world fair to be exclusively concerned with the display and promotion of original works in the decorative arts.

After much debate it had been decided that the full title of this splendid affair should be 'L'Exposition Internationale des Arts Décoratifs et Industriels Modernes' although, because of its original aims, it was usually referred to as the 'Exposition des Arts Décoratifs', or the 'Art Deco Exhibition'. This is the source of the term 'Art Deco', which generally refers to the design style most prevalent at the Exhibition, as opposed to the kitsch copies of these designs, which became popular after the Exhibition had closed and which are more correctly referred to as belonging to the 'jazz age' style.

The main entrance to the Art Deco Exhibition was at the Port d'Honneur, next to the Grand Palais des Beaux Arts, which housed the main part of the French industrial arts exhibition. Nearby there were the special pavilions for North Africa, French West Africa and Indo-China. These were adjoined by a Moroccan diarama, a Tunisian market, a gallery of French shops, the Pavilion of Elegance (featuring the work of the couturiers), the Ruhlmann display, the pavilion of the *Art-Goût-Beauté*

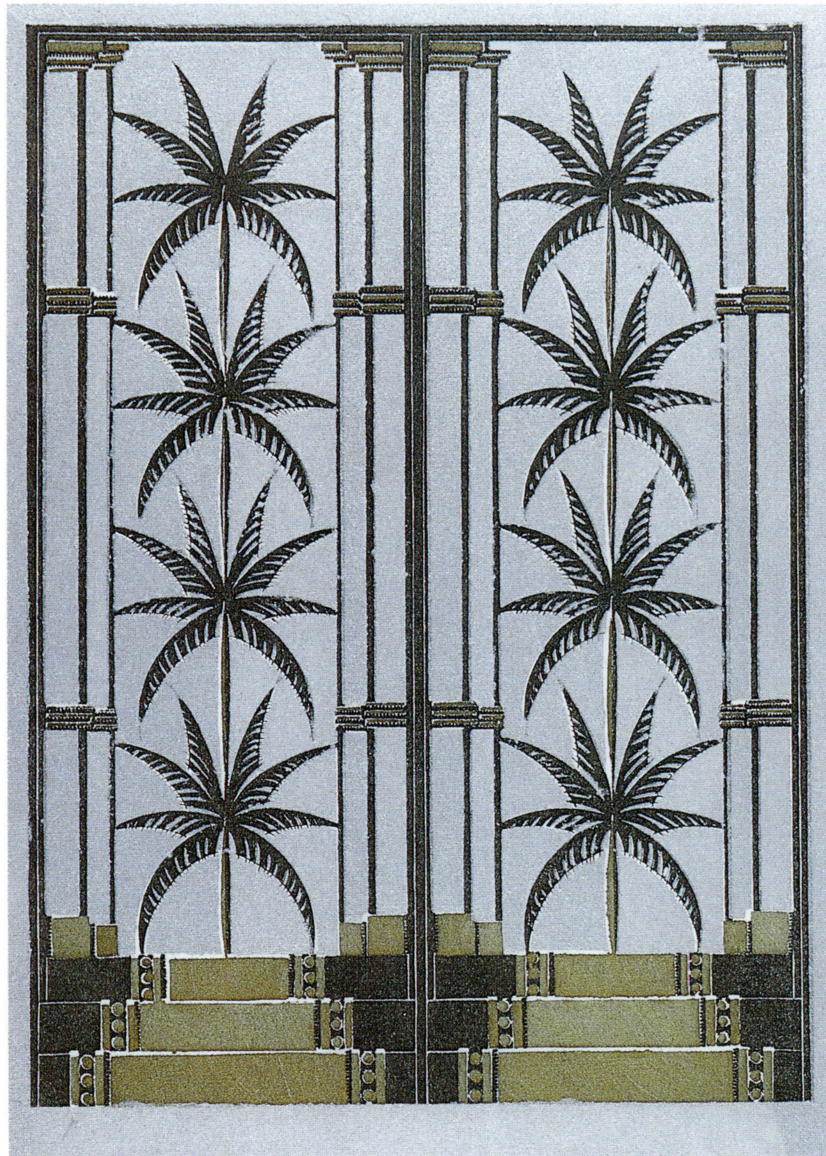

Pochoir illustration *Grille en fer forgé pour le Pavillon de l'Elégance* by Baguès, for *La Gazette du bon ton*. Paris. 1925.

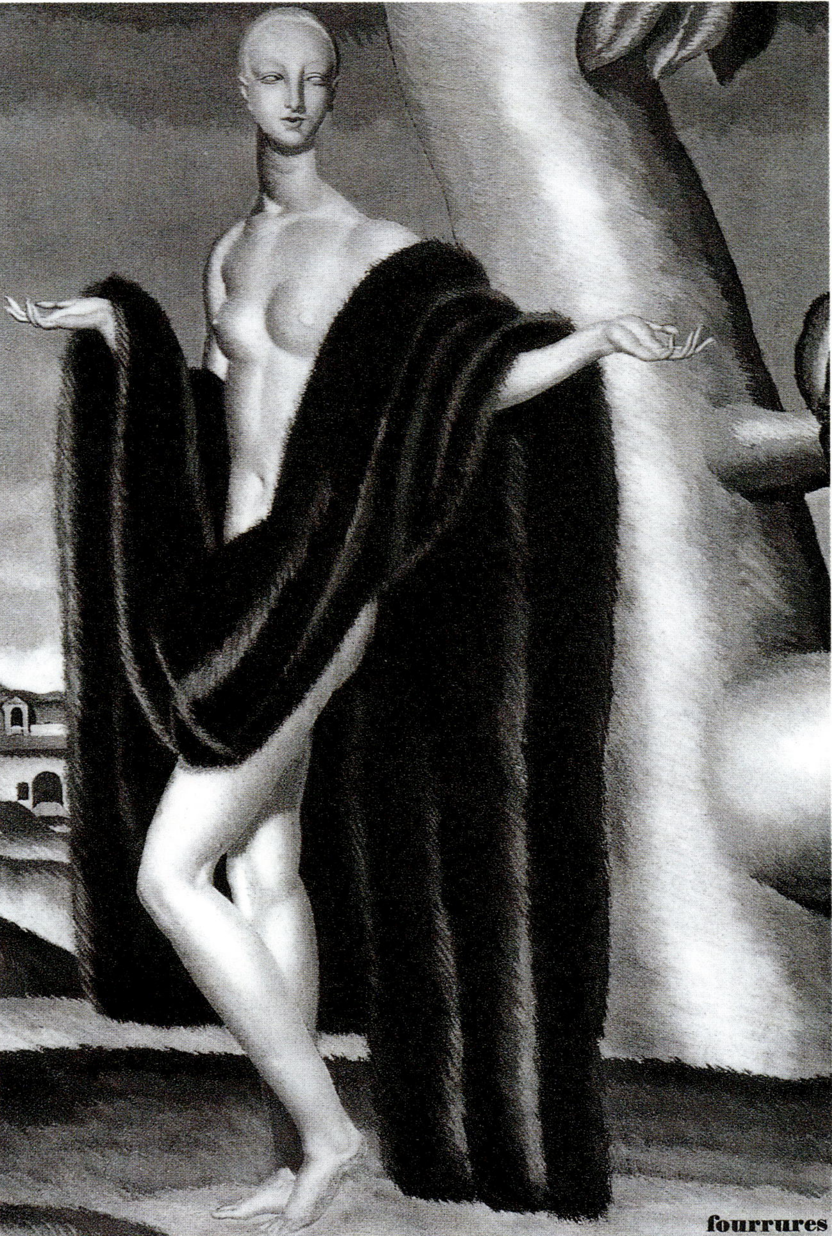

Toi with litho illustrations in black and silver by Jean Dupas and text by Mme Colette. Edition des Fourrures Max, Paris. 1928.

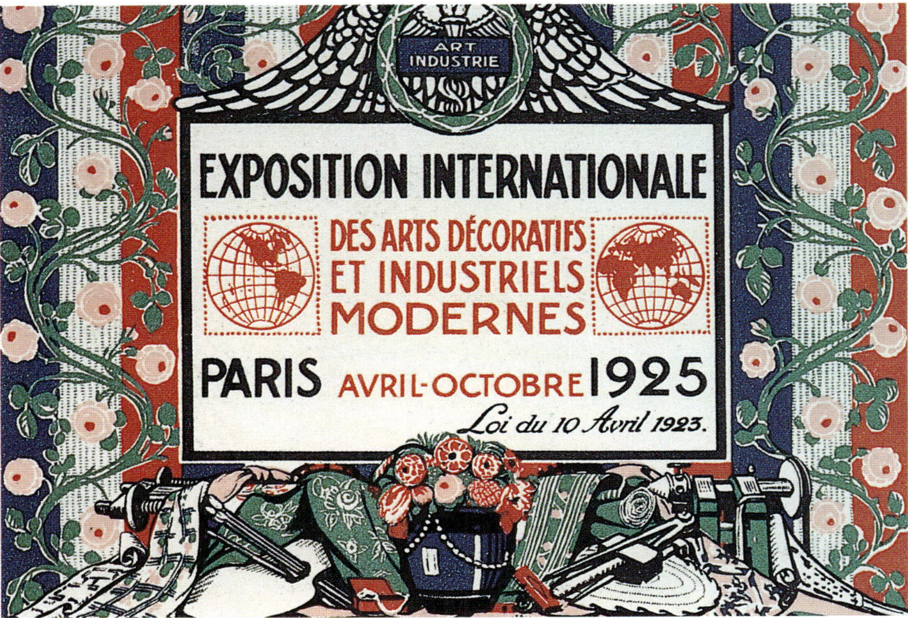

Magazine advertisement for the 1925 Paris Art Deco Exhibition. Paris. 1923.

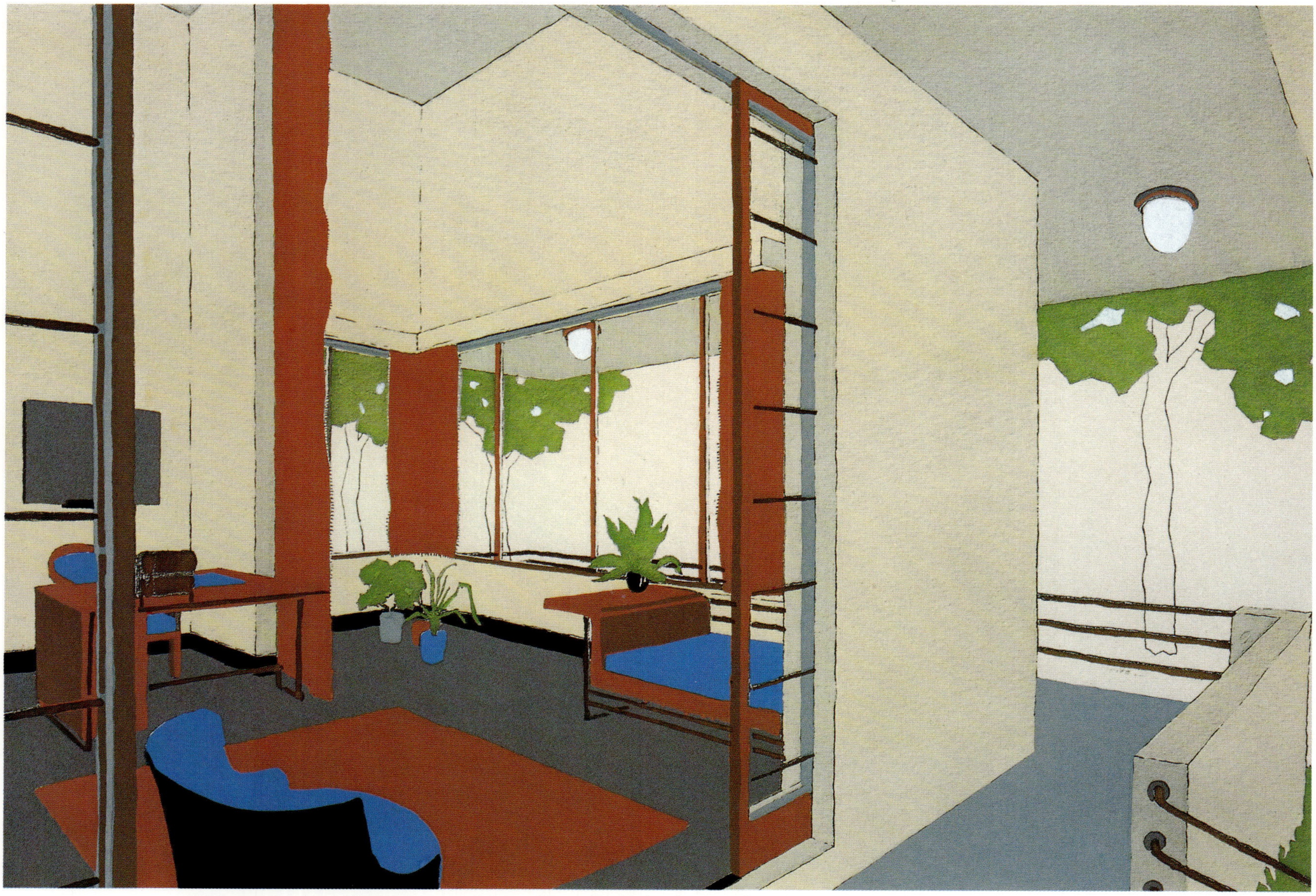

Illustration *Atelier-studio* by Maurice Matet. Printed in *pochoir* by Jean Saudé for *Répertoire du goût moderne*. Published by Editions Albert Lévy, Paris. 1928.

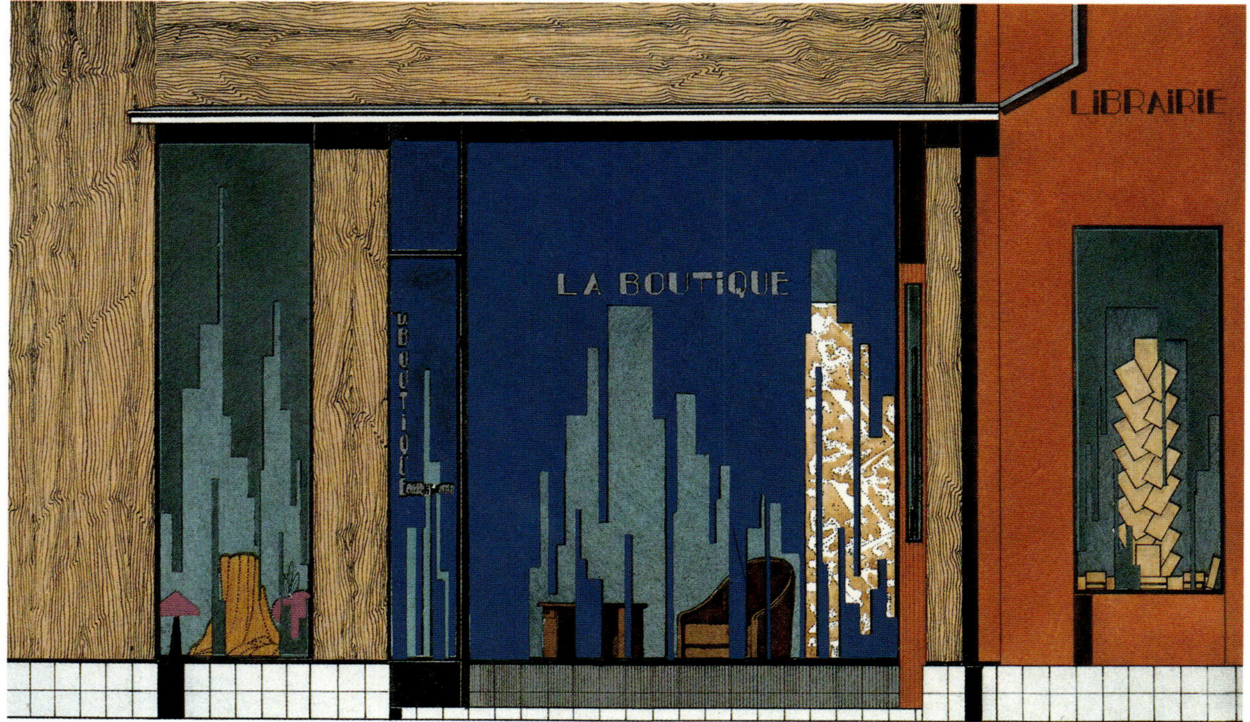

Illustration *La Boutique* by Pierre Chareau. Printed in *pochoir* for *Devantures de boutique*. Published by Editions Albert Lévy, Paris. 1927.

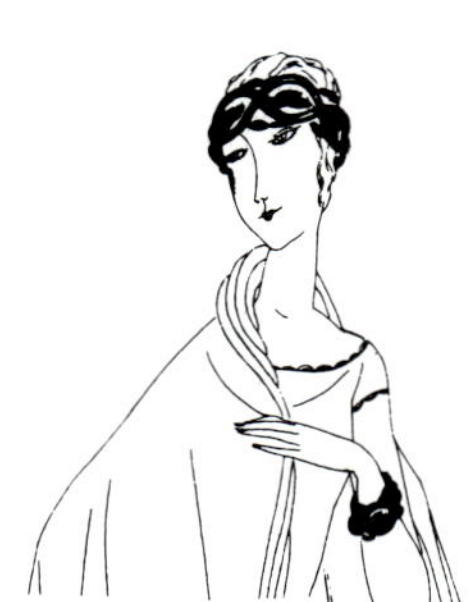

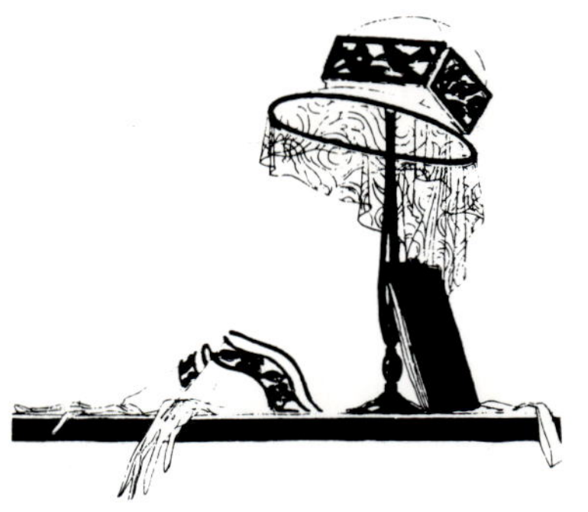

magazine, Paul Poiret's three barges (moored along the banks of the Seine), the Lalique pavilion, and then the pavilions of the Austrian, Japanese, Swedish, Polish, Czech, Netherlands, Belgian, British, Turkish, Danish, Italian, Soviet, Greek, Swiss, Yugoslav and Spanish exhibitors. The United States was not represented in the 33 000 square metres of display space, their only contribution being the dancer Loie Fuller, who appeared at the fashion gala, and the Negro jazz musicians who played at a number of evening events.

The main area of the Exhibition had been planned as a lavish and flamboyant display of new architectural styles from the twenty-eight participating nations. In fact, everything about the Exhibition had been planned to display the variety of modern design styles submitted, so as to impress and excite the hundreds of thousands of visitors who had flocked to Paris from all over the world. *Vogue* magazine described the Exhibition as being full of bold experiments:

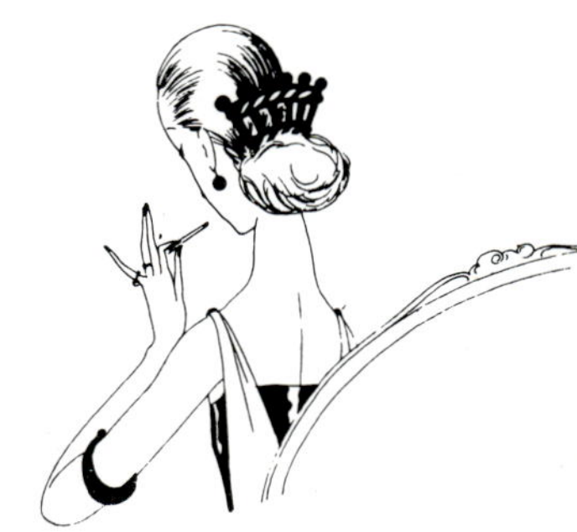

Every shape that the ingenuity of man can conceive has taken concrete form — pavilions parody dinosaurs, kiosks mimic shells . . . enormous fountains of glass play among life-size Cubist trees, and cascades of music wash down upon the alleys from the dizzy summits of four gargantuan towers. And at night, electric lights turn the exhibition into a fantastic spectacle.

Vogue also declared that a new style had been born, which, it thought, combined the influence of the Cubists, the Bauhaus, and Aztec and Mayan architecture. In some of the exhibitions there were also Egyptian motifs inspired by the recently discovered tomb of Tutenkhamen, brilliant colours from the Ballet Russe, and the ostentation of Hollywood. Overall, however, the design styles were well controlled and very definitely within the Art Deco idiom.

As with the Exhibition of 1900, the grounds of the Art Deco Exhibition were landscaped throughout in the traditional French manner, with due regard to balance, classic proportions and decorative detailing. Open spaces were imaginatively sited between the groups of pavilions — attractive gardens with their own specially designed fountains and statues, and with the flowers and shrubs being planted in such a manner as to give each garden a character of its own. There were also fairgrounds for children, with a mixture of merry-go-rounds, stalls and sideshows, and a complete toy village where children could be left to play whilst their parents visited the nearby exhibits.

Special areas were set aside for puppet shows, traditional mime, and dancing groups from many of the contributing countries, and there was a wide variety of special parades, beauty contests, gala events, and frequent night-time fireworks. The Eiffel Tower was decorated with nearly a quarter of a million multi-coloured electric bulbs; René Lalique had created a huge shimmering glass waterfall as a central meeting point in the Exhibition; and there was a special theatre for plays and concerts,

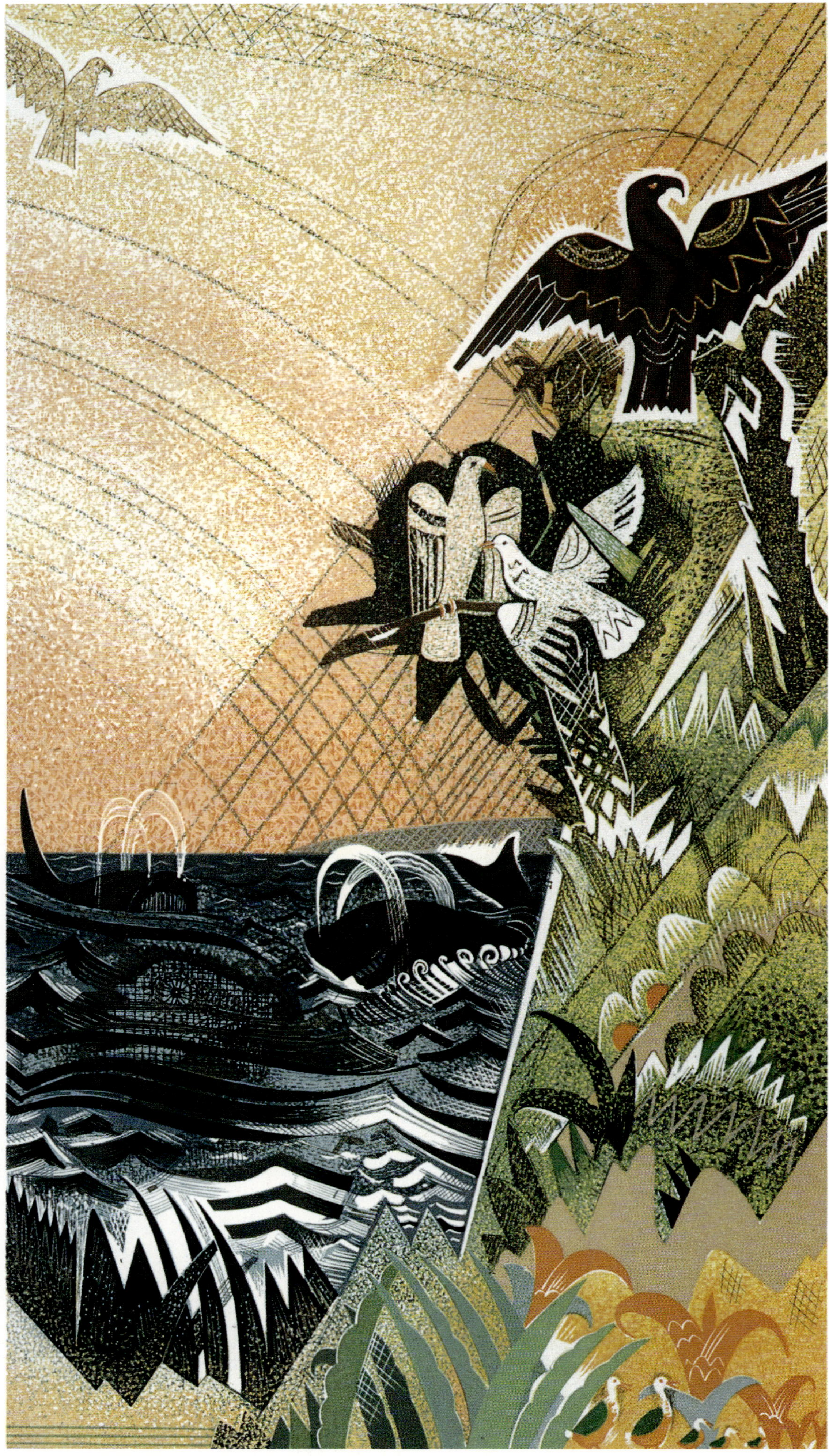

Coloured wood engraving for *La Création* by Dr J. C. Mardrus. Deluxe signed edition of 175 copies. Designed, engraved, printed and published by François-Louis Schmied, Paris. 1928.

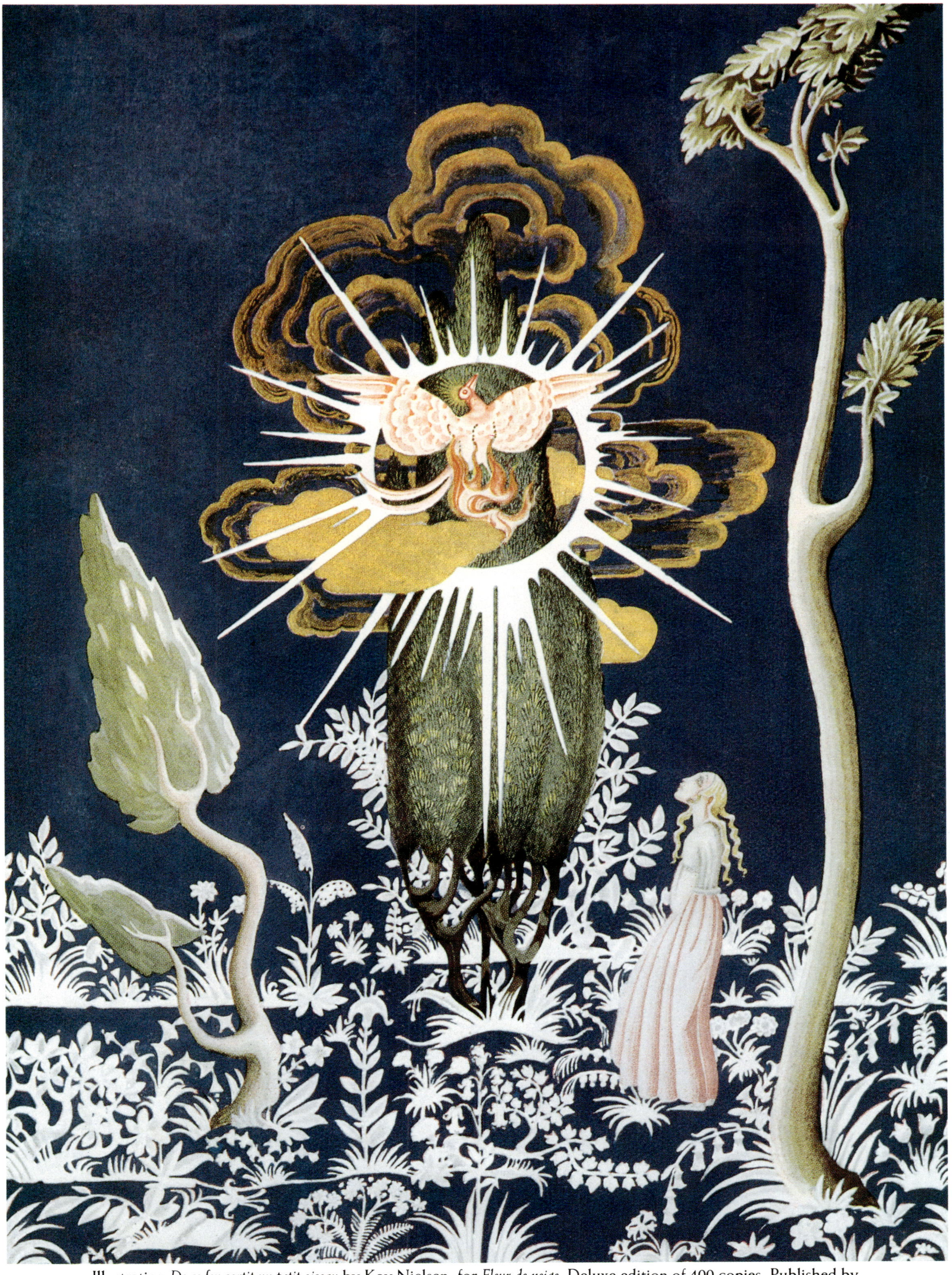

Illustration *De ce feu sortit un petit oiseau* by Kay Nielsen, for *Fleur-de-neige*. Deluxe edition of 400 copies. Published by L'Edition d'Art, H. Piazza, Paris. 1929.

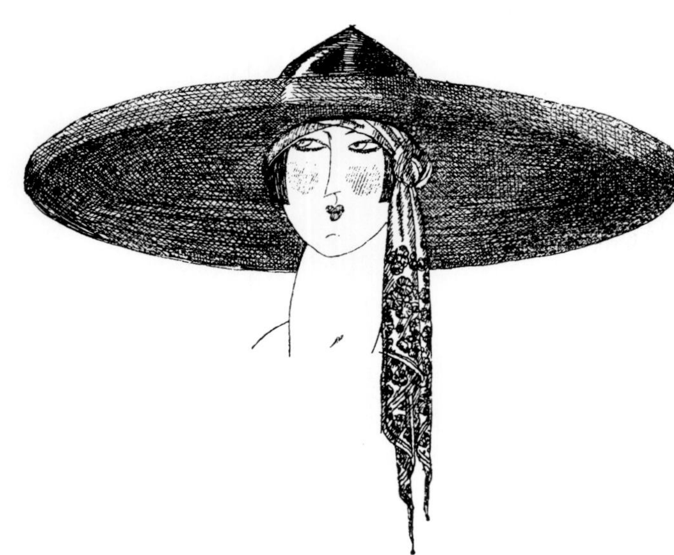

with performers coming from around the world to display their varied talents.

On the evening of 16 June 1925, an extraordinary 'fashion gala' was held on and around the staircase of the Grand Palais; it featured over 2000 dancers, models, actresses, musicians and performers, and opened with a spectacular tableau entitled 'Vision of the East' followed by thirty models wearing full-length ermine coats with seemingly endless trains that totally covered the staircase. There then followed a number of tableaux in the colours of the rainbow, showing designs from the leading couture houses, interspersed with groups of dancers from the Casino de Paris, the Moulin Rouge and the Folies Bergère wearing little more than extravagant displays of feathers and a few sequins. Mademoiselle Mistinguett appeared as a solitaire diamond, wearing a splendid towering headdress and little else; she was accompanied by the Tiller Girls dressed as various jewels. The Russian dancer Ida Rubinstein appeared in an updated version of the costume designed by Léon Bakst for her famous role in *Schéhérazade*, and Loie Fuller danced in her customary single layer of chiffon, with pupils from her school covered in nothing but 'a sea of veils'. There were also Spanish dancers in their exotic frilled costumes, an exerpt from Bizet's opera *Carmen*, an interlude with clowns, and a finale that featured sixty actresses and performers dressed in sumptuous evening gowns supplied by the leading fashion houses.

La Gazette de bon ton published a special edition celebrating the Exhibition and featuring the work of many of the French participants. It was illustrated with ten *pochoir* plates by Lepape, Barbier, Marty and the newcomers Pierre Mourgue, Charles Loupot, Jose Zinoview and Jean Grangier. The *Gazette* proudly declared that 'a new modern world has been created which is worthy of the twentieth century'. An editorial in one American magazine stated, 'The diversity of ideas within the same amazing style is so outstanding that the eyes of the visitors are pulled this way and that in a frenzied effort to understand this frenetic and exhilarating experience.' Other journalists did not agree with these comments and described the Exhibition as 'outraging the established concepts of proportion, composition, balance and harmony of traditional architecture' and 'the most serious and sustained exhibition of bad taste the world has ever seen'.

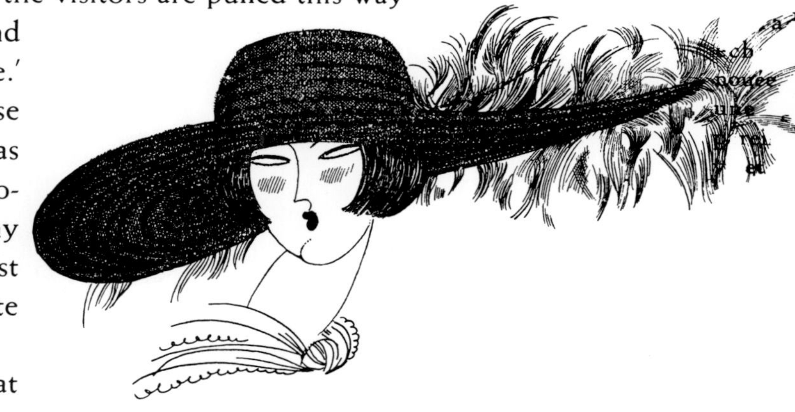

In retrospect, it is possible to see that

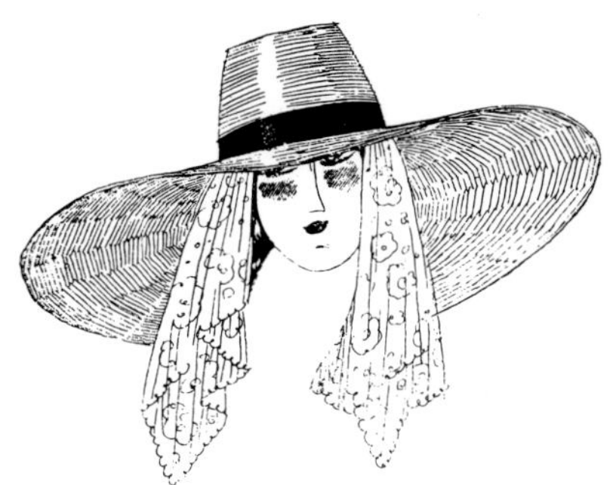

the Art Deco style as displayed in all of its luxury and opulence at the 1925 Exhibition was becoming one of sheer self-indulgence on the part of many of the architects and participating designers, and that a point had been reached at which its creative development could be carried no further. In addition, the point had been reached at which, because of the popular success of the kitsch versions of the products shown in the Art Deco Exhibition, the aesthetic dream upon which the style had been created and thrived was now being shared with too many people and was therefore beginning to be destroyed. It must be remembered that a style of design is not only created to fulfil the aesthetic dreams and aspirations of a particular group of people at a particular time, but that that group of people does not like sharing the results of its dreams with too many other people. This reluctance to share with too many others is a very important ingredient in the mobility of fashion and fashionable styles.

Soon after the 1925 Art Deco Exhibition had opened, superficial copies of products designed in the Art Deco style were beginning to appear in large department stores in the capital cities and towns all over the Western world. This not only diminished the haut monde's ardour, but it also unfortunately lacked the essential aesthetic understanding and quality of craftsmanship that had elevated the original Art Deco designs to a truly modern art form. These new kitsch, or jazz age, products triggered a reaction among the haut monde and the nouveau riche, who had spent vast sums of money on exclusive Art Deco products that they had mixed with antique, oriental and African pieces in stark modern-style interiors. Now they were beginning to look elsewhere for products to purchase. Many of the famous designers and master-craftsmen were also affected by this change in events, and they too began to experiment with other design forms. Soon the inventive flow of designs within the Art Deco idiom began to lessen and the style was no longer pursued with such passion.

This unexpected development, occurring at a time when the aesthetic achievements of the Art Deco designers and master-craftsmen were at their apex, created a strange dichotomy within the world of Art Deco. On one hand, it produced a new breed of avant-garde designers led by

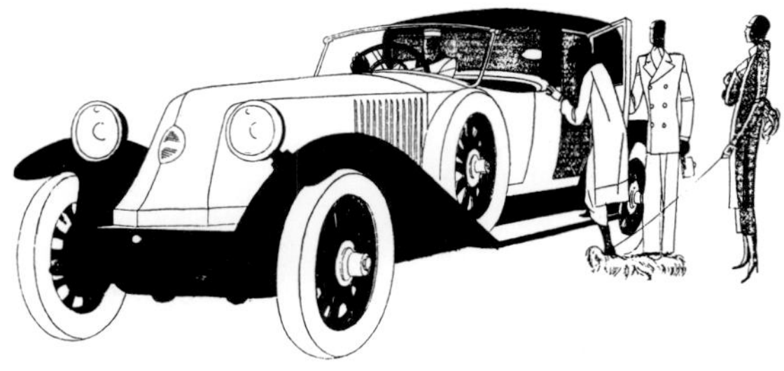

the architect Charles-Edouard Jeanneret — better known as Le Corbusier — whose pavilion at the 1925 Exhibition had been condemned by furious officials as 'too starkly modern' and failing to conform to their standards of 'acceptability'. Le Corbusier later wrote that this conflict was obviously 'a conflict of generations', and added in an article published in 1928, *Right now one thing is sure: 1925 marks the decisive turning point in the quarrel between the old and the new. After 1925, the lovers of the old will have virtually ended their lives, and from now on productive industrial effort will be based on the new. Progress is achieved only through experimentation: the decision in this battle will be awarded to the followers of the new.*

On the other hand, although many established Art Deco designers knew that changes in design style were inevitable, and although they supported the general sentiments voiced by Le Corbusier, they believed that their own designs were still worthy of manufacture as they had in fact elevated their products into recognisable works of art. And despite a slump in sales they continued to make their exclusive products, using the time-consuming methods that they had used before the cheap kitsch copies of their products began to flood the market places of the Western world.

Lacquer work, for example, was a time-consuming and exacting mode of artistic expression much admired during the Art Deco period. First, the pores and grain of the base wood had to be filled and sealed. The wood was then left to dry for about ten days before being sanded and finely ground with pumice stone and calcified staghorn to obtain a really smooth finish. A thin layer of natural lacquer, made from the resin of the Japanese lacquer tree, was then applied to the smooth surface and allowed to dry for between seven and twelve days in a humid room — the humidity causes the lacquer to ferment and this brings about its drying. Seven or eight more layers of lacquer are then applied, each alternate layer being reinforced with fine linen, and being allowed to dry in a humid room for between seven and twelve days before being carefully ground with pumice stone and calcified staghorn. Then the next layer is applied. It is only on the surface thus created — often taking eight to twelve weeks to achieve — that the lacquerist can place his coloured lacquers according to the chosen design. During the application of the colours the lacquerist may also apply inlays of mother-of-pearl, ivory, precious metals, slivers of semi-precious stones, and novelty substances such as sections of crushed eggshells.

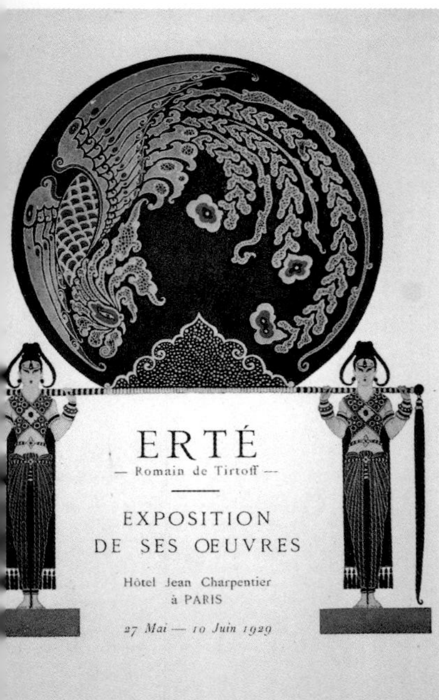

The technique of sandblasting to engrave glass was much used by René Lalique and others. The glass pieces were first blown by hand or produced by the *cire perdue* (lost wax) casting method more usually associated with the casting of small bronze statues. These glass shapes were then engraved using a sandblasting jet, gouging out sections of glass to different depths; the effect could be smooth or rough, matt or shiny, depending upon the intensity of the blast and the coarseness of the sand.

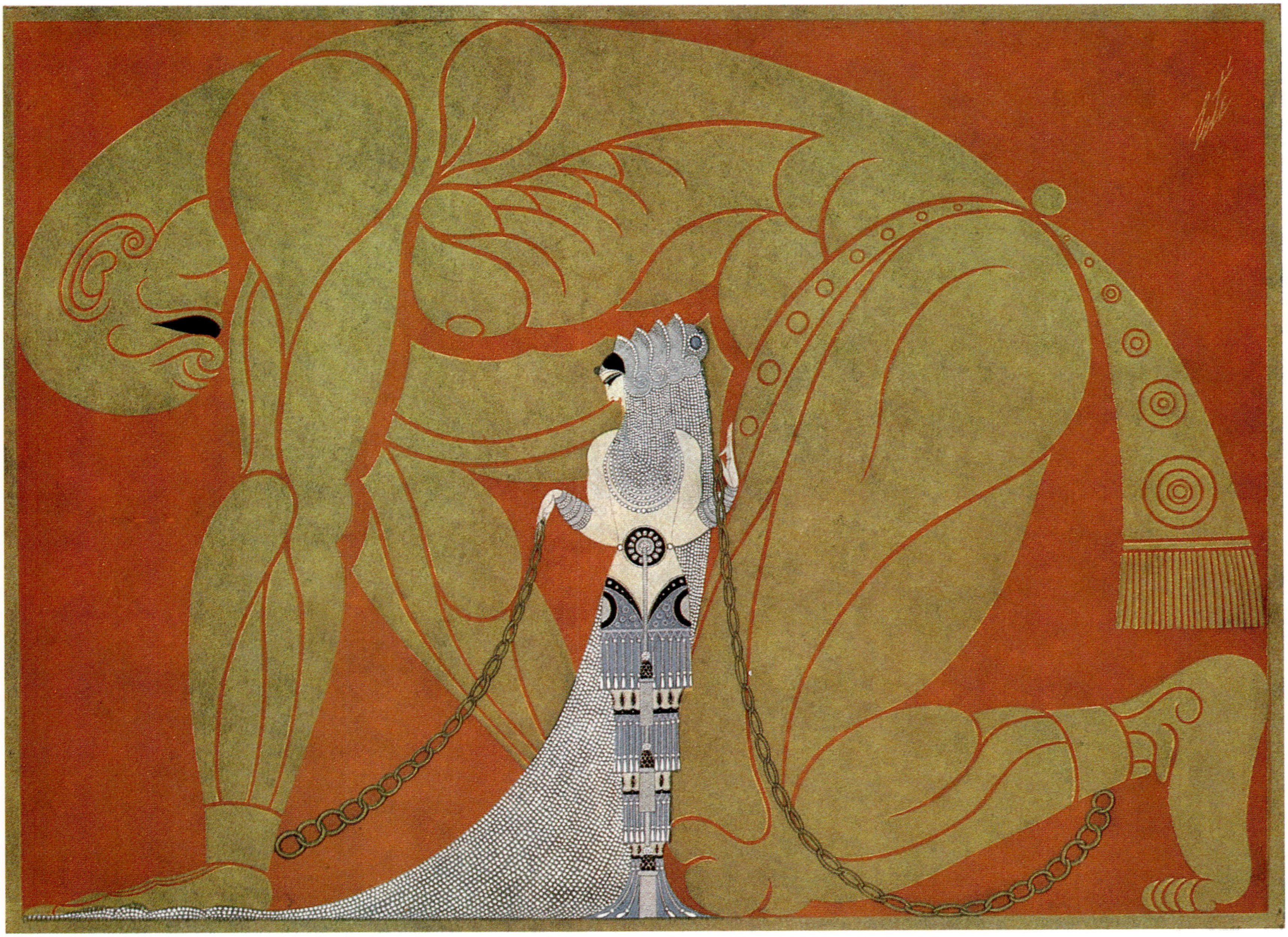

Theatrical illustration by Erté, from the catalogue of his 1929 New York exhibition.

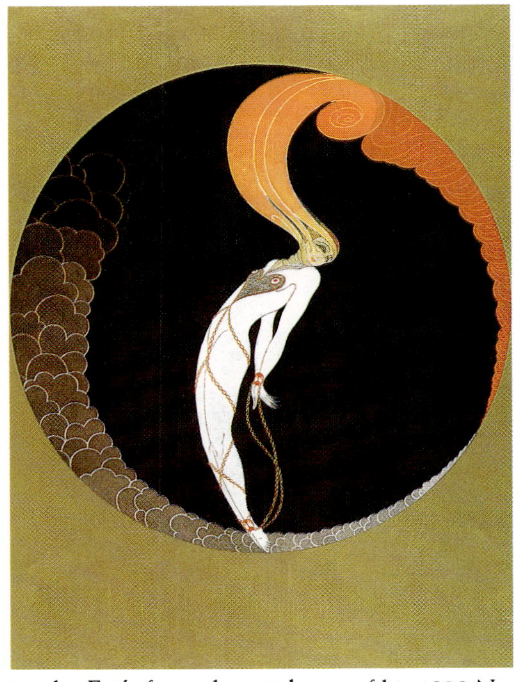

Theatrical illustration by Erté, from the catalogue of his 1929 New York exhibition.

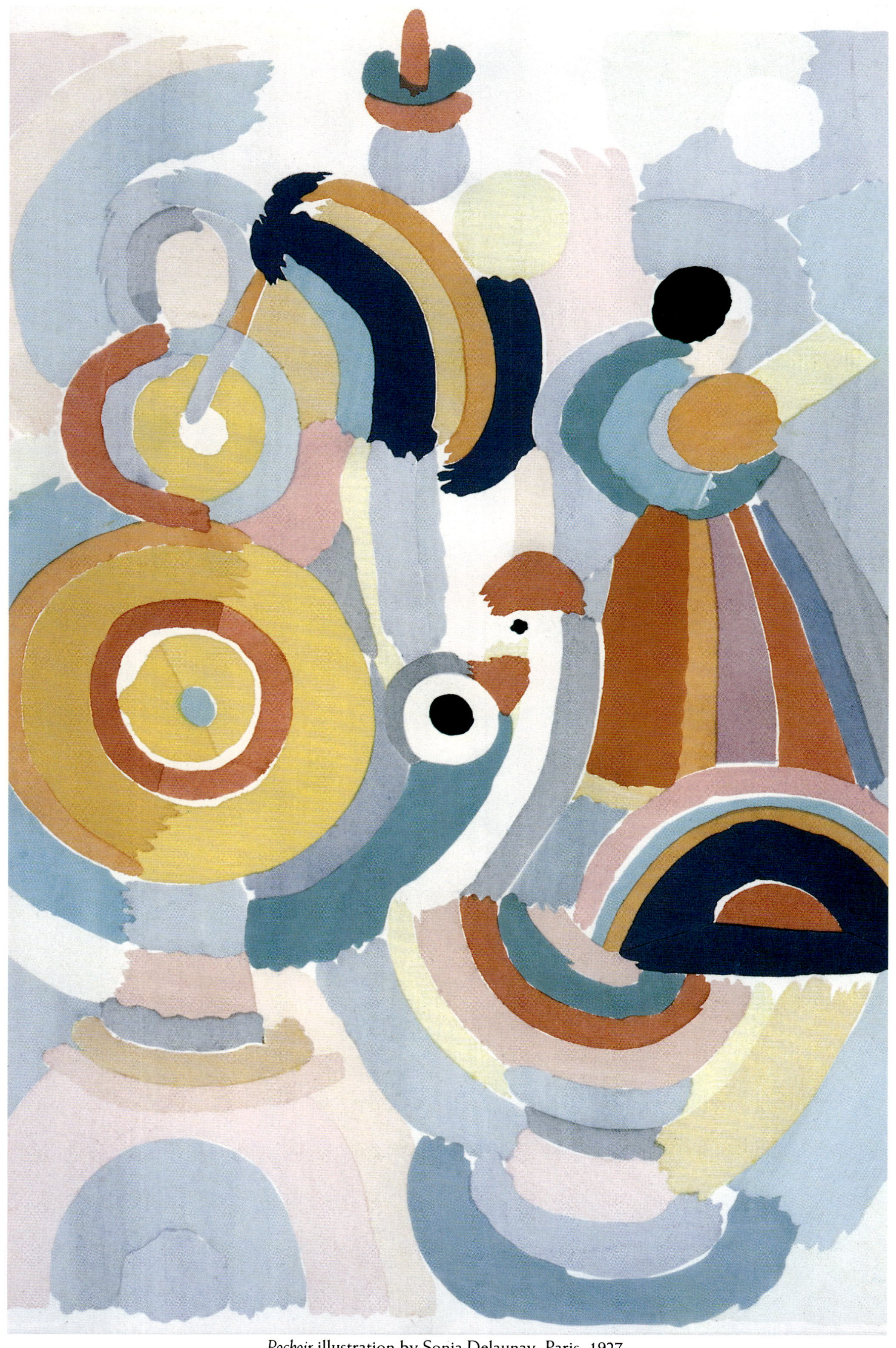

Pochoir illustration by Sonia Delaunay. Paris. 1927.

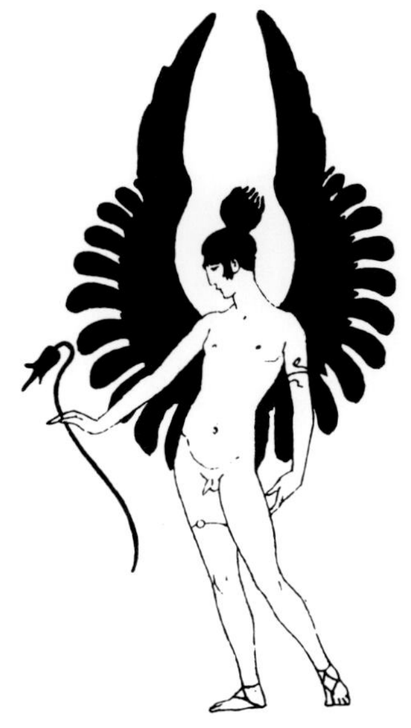

The exclusive pieces of furniture made by Ruhlmann and others from rare and expensive woods and featuring inlays of ivory and shagreen should not allow their usefulness to belie their artistic merit. This is also true of much of the wrought ironwork that was designed for use as door panels, screens, lamp fittings, archways, and many other decorative purposes; and it was true too of the stylised silverware of the period.

Ironically, the artistic merit so often associated with this period is that projected by chryselephantine statuettes. These were in fact generally mass produced, and originally were chosen for their decorative effect — a tendency that produced some interesting stylisations of the female form but did not aim very high in aesthetic terms. Like other popular forms of Art Deco, these chryselephantine statuettes — the word 'chryselephantine' coming from the Greek word referring to the combination of ivory and gold such as is said to have been used in the statue of the Athena Parthenos on the Acropolis — did not represent the best work of the artists of the period, even though the makers did attempt to incorporate many artistic innovations.

During the Art Deco period changes also occurred in the way in which legitimate forms of sculpture and paintings were used. In the nineteenth century, successful painters and sculptors exhibited their works at the annual salons. The purchasers were invariably large institutions, and the artists often received a variety of commissions for decorating buildings with large naturalistic or mythological paintings and lavish sculptured friezes. But in the twentieth century buildings were becoming less ostentatious, and painters and sculptors were more often required to produce small pieces for easy display in the houses and apartments of collectors. Many of the more successful artists worked very closely with interior designers, who commissioned works of specific size and shape for inclusion as an integral part of the design plan.

Other artists, in order to make a reasonable livelihood, became designers, thus blurring the previously rigid European distinction between art and design. Still others became illustrators, and their illustrative work influenced both designers and other artists. Some illustrators became fashionable painters, whilst others designed jewellery, carpets or decorative statuary. Picasso, for instance, and Natalia Goncharova, designed carpets and costumes for the Ballet Russe; Jean Lurçat and Raoul Dufy designed textiles, and Benito became a fashionable portrait painter. The whole field of visual creativity was becoming one of interdependence, and no single area was considered more important, or more artistically valid, than another. This was particularly vivid in the case of illustration and the printed image.

Unfortunately, today there seems to exist a prejudice against design in general, and fashion in particular, in the matter of their being regarded as legitimate forms of artistic expression. This is also so with printed

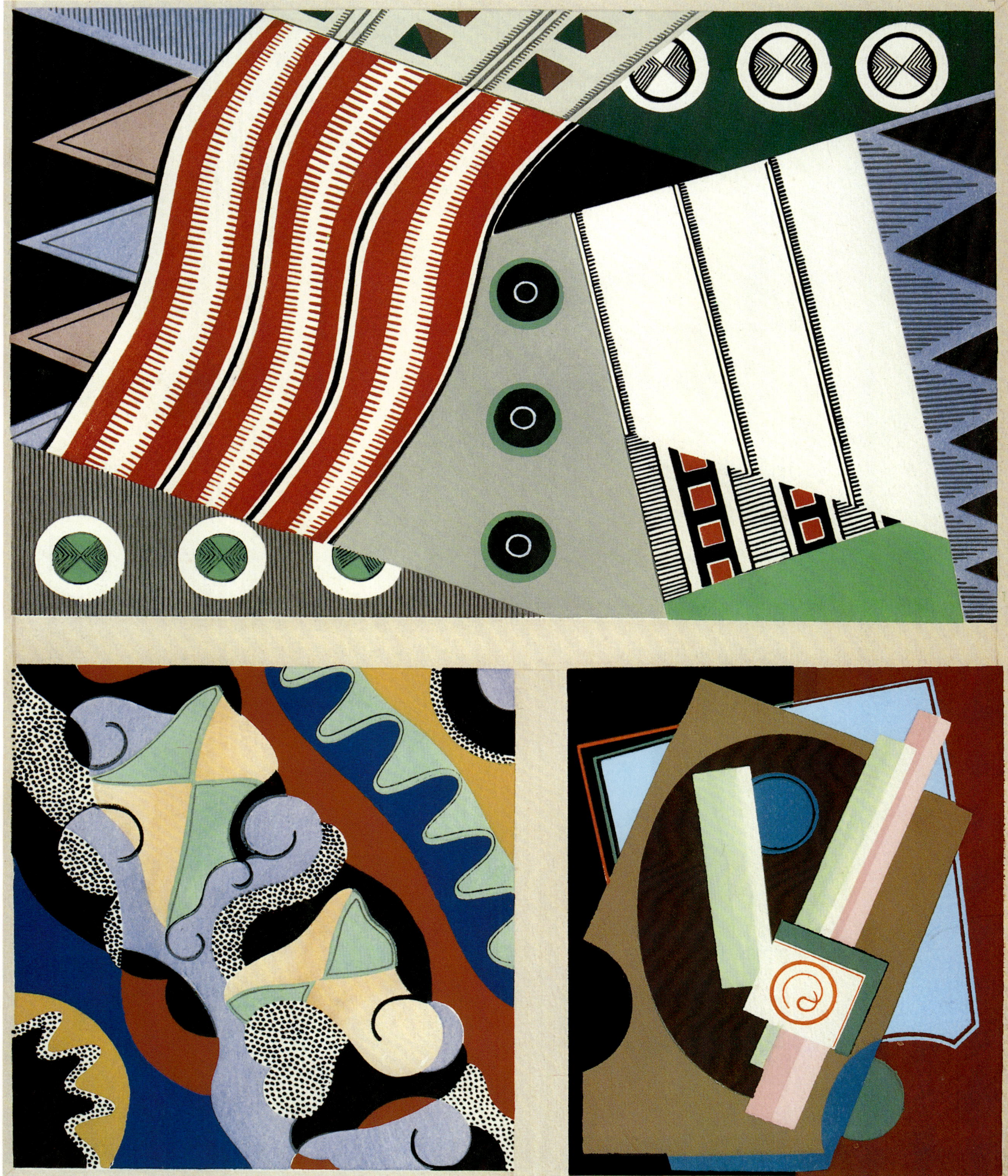

Collection of designs *Décors et couleurs* by Georges Valmier. Printed in *pochoir* by Jean Saudé for Editions Albert Lévy, Paris. 1929.

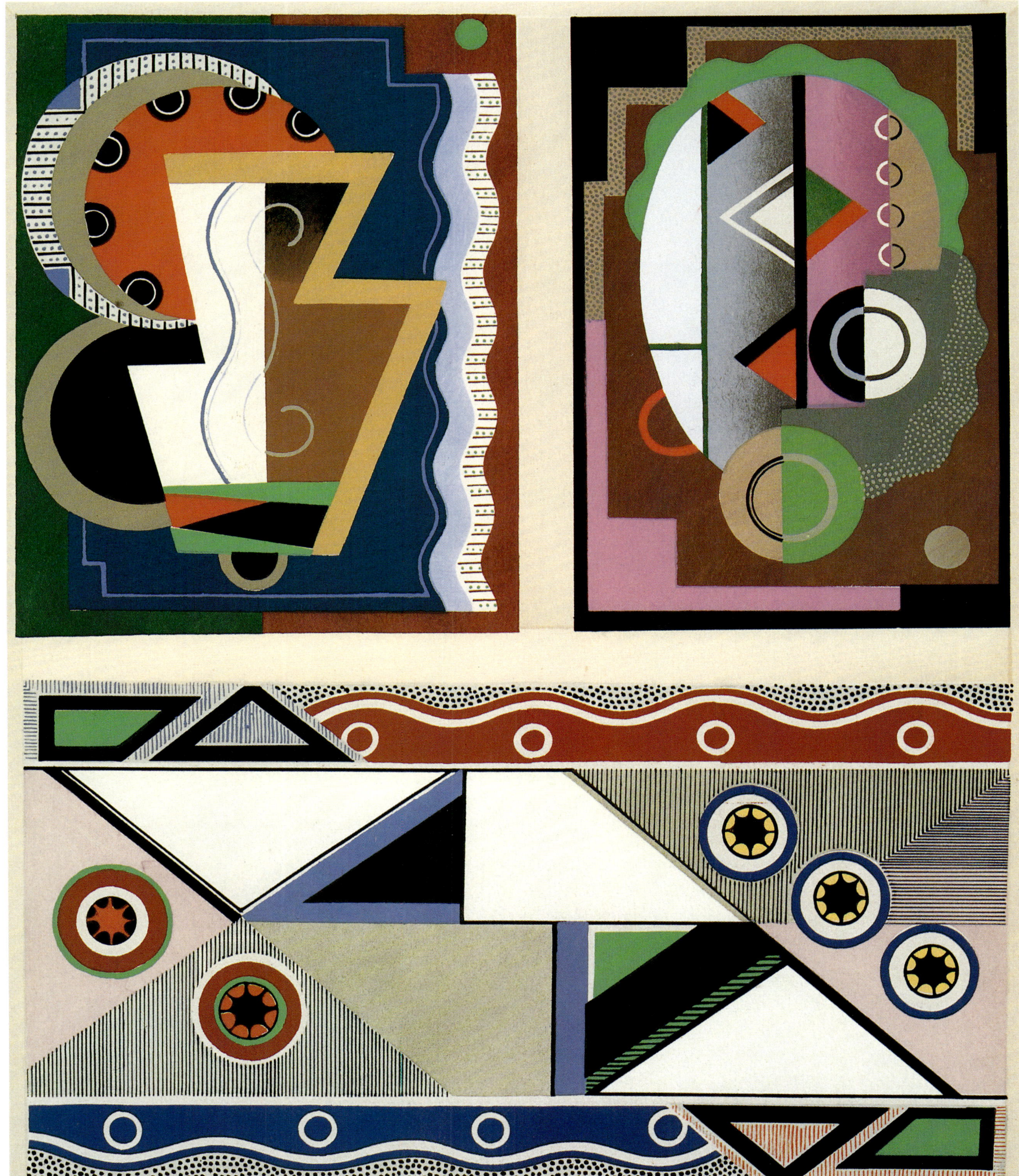

Collection of designs *Décors et couleurs* by Georges Valmier. Printed in *pochoir* by Jean Saudé for Editions Albert Lévy, Paris. 1929.

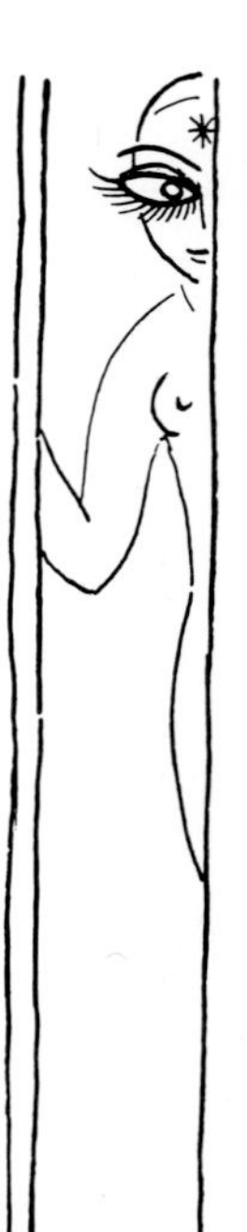

images, the word 'print' seeming to suggest that it is a purely commercialised product requiring only elaborate mechanical activity to produce a vast output. In addition, the word 'print' has become associated with sensational journalism, middle-class magazines, and commerce in general; the association does not suggest an acceptable medium for a work of art.

As with many other modes of expression, during Victorian times the printed image had fallen into disrepute under the weight of men of meagre talent and sensibility. In the latter part of the nineteenth century, however, with the talent of Whistler, Crane, Beardsley and Morris, a revival began, reaching its peak in works published by the Kelmscott Press, which re-established a visual unity and aesthetic sensibility for the printed page. This unity was further developed during the Art Nouveau and Art Deco periods: designer, engraver and printer François-Louis Schmied became the acknowledged master of woodblock printing, and Jean Saudé became a master of the deluxe *pochoir* process; both of these legendary men printed many fine books, portfolios and albums during the latter part of the 1920s.

Jean Saudé had already achieved a large following for his work on such books as *Le Jardin de caresses* and *Le Chariot de terre cuite* from illustrations by Leon Carré, *Hassan Badreddine el Bassraoui* from illustrations by Kees van Dongen, *Sports et divertissements* from illustrations by Charles Martin, *Le Bonheur du jour pour 1920* from illustrations by George Barbier, numerous issues of *Falbalas et Fanfreluches* and *La Guirlande*, and his *Traité d'enluminure d'art au pochoir*, which was displayed in the 1925 Art Deco Exhibition. He then turned his talents to printing portfolios of designs of new furniture styles, carpets, light fittings and glass pieces, shop fronts, new architectural styles, collections of sculpture and paintings, and a huge array of other works. His *pochoirs* for M. P. Verneuil's abstract *Kaleidoscope* published in 1926; for *Décors et couleurs* by Georges Valmier published in 1929; for the remarkable collection of *pochoir* images in *Tapis modernes* with designs by Picasso, Arp, Léger, Lurçat, Bruhn, Goncharova; for the fine five-volume set *Répertoire du goût moderne*; and for the belated *Relais 1930* with illustrations by Eduardo Bénédictus are some examples.

François-Louis Schmied had achieved a large following for books he had worked on with George Barbier and Paul Jouve, notably *Le Chanson de Bilitis* and *Le Livre de la jungle*, but from the mid-1920s he produced his best work alone. *Daphne*, *La Cantique des cantiques*, *La Création* and *Histoire de la Princesse Boudour* are among his greatest works — not only did he design all the illustrations, the layouts, the cameos, tailpieces and initials, but he also designed an original typeface for each new title. In addition, he engraved the woodblocks for each of his own illustrations, using as many as forty-five blocks to achieve the effect he desired for just one printed image. All the printing for these books was done on individual double-page spreads in the traditional hand press; some limited editions of only

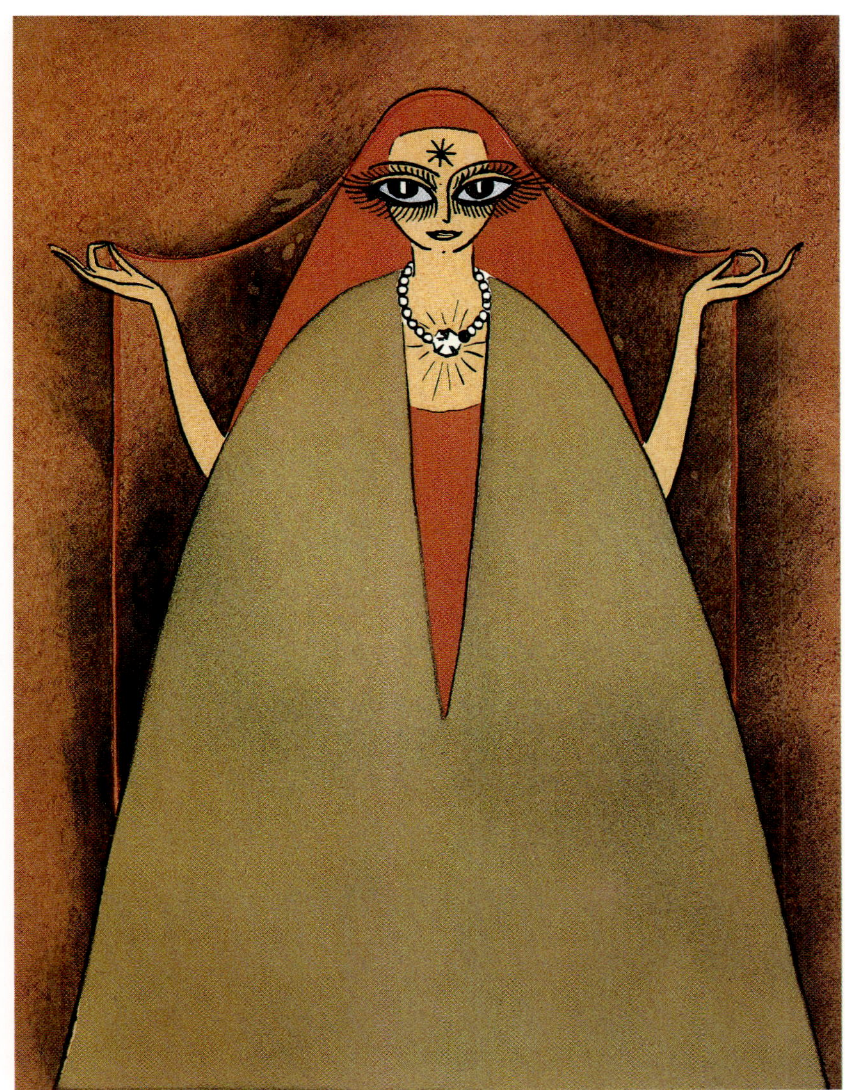

Pochoir illustration by Kees Van Dongen, for *Hassan Badreddine el Bassraoui*. Deluxe edition printed by Jean Saudé for Les Editions de la Sirène. Paris. 1926.

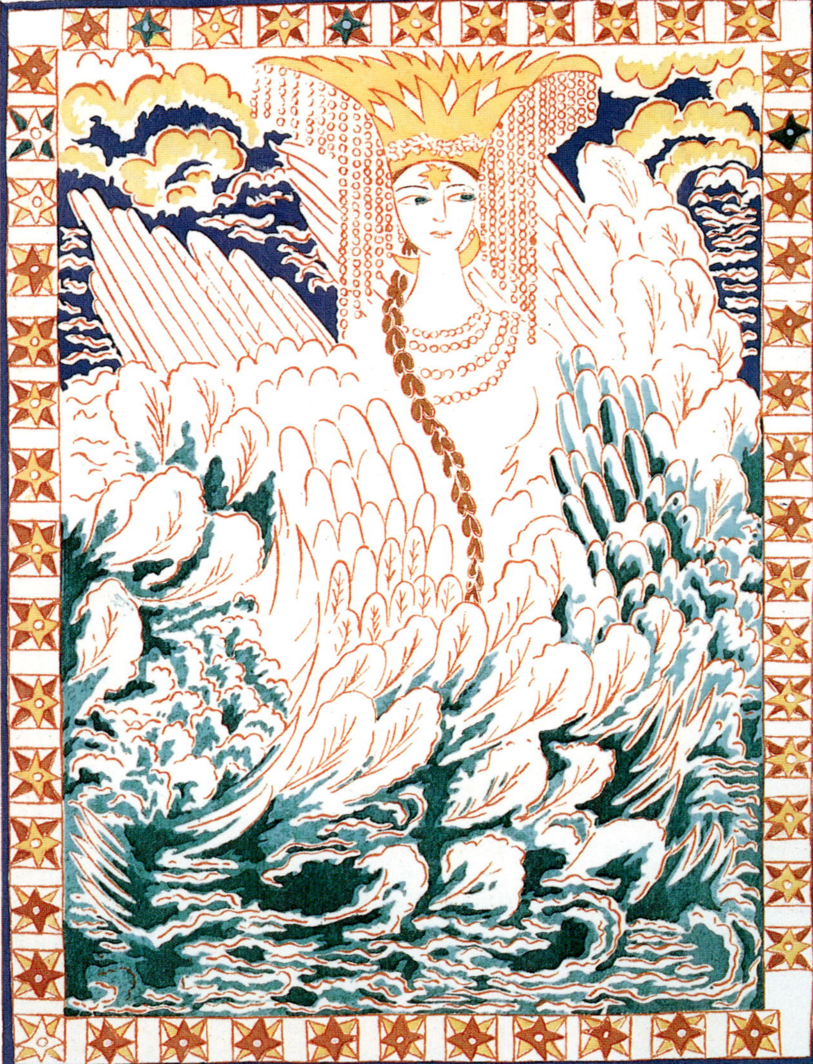

Pochoir illustration by Natalia Goncharova for *Conte de Tsar Saltan*. Deluxe edition of 500 copies. Editions de la Sirène, Paris. 1921.

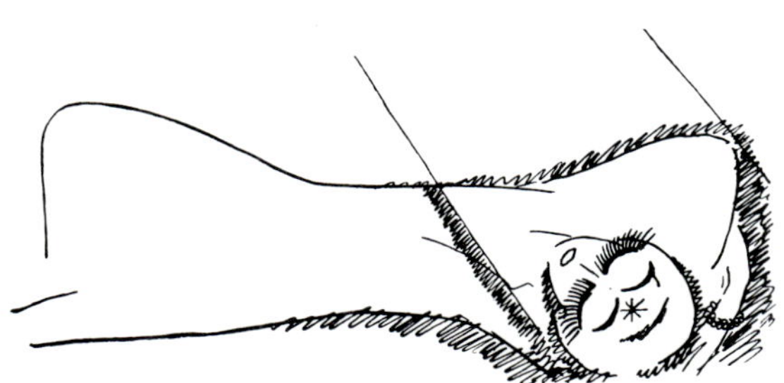

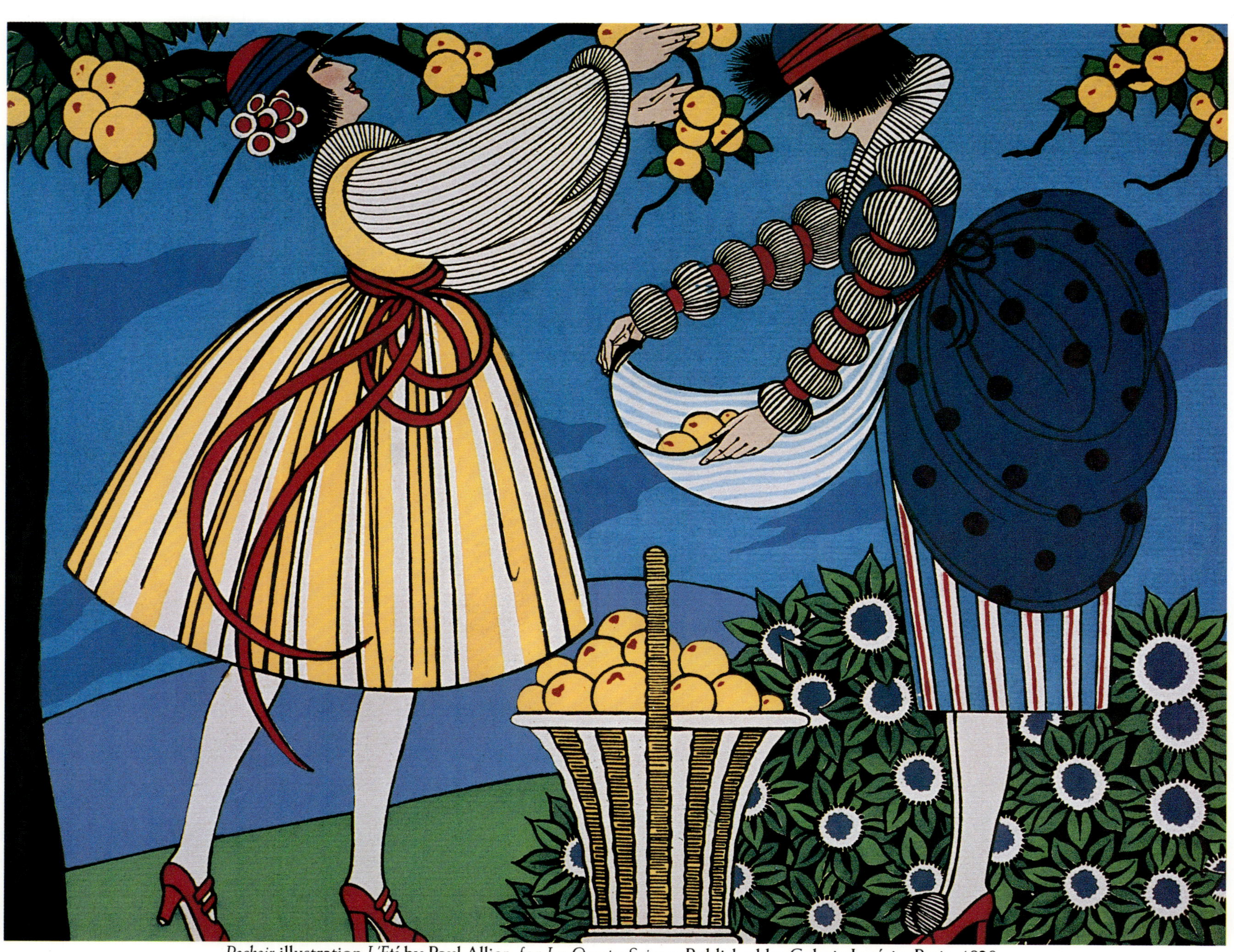

Pochoir illustration *L'Eté* by Paul Allier, for *Les Quartre Saisons*. Published by Galerie Lutétia, Paris. 1928.

110 copies would take one year to print, and some double-page spreads featured complex images requiring several days' work. Schmied also used special handmade paper for his various projects and he had the finished copies bound by the leading bookbinders, often incorporating lacquered panels by his friend Jean Dunand.

In 1927 Schmied held an exhibition of his work in New York and was hailed as 'the magnificent creator of the modern beautiful book'. Henry L. Bullen wrote in the foreword of the exhibition catalogue,

We are fortunate to have the work of François-Louis Schmied, whom we regard as the greatest living master of the art of the book. He designs and paints the illustrations, decorations and initials of his books. He reproduces his designs himself by means of complex wood engravings, composes the type and mixes the ink . . . He in fact designs and controls everything, even designing special typefaces to suit each book so that they are compatible with the effect desired from the illustrations.

A year earlier, in 1926, an exhibition had been held in New York which had featured a special collection on loan from the previous year's Art Deco Exhibition. The intention of this exhibition was to persuade Americans to buy the works of the French designers. It opened at the New York Metropolitan and then toured the major cities. Although it did indeed have a dramatic effect on those who came to see it, its effect on potential customers was not what had been hoped; instead, it influenced the new breed of young American designers who had also been influenced by the Hollywood Deco style common in the mid-1920s.

In 1927, Macy's department store in New York held a follow-up Art Deco exhibition called Art in Trade. This included many items designed by local American designers whose products were beginning to show evidence of a mixture of French Art Deco, a new streamlining, and distinct theatrical overtones inspired by Hollywood.

The design scene was also beginning to change in Paris. Many of the smaller ateliers were being forced to close for want of orders, or they were beginning to produce other forms of more saleable merchandise. *La Gazette du bon ton* had also been closed by its new American owners, Condé Nast, because the number of subscribers dropped dramatically at the end of 1925. But the talented illustrators were not out of work: most of them were offered work on the French and English editions of *Vogue* and on *Le Jardin des modes*, both of which were also part of the

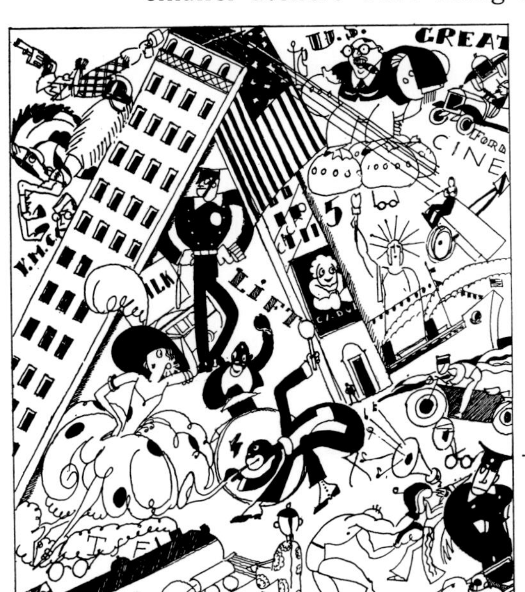

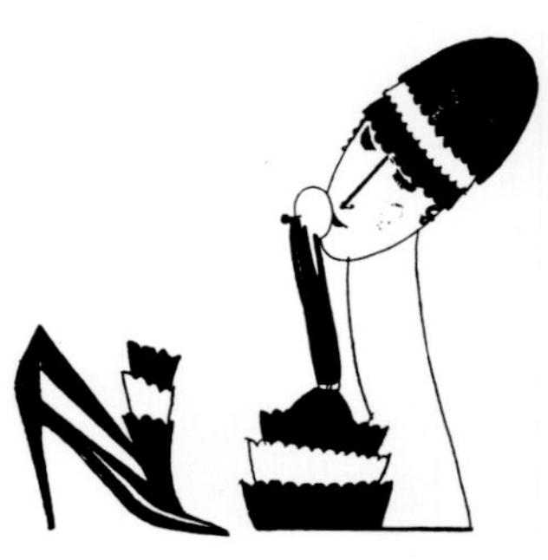

Condé Nast publishing empire; other illustrators worked on small albums of fashion designs such as Paul Allier's *Les Quartre Saisons*, Carlos Bady's *La Journée de Mado*, and Tito's *Quatre Proverbes*.

The fashion scene was changing, too: *Art-Goût-Beauté*, the only remaining deluxe fashion monthly published expressly for the haut monde, reported, 'One of the signs of the times is that fashions are being steadily modified through the new taste for sport which has become more pronounced this autumn season. Dresses continue to be made very smart in the Rue de la Paix, but at the same time they are now more practical'. It went on: 'One of the newest crazes is to wear a divided golfing skirt with a man's velvet smoking jacket, a monocle and high leather boots when going to a downtown nightclub'.

The large glossy magazine *Paris chic* informed its readers of 'the flash and splendour of diamantes worn for cocktails', whilst for evening wear and afternoon race attire it advised 'diaphanous silk chiffon, tulle and lace, with the décolletage being cut very low'. The new very short dance dresses were, we are told, made 'from a single layer of chiffon, handsomely beaded' and worn with a slimly cut flesh-coloured slip that had a buttoned crotch, called a *chemise-culotte*. This was to be worn instead of the usual French knickers, or any other forms of underclothing, even when dancing the charleston or the shimmy — there was not much more than a couple of centimetres of silk fabric protecting the wearer's modesty, and even that was loosely fitted.

An editorial in a 1928 edition of *L'Art et la mode* pointed out that, despite the vogue for eating out, plump women with full, rounded shoulders, heavy breasts and well-developed *derrières* were no longer in fashion. This was reinforced by an article in *La Femme chic*:

Women are no longer being classified by age, but according to their body shapes. Bodies should be kept supple and lithe by continuous exercise and by diet, which thankfully is no longer a scientific mystery as it was in our mothers' day. In the theatre physical beauty has always been demanded, and expected, and therefore provided. Go to a good revue or a musical comedy and you will find an excellent object lesson in physical culture. Here are beautiful human bodies perfectly trained.

If perchance you just happened to be in Paris that year you could have seen the much admired, and much displayed, lithe body of the Afro-American Josephine Baker, who was then being hailed as the Queen of Jungle Jazz, Harlem's Hot Spot, and the Dynamo of Syncopation. In her new Negro revue, *Blackbirds*, she is said to have danced as if in 'a savage frenzy inherited from her distant African ancestors', wearing a skimpy diamante-trimmed black maillot and long red gloves that one reporter described as 'up to the wildest imagination of Beardsley'.

In 1928 fashion reporters praised the increasing popularity of wearing lizard and snake skin shoes to draw attention to the wearer's shapely legs, and thought the fashion for the new decorative garters and for rouging

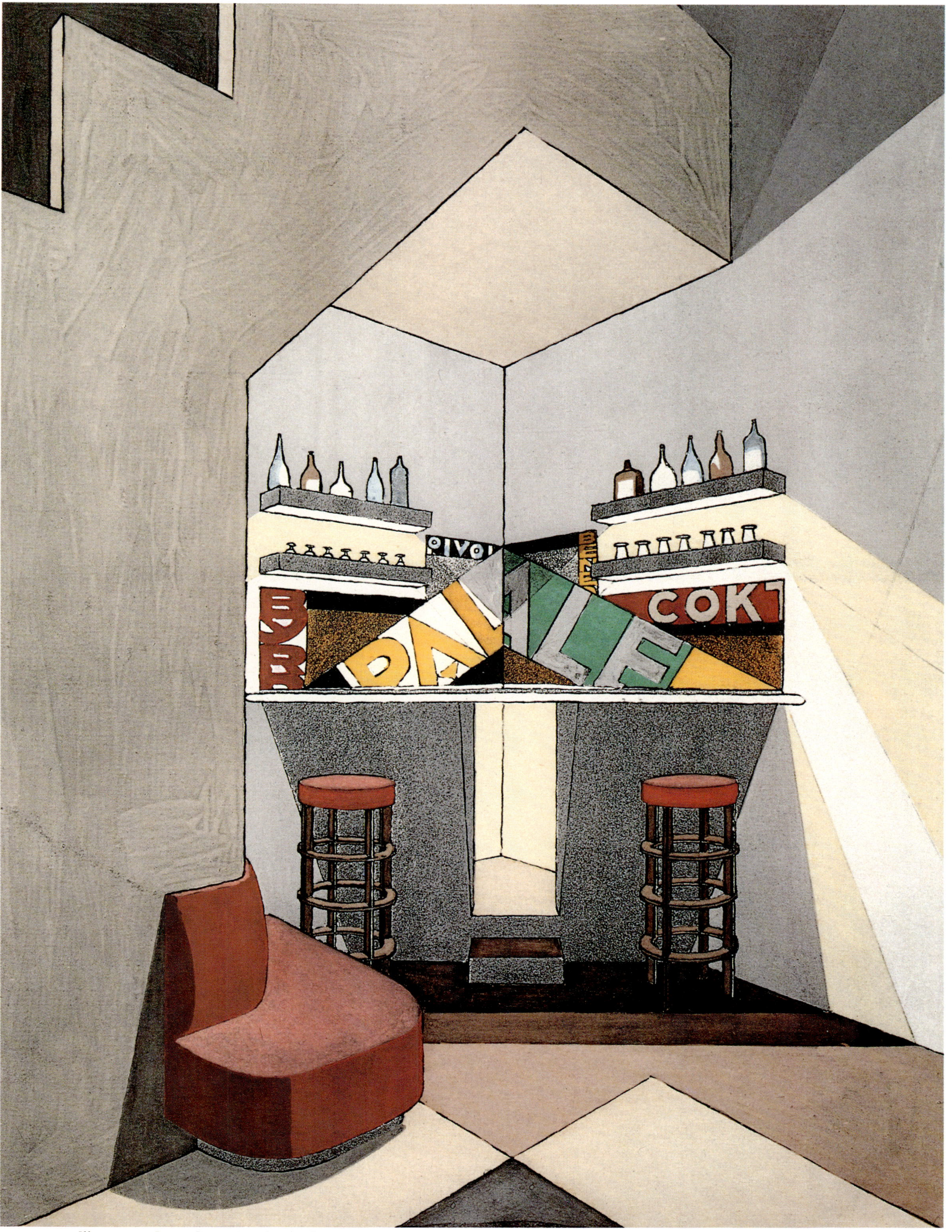

Illustration *Living Room, Petit Bar* by Djo-Bourgeois. Printed in *pochoir* by Jean Saudé for *Répertoire du goût moderne*. Published by Editions Albert Lévy, Paris. 1928.

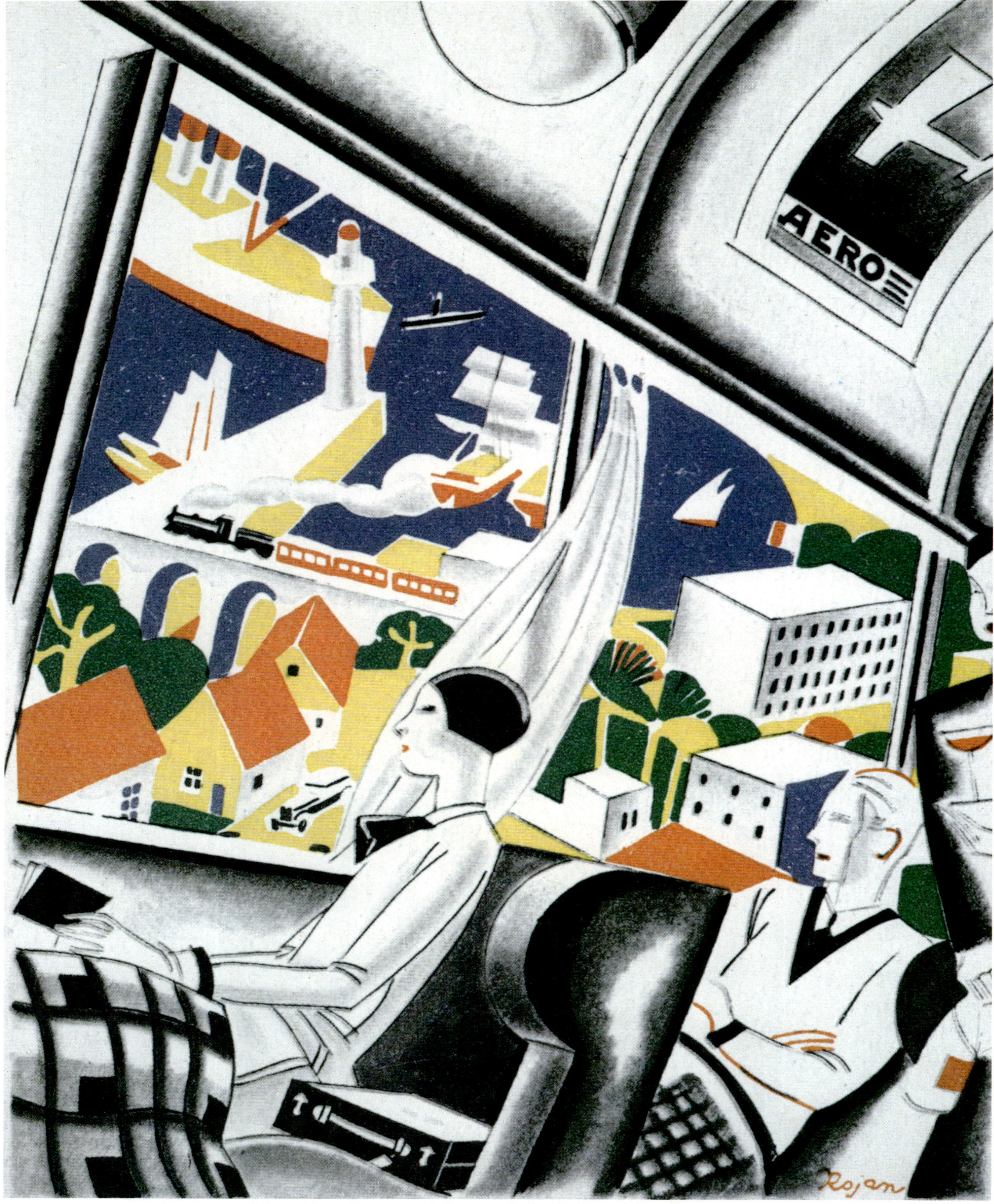

Coloured litho illustration M. Rojan for *La Grande Maison de blanc*, Paris. 1929.

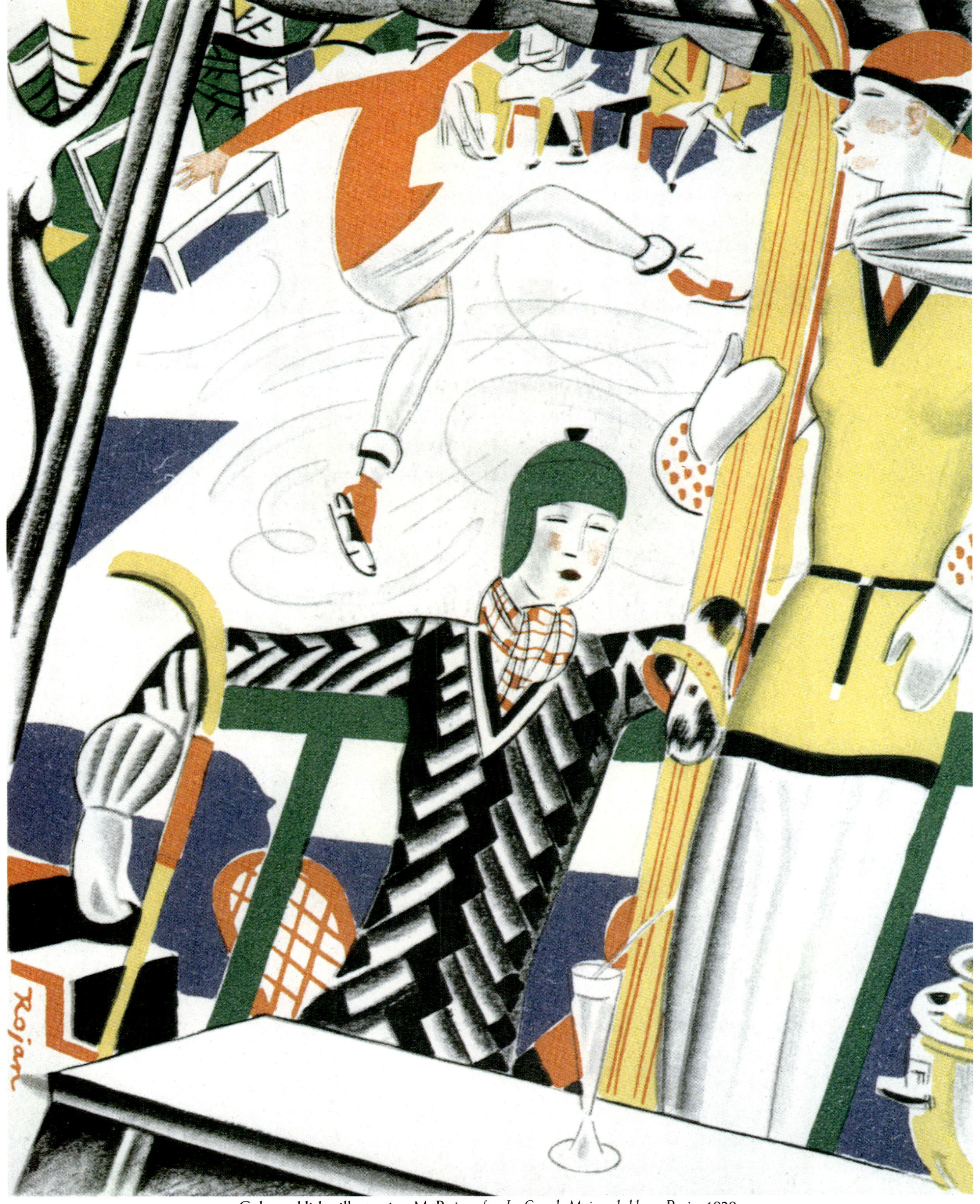

Coloured litho illustration M. Rojan, for *La Grande Maison de blanc*, Paris. 1929.

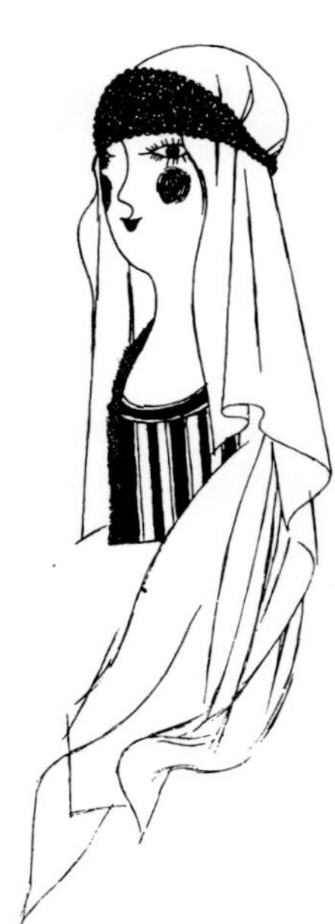

the knees was 'most becoming'. They staunchly supported Coco Chanel as the designer of 'youthful chic'. They cooed approvingly when the new fashions had hemlines that dipped slightly to one side, giving an asymmetrical look, or dipped on all sides and had inset godets to give a handkerchief hemline. They acquiesced at the reintroduction of the corset, even in the youngest of women, to achieve a smooth, unbroken line for the new curved sheath dresses. They praised the new resort fashions for silk pyjama trousers worn with a casually tied silk jacket. And they drooled over the new evening wraps made from gold and silver lamé, metallic brocades and silk moirés lavishly trimmed with monkey fur and garnished with the latest Cartier jewels.

Editorials also appeared for men, advising them that the woman of fashion wanted her escort to be 'correctly attired on every occasion and at all times': woe betide the man 'who, although wealthy, by being incorrectly dressed according to the unwritten laws of good society, shows himself ignorant in the manners of good breeding'. Another reporter wrote,

With the exception of evening dress, formal afternoon clothes are the most important in a man's wardrobe. Certainly, a man never looks better than when he is well turned out in a top hat, cut-away coat and striped trousers. Like one's evening tail-coat, the cut-away must fit impeccably, otherwise the entire ensemble loses all of its distinction and smartness.

And to fit really well, the columnist advised, 'the cut-away must follow closely the lines of a slim figure and set snugly at the waistline, a feat,' she concluded, 'which could only be achieved by the best tailors of London's Savile Row.'

Obviously, just as it had been throughout the nineteenth century, it was the duty of a man of fashion to conform to the rules of society so that he could display his wealth, social position and breeding. Before the French Revolution, the fashionable man of wealth and good standing had, like his sisters, worn a wide variety of fashions made from satins, velvets and other fine fabrics decorated with embroidery and beadwork. But during the latter part of the eighteenth century, when there was unrest throughout Europe and the French Revolution was at its bloodiest, any

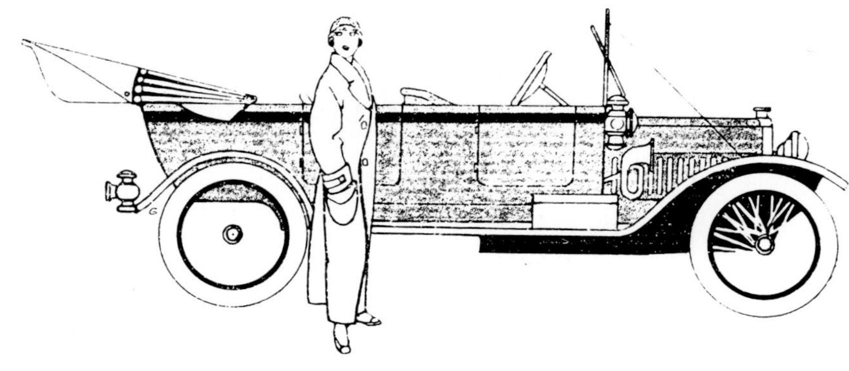

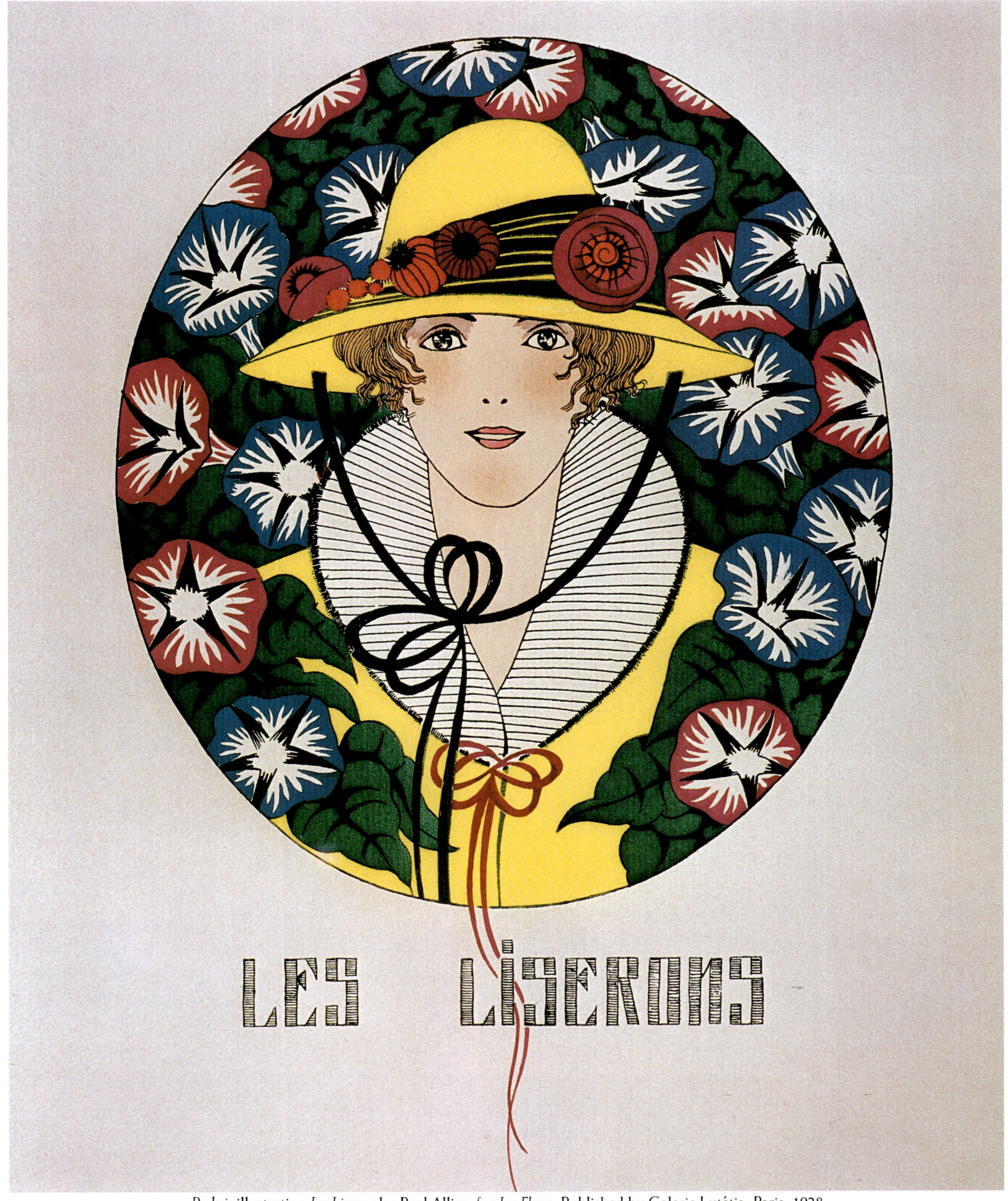

Pochoir illustration *Les Liserons* by Paul Allier, for *Les Fleurs*. Published by Galerie Lutétia, Paris. 1928.

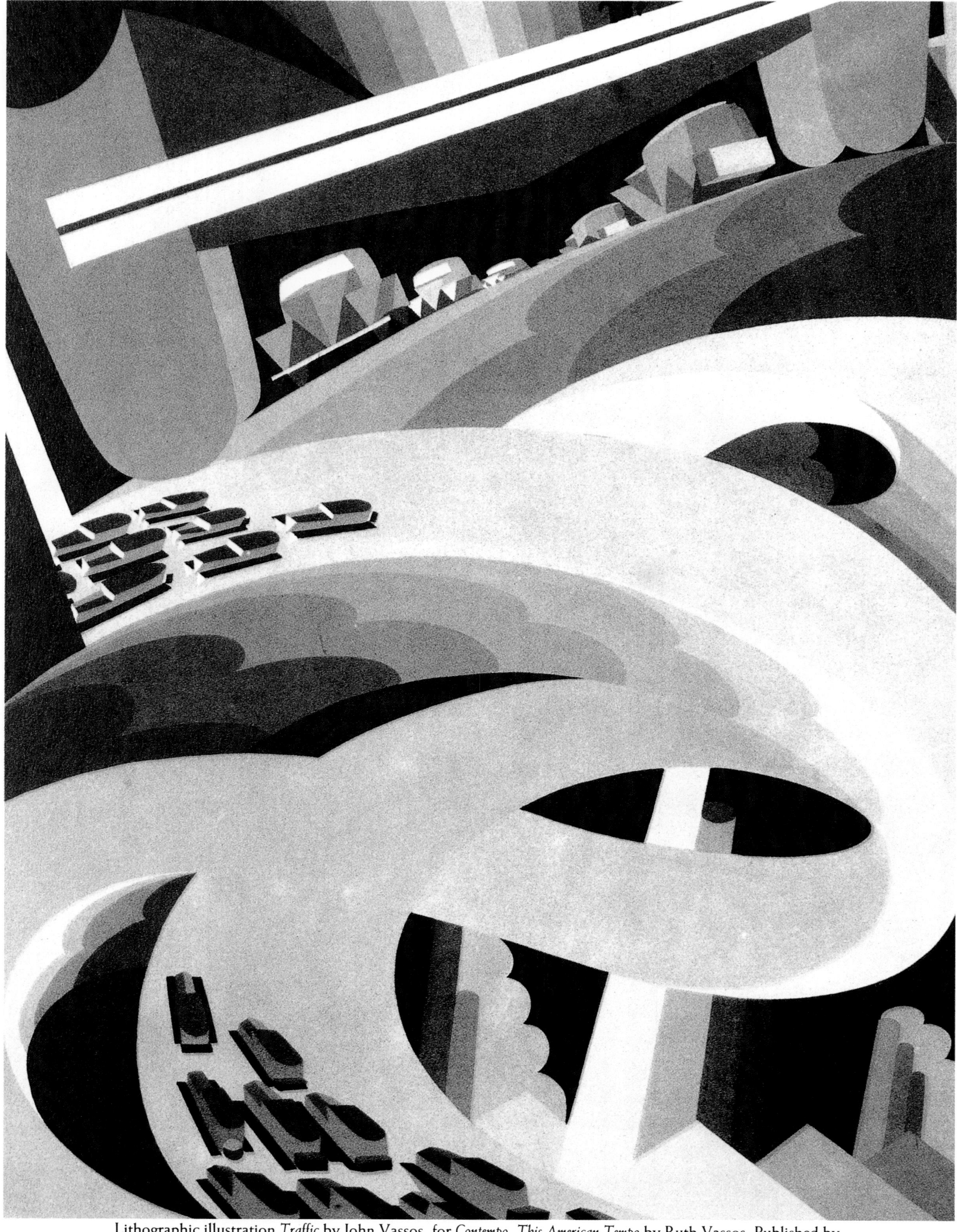

Lithographic illustration *Traffic* by John Vassos, for *Contempo. This American Tempo* by Ruth Vassos. Published by E. P. Dutton & Co. Inc. New York. 1929.

male who dressed in a fanciful manner was immediately suspected of being an aristocrat and was liable to summary execution, or at least imprisonment. Male costume came under the rigid control of social politics; it became increasingly conservative, and any male who dared to dress outside the dull conventions of black and grey was liable to be ostracised from society.

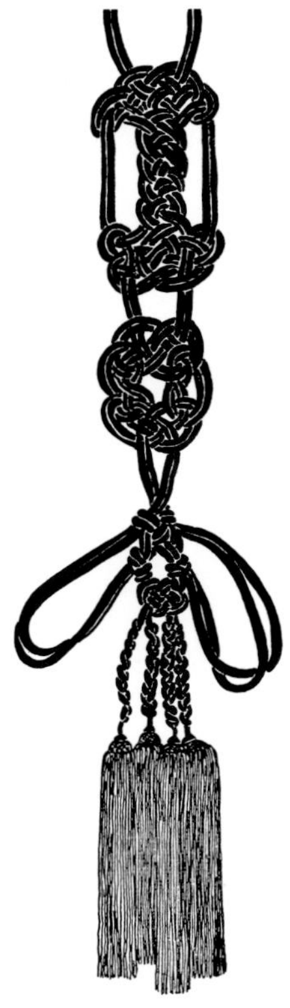

In the late 1920s, however, it seemed for a time at least that some men were being unleashed from the chains of conventional dress. Male Hollywood stars began to influence the new male modes, and editorials began advising their male readers that they should change their ways.

You are beaten, outwitted, outvoted, outplayed and you have lost the privilege of being ugly and out-of-date. So get pretty or beat it. If you want to be loved by one of today's fair maidens, have your hair curled, give your skin that sun-kissed look, and visit the beauty salon to acquire the cared-for look of the new Hollywood stars.

But the majority of reporters thought that the traditional pre-eminence of English men's tailoring was quite unshakable:

. . . to the despair and confusion of those tailors and chemisiers of Paris and New York who have developed a style of quite the wrong kind. It is true that in the Rue de la Paix and Fifth Avenue can be found undeniably pretty clothes for men, but these items, when worn with bright-hued accessories by the willowy young men who prefer to inhabit bars and night clubs, are to us in very bad taste — what the French call chi-chi . . . and what would cause any young woman of fashion to die of embarrassment if seen being escorted by one of these new lounge lizards to Ascot, Wimbeldon, or the theatre.

Despite this opposition, though, men's casual clothes, given the seal of approval of the Prince of Wales, due to be crowned King Edward VIII, did become slightly less rigid and more colourful.

Language was also undergoing a dramatic change during the final two years of the 1920s. The word 'chic', for example, was continually used in conversation and it appeared over and over again in all sorts of publications. The word had in fact originated in modern parlance in Hollywood, as a reference to Rudolf Valentino in his famous role as *The Sheik*; it came to be used to denote anything that resembled the new daring and charm of 'Rudi'. But many people were ignorant of its origins and pronounced it 'chick'; the French, of course, pronounced it 'sheek', as they had always done. Thus it was that by 1928 'chic' came into vogue: not to use it would have been very un-chic. Copywriters began to exploit this evocative word. It was used to sell anything from the new cami-knickers to expensive limousines, and gradually it came to mean what was in the minds of its users: stylishness and a kind of extravagant, risqué elegance.

In the America of 1929, automobiles, movies and bootlegging were said to be the three biggest industries. After these, I suspect, came fashion and beauty. A look through the advertisements pages of any popular American magazine of that year reveals at least one page in every three

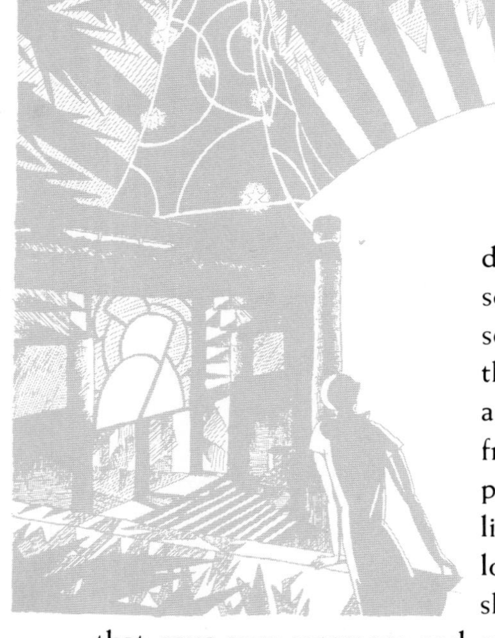

devoted to new fashions and to beauty: scented soaps, skin foods, lotions, hair preservers, hair removers, hair lotions, pills that claimed to dissolve fat from the inside, and bath salts that claimed to dissolve fat from the outside. There were powders, paints and pastes of all colours, kiss-proof lipsticks, foods that guaranteed to make you lose weight, machines that gave you electric shocks to stimulate your nerves, engines that gave you massages and exercised your muscles. There were advertisements for beauty parlours, beauty specialists and masseurs, and for new styles in lingerie, dresses, coats, shoes, accessories, hats, 'resort wear' and travel clothes, and even specialists who would refurbish last year's Rolls Royce to suit the styles and colours of the latest fashions.

Fashionable jewellery was also beginning to change its style, financed by the fortunes then being made on Western stock markets. It began moving towards new, more sculptural forms, in which the idea often took precedence over function. The sophisticated woman could have her jewels redesigned to suit her latest mode of dress, and the couturiers were introducing collections of disposable costume jewellery made from semi-precious stones.

The decade was nearing its end, and vast sums of money were being spent to finance the elite's increasing demand for new jewels, new clothes, world-wide travel, new business ventures, lavish entertainments, new furnishings, more and more of everything.

Then the crash came. Like a bombshell, that unforgettable 'Black Tuesday' of 29 October 1929 arrived without warning: the American stock exchange collapsed and stocks and shares that had been trading at unparalleled levels dropped in one day to less than one-tenth of their value. Vast fortunes were lost overnight. Confusion and uncertainty spread across America, and then throughout the Western world.

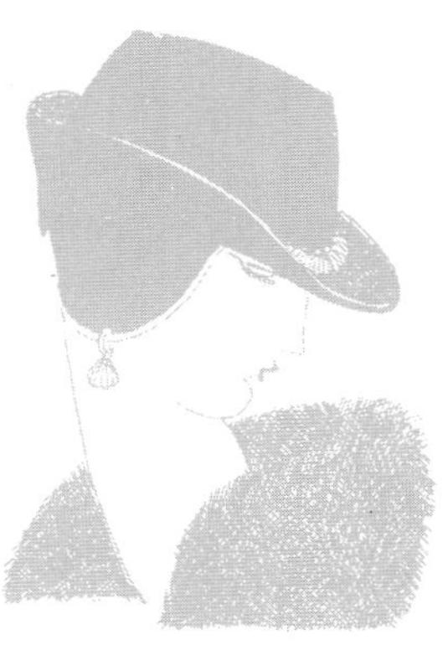

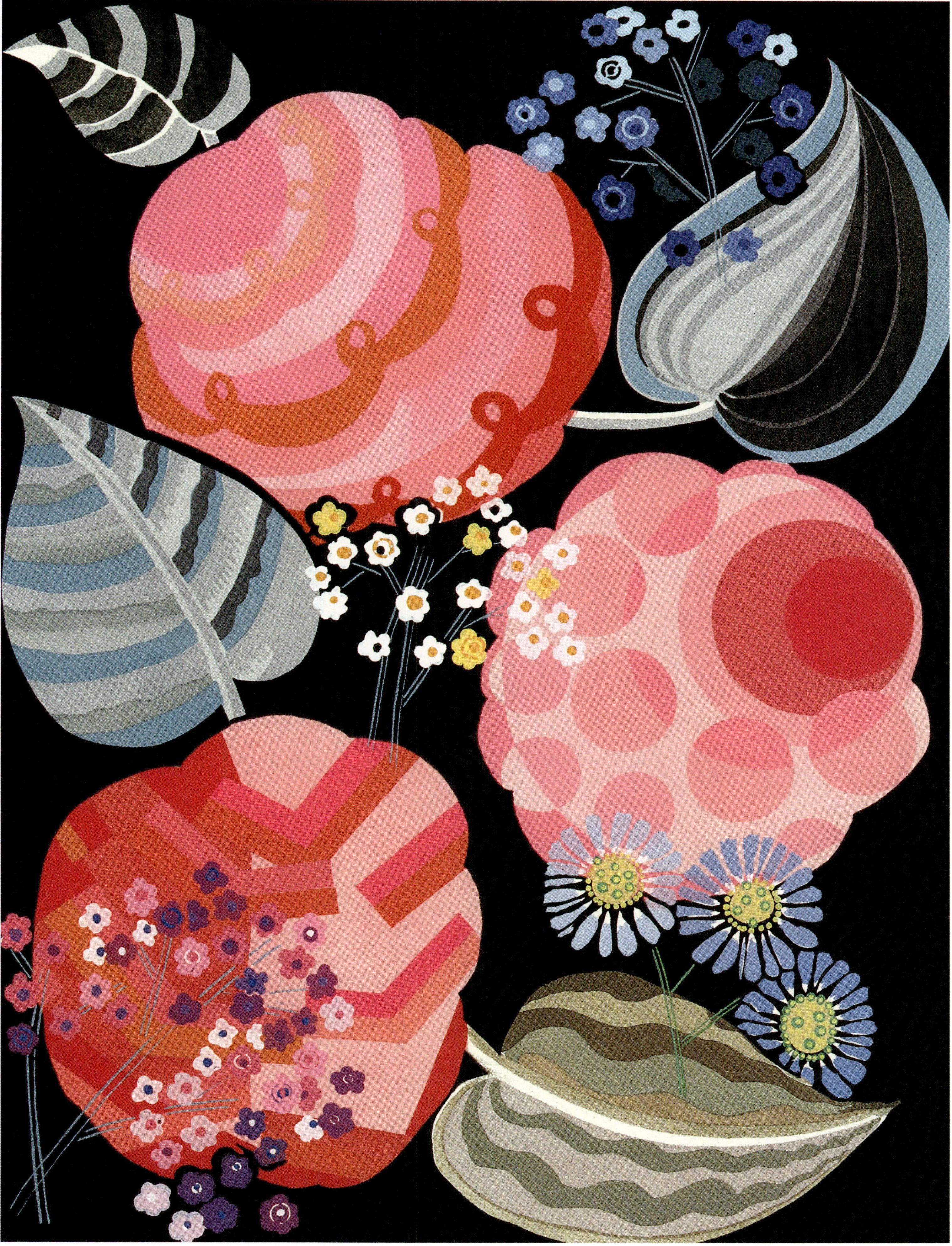

Design ideas *Relais* by Bénédictus. Printed in *pochoir* by Jean Saudé, for *Relais 1930*. Published by Editions Vincent, Fréal et Cie, Paris. 1930.

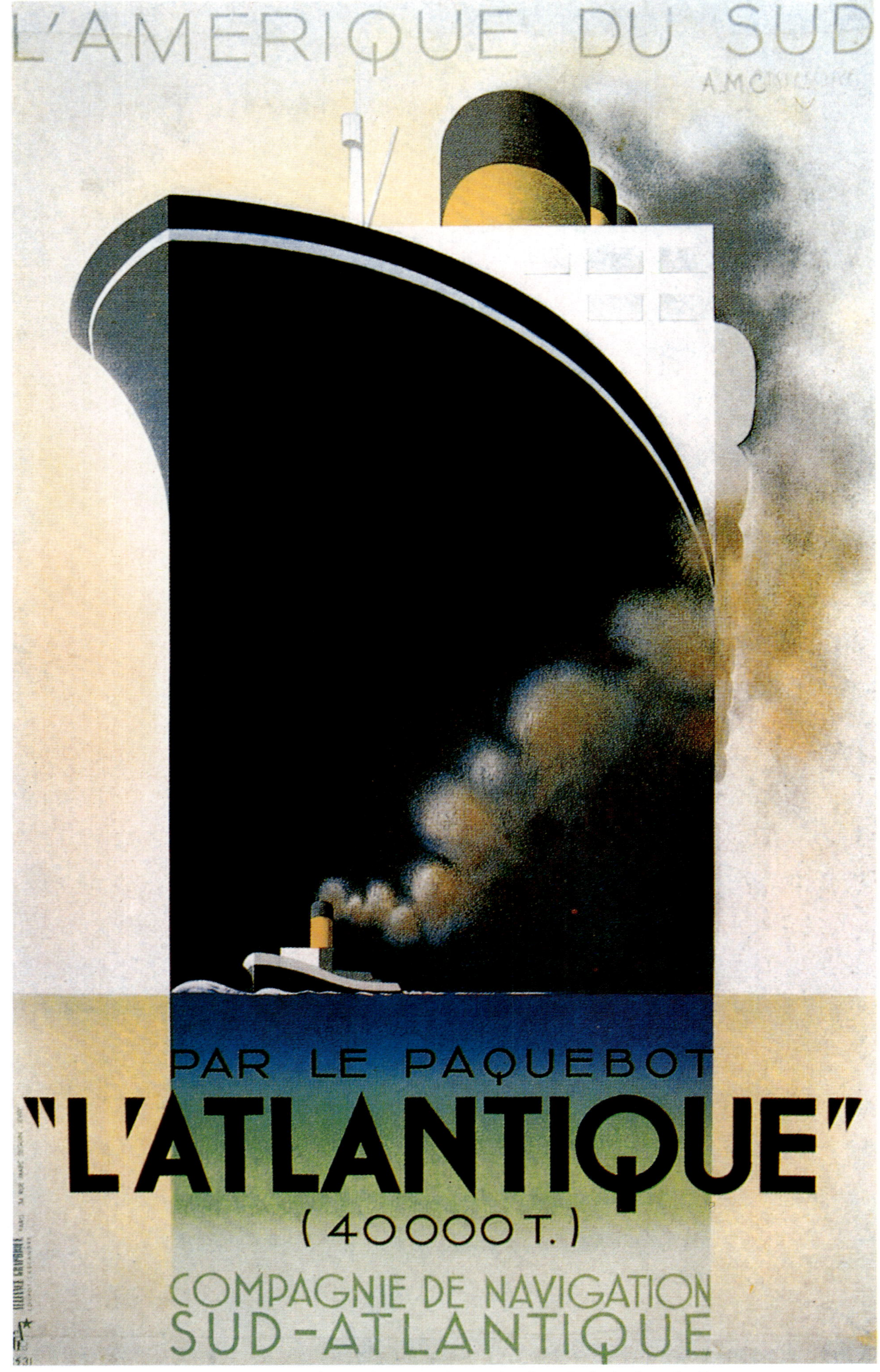

Magazine advertisement *L'Atlantique* by A. M. Cassandre, from *Le Jardin des modes*. Paris. 1931.

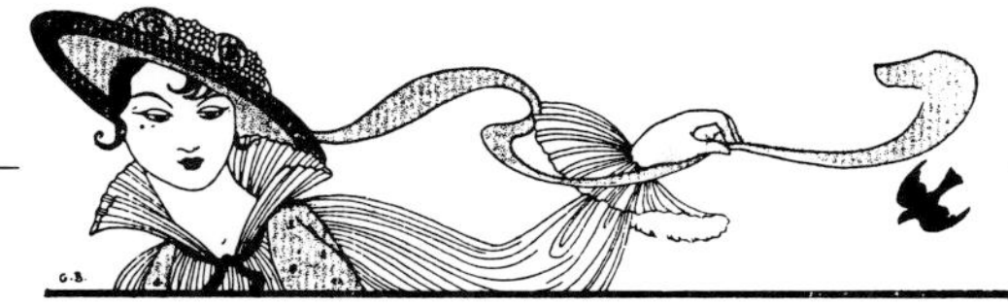

THE STREAMLINED DESIGN STYLE

In the years of financial chaos that followed the great Wall Street crash of October 1929, during the period known as the Great Depression, Western society began to strive for social progress and industrial proficiency. In design, the geometric shapes and clear colours of the Art Deco style of the 1920s gave way to the mass-produced streamlined teardrop shape — the new symbol of optimism and hope. Evolved from the scientific quest for speed and mechanical efficiency, this shape had been first employed during the late 1920s by engineering designers seeking to create a new generation of streamlined aeroplanes, automobiles, coaches and trains.

Having established the principles of the teardrop shape, product designers began to adopt streamlining as a non-functional stylism. This then quickly became identified with the new mass-market trends in furniture design, radios, bathroom fittings, electrical gadgets of all kinds, and clothing, even when speed and efficiency were irrelevant.

During these first few years of the 1930s, many of the famous Art Deco designers who had reached their peak of creativity five years earlier, when their finest products were displayed in the 1925 Art Deco Exhibition, were being replaced by a new breed of industrially orientated designers: Walter Dorwin Teague, Marcel Breuer, Le Corbusier, Henry Dreyfuss, Richard Buckminster Fuller, Norman Bel Geddes and Ludwig Mies van der Rohe were applying the new principles of streamlining and modern methods of production to buildings and mass-produced goods, making them more attractive, safer, more functional, easier to produce, and cheaper.

The roots of the streamlined teardrop shape, like the roots of the

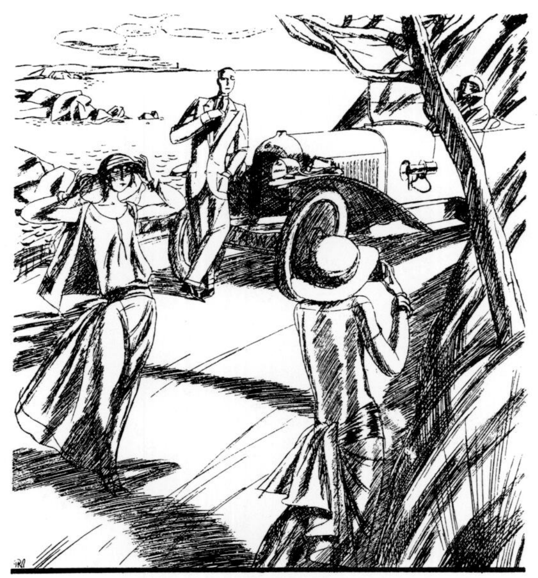

very early Art Deco design style, are to be found in the writings of the eighteenth and early nineteenth century industrial philosophers, some of whom had studied the effects of hydrodynamics and aerodynamics on sailing ships and horse-drawn carriages, particularly those made for racing. But at that time it was difficult to undertake useful experiments to prove the theories these industrial philosophers propounded: testing facilities were very limited and rather crude. Daniel Bernoulli does mention some experimental work on hydrodynamics in his book of 1738, and later Sir George Cayley writes of developing from his study of fish and birds a streamlined shape for the hull of a boat, which he thought 'would travel equally well in water as it would in air'. Cayley developed his theory further after making detailed studies of trout and seagulls, and in a paper on aeronautics published in 1804 he proposed that in a form designed for least resistance whilst travelling through water or air 'the trailing end was as important as the curved front end'. He also correctly predicted the eventual acceptance of streamlining for all man-made moving objects, which he pronounced had been 'created by a better designer than man'.

In 1850 Cayley devised a whirling-arm apparatus for testing his various theories of streamlining, but his ideas, and those of Bernoulli, could not be tested with any accuracy until the development in the 1870s of the first wind tunnel, at Greenwich in England. Experiments in streamlining continued throughout the 1870s and 1880s, and by the early 1890s many new discoveries were being made about the ideal shape of rigid-framed airships and trains. Similar tests were also being undertaken in water tanks to assess the streamlining effect on ships' hulls, and for designing submarines and torpedoes. But the real breakthrough in the development of streamlining came in America in the mid-1920s, with research being carried out for developing a new generation of intercity passenger trains, intercontinental aeroplanes, and new styles of automobiles — all of which promised very profitable markets for those who succeeded in developing a form that captured the public imagination.

Always quick to pick up an idea that represented a new trend in commercial life, the Hollywood film industry began in the mid-1920s to incorporate its ideas about streamlining into set designs, thus starting to influence public taste. The trend was also beginning to be reflected in advertising graphics and in small mass-produced artifacts.

As sales of manufactured Art Deco-inspired goods began to slump in the Western world, largely as a result of over-production, manufacturers turned to their sales executives for advice about changing the surface

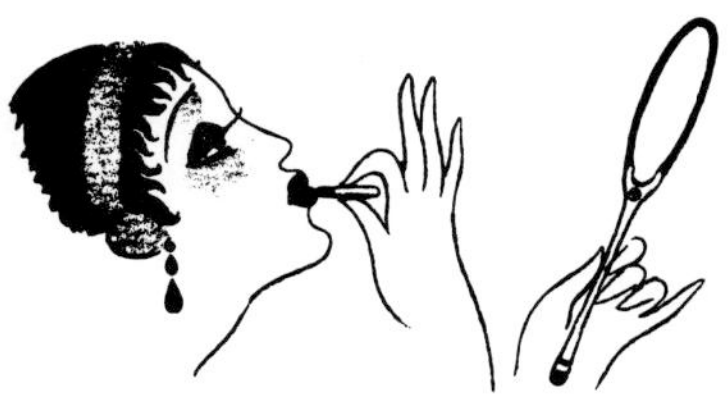

appearance of their products: this might boost flagging sales but obviate the vast expense of the retooling involved in producing completely new designs. Advertising agencies were called in to help restyle the surface treatment of many consumer items, to make them more attractive and to give them a look of modernity. And the agencies employed the only specialists they had: an army of advertising illustrators, packaging artists, graphics experts, and theatrical designers. These specialists, adept at the art of visual persuasion and understanding the temporary nature of popular taste, were able to absorb the need for a streamlined fashion; they concentrated their efforts on redesigning products according to the mode they had seen in Hollywood films and read about in books and advertisements. They were the first generation of American 'design stylists'.

The years 1929–33 witnessed some remarkable achievements in restyling consumer products in America. Sales of many items such as electric kettles and toasters, food mixers, radios and refrigerators increased up to sevenfold after the products were restyled. Gradually, too, the stylists began to influence new products which, on the basis of their increased profits, manufacturers planned to introduce. In collaboration with market analysts, production engineers, and a host of other specialists, they created totally new streamlined design concepts.

One of the first, and certainly one of the most successful, designers employed in restyling American consumer products was erstwhile film and theatrical designer Norman Bel Geddes, who between 1919 and 1926 had designed the sets for over fifty theatrical productions, several operas, and for films of both Cecil B. DeMille and D. W. Griffiths. Geddes and his specialist staff of twenty assistants were employed to restyle in the streamlined mode an enormous range of items, from luxury interiors complete with custom-built furniture for several multi-million dollar corporations, to industrial weighing machines, portable kitchen units, and electrical items intended for mass sale. When his designers were not fully occupied on an industrial project they were put to work on so-called development work, predictions of future needs that Geddes then published in his promotional work and in his 1932 book *Horizons*. This book became an important reference for all streamlining enthusiasts, particularly those who wished to project into the future: Geddes had included ideas for vast intercontinental airliners with all the features of a modern hotel, for a rotating innercity restaurant on top of a gigantic tower surrounded by streamlined skyscrapers and a dome-like building complex, and for many variations of streamlined cars, intercity coaches, ocean liners, trains, rolling stock, and so on.

In the late 1920s Henry Dreyfuss, who had been a theatrical designer as well as a successful graphic artist, and Walter Dorwin Teague, previously an illustrator and advertising artist, also began redesigning various consumer products for the American market, applying aerodynamic

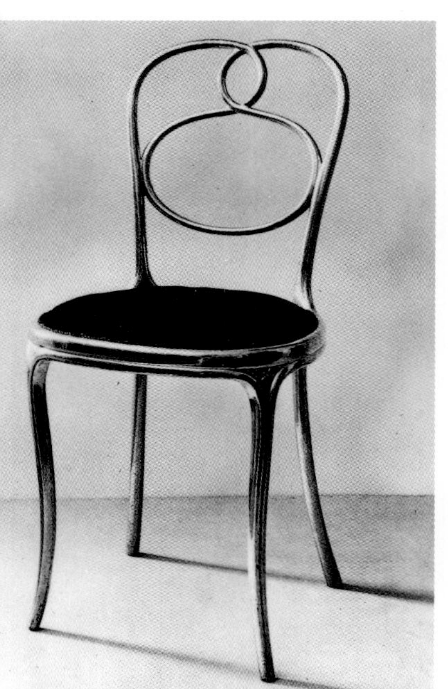

Proto-modern design by Michael Thonet for the Liechtenstein Palace, Vienna, 1843–46. (Photo courtesy Gebruder Thonet, Frankenberg.)

theories to telephones, cameras, perfume bottles, office machinery, household appliances of all sorts, and interior schemes for ocean liners, trains and big corporations. The architect and industrial engineer Richard Buckminster Fuller concentrated his efforts on designing buidings with geodesic domes that combined maximum floor space with minimal structural weight for minimum cost.

Fuller developed the 'Dymaxion' concept, in which 'rational action in a rational world demands the most efficient overall performance per unit of input in every social and industrial operation'. Using this concept, he designed a prototype city car that was capable of easy parking, had a very tight turning circle, and was capable of travelling at speeds of up to 190 kilometres per hour. He also began developing the 'zoomobile', an auto-aeroplane that could lift off the highway to fly over flat stretches of land between cities and yet would travel around the inner city like an ordinary car.

In Germany, the Bauhaus had produced a crop of inventive designers who combined *Sachlichkeit* with talent and skill to produce new concepts in furniture, light fittings, ceramics, textiles, graphics, and theatrical design and architecture. The most notable work came from Ludwig Mies van der Rohe and Marcel Breuer, whose influence still lingers on. But the authorities saw the influence of the Bauhaus as disruptive and in 1925 it was forced to move from Weimar to Dessau; then, because of what were termed 'subversive activities', it was moved to Berlin before being finally closed down in 1933 by the newly elected Social Democratic Party. Some staff members were obliged to leave Germany for America, where they set up a new Bauhaus in Chicago.

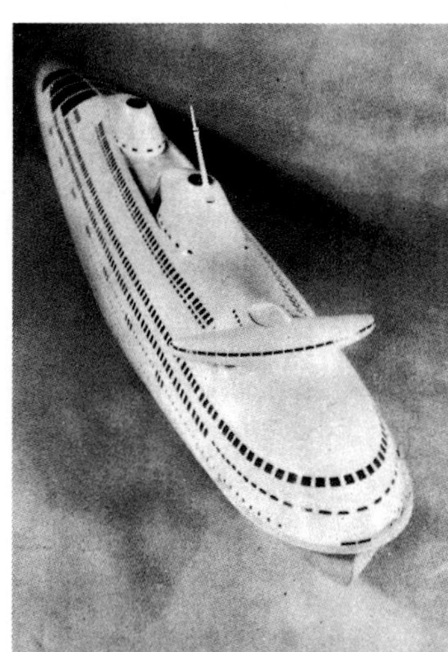

Photograph by Maurice Goldberg of Norman Bel Geddes' streamlined ocean liner. From Geddes' *Horizons*. Published by Little, Brown & Company, Boston. 1932.

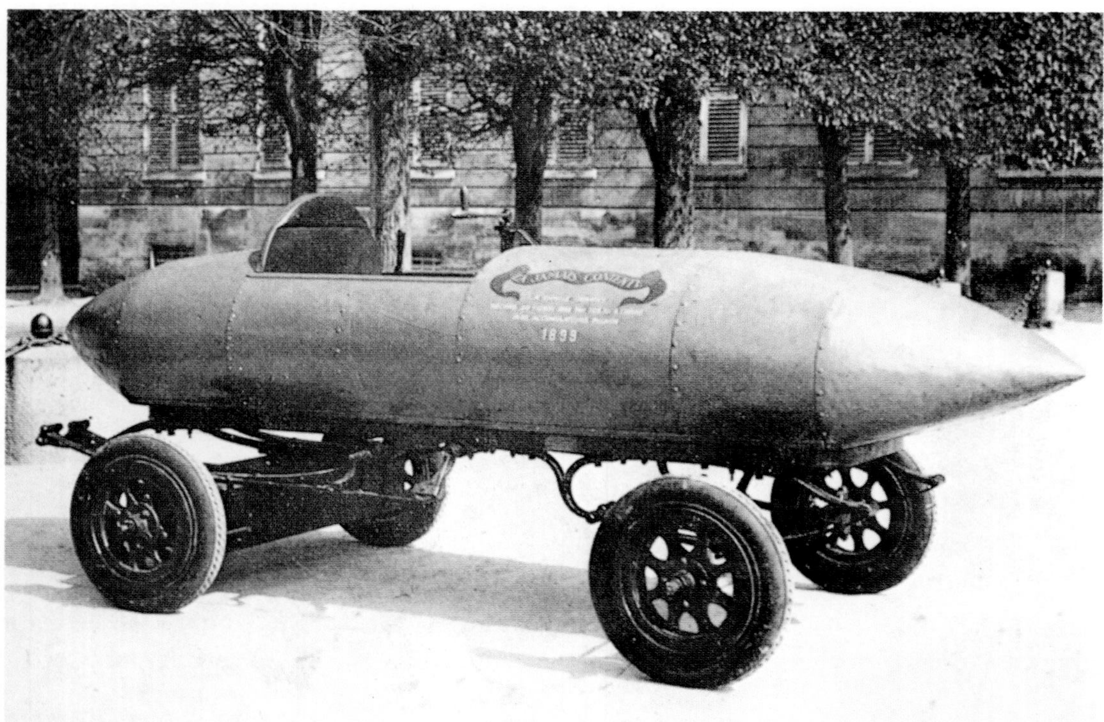

La Jamais Contente — at 104 kilometres per hour the world's fastest car. An early example of streamlining. 1899.

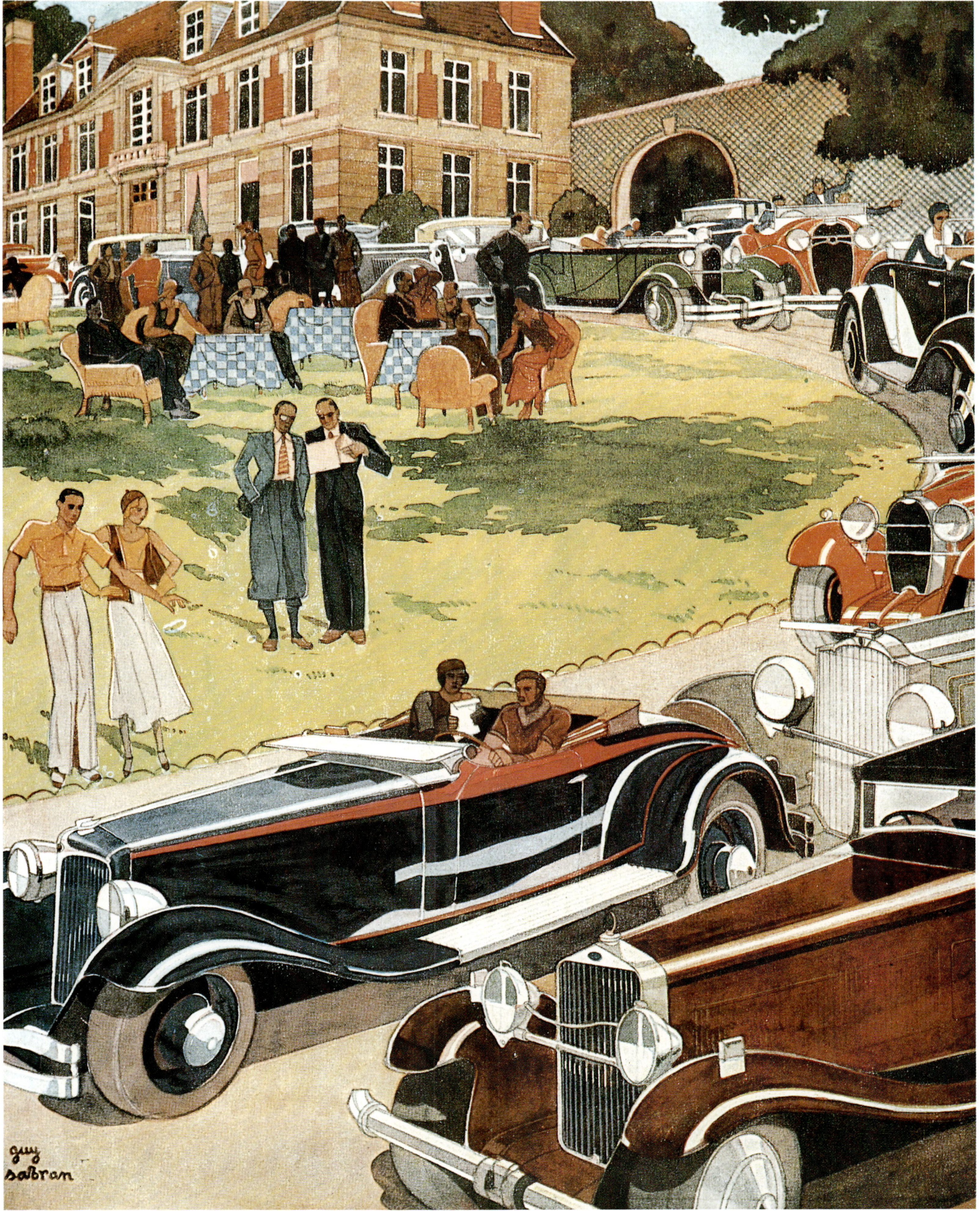

Magazine illustration *Le Départ d'un rallye automobile* by Guy Sabrain, for *L'illustration*. 1932.

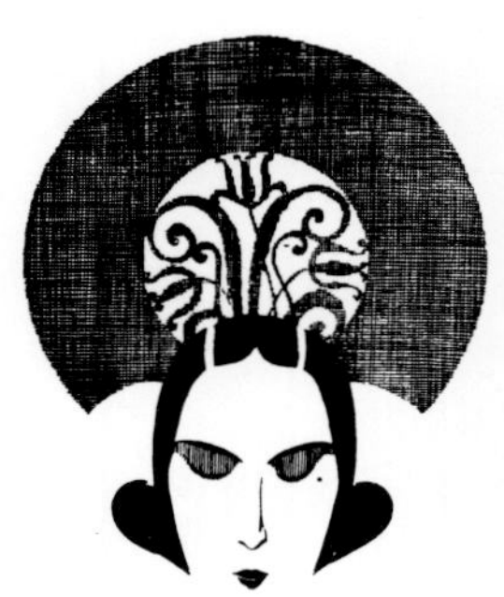

The French architect Le Corbusier, author of *Vers une architecture*, had become well known for his starkly modern pavilion at the 1925 Art Deco Exhibition and by 1932 he had started to build houses and office blocks in stark white concrete in Europe and the United States. The press reported that these buildings were 'suggestive of modern steamships', with the interiors being 'simple, unfussy and hygienic, bare of useless objects, free from meaningless ornament and arranged with convenience for modern living as their principal objectives.'

Throughout the Western world women began to streamline their clothes, and the press declared that the 'hard, crisp, shiny, chic era of the fashionable woman of the 1920s, with her obligatory Eton crop, short skirt, long cigarette holder and flattened bustline, was dead'. One journalist mused, 'How marvellous it would be to be naked with a cheque book in order to buy the new figure revealing fashions'; others proclaimed the arrival of 'the most feminine fashions for years', cut on the bias of the fabric *à la Vionnet* so that they clung to the body, revealing every contour and dimple.

Illustrative styles were changing too: surrealism was hailed as 'a unique invention characteristic of our time'. Cinema had changed dramatically since the introduction of the 'talkies' in the latter part of the 1920s. The 'all singing and all dancing' musicals directed by Busby Berkeley created a new genre that saved Hollywood from bankruptcy and greatly influenced the direction of the industry. D. H. Lawrence published his controversial book *Lady Chatterley's Lover* in the late 1920s and was roundly denounced by the press as too sexually explicit. By the mid-1930s the Museum of Modern Art in New York had been opened, testimony to the cultural acceptability of new art forms. Trotsky was exiled from Russia, and in 1932 Franklin D. Roosevelt was elected President of the United States on the promise of a 'new deal' that would, he said, 'get the economy moving again'.

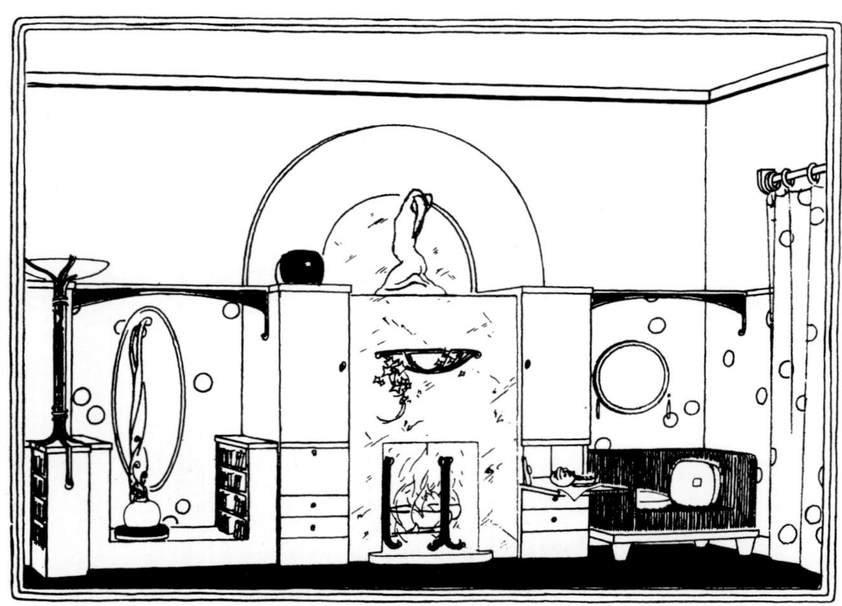

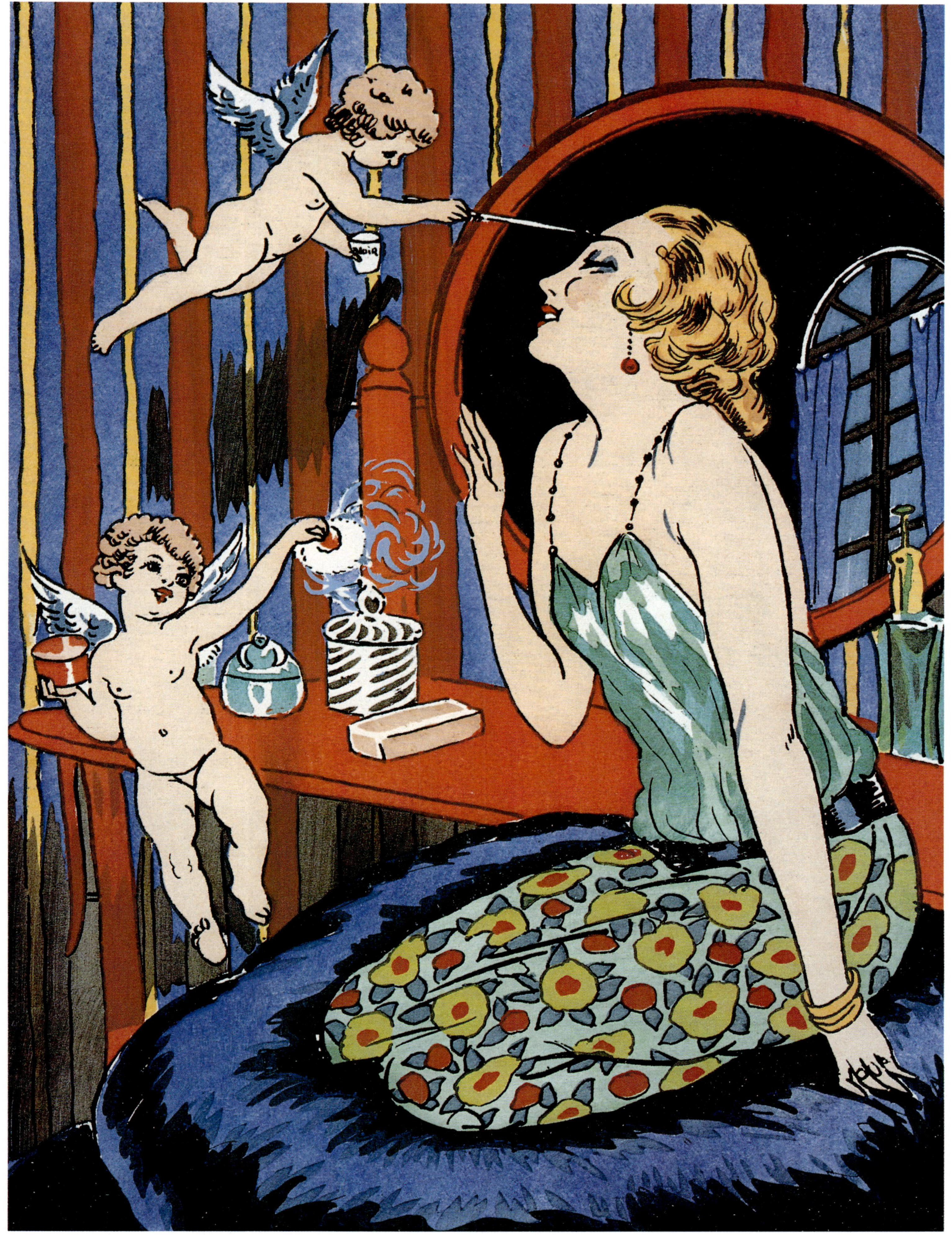

Pochoir illustration *Mado se maquille* by Carlo Bady, from *La Journée de Mado*. Published by the Galerie Lutétia, Paris. 1932.

The popular music industry also underwent a dramatic change: sales of records had plummetted from 100 million in 1928 to just 6 million in 1931. The music industry began to look for a new sound to replace the dated 1920s jazz; what was needed was an expression of the new streamlined era. The answer was 'swing music', in which the basic melody could be broken up by improvisations from the expert jazz soloists who, like so many 1920s designers and creators, were out of work and were more than willing to conform to the new rhythms. The beat of Benny Goodman, known as the King of Swing, epitomised the early to middle 1930s.

The new swing rhythms elicited new modes of dancing: the 'Lindy hop' led to the 'jitterbug', in which young dancers displayed a frenzied athleticism in spectacular jumps and turns that were criticised as being hazardous to the performers and other dancers. In many dance halls this form of dancing was in fact banned, labelled sexual and exhibitionist, but the young flocked to places where it was allowed and the dancers enjoyed flaunting their bodies and their skills as they whirled each other into the air to a chorus of calls and claps from the other dancers.

Transportation was revolutionised. The cigar-shaped *Graf Zeppelin* could travel from Frankfurt in Germany to New Jersey in the United States in less than fifty hours and its passengers enjoyed all the comforts of a deluxe hotel. Its smooth, relaxing flight was reported as 'giving that feeling of luxury which will surely make this the ideal way to travel'. New

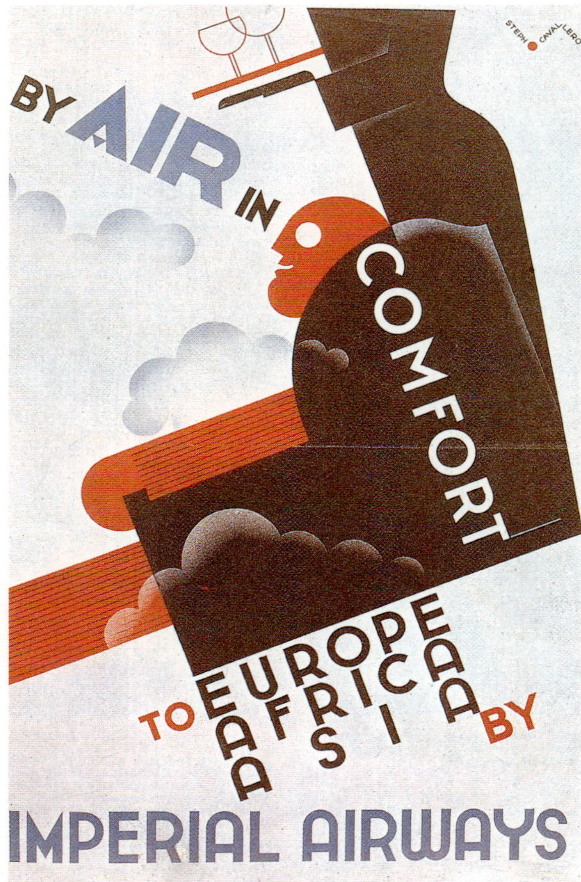

Magazine advertisement for Imperial Airways, by Stephen Cavellero. 1934.

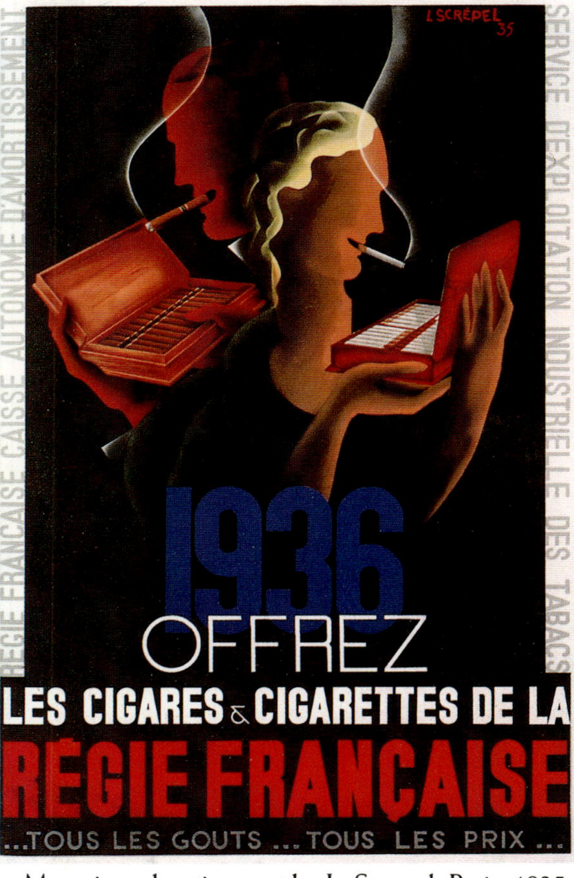

Magazine advertisement by L. Screpel. Paris. 1935.

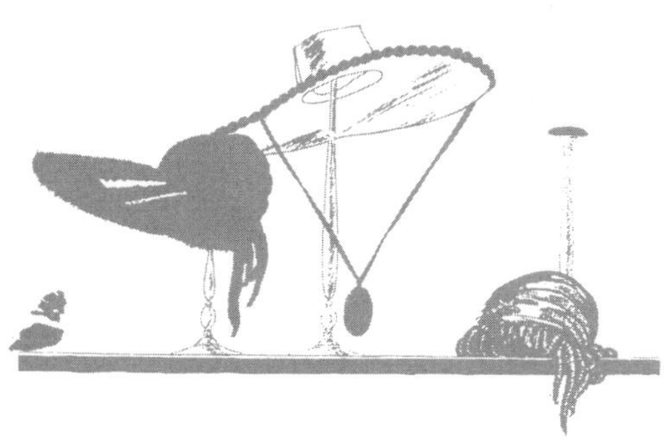

streamlined rigid-framed aeroplanes were also beginning to be introduced, allowing passengers to travel from New York to Los Angeles in just over one day. International passengers could fly from Paris to Budapest in time for lunch, and from Budapest to Rome in time for dinner. Or they could be in Calcutta within five days, in Singapore within eight, or on a Pacific Island or in Australia within ten days.

In women's fashion, the main reason for the change to slender, reed-like figures was undoubtedly the influence of sportswear, which had become very popular as a result of the efforts of three French couturiers — Coco Chanel, Lucien Lelong and Jean Patou. The sportswear they designed was not particularly French in character: it was aimed more towards the American and the English markets, and their new designs were generally displayed on American or English models, who had longer legs than their French counterparts. In addition, these American and English models were from 'good backgrounds' and were well connected, which made what they wore and how they looked acceptable to most of the haut monde customers. French models were often regarded with suspicion because no French girl of good breeding would have been allowed to undertake the job of mannequin: the displaying of clothes was still closely associated with the profession of the demi-mondaines of the pre-war years, and naturally their mothers were determined to protect their daughters from such a 'shameful' occupation.

American girls were also being admired on the screen, particularly those who were featured in the chorus lines of the Busby Berkeley musicals of the time — *Dames, Forty-Second Street, Roman Scandals, A Kid From Spain*, and *Making Whoopee*. Each week millions of people all over the world flocked to see the latest Hollywood films, to erase for a time the thoughts and the hunger of the Great Depression. As George Raft later said in *The Golden Age of Hollywood*,

All you had to do in those days was to go to a movie. Busby Berkeley would do the rest. He'd get you a date with a great looking dame. Give you a top hat and tails. Put plenty of green stuff in your pocket. And get you to hit all the right joints on the Great White Way.

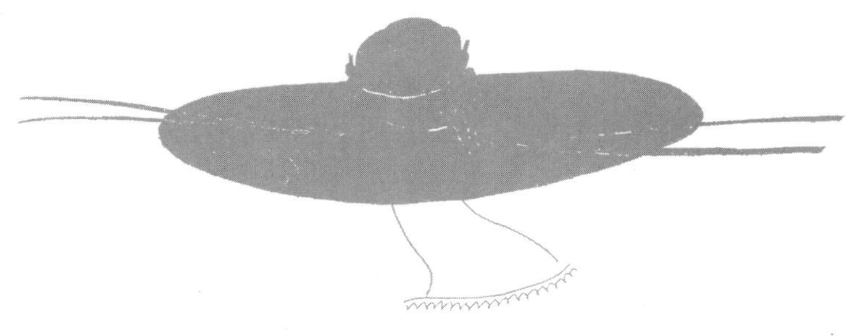

The audiences loved to see the lead actors and actresses dancing, and they loved the high kicks of the chorus line. They also loved to see Cecil B. DeMille's heroines disrobing, or appearing on screen wearing little more than one layer of muslin. Disrob-

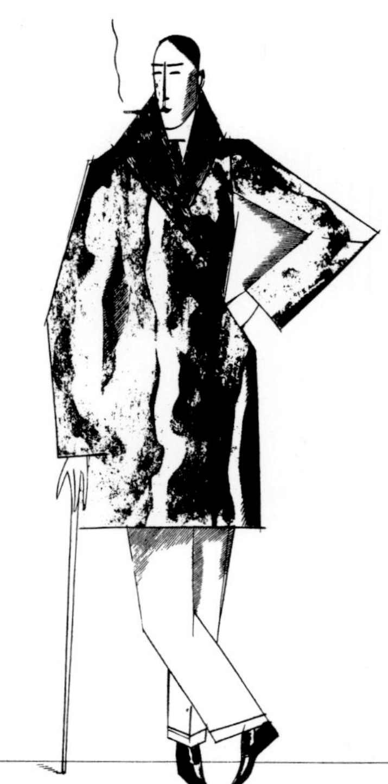

ing and appearing on screen semi-nude had, in fact, developed into quite an artform under DeMille, but he was also aware that full clothing had to be worth wearing and worth watching. DeMille's brother William wrote of these clothes, which often became new fashions almost overnight,

Before this, Paris fashion shows had been accessible only to the chosen few. 'CB' revealed them to the whole country, the costumes his heroines wore being copied by women and girls throughout the land, especially by those whose contact with the centres of fashion was limited.

DeMille's philosophy in dress, as in all the other areas of design, was to employ only the very best artists he could find: the gowns, lingerie, shoes, hats, and even the seemingly casual wrap-around layers of muslin, that were shown in his films, were all specially designed in order to gain maximum effect. But DeMille also realised that such designs had to be produced at least six months before they would be shown, and this meant, of course, that they could not be in the current mode: on release his films would have looked six months out of date. He overcame this, as did many other directors who had been caught by surprise at the end of 1929, when Paris hemlines had dropped to ankle length overnight, by calling for sensational styles. He insisted that his designers exaggerate the mode far beyond that of normal wear and, as far as expense was concerned, there was no limit.

The DeMille films of the 1920s and 1930s provided audiences with a visual feast that was only possible on the screen. At the beginning of 1919, when directing *Male and Female,* he brought artist–designer Paul Iribe across from Paris to create the sets and costumes for his female lead, Gloria Swanson. Iribe's designs for Swanson were reported as 'quite brilliant', and movie historians agree that 'Miss Swanson's intricate pearl costume with a long peacock train and head-dress crowned with jewels and displaying a fortune in white aigrette feathers designed by Paul Iribe had rarely been equalled for sheer Hollywood magnificence'. Iribe's artistry brought film costuming to a new level of the fantastic and, by accepting DeMille's demands, Paramount became the first studio in Hollywood to acknowledge the importance of creating special costumes for its stars.

DeMille also discovered the great Hollywood costume designer Adrian — Adrian Adolph Greenburg — who had been born in Naugatuck, Connecticut, in 1903. After studying in New York, Adrian had gone to Paris to study design and when he returned he worked for a time on Broadway with Irving Berlin. He then went to Hollywood, assisting Natacha Rambova on two Valentino films. In 1925 he became a contract designer to DeMille, who used him for *The Road to Yesterday, The Volga Boatman, King of Kings* and, with Iribe, *Madame Satan.*

Adrian changed his allegiance to MGM in 1930 and his name soon

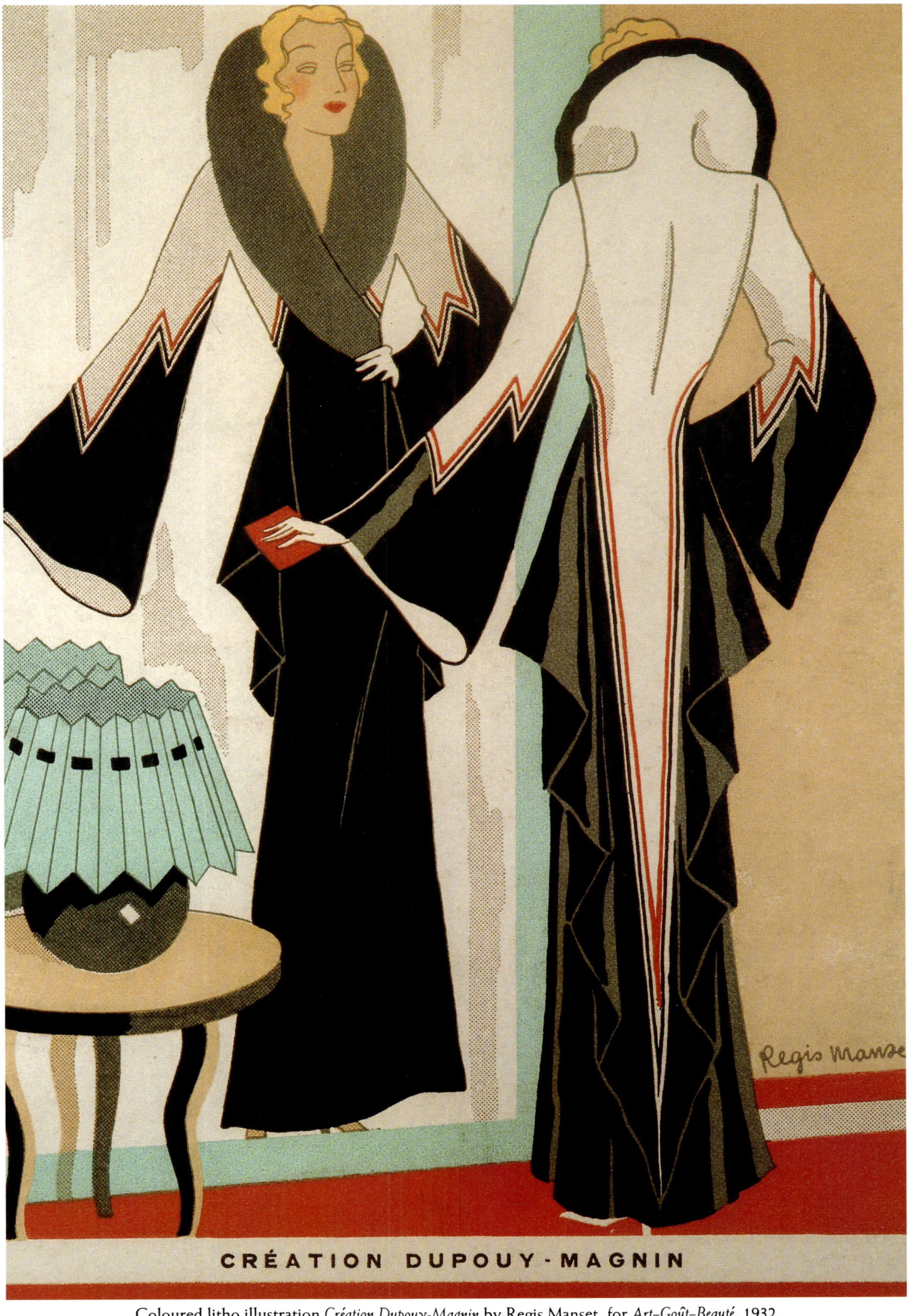

Coloured litho illustration *Création Dupouy-Magnin* by Regis Manset, for *Art-Goût-Beauté*. 1932.

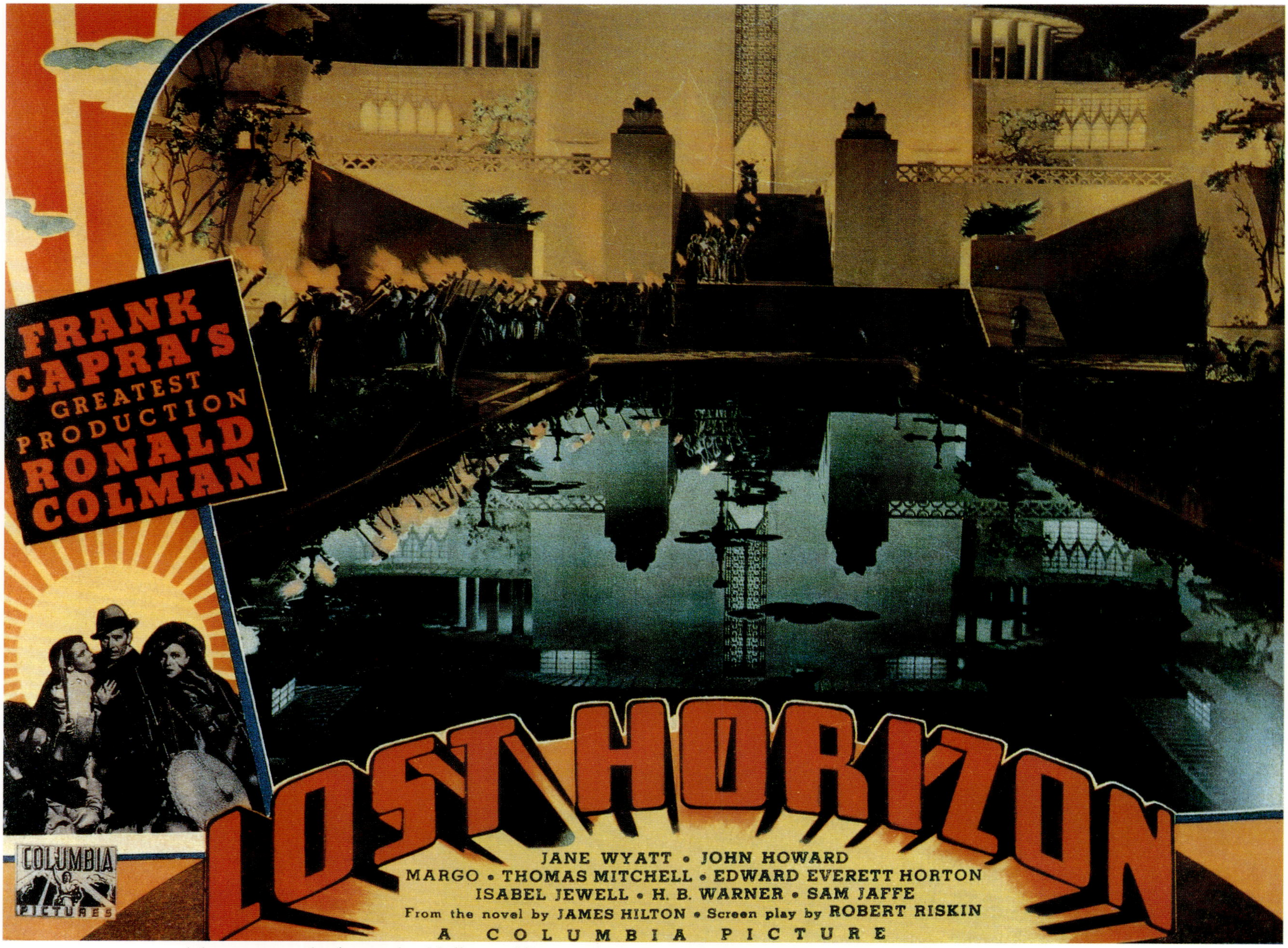

Advertisement display card in Hollywood Deco style for Frank Capra's *Lost Horizon*, starring Ronald Colman. 1937.

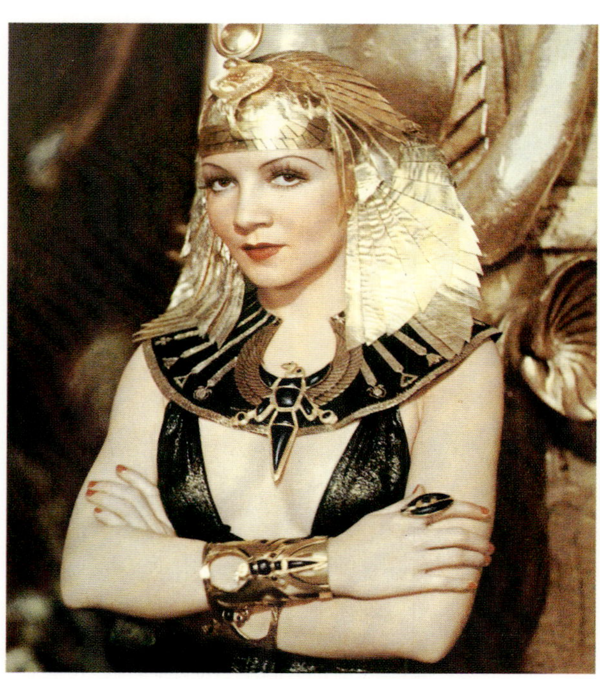

Hollywood Deco as designed by Travis Banton for Cecil B. De Mille's 1934 epic *Cleopatra*, starring Claudette Colbert. (Photo courtesy Kobal Collection.)

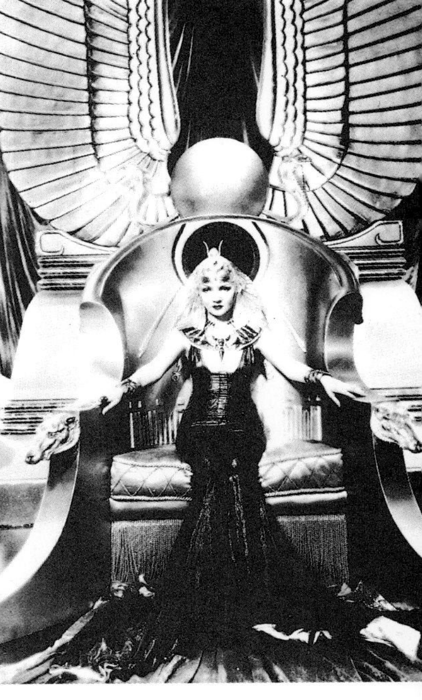

became synonymous with the fashions of Greta Garbo, Joan Crawford, Jean Harlow, Norma Shearer, Hedy Lamarr and Lana Turner. As chief costume designer, he was responsible for such films as *Mata Hari*, *Grand Hotel*, *Dancing Lady*, *Naughty Marietta*, *Broadway Melody of 1936*, *The Great Ziegfeld*, *Camille*, *The Wizard of Oz*, and *The Women*. His film fashions became the fashions worn by millions of women, and in 1932 one particular dress — the famous beruffled *Letty Lynton* dress worn by Joan Crawford — is reputed to have sold over half a million copies in Macy's New York store alone.

Adrian's competitors in the film world in the early to middle 1930s were Travis Banton, Walter Plunkett, Milo Anderson and Bernard Newman. Banton started his film career designing the flamboyant costumes for the 1925 production *The Dressmaker from Paris* and then working on lavish wardrobes for Pola Negri, Clara Bow, Carole Lombard, Marlene Dietrich, Kay Frances, Claudette Colbert, Mae West, and many other famous Paramount stars. Walter Plunkett designed most of the costumes for the stars of RKO; Milo Anderson designed many of the costumes for the Busby Berkeley musicals; and Bernard Newman became famous for his Ginger Rogers costumes in such films as *Roberta*, *Top Hat* and *Swingtime*. These four designers also had a profound effect on the women's fashions of the time.

Hollywood-style glamour as personified by the stars was of major importance throughout the 1930s. Advertisements and articles appeared weekly, advising readers how to improve their looks, how to become more beautiful, and how to look like their favourite actor or actress. Readers were also told that the new cosmetic products would do 'wonderful things for their skin', they would reveal their own 'hidden beauty', and make them 'interestingly different'. The Hollywood stars, they were told, did not want to look exactly like one another: they wished to 'individualise their attractiveness' and this they did by the use of powder, rouge, lipstick and mascara, to 'dramatise the individual charm of every star, making each one so glamorous, so perfect, so desirable, that you gasp and ask yourself — is she real?'

Other articles about beauty products promoted them as if they had supernatural qualities that would instantly give the user the lips of Clara Bow, the allure of Carole Lombard, the radiance of Ginger Rogers, or the sex appeal of Jean Harlow; perfume copywriters called upon the wizardry associated with the primitive senses or the lustre and splendour of ancient history: 'Cleopatra didn't just dab a little ashes of violets behind her ears to entice Mark Anthony. Instead she used rare perfumes in greater quantities than any woman before or since'.

Illustrators had to try to capture all this feeling, the changing ideals of the readers, and the new styles themselves. A few illustrations were still being printed in *pochoir* in the deluxe magazine *Art–Goût–Beauté* and in the

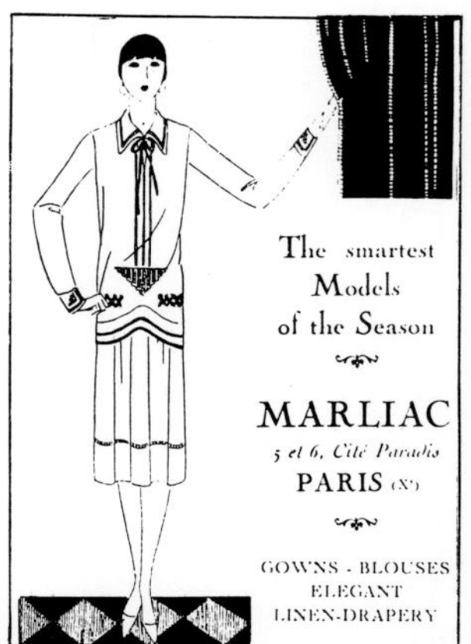

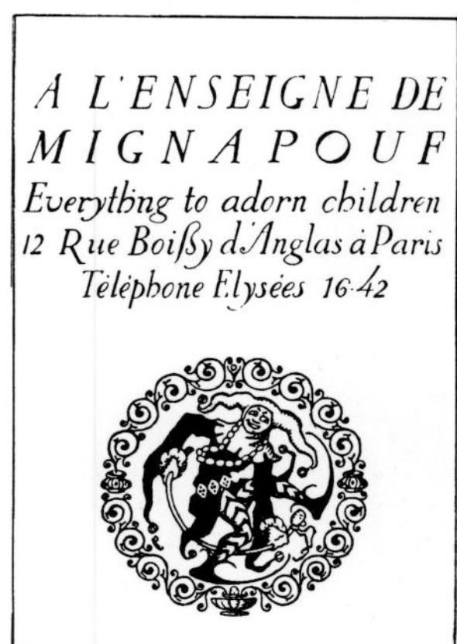

few remaining limited-edition folders, but most of them were appearing in glossy magazines such as *La Femme chic*, *Vogue*, *Harpers Bazaar*, and *Excelsior Modes*. To survive, the artists had to be versatile, and it was fortunate that the exploratory use of illustrative techniques had always been the hallmark of the great Art Deco illustrators.

Until this time illustrators had been encouraged to undertake a commission as they saw fit, creating an image that reflected their view of the subject and using the technique they thought most suitable. But now, in the age of the streamlined style, their creative ability was being put to the test by the new breed of magazine editors and art directors, who often specified exactly what they wanted and refused to accept an illustration if it did not conform to their original brief.

The magazines of the early 1930s were being designed by the art directors and editors as a complete ensemble, with as much regard being given to the novelty of the layout, the balancing of text and the placement of advertisements, and so on, as was given to the content of the illustrations and the text. The illustrator was to do his one-man job only under the art director's watchful eye because what he did had to be compatible with the director's idea of the final layout. If the finished product met with the displeasure of the editor or editor-in-chief, all of the layout work including the illustration would have to be done again for no extra fee.

This was certainly a contrast to the ideas and ideals of Lucien Vogel and the other innovative publishing entrepreneurs back in 1912, when the artists themselves were commissioned to design the layout and decide the subject for their illustrations. The artists also created the mood for the magazine, rather than working from the art director's concept, and in many cases they also designed the object being featured. But by 1933 *Vogue* had already signalled the end of the reign of the illustrator: it began to use photographic covers, the first being a bathing beauty photographed by Edward Steichen. This was *Vogue's* first photographic cover since 1909, and within a few months most other magazines followed suit. At first, these covers were a great novelty, but within a year they had become a matter of expediency, serving the magazines efficiently enough at the time but tending to fade from memory once the novelty had worn off. Few were really memorable.

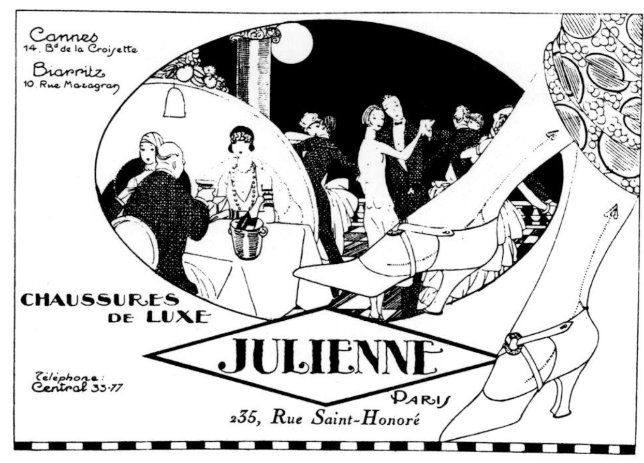

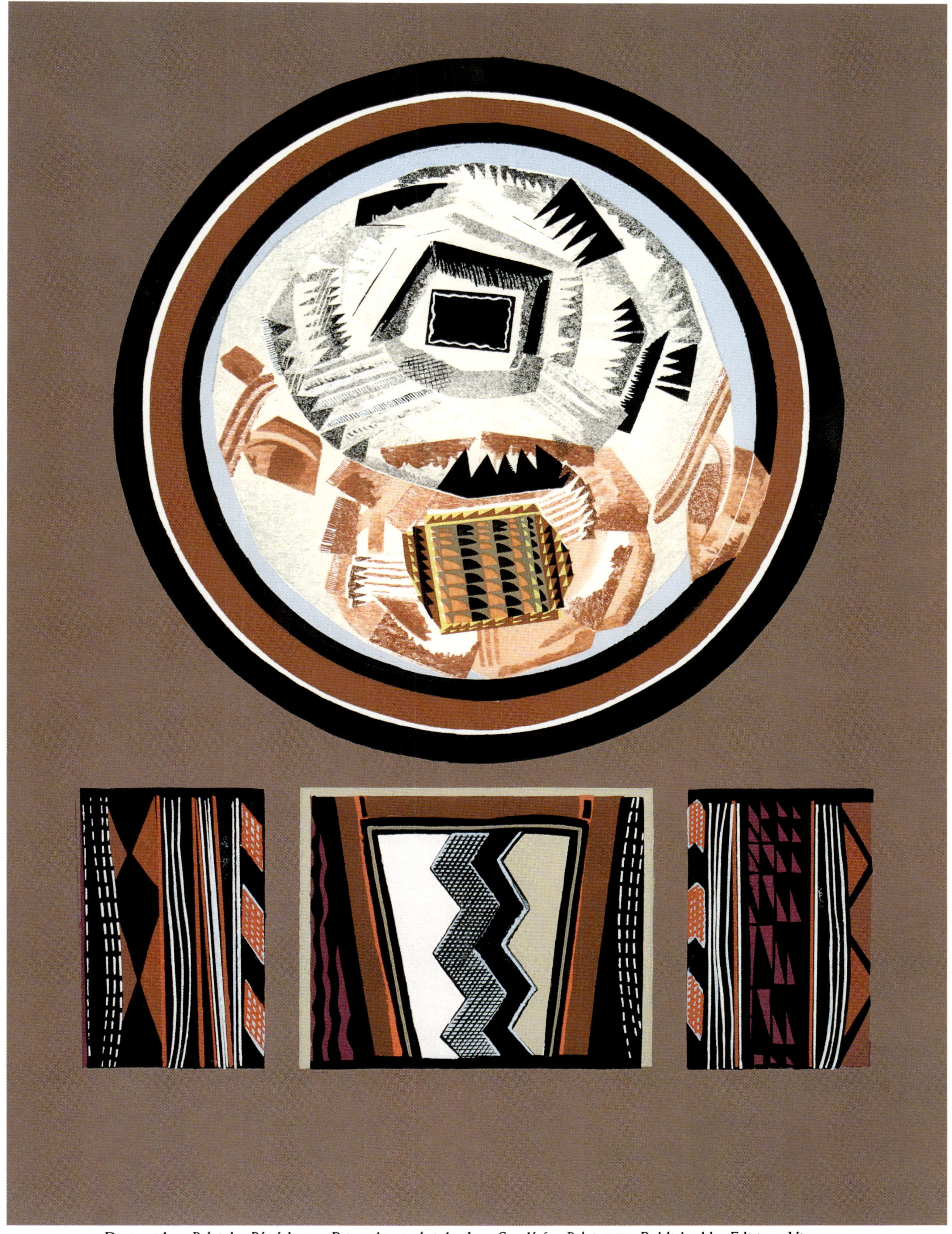

Design ideas *Relais* by Bénédictus. Printed in *pochoir* by Jean Saudé for *Relais 1930*. Published by Editions Vincent, Fréal et Cie, Paris. 1930.

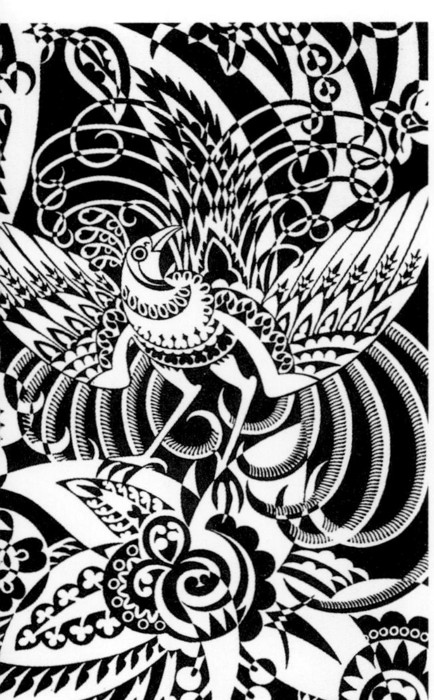

Book illustrations by Boris Artzybashoff, for *Creatures* by Padraic Colum. Published by Macmillan & Co., New York.

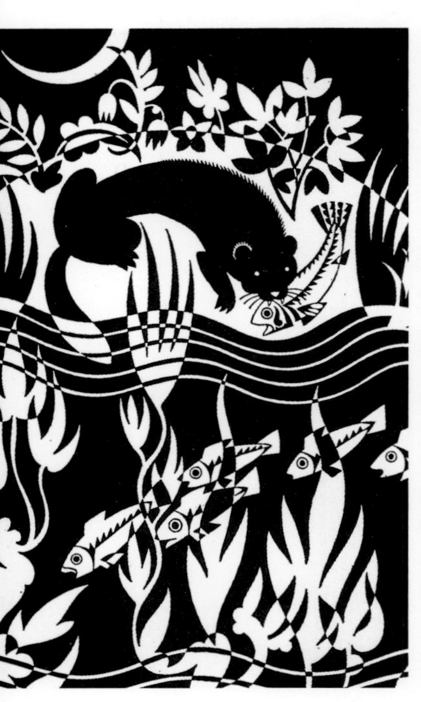

Fortunately, though, illustrative covers did not completely disappear, and covers by Lepape, Erté, Mourgue, Brissaud, Benito, Marty and Dufy appeared from time to time, as did covers by the young artists Bérard, Eric, Bouché, Dali, Benigni and Demachy. Illustrative commissions for the internal pages of magazines were also fewer because art directors preferred working from a selection of photographs rather than with a single illustration that might have taken days to prepare. The number of advertisements using illustrations diminished, too, as did illustrative commissions for deluxe-edition books.

Commercialised forms of photography began to thrive. The consummate professionalism of Steichen, Horst, Baron Gayne de Meyer and Baron George Hoyningen-Huene produced inventive images that generally proved to be a very persuasive commercial argument in favour of the use of photographs. And readers liked looking at these images, especially those printed in colour, because they could more easily identify with the image of a real object, rather than with an illustrative interpretation that often presented an idiosyncratic point of view.

Both Baron Gayne de Meyer and Edward Steichen had been employed as professional photographers since before World War I, and they had become noted for developing original techniques that enabled them to capture some of the mystery and illusion of the modes that were published in the glossy magazines of the time. Then, in the early 1920s, they began to employ diffused studio lighting and soft focus to capture the elusive quality of the new fashions for *Vogue* and *Harpers Bazaar* which gave the haut monde something to which they could aspire, and at the same time made the fashions seem accessible even to poorer working-class girls.

Throughout the 1920s Steichen and de Meyer continued working for the leading glossy magazines, producing cleverly lit, beautifully posed and very formalised photographs that suited the great age of Art Deco design. De Meyer in particular perfected his remarkable style of back-lighting his subject, producing an almost three-dimensional effect with an aesthetic appeal very similar to that of a hand-painted illustration. His technique was adopted by several of the new generation of photographers who were by the end of the 1920s arriving on the scene.

George Hoyningen-Huene was one of the best of these new professional photographic image-makers and he had managed to retain a remarkable aesthetic quality in his commercial work. He was also the first magazine photographer to rid his images of the apparent constraints of the studio, giving his printed pictures the look of everyday life. His models were photographed in bathing costumes, lying on the sand, shaded by umbrellas and surrounded by admirers. Sometimes they

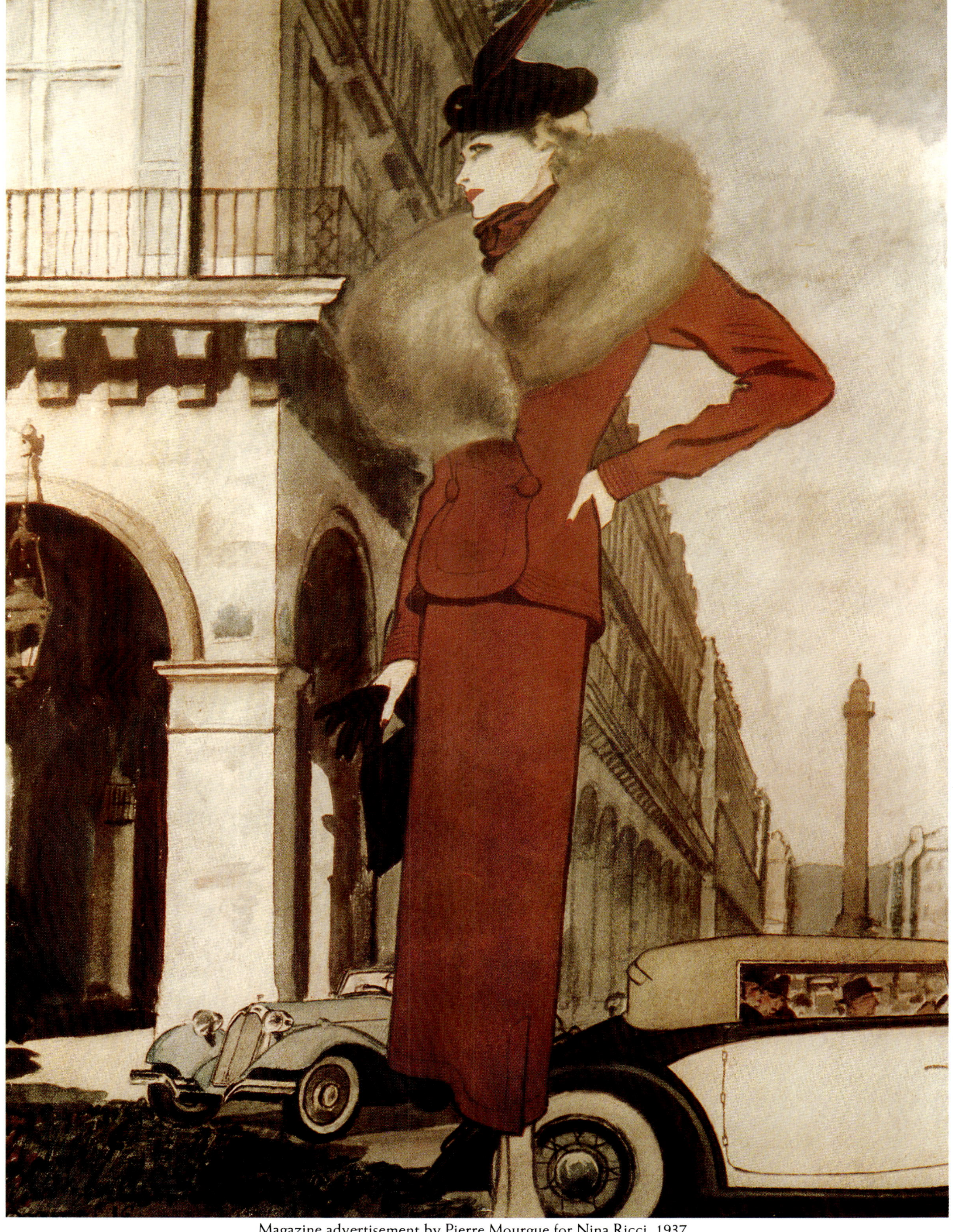

Magazine advertisement by Pierre Mourgue for Nina Ricci. 1937.

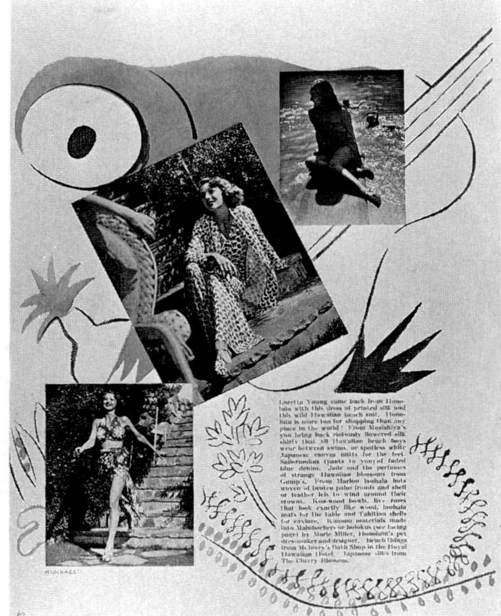

Loretta Young came back from Honolulu with this dress of printed silk and this wild Hawaiian beach suit. Honolulu is more fun for shopping than any place in the world! From Musishiya's you bring back riotously flowered silk shirts that all Hawaiian beach boys wear between swims, or spotless white Japanese canvas mitts for the feet. Sailormokus (pants to you) of faded blue denim. Jade and the perfumes of strange Hawaiian blossoms from Gump's. From Marlou lauhala hats woven of beaten palm fronds and shell or feather leis to wind around their crowns. Kou-wood bowls, live roses that look exactly like wood, lauhala mats for the table and Tahitian shells for exclure. Kimono materials made into Mahuhochers or holokus (see facing page) by Marie Miller, Honolulu's pet dressmaker and designer. Beach things from McInery's Bath Shop in the Royal Hawaiian Hotel. Japanese silks from The Cherry Blossom.

Fashion photography by Munkasci, combined with line drawing, featuring Loretta Young in Honolulu. *Film Fashions*. 1937.

appeared in smart day dresses, getting into or out of expensive cars, or in cocktail or evening dresses in an array of original but never overstaged situations, all of which were created inside the film studio so that he could still use the studio lights which were so essential for obtaining the sharpness required for magazine reproduction.

In the meantime, the Seeberger brothers were still at work photographing the haut monde at the fashionable French resorts and although their photographs were reproduced in the occasional magazine, the quality was such that few magazines were able to reproduce their images successfully. It is only in recent years, with improvements in printing technology, that their images have been able to be enjoyed by more than a handful of devotees.

During the later part of the 1930s other young photographers also managed to create unconventional and eye-catching images with their experimental use of new and more adaptable cameras and new kinds of film stock, including the newly introduced colour film. Martin Munkasci had his models leaping around so that he could capture the movement of the new clothing styles; Erwin Blumenfeld made a notable impact by photographing his surrealistic-looking ladies in stunning hats; Man Ray was experimenting with positive–negative images and the unique use of fashionable figures that were interestingly confined into the space of his photographic frame; and Anton Bruehl arranged his models in Art Deco patterns reminiscent of Busby Berkeley.

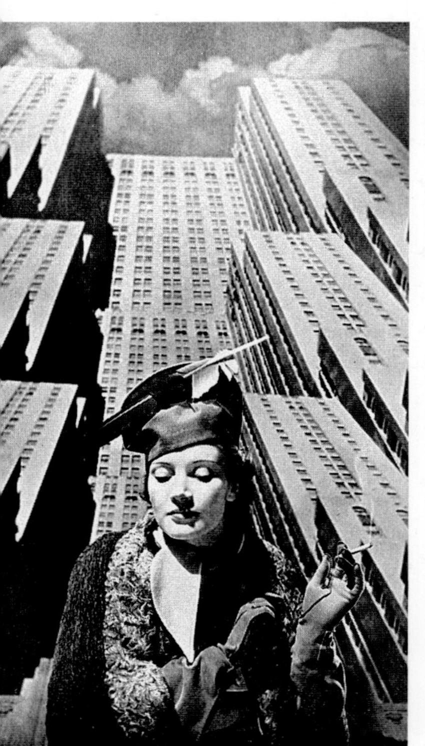

Magazine photograph by Meerson (hat by Maria Guy; Rochas tweed suit).

Surprisingly, though, after the initial impact of the photographic image in the early 1930s (which changed the visual message from the deluxe *pochoir* Art Deco styles to the mass-produced streamlined images of the new decade) the images actually slowed down the progress of change in the promotion of new design styles. The reason was that the new images could only be made from a product that had already been created, whilst hand-drawn illustrations could be used to convey an idea of what a new product was going to look like or to try out variations of a new design before the final product was decided upon.

Hollywood, of course, played a part in this experimentation, introducing an ever-changing array of ideas in the luxurious Hollywood Deco style, which kept some of the Art Deco aesthetic ideals simmering on well into the mid-1930s. Once magazine art directors and editors realised that these aesthetic ideals were still alive and that illustrative images still had a valuable function to perform, they began to change their views and give the illustrators more freedom to draw again the sort of images for which they had become famous.

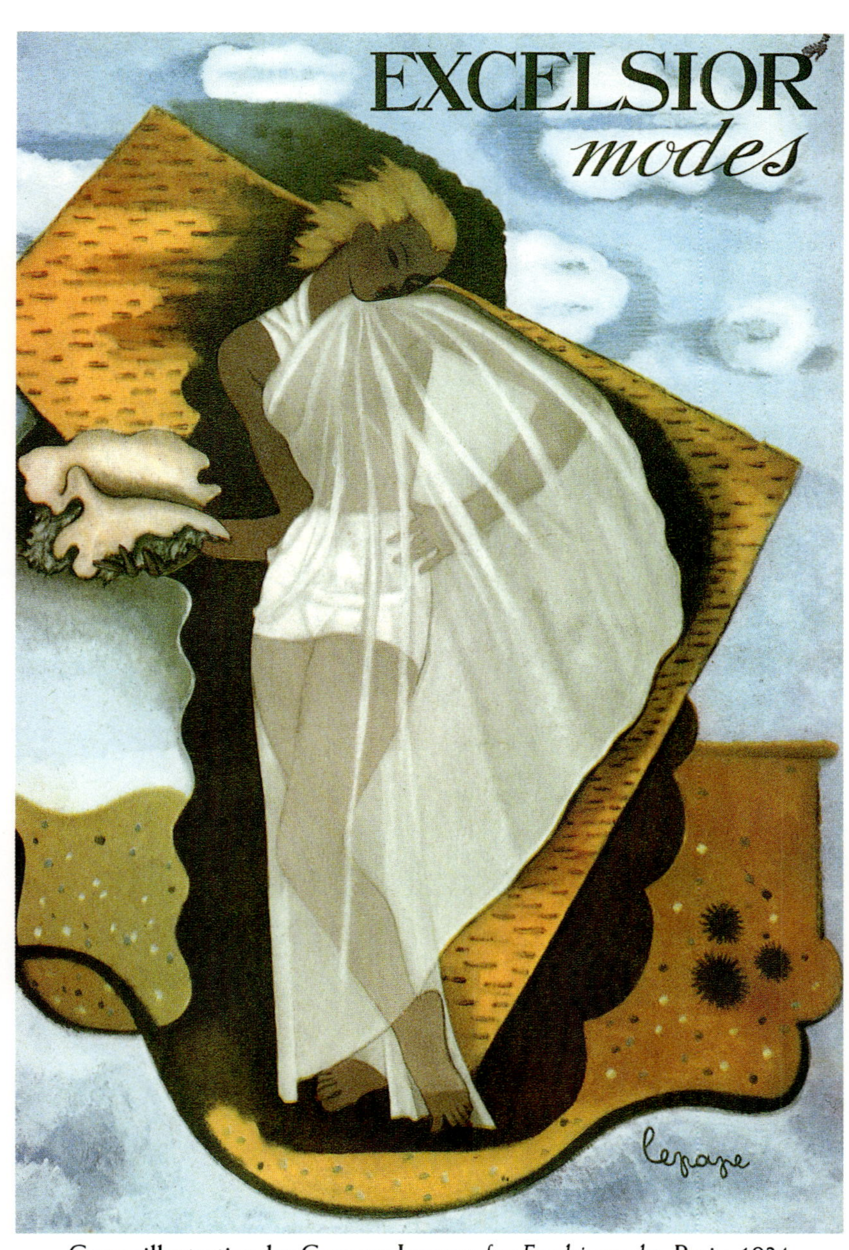

Cover illustration by Georges Lepape, for *Excelsior modes*. Paris. 1934.

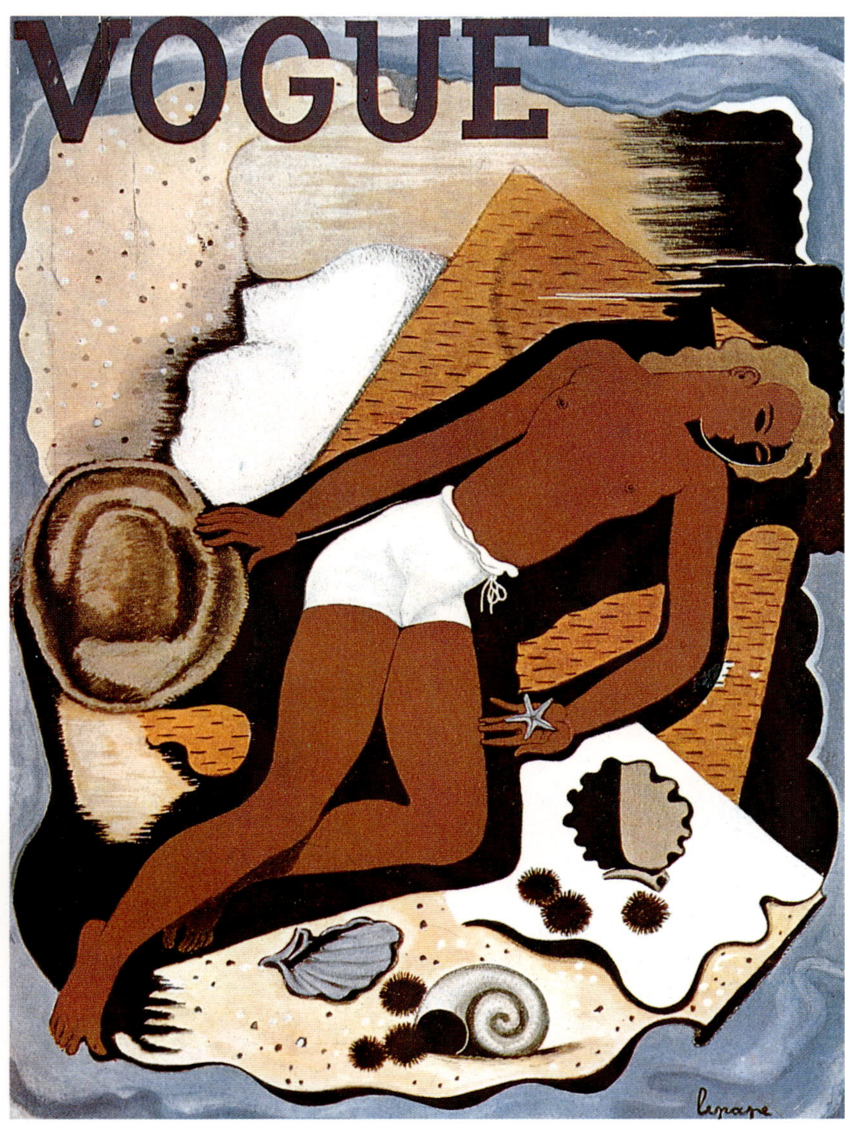

Cover by Georges Lepape, for French *Vogue*. July 1934.
(Courtesy of French *Vogue*.)

A new group of illustrators was emerging and by 1936 the doyen of pictorial illustration was the Swedish-American Carl Ericsson — better known as Eric — who had joined the group of *La Gazette du bon ton* illustrators in 1925, shortly before it closed. He subsequently joined the staff of *Vogue*, and the people he drew for this now fashionable glossy magazine were healthy, beautifully dressed, intelligent and cultivated, always seeming to be laughing, whether lunching at the Ritz, playing baccarat at Cannes, shopping on the Champs Elysées, or adjusting their skis at St Moritz. Eric's drawings always had the appearance of being taken directly from life, although they were actually the result of much study and many preliminary sketches.

Other important illustrators of the period were Eric Frazer, Léon Benigni, Christian Bérard, Jacques Demachy, Count René Boute Willaumez, Guy Sabrain, Marcel Vertès, Reynaldo Luza, Alberto Vargas (who was to become famous in the early 1940s with his *Esquire* pin-up girls) and the incomparable Georges Lepape, with his uncanny instinct for modernity and knowing exactly what was 'right' for the time. Lepape continued to create impressive and appealing images into the early 1940s, as did his compatriots André Marty, Pierre Brissaud and Bernard Boutet de Monvel.

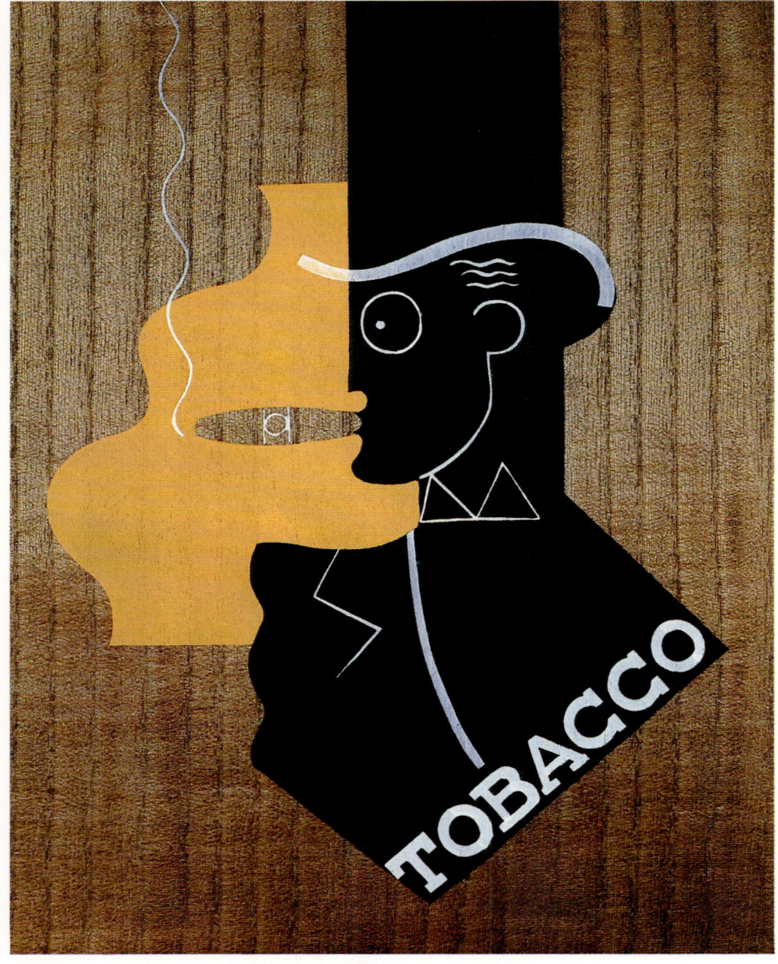

Illustration from A. Tolmer's *Mise en Page: The Theory and Practice of Lay-Out*. Printed by A. Tolmer, Paris, for The Studio, London. 1931.

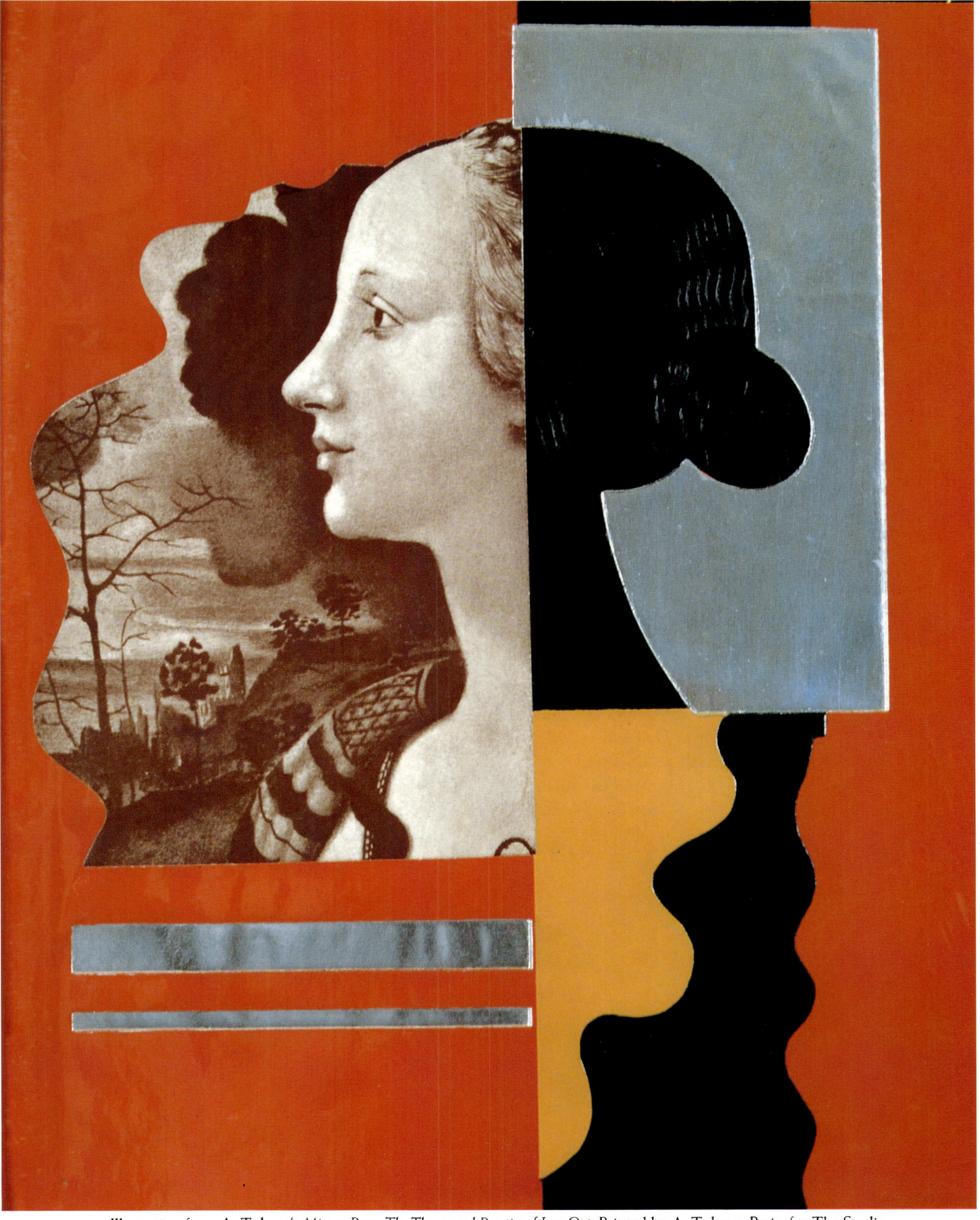

Illustration from A. Tolmer's *Mise en Page: The Theory and Practice of Lay-Out*. Printed by A. Tolmer, Paris, for The Studio, London. 1931.

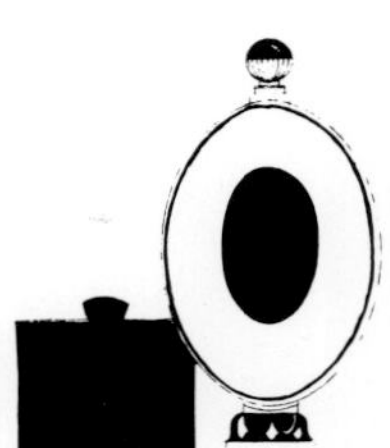

New forms of architecture were also being promoted throughout the Western world. The ideas of Frank Lloyd Wright, Norman Bel Geddes, Le Corbusier, Richard Buckminster Fuller and Ludwig Mies van der Rohe radically changed building techniques and became a feature of the 1939 New York World Fair.

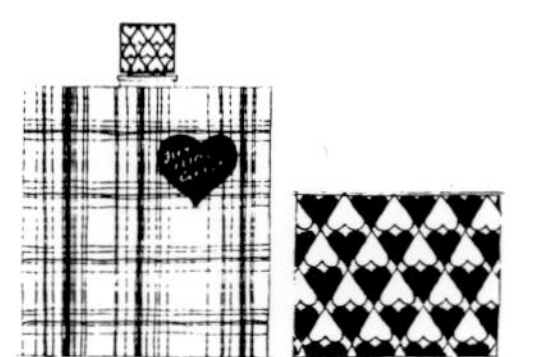

The Vincent Korda visuals for the H. G. Wells film *Things to Come* provided a vision of the future. In 1936 a journalist described the illusion created,

Deep in a sunless cavern a new society, clad only in garments containing complete radio telephone systems, inhabits windowless buildings, strolls along avenues from which automobiles are conspicuously absent and stands on broad flights of anachronistic steps. Transportation seems to be largely by means of suspended railways and elevators, mysteriously rising and descending in mammoth tubes of glass, to give access to the different levels.

This image of the future was reinforced by Norman Bel Geddes in his 'Highway and Horizons' building for General Motors at the 1939 New York World Fair. It featured a spectacular 'futurama' that became the most popular of all the displays. The futurama gave the spectator 'a flight through time and space' and was designed to demonstrate 'that the world, far from being finished, is hardly yet begun. The job of building the future is one which will demand our best energies, our most fruitful imagination; and with it will come greater opportunities for all.'

By the end of the 1930s streamlining was beginning to lose its visual impact: people were tiring of seeing the applied streamlined stylism used in all places, on all occasions, for all manner of things, whether necessary or not. Just as had happened with the earlier curvilinear style, its symbols became yet another form of applied stylism for indiscriminate use on pencil sharpeners, cocktail cabinets and car fenders. Streamlining was losing its aesthetic appeal. Another style of design began to emerge, one more suited to the times.

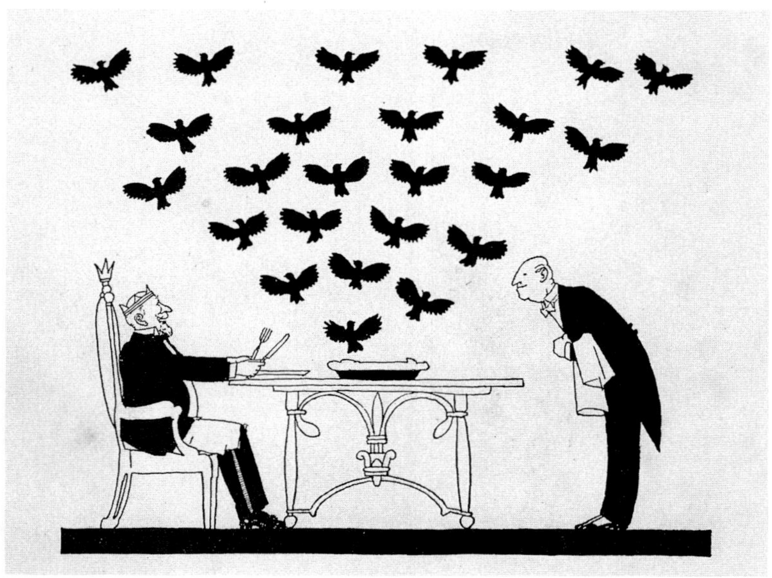

Illustration by Willy Pogany for *Mother Goose and Other Nursery Rhymes*. Published by Thomas Nelson & Sons Ltd., New York. 1931.

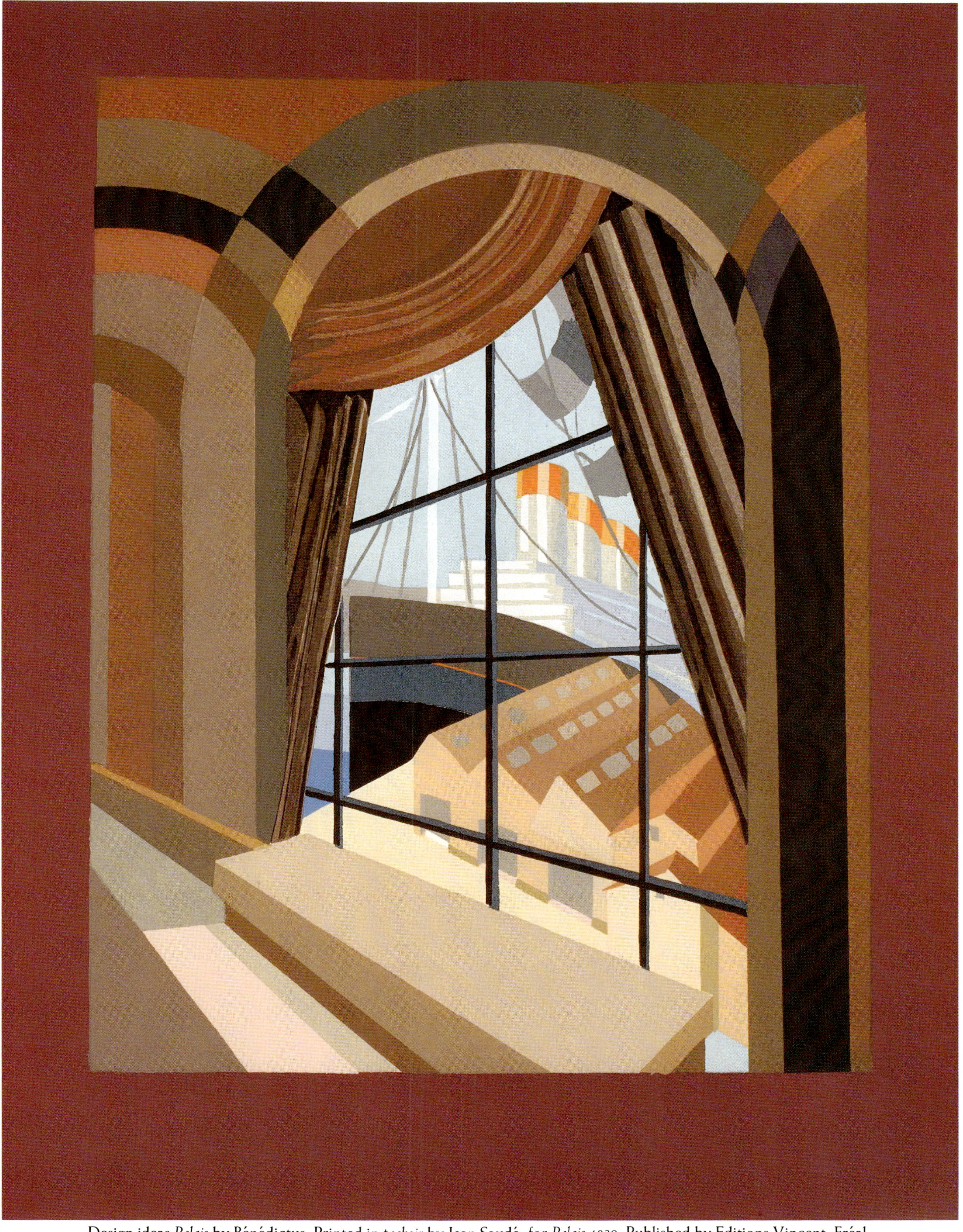

Design ideas *Relais* by Bénédictus. Printed in *pochoir* by Jean Saudé, for *Relais 1930*. Published by Editions Vincent, Fréal et Cie, Paris. 1930.

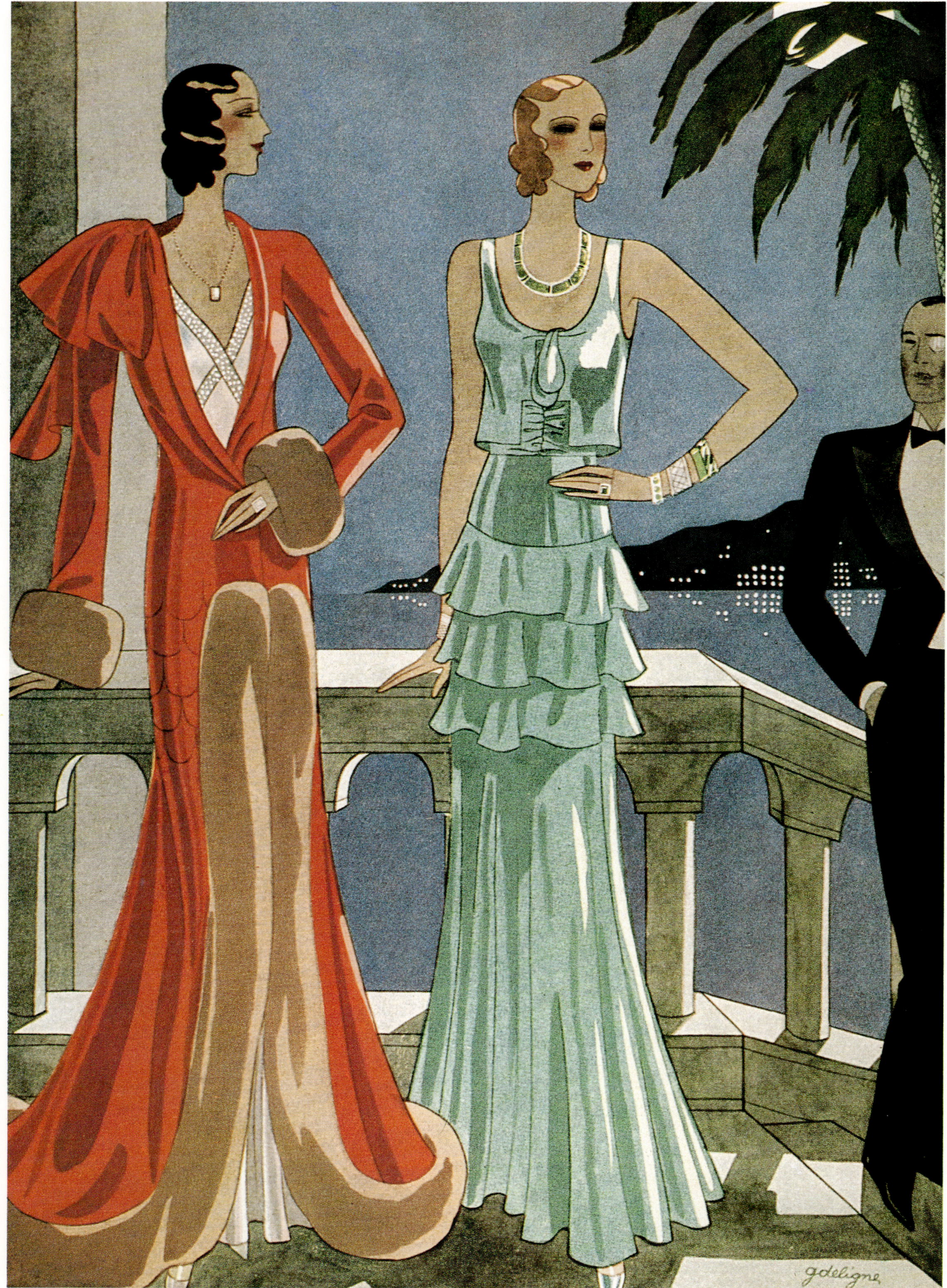

Magazine illustration by George Deligne for *Harpers Bazaar*. 1932. (Courtesy of *Harpers Bazaar*, London.)

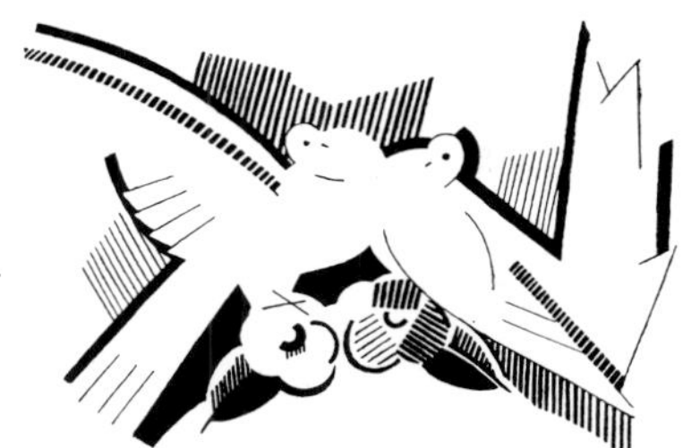

POSTSCRIPT: THE CONTINUING I·N·F·L·U·E·N·C·E

After the collapse of the New York Stock Exchange in October 1929 many lesser Art Deco ateliers were obliged to close for want of regular orders, and many of the small workshops started producing a cheaper range of designs in the new streamlined style. But a number of the better known designers — notably Lalique, Dunand, Ruhlmann, Schmied, and the couturiers Vionnet, Lanvin, Paquin, Callot Soeurs, and Patou — were able to continue producing their highly specialised and expensive merchandise for discerning clients who had not lost their fortunes and still travelled to Paris twice a year to purchase their clothes and other fashion requirements.

Between 1919 and 1929 the prosperity of the Western world had depended greatly on America's high rate of consumption of manufactured products, including the expensive Art Deco products that were mainly being manufactured in Paris. But American consumption fell during the Depression and manufacturing industries began to close down. The Americans' ability to purchase expensive European merchandise also fell sharply, as did the purchasing power of other Western nations.

The French economy, however, was still mainly agriculturally based, unlike the economies of most of her European neighbours; this meant that overall France suffered comparatively less and the value of the franc remained firm, which in turn posed great problems for the country's export industries. The luxury trades of Paris lost a large percentage of their export trade and by the end of 1932 many of the Art Deco designers were becoming more and more reliant on official, as opposed to private, patronage. This official work involved the Art Deco designers in satisfying the varying needs of such prestigious schemes as equipping the luxury

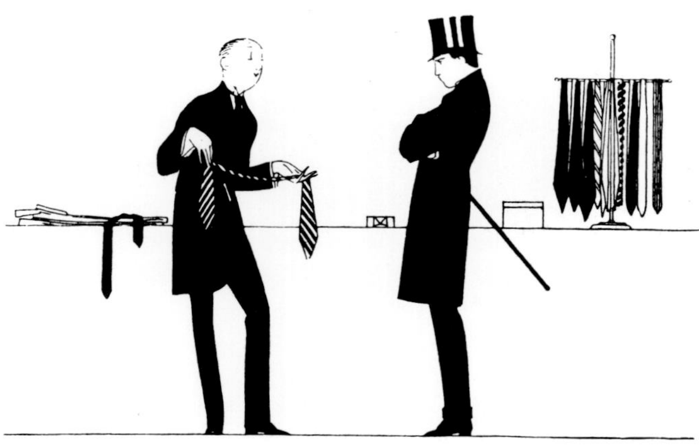

liner *Normandie* and the Radio City building complex in New York.

Both of these schemes and several others required giant murals to be made by Dunand, enormous glass panels to be manufactured by Lalique, huge pieces of furniture to be designed by Ruhlmann, imposing metal screens and balustrades to be supplied by Baguès, and a multitudinous array of light fittings, display panels, table services, textile drapes, carpets, decorative artifacts and fixtures that kept many designers and ateliers busy for several years.

But Art Deco had originally been patronised by a small and fastidious clientele, and when the designs were enlarged for official use on the *Normandie* or as part of the vast interior scheme for the Radio City building they began to lose their individuality and identity. They also began to lose their exclusiveness because the refined detailing and use of rare and expensive materials such as ivory and shagreen were not appropriate for these large-scale official schemes. Gone, too, were the small lacquered and enamelled pieces, the variety of objets d'art, and the hand-printed deluxe books of Schmied and Saudé that had marked the earlier Art Deco period as one of the great innovative and aesthetically successful periods of Western culture.

In order to regain some of this lost inventiveness and to help promote the work of the remaining designers, a new Paris exhibition was planned for 1937; the organisers hoped it would revive world interest in the French decorative and luxury arts. But much had changed since the 1925 Exhibition and, although the new exhibition was promoted as being 'like a jewel set in the very heart of Paris' and featuring products that were 'of modern inspiration and truly original in design . . . with all copies, imitations and old-fashioned products being excluded', it was not a financial success. The Art Deco design style continued to decline.

Despite being severely affected by the loss of many of its traditional clientele, Parisian couture did not decline to the same extent as the design ateliers: fortunately, there was nowhere else in the world so well organised to cater for the sartorial needs of the remaining members of the haut monde and of the nouveau riche.

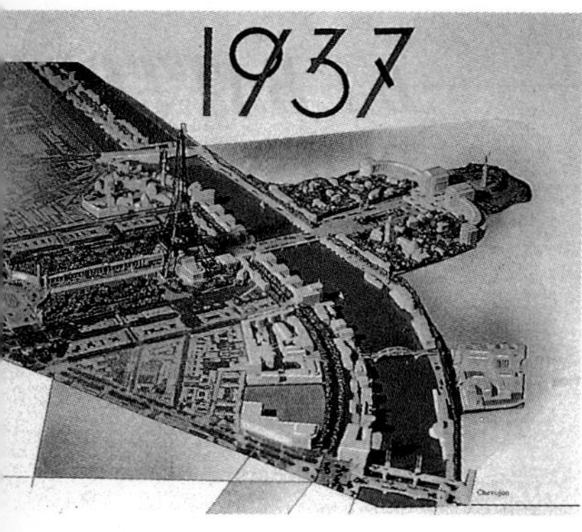

By 1933 the major Paris couturiers were once again being patronised by a steady flow of customers from all over the Western world. These people were willing and able to pay Paris prices, particularly for glamorous evening dresses. (The morning and afternoon styles that had sold so well previously lost some popularity, the exception being those of Chanel, whose sporty day clothes continued to sell as well as ever.) The couturiers also found that their new customers were generally younger

Advertisement *Mistinguett at the Casino de Paris,* by Zig. Paris. 1931.

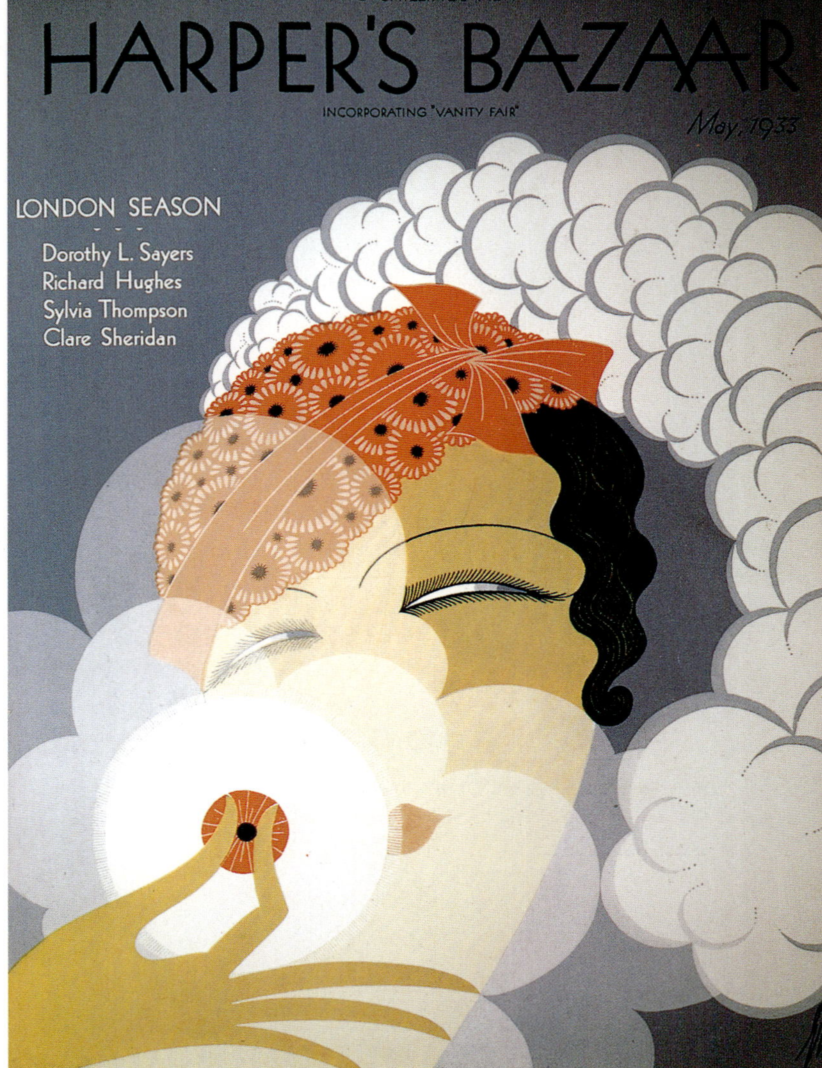

Erté's cover for *Harpers Bazaar*. May 1933. (Courtesy of *Harpers Bazaar*, London.)

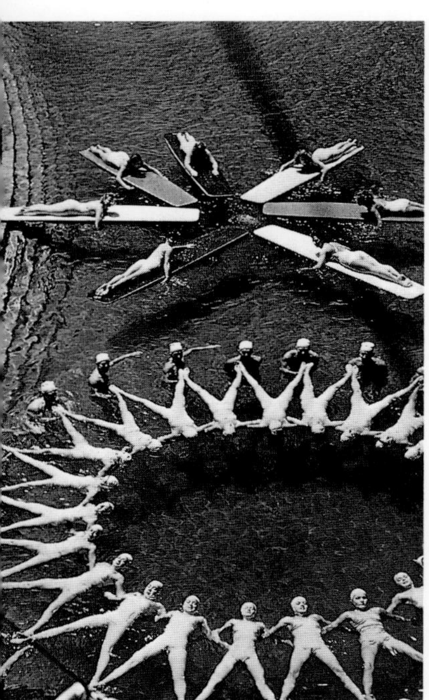

than in the pre-1929 days, and they preferred figure-clinging clothes cut on the bias of the fabric, *à la Vionnet*. In addition, they were more daring in their choice of styles, preferring to show parts of their bodies that previous customers had wished to conceal, encouraging the couturiers to design more revealing modes. Such styles became the hallmark of the 1930s, and they were beautifully captured in the photographic images of Hoyningen-Heune, Horst, Blumenfeld and Man Ray.

Several new couturiers had also emerged and their design styles reflected much of the change then taking place in the arts and design in general. Among the most notable of these new couturiers were Italian-born Elsa Schiaparelli and Nina Ricci, American-born Mainbocher, and French-born Marcel Rochas, Maggy Rouff and Madame Grès, who initially used the name 'Alix'. This group of innovative 1930s couturiers was joined a little later in the decade by the Egyptian-born Jean Dessès and the Spaniard Christobal Balenciaga. Balenciaga, Schiaparelli, Poiret and Vionnet, and the 1940s designer Christian Dior, are arguably the five greatest couturiers of this century. Their work is now being avidly collected by art galleries and museums around the world for display alongside other twentieth century examples of art and design; the Art Deco designs of Madeleine Vionnet and Paul Poiret usually take pride of place in such collections.

During the past ten or so years there has, in fact, been great interest in the revival of Art Deco fashion and fashion illustration. The Metropolitan Museum of Art in New York, the Victoria and Albert Museum in London, and the Museum of Fashion Art in the Louvre have all held major exhibitions on the subject. There have also been a number of authoritative books published on both Art Deco fashion and Art Deco fashion illustration which have had a strong influence on many of the clothes worn by a new generation of Art Deco devotees and have generated much interest in other forms of Art Deco design.

The Art Deco style of design is also remembered for its contribution to the enormously popular Hollywood Deco style, which was extensively used in the lavish film productions of the late 1920s and early 1930s. Cinemas built in the early to mid-1930s also reflected the popular taste for Hollywood Deco; the intention was to heighten the patrons' sense of well-being as they entered a glamorous world of luxury and extravagance previously reserved for the world's wealthy elite.

Hollywood Deco successfully managed to capture the visual essence of the elite Art Deco style and project it into the drab, depressed world of the 1930s. But not everyone was impoverished, and nor did elitism disappear. It was simply that those who had money redirected their priorities, away from the Art Deco style of furniture and small artifacts and into more visible signs of wealth and status — international travel, new clothes and, in particular, new motor cars with custom-built

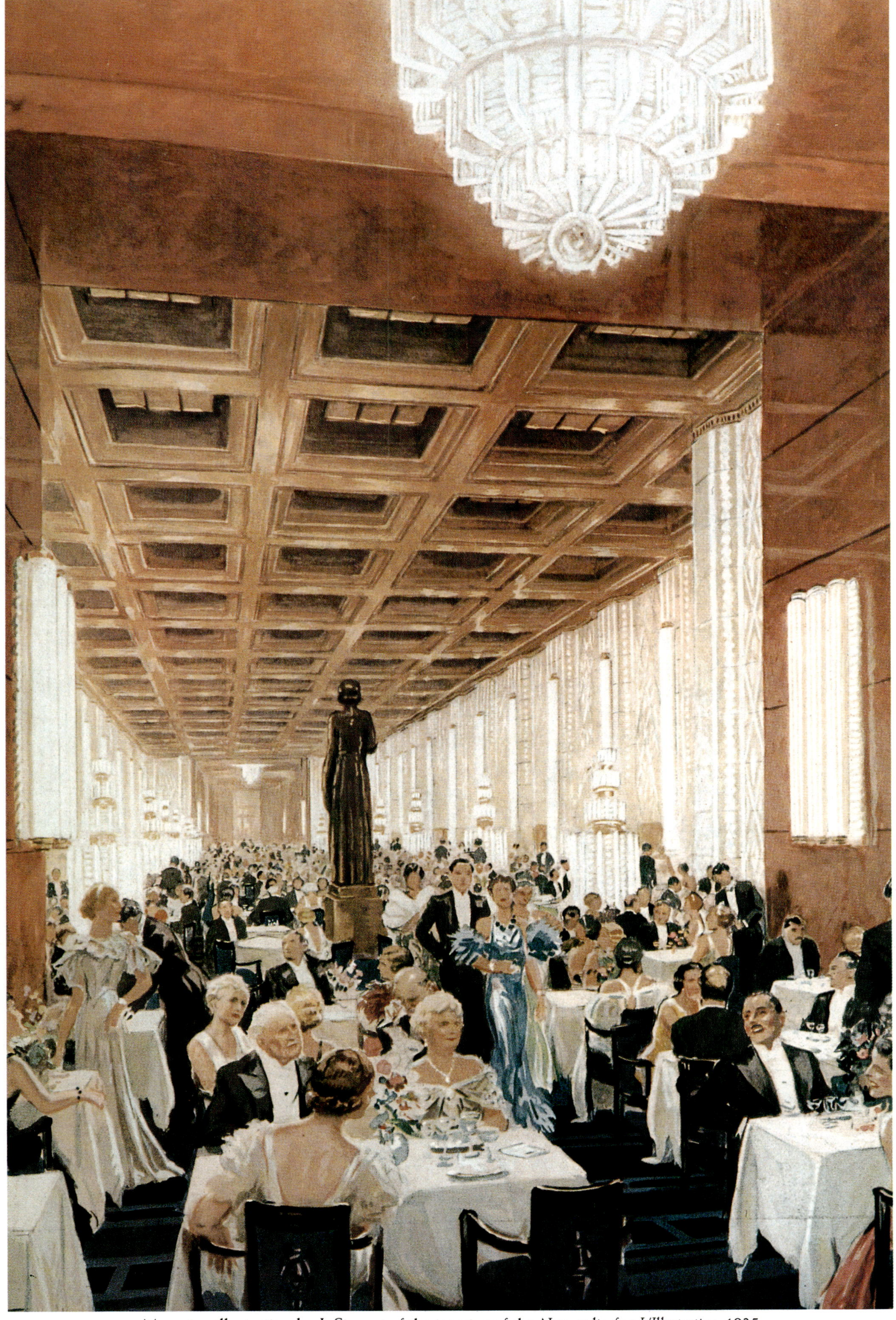

Magazine illustration by J. Simont of the interior of the *Normandie*, for *L'Illustration*. 1935.

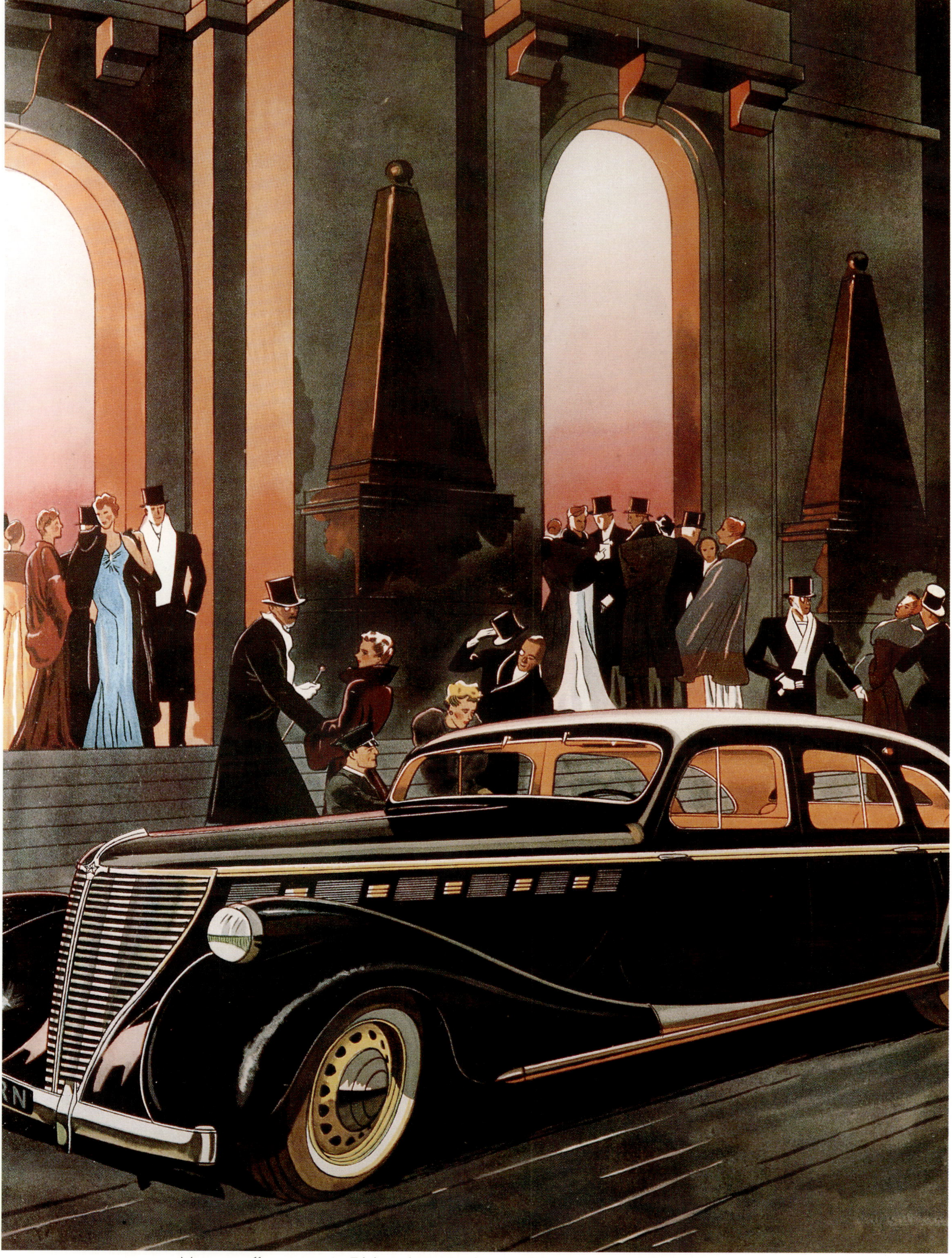

Magazine illustration *Au Fil de nos heures Mesdames par Renault* by Guy Sabrain. Paris. 1939.

coachwork by such designers as the American Raymond Dietrich. He designed exclusive cars for the great Hollywood stars of the 1930s and continued the Art Deco traditions of luxury and visual extravagance. So did Cartier jewels, furs by Fourrures Max, luxury yachts and numerous other items chosen by the elite as symbols of privilege.

Today, interest in Art Deco design is increasing. Collectors are once again purchasing selected items to display alongside their eighteenth century antiques, medieval paintings, Renaissance pieces, Grecian and Egyptian antiquities, and pieces of African and oriental art. They have recognised that the Art Deco style of design was without doubt the most important, the most aesthetically satisfying, and the most influential style to emerge in the Western world during the past two hundred years.

Many collectors are also purchasing deluxe edition books, albums, and portfolios that contain the *pochoir* illustrations of this unique period. In fact, during the past thirty years, since I started to collect and deal in rare *pochoir* publications whilst a student at the Royal College of Art in London, I have been fortunate to travel the world to advise, value, purchase and sell examples of these unique illustrative works. And I have been pleasantly surprised to discover how many collectors are devoted to this distinctive and resplendent style.

It is also interesting to observe how the Art Deco illustrative influence of the 1920s has begun to reappear in everyday graphics — not exactly as before, but nevertheless distinctive enough to add a touch of excitement to an otherwise mundane depiction. This influence has also reappeared in contemporary jewellery design, fashionable accessories, cinema and many other aspects of everyday life.

In the hope that this trend will continue, I dedicate this book to all the talented individuals who helped to create a unique design style, and to the artists who produced the wonderful illustrations that promoted the style throughout the Western world. In so doing, they captured the essence of a period of glorious creativity, the like of which may never be seen again.

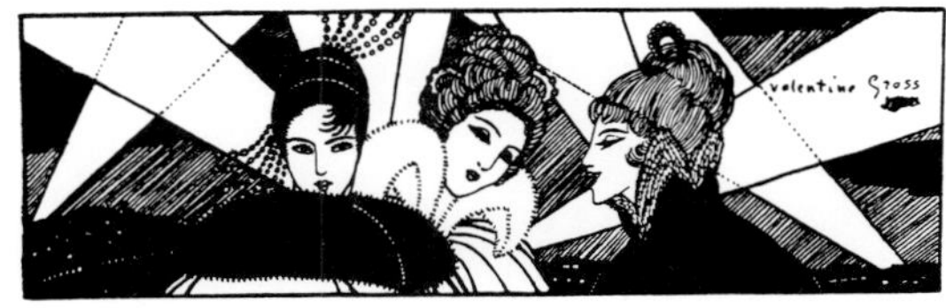

INDEX

INDEX OF PUBLICATIONS

GENERAL INDEX

A

B

C

D

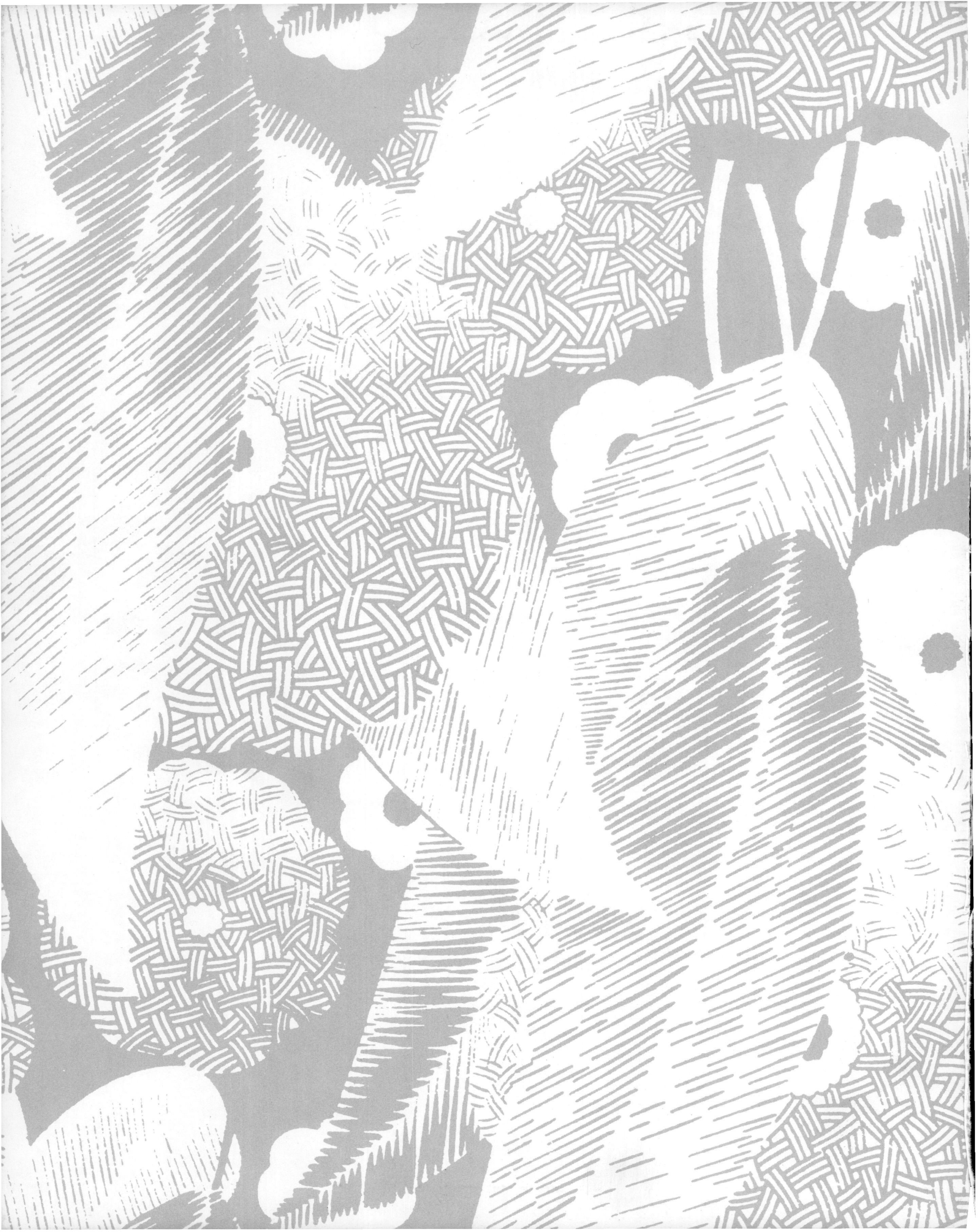